D0373493

Jessie Benton Frémont. From the portrait by T. Buchanan Read.

JESSIE BENTON FRÉMONT
A WOMAN WHO MADE HISTORY

BY

CATHERINE COFFIN PHILLIPS

AUTHOR OF

CORNELIUS COLE
A CALIFORNIA PIONEER AND UNITED STATES SENATOR

PORTSMOUTH PLAZA
THE CRADLE OF SAN FRANCISCO

Introduction to the Bison Book Edition
by Christine Bold

University of Nebraska Press
Lincoln and London

Introduction to the Bison Book Edition copyright 1995
by the University of Nebraska Press
All rights reserved
Manufactured in the United States of America

⊗ The paper in this book meets the minimum requirements of American National
Standard for Information Sciences—Permanence of Paper for Printed Library Materials,
ANSI Z39.48-1984.

First Bison Book printing: 1995
Most recent printing indicated by the last digit below:
10   9   8   7   6   5   4   3   2   1

Library of Congress Cataloging-in-Publication Data
Phillips, Catherine Coffin, 1874–1942.
Jessie Benton Frémont: a woman who made history / by Catherine Coffin Phillips;
introduction to the Bison Book edition by Christine Bold.
p.   cm.
Previously published: San Francisco: J. H. Nash, 1935.
Includes bibliographical references and index.
ISBN 0-8032-8740-2 (alk. paper)
1. Frémont, Jessie Benton, 1824–1902.   2. Frémont, John Charles, 1813–1890.
3. Women pioneers—United States—Biography.   4. Politicians' spouses—United
States—Biography.   5. Pioneers—United States—Biography.   I. Title.
E415.9.F8P48   1995
973.6'092—dc20
[B]
94-43803   CIP

Reprinted from the original edition published in 1935 by John Henry Nash,
San Francisco.

Introduction to the Bison Book Edition

Christine Bold

From the furious debates over Hillary Rodham Clinton at one end of the public spectrum, to burgeoning revisionist scholarship on Eleanor Roosevelt at the other, "political wives" are an intensely topical subject. It is to this lineage that Jessie Benton Frémont belongs. Daughter of one famous expansionist—Senator Thomas Hart Benton of Missouri—and wife to another the western surveyor John Charles Frémont—she was a brilliant, indefatigable, and charming woman who occupied, for much of the nineteenth century, that ambiguous position associated with high-profile First Ladies of more recent decades.

She was present at some of the defining moments of America's expansionist phase: the opening of westward emigration routes; the gold rush; California's statehood convention; the birth of the Republican party and its first presidential campaign, with Frémont as candidate; the Missouri theater of conflict during the Civil War. Yet her precise impact on these events defies accurate measurement. Confidante and mediator to the inner circle of national politicians, she held no appointed or elected office. She can be understood as, alternately, a wielder of significant behind-the-scenes influence or a mere sounding board for those with real power, cast by the proprieties of her age in a supporting role. In reading Jessie Benton Frémont's remarkable story, we are also challenged to appreciate the significance of women who accompany their mates into the political arena and to assess their functions, their spheres of influence, their larger meanings in American culture.

One thing is clear: Jessie Frémont was a key player in the production and maintenance of her husband's image. In this sense, the subtitle of this biography is precise. Without Jessie, Frémont might well have mapped routes for America's westward movement; he almost certainly would not have inscribed his adventures into the nation's recorded history. According to Catherine Coffin Phillips and others, Frémont found himself spent at the end of his first topographical expedition to the Rocky Mountains, utterly unable to compose a coherent report for Congress. It was Jessie who coaxed the stories out of him and wrote them down, in the process injecting anecdotal energy and dramatic visualization into the itemization of scientific data. These qualities persuaded the Senate to make the account publicly available and won a vast readership among emigrants needing a practical guide and stay-at-homes seeking imaginative contact with the rugged West. The volume was likened to *Robinson Crusoe*, and it made heroes of Frémont and his guide, Kit Carson. Jessie's role as amanuensis had transformed Frémont into a public figure, thenceforth available as a symbolic hero for an expansionist nation: as mapper of westward trails, as leader of the Bear Flag rebellion when California was Mexican territory, then one of the first senators for the new state, as unswerving Free Soiler, as presidential candidate, and as Civil War general and author of the first emancipation proclamation for slaves (swiftly revoked by Lincoln). Jessie gave Frémont access to those levels of influence by helping him to establish an attractive and authoritative public voice. She continued to sustain his image, through his triumphs and his embarrassments—political, military, and financial—with her contributions as political ally and advisor, her social skills as *saloniste*, and, later, her own published writings.

With these activities, Jessie challenged the conventional limits of women's "separate sphere" in the nineteenth century; her case also confounds the demarcations of Western American historiography today, in both its traditional and revisionist forms. Traditional interest in the "great men" of western exploration and settlement elides the contribution of women such as Jessie Frémont. New western scholarship has established more inclusive practices by attending to women's roles as homemakers on the westward trail and the frontier of white settlement, as professional participants in the establishment of new western societies, and as alternative myth makers.[1] Jessie played these roles, surviving (just barely) the perils of the westward route by Panama in the mid-1800s, adapting to spartan and dangerous living conditions on the West Coast, taking a hand in the education and welfare of children, and producing her own tales of the West in both adult and juvenile publications: over fifty travel pieces, stories and articles, and three books, characterized by Pamela Herr as belonging to the woman's genre of "fireside history."[2]

But Jessie's meaning is not quite contained by any of these roles. She was also, indelibly, the Washington political animal, raised within the inner circle of power: familiar with leading statesmen of the Jacksonian era. They frequented the Benton home and indulged the precociously talented child, who was favored over her brother by Benton, to be educated, initially, in the forms of privileged male discourse. Nor can she be easily aligned with the proto-feminism of her day. Her prominence in the 1856 Republican presidential campaign—gracing Frémont's side in political cartoons and campaign songs—attracted the support of the women's rights movement, whose position on abolition she had long shared.

When Elizabeth Cady Stanton and Susan B. Anthony courted her ten years later, however, seeking her support for women's suffrage, she rejected their overtures on the grounds that women were better off without the vote.[3] In other words, Jessie Benton Frémont straddles our analytical categories: as both domestic worker effaced by recorded history and political actor profiting from the male sphere of power, as one who bent but refused to break the boundaries of established power structures, she does not quite fit the paradigms of revisionist inquiry.

Jessie herself recognized her position *entre deux mondes*. Phillips quotes a letter that she composed during her husband's absence on his second western survey. Writing from the St. Louis family home, where she was tending her ailing mother and her young daughter Lily, to her father in their Washington residence, she recounts how, walking alone by the Missouri River, she came across an emigrant wagon:

> *No men were about, but seated on an overturned tub near the wagon was a young woman my age, nursing her baby. Her laughing blue eyes peeped up at me from a pink ruffled sunbonnet. A strand of wavy yellow hair, loosed from its coil, lay shimmering on the shoulder of her brown linsey dress. We talked for some time while the baby "John," named for his father," lay asleep in her bosom.*
>
> *I didn't tell her who I was. Finally, she rewarded my interest with, "Wouldn't you and your folks like to come along? There are three wagons of us. Did you know you can get a whole section of good land to yourselves and save your children from a life of wages?" I said, "I can't go because of my sick mother, but how I wish I might." Then I walked away quickly, for I was crying. If it weren't for mother, I would take Lily and go with them. I am strong and not afraid, and waiting grows harder every day.* (see pp. 80–81)

Both the idealization of the traveler's beauty and the tone of intense regret suggest that Jessie knows herself to be inescapably different from this woman and that, for all her Benton privileges, it may well be the woman with baby at breast and husband by her side who is the luckier. But Jessie also distanced herself from an absolute identification with the social class into which she was born. When she eloped, at seventeen, with Frémont, she defied both her father's decrees and her society's expectations. As the illegitimate son of a romantic but legally unsanctioned union between a Southern society woman and an impecunious French teacher, Frémont was not at all the match prescribed by Jessie's social set. She retained the desire to empathize across both class and cultural lines. Herself multilingual in her verbal skills and multicultural in her sympathies, she was critical of the narrowness of so many federal representatives: "Washington especially should speak many languages" (p. 160). And she knew too well the double standard that denied her the range of public voice available to men of her class. Lampooned by the press for her overweening role as "General Jessie" in Civil War

Missouri, dismissed by President Lincoln in her efforts as messenger from the war front to the White House, Jessie dryly remarked, "Strange, isn't it, that when a man expresses a conviction fearlessly, he is reported as having made a trenchant and forceful statement, but when a woman speaks thus earnestly, she is reported as a lady who has lost her temper" (p. 253). Most revealing of her ambiguous position, perhaps, was her disappointment at giving birth to a daughter.

If this liminal position suggests Jessie's tenuous contact with the reins of federal power, it can also point to the centrality of her role on the frontier. Annette Kolodny, one of the first feminist scholars to reorient western studies toward the recognition and analysis of women's agency, has recently issued a call for the further redefinition of the field.[4] Eschewing the traditional representation of the frontier as boundary or leading edge of American progress, Kolodny argues for the reconceptualization of the American West as "borderlands, that liminal landscape of changing meanings on which distinct human cultures first encounter one another's 'otherness' and appropriate, accommodate, or domesticate it through language . . . an inherently unstable locus of environmental transitions and cultural interpenetrations."[5] From this perspective, Jessie's role as translator, mediator, and hostess to a sweeping range of cultural types looks newly significant. According to this interpretation, she becomes a linchpin in the hybrid formations distinctive to the western region.

At the same time, Jessie's story makes palpable the costs of "winning the West," even for members of the dominant culture, for those closely connected to the inner circle of influence and policy making. Like many an anonymous woman emigrant, Jessie endured the loneliness of life with a peripatetic husband, the high price of frontier-making in troubled pregnancies and infant mortality, the hardship of survival in rudimentary western conditions, and the unwonted proximity to male violence. Observed one commentator, startled by the appearance of this woman with such political connections and public distinction: "Pioneering is hell on women. That child is all eyes and grit. Nothing else left" (p. 170). Her story also exposes the weaknesses and blindnesses of "great men"—Benton, Frémont, Lincoln, among others—as we see her suffer the consequences of their rivalries, vanities, and unbridled lust for fame. One of those consequences was a fall from privilege: Frémont's expansionist dreams led him to rash political acts and speculative business deals, a combination that ultimately led the family to penury and Jessie to the career of author, in the search for economic support. To this extent, her story does fit the feminist injunction, that "the personal is the political." Her personal story is one face of Western expansionism too easily overlooked.

Her story also encourages us to redefine the nature of political power. As recent work in International Relations insists, power isn't derived or wielded in a social vacuum; we need methods for recognizing and analyzing the collaborative production of public influence.[6] Reading Jessie's story helps us to reflect on the dimensions and limitations of the invisible power—in nineteenth-century America, the woman's domestic domain—that undergirds visible leadership—the male's public authority. Crucial to the woman's position was her ability to disguise the demands of the self, to present her power as other-directed. Catherine Coffin Phillips identifies "that salient characteristic of Jessie Frémont's which was to exercise its spell over everyone, old or young, who came in contact with her throughout the seventy-eight years of her life, her power 'to make others shine in their qualities.'" Henry Ward Beecher said, more prosaically, "How she makes us pleased with ourselves!" (p. 69) Jessie was also instrumental in fostering the careers of young writers and speakers, such as Bret Harte and Thomas Starr King. That altruistic work, however, takes on a different cast if we define it as power-broking, a quality which Jessie herself openly admired in others. Of her audience with Queen Victoria, she reported: "I felt myself not a Democrat bowing the knee to royalty but an American paying homage to a figure of womanly goodness and power" (p. 183). Phillips's account also reveals the "long procession of women" (p. 341) on which the Benton and Frémont dynasties depended: no John Charles Frémont without his mother's daring adultery, no Benton clan without the strong pioneering efforts of the wives and mothers; and, of course, no Frémont myth without Jessie.

We read Jessie's story here through the lens of Catherine Coffin Phillips, herself a particular woman writing at a particular historical moment. One way of assessing Phillips's version is to compare it with the 1987 biography by Pamela Herr.[7] The two biographers share the drive to make visible the contributions of women to American history. But Herr's work is more openly engaged with the costs of public life for nineteenth-century women. Phillips is a woman of the 1930s, both in her devotion to grassroots history and in her confidence about American expansionism. Her unquestioned touchstones—the West's "virgin soil" and its melting pot effect on collective identity, for example—had become subject to fierce interrogation by the 1980s. While Phillips celebrates Jessie for seizing the opportunities of nineteenth-century womanhood, Herr portrays her as chafing against the same limitations, channeling her thwarted ambition and energy into her husband's career. Herr exposes more of the hidden history of Jessie's personal life, dwelling on both the illegalities of Frémont's parents' union and on Frémont's own sexual philandering—a topic unacknowledged by the proprieties of the 1930s biography. And Herr is much more skeptical of Jessie's accounts, suspecting that her subject overdramatized her own influence on crucial events, as consolation for her lack of real power. Ultimately, Herr's sympathies seem to be with those friends who dubbed Jessie's unswerving loyalty to Frémont "Jessie's insanity" (p. 416).

Yet Phillips's account may not be quite the sentimental celebration that such a superficial comparison suggests. The costs of expansionism are imprinted on her tale, despite the lack of explicit commentary. For all the emphasis on Jessie's achievements, the biographer repeatedly represents her as a plaything of fate, ultimately unable to control her destiny. Jessie is also made to articulate the costly paradox of western heroism. At one point she is quoted staunchly celebrating her husband's accomplishments: "John C. Frémont's name can never be erased from the most colorful chapters of American history. From the ashes of his campfires, cities have sprung" (p. 325). At another, Phillips imputes to her the realization that expansionism had ruined him: "At the worst, she felt his dreams to have been a little mad, his mind so filled with visions of those shining steel paths across the territories to the Pacific that he walked blindly along the dark alleys of tricky speculation with his associates" (p. 292). Phillips's acceptance of Jessie's viewpoint results in a biography partisan in Frémont's favour and close to hagiography in its idealization of Jessie. These qualities also, however, carry a salutory significance. More directly than Herr's, this account is what 1970s feminism punningly labeled "herstory," the product of a community of women's voices. Phillips's source material was Jessie's letters, the newspaper clippings carefully preserved by her and Lily, and the direct contact between the biographer and Jessie in her last six years and between Phillips and Nelly Haskell, a confidante of Jessie's, in her old age. What we hear is Jessie's voice, refracted through her advocates; it is a valuable contribution, though one that modern scholarship teaches us to handle with care.

When Phillips produced her biography in 1935, Nelly Haskell welcomed it as the first account of a forgotten woman. When Herr published her biography fifty years later, reviewers heralded its attention to a long neglected figure. The repeated forgetting of Jessie Benton Frémont suggests, again, the challenge that she poses to our mapping of the West. Phillips reports Jessie in her final days, at the turn of the century: "This is truly *fin de siècle*," she would say, "but I have a robust faith in youth. . . . I only hope that the youth of this country will learn to evaluate the past in the light of our heroes' dreams as well as their achievements, and this for their own sakes, since by the largeness of our dreams do we truly live" (p. 344). The sentiment can be read as one final apologia for the dreams of Frémont that ultimately consigned husband and wife to poverty. It can equally be understood, however, as a prophesy from her *fin de siècle* to ours: an avowal of the need to assess both manifest and hidden forces in setting the historical record straight.

NOTES

1. Recent work in the more traditional vein of frontier scholarship would include William H. Goetzmann and William N. Goetzmann, *The West of the Imagination* (New York:

Norton, 1986). New Western History projects are pursued in William Cronon, George Miles, and Jay Gitlin, eds., *Under an Open Sky: Rethinking America's Western Past* (New York: W. W. Norton, 1992); Patricia Nelson Limerick, Clyde A. Milner II, and Charles E. Rankin, eds., *Trails: Toward a New Western History* (Lawrence: University Press of Kansas, 1991); and Richard White, *"It's Your Misfortune and None of My Own": A New History of the American West* (Norman: University of Oklahoma Press, 1991). The burgeoning new literature on women's contributions to frontier life include Susan Armitage and Elizabeth Jameson, eds., *The Women's West* (Norman: University of Oklahoma Press, 1987); Anne M. Butler, *Daughters of Joy, Sisters of Misery: Prostitutes in the American West, 1865–90* (Urbana: University of Illinois Press, 1985); Lillian Schlissel, *Women's Diaries of the Westward Journey* (New York: Schocken, 1982); and Lillian Schlissel, Byrd Gibbens, and Elizabeth Hampsten, *Far From Home: Families of the Westward Journey* (New York: Schocken Books, 1989).

2. Pamela Herr, *Jessie Benton Frémont: A Biography* (New York: Franklin Watts, 1987), 414.

3. Herr, 277.

4. Annette Kolodny's decisive intervention in the study of Western mythology was *The Land Before Her: Fantasy and Experience of the American Frontiers, 1630–1860* (Chapel Hill: The University of North Carolina Press, 1984).

5. Annette Kolodny, "Letting Go Our Grand Obsessions: Notes Toward a New Literary History of the American Frontiers," *American Literature* 64 (March 1992): 9–10.

6. See, for example, Cynthia Enloe, *Bananas, Beaches & Bases: Making Feminist Sense of International Politics* (Berkeley: University of California Press, 1990).

7. Recent publications on Jessie Benton Frémont, in addition to Herr's biography, include Pamela Herr, "Besieged at Las Mariposas: New Insights into the Frémonts' Bittersweet Marriage," *Californians* 5 (1987): 8–17; Pamela Herr, "Jessie Benton Frémont," *American History Illustrated* 22 (1987): 20–29, 56; Pamela Herr and Mary Lee Spence, "'I Really Had Something Like the Blues': Letters from Jessie Benton Frémont to Elizabeth Blair Lee, 1847–1883," *Montana* 41 (1991): 16–31; Pamela Herr and Mary Lee Spence, eds., *The Letters of Jessie Benton Frémont* (Champaign: The University of Illinois Press, 1993); and Mary L. Spence, "Jessie Benton Frémont: First Lady of Arizona," *Journal of Arizona History* 24 (1983): 55–72.

CONTENTS

ILLUSTRATIONS

INTRODUCTION

The trend of modern social thought is to recognize woman in her own economic and cultural significance as an essential factor in the evolution of society. From Mistress Margaret Brent to Jane Addams, there is a lengthy list of noble and courageous women who participated in the great social movements in the United States and who bore their full share of labor and responsibility in every crisis of the nation's history.

Among these women, Jessie Benton Frémont stands preeminent. A direct descendant of Anne Benton of Tennessee and of Mary McDowell of Virginia, she had pure pioneer inheritance. As the daughter of Senator Thomas H. Benton, scholar, statesman, and dynamic force in national affairs for thirty years, she grew up in Washington official family life. She received broad cultural opportunities, and while still very young, was a belle of acknowledged wit and beauty. As the wife of John Charles Frémont, noted explorer, the first Senator from California, and the first Republican candidate for the Presidency, the course of her life was highly dramatic. She was fitted by temperament and education to adapt her-

self with grace and fortitude to every phase of Frémont's stormy career. Thrust with him into the open, sharing with him the initiative in policy, she was destined to have but short intervals in which she could watch from the audience the drama of public affairs. Her part in that drama carried her from Washington and the courts of Europe to the pioneers' California of '49; from a New York mansion to a cabin in a Sierra mining camp; from wealth to poverty.

She was identified with the transition of California from a territory to a free-soil state. A member of a slave-holding family who freed their slaves before the war, she was tireless in working for the abolition of slavery. The mother of five children, she was associated with the earliest official movements for child welfare and education in America.

Jessie Benton Frémont was a prolific and witty correspondent, as well as a writer of trenchant articles and delightful memoirs. Her letters to poets, diplomats, and politicians reveal a bold intellect, a fearless spirit, and on occasion, a power of invective which merits the sobriquet, "a Benton in petticoats." However, it is in her letters to her husband and children and to a beloved protégée, Nellie Haskell Browne, that her lively fancy, her gayety, and her tenderness are fully revealed. Her life was a colorful fabric woven with a fast-moving shuttle, and through its sturdy warp and weft runs the richly toned thread of a romance which ranks with the world's great love stories.

Her proud, unswerving loyalty to John C. Frémont found justification for his every act, explanation for all seeming blunders. Her militant pride in him admitted no questioning of motive. Her faith sustained him equally amid the shouts of popular acclaim and the whispers of scandal, working with him in that identity of purpose which is itself a fortification against adverse circumstance.

It is to be hoped that even those to whom Frémont's career is a highly controversial subject will find him, as seen through her discerning eyes, not lacking the elements of greatness.

She survived General Frémont twelve years, and while spending her old age in Los Angeles, was still a personage, holding her place in the regard of the nation. To the very last, her self-imposed retirement was broken in upon by her friends, often the great of this and other lands, come to pay homage to a truly noble woman, one who bore her triumphs without arrogance and her defeats without bitterness.

CHAPTER I

The Widow Benton's Settlement

N A June morning in the year 1798, Anne Gooch Benton stood in the doorway of her home near Nashville, Tennessee, directing the unpacking of household goods. Her eight slaves, strong young negroes, lifted the last of the heavy boxes from the wagons. Her three small daughters ran back and forth putting articles in place. Her two younger sons carried the choicest provisions to the storeroom. Thomas, the eldest, a tall boy with a shock of reddish-blond hair and warm gray eyes, smiled up at her from his work of unpacking books. She joined him in this task so congenial to both, the handling of the precious volumes packed a month before in the library of the family home at Hillsborough, North Carolina.

Six weeks earlier, Anne Benton had taken final stand against the Hillsborough relatives assembled in a body to dissuade her from "this foolhardy adventure into the back country, full four hundred miles away." Her husband's brother William had been most eloquent in declaring that the proper place for a delicately reared lady was in the country where her husband's career as secretary to Governor Tyron was held in honored memory. "And what more seemly," William had urged, "than for a young widow to be spared the cares of business until her sons are old enough to manage for her?" This plea failing, he had pointed out the discomforts and dangers of overland travel, the heavy wagons jolting their way for long distances over rocky roads, crawling precariously down into dark ravines and upward across narrow passes, and always the cattle and pack train menaced by Indians, even though her own wagons were part of a caravan protected by outriders. Once arrived in the blue-grass country, though it proved as beautiful as her husband had described, she would find herself in a ramshackle old house, a lone settler on forty thousand acres of wild land lying at the very edge of the Creek Indian country.

Although she had listened with the respect a gentlewoman owed to the superior judgment of her menfolk, Anne Benton had her own sufficient reasons for persisting in her plan. Hillsborough had become hateful to her. Her Scotch Puritanism disapproved the gambling, hard-riding, hard-drinking young bloods among whom her brother-in-law was a leader. Her son Thomas admired and already wished to emulate his popular uncle.

Thomas had his father's height, his blond good looks, his courteous bearing, his scholarly tastes. Anne Benton's heart was set upon her son's becoming an eminent lawyer as his father had been. At seventeen, after two years at the University of North Carolina, he was an excellent Greek and Latin scholar with some knowledge of English literature, history, and law. But at seventeen he also showed strong liking for the lusty pleasures of his class. He needed discipline, responsibility. His mother had heard that large opportunity awaited ambitious young men in Tennessee. Those rich lands purchased by her husband lay in the heart of the blue-grass region with its trails converging on Nashville. Already a sizable house, a few negro cabins, and forty acres of cleared land awaited her. There she and her daughters would make a home; her sons would develop the plantation and become strong, God-fearing citizens. Setting aside all pleas, she had sold her property, bought equipment for moving, and joined six other families traveling to Tennessee.

No one was the wiser if Anne Benton regretted her decision as the long line of wagons moved slowly through the Carolina mountains, down the valley of the Holston to Fort Campbell, through immense stretches of gloomy forest, into the valley of the Cumberland, and on over the rough roads of the blue-grass region toward Nashville. If dismal apprehension seized her, she did not betray the fact. Long afterward her children recalled her on this journey, pointing out to them the beauties of nature and teaching them to identify the trees, shrubs, and varieties of birds and small game along the water courses. At night as they sat about the campfire after supper, she repeated psalms to them and bade them recall their blessings.

Jessie Benton Frémont: a Woman Who Made History

Her destination reached, Anne Benton's courage did not fail her as she looked out over her vast acreage of wilderness broken only by this stout old stone house and a few negro cabins. All day long the unpacking and settling continued. At twilight while the negroes prepared supper of bacon, corn bread, and stewed apples, she called her sons to the porch, and pointing to the cleared land about them, outlined her plan for "a church and a schoolhouse to be built at the cross-roads after we have built the roads." On that day Anne Benton began writing her family history upon the virgin soil of her country.

The day following the family's arrival was a memorable one for Thomas. In deadly fear of Indians, he watched with shaking knees and chattering teeth while his mother stood in the doorway smiling pleasantly at a pair of young bucks "who looked eight feet tall." With a little French, a little English, and many signs she made them understand that they might keep their war trails open across her land and might fish in her streams and that she would pay them in sugar and tobacco for certain medicinal herbs. She made good these promises by giving them in advance a small quantity of sugar, ground corn, and tobacco. They met this procedure with grunts and gestures indicating that she and her household would never be molested.

After the Indians had gone, Thomas hastened to express his admiration for his mother's courage and to admit his own cowardice. Her reply acknowledged and rewarded a salient trait of his character—moral courage. Thomas Benton's sharpest recollection of himself was as a boy of eight, sitting on a log in the woodlot the day after his father's funeral and crying into his Greek testament from which the Reverend Mr. Micklejohn was teaching him to translate: "Blessed are they that mourn." The rector was urging him to be brave and reminding him that as the eldest son he was now the comfort and mainstay of his mother. He had "remembered" throughout his boyhood, and his reward now came in her reply to his confession of cowardice: "You have often showed the kind of courage that faces worse danger than Indians. I have come here because I can depend upon you to work with me for the good of the family."

Under his mother's direction Thomas superintended the clearing of the land and the planting of crops; he helped the slaves in the building of bridges and log houses for small-lease tenants. Within a year Anne Benton's plans materialized in a horse gristmill, a general store, a schoolhouse, and a church, which drew many incoming settlers to the neighborhood. She identified herself with the life and interests of her neighbors even to the extent of "turning Methodist" and refusing to allow cards or whiskey in the house. Her superior talents were exercised to such purpose that this community, last outpost between civilization and the southern Indian tribes, became known afar as the Widow Benton's Settlement.

The education of Thomas was continued under his mother's supervision. All the resources of her exceptional mind were brought to bear upon a plan of study best calculated to fit him for a legal career. He had been well grounded in Greek and Latin. He had access to the volumes of her own library, which held Plutarch's *Lives,* Shakespeare's plays, and the French classics. These, together with the folios of the *British State Trials,* formed the backbone of his training. While studying, Thomas occasionally taught a term at the crossroads school.

The happy family life of the Bentons in their new environment lasted only a few years, for consumption, that scourge of pioneer America which had caused the early death of Anne Benton's husband, took her three daughters within a year of each other. They were buried high on a hillside, and "the graves of three sisters" became a local landmark. Within another year two of her sons had died of the same disease. Thomas Benton's respect for his mother was heightened to awe as he watched her bear these sorrows with the calm stoicism of the Puritan. With unbroken spirit she continued to care for her household and visit the sick. She set an example for good treatment of the negroes by herself waiting upon the ailing among her slaves. A visitor from Hillsborough, her old home, wrote of her at this time:

Anne is still beautiful, though her hair is snow white, and her eyes are the saddest I ever saw. She always dresses in black, with neck- and wrist-bands of white, like a nun, and in truth she is mother confessor to the whole countryside.

Anne Benton's desire to make a lawyer of her eldest son was aided by his growing distaste for farming. When the cotton crop brought fifteen cents a pound, and he could return from Nashville with necessaries for the household and special delicacies for his mother, he was content; but when frosts and blight cut profits in half or destroyed them altogether, he became disheartened. After one of these disappointments he declared to his brothers: "You may have this land. I am through with a pursuit in which I can't influence results. Hereafter, it is law alone for Tom Benton."

While studying with St. George Tucker of Nashville, Benton was greatly influenced by the rugged and picturesque men about him who were later to shine in the annals of the West; Davy Crockett, member of the Tennessee Assembly; Peter Cartwright, the dynamic backwoods preacher; and Sam Houston. These men he admired, but it was the rash and roistering Andrew Jackson to whom he was irresistibly drawn. As a former Senator and now as a Judge of the State Supreme Court, Jackson was a heroic figure. He was noted for his common sense and the impartiality of his court decisions; and his courage in the frequent shooting affrays which characterized the social life of the time had long been remarked. The uncouth choleric Jackson was much taken with the fastidious young law student who admired his vigor and fearlessness.

Early in 1806, Benton was admitted to the bar under the patronage of Jackson. While Benton was practicing in Nashville, he often drove out beyond Stone River to spend a few days with the Jacksons at Hermitage Farm. Here he met Mrs. Jackson, stout, florid, unlettered, but reputed to be "the only person who could do anything with Andrew." As "Aunt Rachel" Jackson she was hostess to half the county. She made everybody comfortable, and despite the constant stream of visitors, managed to secure to her husband and his favorite guest some measure of privacy for the discussion of local news and wider political affairs.

Seated before a blazing log fire, Jackson and Benton often talked far into the night. Their political views were identical. They considered themselves Westerners and thought in terms of the Union. Though Jackson was fifteen years Benton's senior, he listened with respect to the younger man's estimates of John Adams, Thomas Jefferson, and John Randolph, whose characters and aims Benton understood quite as well as did Jackson, who had known all three during his term as Congressman in 1798. These two analyzed, weighed, and prognosticated, little dreaming how closely connected with their own future careers these men they discussed would become.

Benton's popularity, growing out of his keen sense of justice and his unyielding tenacity to an idea once he felt it to be right, soon carried him into politics. In 1809 he was elected to the lower house of the Tennessee legislature. Here he began in earnest to exercise those salient characteristics which were to mark his long political career. In his single term of service he pounded through two unpopular measures: one, a bill introducing the circuit system into the state judiciary, a reform of special benefit to the poorer class of litigants; the other, a law which gave the slave the same right to jury trial as the white man. He also advocated the right of preemption to the actual settler on public land. At the close of his term, his office was besieged by settlers from creek head and mountain gorge, whose homes secured through untold privations were now menaced by speculators. Benton interested himself in their plight and succeeded in gaining the enactment of the first preemption law known in Tennessee.

During this period when Presidents Jefferson and Madison were engaged in "the struggle for neutrality" and when the Easterners were favoring England rather than France, Benton and his associates were among those dubbed Western Warhawks. Representatives of a sectional civilization highly democratic, imbued with Jeffersonian ideals, they repeatedly inveighed against England's sea-power aggressiveness. They prophesied war and declared that in such event Andrew Jackson was the logical leader of an important command. Jackson was already a Major-General of Militia in Tennessee, and Benton his aide-de-camp. The dream of both was the conquest of Florida.

On a raw February day in 1812, as Benton sat in his law office, the tardy mail brought news that President Monroe had been authorized by Congress to accept organized bodies of volunteers to the number of fifty thousand to serve for one year and to be called into service as emergency required. Here was a chance for quick action. Mounting his horse, Benton rode through a sleet storm thirty miles to Jackson's home, the Hermitage. Quickly he outlined his plan for raising volunteer companies. Jackson adopted it at once, and within a few days Benton's impassioned speeches were bringing enlistments from loyal planters and merchants.

A joint resolution was passed by Congress on June 18, 1812, declaring war against Great Britain. Scarcely had Billy Phillips, the Paul Revere of the South, ridden through Nashville shouting, "Wake up! War! War with England!" before Jackson was dispatching a courier to Washington, offering the services of two thousand volunteers and assuring the President that he could depend upon the Tennesseeans "to stay on duty till we or the last armed foe

Thomas H. Benton. From original in the Southwest Museum, Los Angeles.

expires." The authorities at Washington, fearful of a British attack on New Orleans, accepted this offer with alacrity.

In November the troops were mobilized. General Jackson could deliver a rousing speech but hated writing one; so the address to his assembled troops was written by Benton and expressed to the letter Benton's convictions:

The Major-General has now arrived at a crisis where he can address the volunteers with the feelings of a soldier. The state to which he belongs is to act a part in the honorable contest of securing the rights and liberties of a great and rising Republic.... Every man of the Western country turns his eyes intuitively upon the mouth of the Mississippi. There he beholds the only outlet by which his produce can reach the markets of the Atlantic states and foreign nations. Blocked up, the fruits of his industry rot upon his hands; open, he carries on a commerce with the nations of the earth.... Brave volunteers, it is to the defense of this place you are ordered to repair.... By the alacrity with which we obey the orders of the President let us demonstrate that the people of Tennessee are worthy of being called to the defense of the Republic.

Jackson was cheered to the echo as he ordered the men to rendezvous at Nashville on December 10, 1812.

That day was unusually cold, with deep snow on the ground. The two thousand men had arrived on time and pitched camp as best they could. They had also conformed to the liberal ruling as to equipment: their own rifles, dark-blue or brown suits, hunting shirts or coats at option of the wearer. The command consisted of one regiment of cavalry under Colonel Coffee and two regiments of infantry commanded by Colonels Hall and Benton. In the latter's regiment Sam Houston was a Corporal.

In the interim before the departure of the troops, Benton went home for a few days' stay. At sight of him his mother asked in great alarm as to his health. He finally admitted that he was suffering from fever, cough, and night sweats, the dread symptoms of the family scourge. Then for the first time he saw her yield to fear as she exclaimed in tears: "Now is the end of all hope in my life." She begged him to remain home in bed on a chance of improvement.

His reply was characteristic: "In this disease there is no chance. Better to go, to give my life for a purpose than to wear it out here." In this fatalistic spirit Benton bade the family goodbye and returned to his command.

By January, 1813, "the heart of Western Tennessee" was on its way south, the infantry on flatboats, the mounted riflemen by land. During the southward march, Benton did not neglect remedial measures as to his health. He supplemented the coarse army fare with fresh milk and large doses of quinine. He bathed in the streams, rubbing his body vigorously with rough towels, and rode all day with throat and chest exposed to the sun. Within a short time he showed marked improvement. His conviction that Jackson was on his way to conquer Florida kept him in high spirits and doubtlessly aided his recovery.

The movements of Jackson were so much more effective than those of the officials at New Orleans that the little army had to be stopped at Natchez. Here in February, 1813, they encamped awaiting further orders. Weeks passed. Near the end of March an express rider from Washington appeared at headquarters, bearing a message from the Secretary of War. Congress had authorized the President to take charge of Mobile and Western Florida; an army was no longer needed. General Jackson was ordered to disband his troops.

Jackson's militant spirit was dashed; his pride was in arms. Enraged, he sent for Benton and handed him the message. Benton's spirit too was dashed, but his militant pride in his commander suggested instant action. Carefully reading the order again, he said:

This is dated February 6. The Secretary of War expected it to reach you before we were so far from home. We are now full five hundred miles from Nashville. It is scarcely disobedience for you to hold your command together until you reach there. If we disband, Governor Wilkinson and his recruiting officers at New Orleans will get hold of the best lot of crack riflemen in the West. This is General Jackson's army. It should be marched home under Jackson. We can appeal to Wilkinson for money to transport the sick, and treat with the merchants here for stores.

Jackson acted upon this advice to such purpose that upon Wilkinson's refusal to allow funds, he pledged his own credit for everything needful; and his army, supplied from the local stores of Natchez, was soon on its way north.

[9]

His courage and initiative were so admired by his "crack riflemen" that they promptly gave the name Old Hickory to Jackson, the first political hero of the pioneer.

The disbanding of the army took place at Nashville on May 22. Anne Benton welcomed home the son she had not expected to see again, and Rachel Jackson listened with hearty approval to her husband's admission of having pledged his last cent to get his men home.

A month later, the notes given to Natchez merchants fell due. Jackson was unable to meet them and they went to protest. As Benton saw Jackson facing ruin, he arranged for the suits to be delayed until he himself could go to Washington. Upon arrival, he appealed to the Secretary of War, declaring that those volunteers were drawn from the bosom of almost every substantial family in Tennessee and that the whole state would be lost to the administration if Jackson were left to suffer.

The Secretary reported regretfully that relief would have to be given by Congress. Benton was prepared for this evasion. He suggested that General Wilkinson, Quartermaster of the Southern Department, be given an order to pay for so much transportation as General Jackson's command would have been entitled to under regular orders. Without demur the Secretary wrote the order and expressed to Benton his hope that this would effectively relieve the pecuniary distress of the General. Benton upon his return made a speech in which he stated that "Tennessee could now in honor remain firm to the administration."

Despite Benton's admiration of Jackson, he and his brother Jesse were later drawn into an affray with him at the City Hotel in Nashville. The quarrel grew out of the fact that Jackson had acted as second for William Carroll in his duel with Jesse Benton. Garbled reports reached Thomas Benton upon his return from Washington, and the partisans on both sides soon fanned the embers into full blaze. Of the later encounter between Jackson and Benton, as many versions were reported as there were participants and spectators. No two agreed as to the merits of the three-to-a-side fracas, but all admitted the fact that Jackson was shot in the shoulder and that Benton was pitched headlong down a flight of stairs. One curious incident of this encounter was that a stray bullet plowed through the thin partition of a bedroom in which lay a nine-months-old boy, John Charles Frémont, whose parents chanced to be staying at the hotel. Despite much gossip and recrimination following the Jackson-Benton affray, it soon became known that the mutual loyalty of the two principals could outlast bullet wounds and bruises, for the quarrel was later patched up and their friendship continued henceforth unbroken.

Thomas Benton's experience in the state legislature and his successful visits to Washington had given him a glimpse of new political horizons. In 1815 he decided to open a law office at St. Louis in the Territory of Missouri. He faced the difficult task of persuading his mother to accompany him. Though her house was lonely, she dreaded leaving the settlement now called Bentontown, which she had helped to build. When he promised her "a new home and her devoted Nancy to care for her," she walked to the window, and looking toward the hillside with its five graves, said: "And who will care for those others if I go to make a home for you?"

After further pleas, she bade him go alone, promising to join him in the near future. He left home a few weeks later with four hundred dollars in his pocket and with a dozen boxes of books and clothing. He arrived on a Sunday evening at the east bank of the Mississippi opposite St. Louis. He and his luggage were ferried across the rushing current in a keel boat manned by expert French oarsmen. He knew no one in the town but soon found comfortable lodgings with a French family and within a week had opened a law office on Rue de la Tour.

Benton soon saw in the cosmopolitan little city of St. Louis adequate field for his talents. The Territory of Missouri was now the Far West, flanked on all but the river side by vast stretches of wilderness inhabited by Indians. Steamers and flatboats were operated on the Mississippi, but the adventurous woodsmen and plainsmen, not content with traffic along the river towns, were organizing trading expeditions across the wilderness to the Mexican settlements on Rio del Norte. These caravans, while bringing back precious metals and furs along the track later to be known as the Santa Fé Trail, brought what was to prove of greater value than all their treasure: fabulous stories of the wonders of that rich uncharted region to the west.

St. Louis was the outfitting post for these expeditions. Among her six thousand citizens were a few doughty survivors of Augustine Chouteau's original trading-post party of 1764, as well as scores of Scotch, Irish, and German settlers who had left Illinois to escape English rule. Here also were descendants of the early Spanish and French officials, traders, trappers, and friendly Indians.

Benton found the dominant feeling of the town French, and at once set himself to perfecting his speaking knowledge of the language. Soon he was doing a highly profitable law practice among the French residents as well as among the New Englanders, Kentuckians, and Virginians, who formed this colorful cross-section of the new America. His wealthier clients lived in homes along Rue Royale and Rue de la Tour, streets beautifully shaded but unpaved.

Among these homes was that of Colonel Auguste Chouteau. Built of stone with a pillared portico, it was surrounded by a wall two feet thick and ten feet high, with portholes through which to shoot Indians in case of attack. The interior was elegantly furnished with floors of polished black walnut, chair coverings and curtains of red brocade, and walls adorned with mirrors and paintings. Guests came and went at all hours, and the sound of music echoed through the halls by day and night. At the dances and dinner parties here and in similar homes, Benton was introduced to a life which charmed him with its freshness of enjoyment, its light-hearted rather than stoical acceptance of experience. His own scholarly qualities and gracious high-bred manner made him a welcome guest.

Soon his letters home enlarging upon the kindly nature of the townspeople brought encouraging replies from his mother. He built a house and then departed for Bentontown to visit her. On a June morning in 1817, Anne Benton again turned her face resolutely toward a new life. She and Thomas, accompanied by her orphaned grandchild Sarah, stood in her dooryard surrounded by tearful neighbors. In the background a dusky crowd of lamenting plantation negroes formed a chorus. Anne Benton wept with them but held to her purpose. After a pleasant journey to St. Louis by carriage and steamboat, she found awaiting her a commodious brick house on a block of ground surrounded by trees. Here with her old servants to care for her, Anne Benton was established, her own furniture about her, the shelves filled with her favorite books. Here she was to live for twenty years, watching with pride the career of the son for love of whom she still found life sweet.

Among the first visitors to the Benton home was General William Clark, Governor of the Territory. Through his influence Benton was urged to accept the appointment as member of the first board of school trustees. From the policies of this board originated the Missouri system of public education. Benton was held to be "a man of ideas sound though advanced."

The Romantic Movement, begun long before in Europe, was now in full swing in the United States. In New England, the South, and the West, men's minds had broken with tradition. Attuned to change, they were pursuing adventure in every line of thought: theology, education, economics, and politics. The old America was passing. On the frontier, a sturdy ambitious people of romantic mind was visioning new fields for planting toward a new harvest. Men of widely divergent background were rapidly becoming fused into a group with identical aims and ambitions. Already they called themselves Westerners, children of a destiny which intended them to own all frontier America; their heritage, ready for the taking, waited only leaders of courage and enterprise.

In Thomas Benton they found a man of integrity, educated, resolute, proud of his country, confident of her capacity for development. They hailed him as their leader, their man of vision. In 1819 as editor of the *St. Louis Enquirer*, he was writing trenchant articles advocating trade expansion, expressing his belief that we should penetrate the farthest wilderness, make good our title to it, and "place it forever under the domination of our people."

Benton's popularity soon took him into the Senatorial contest of 1819, when Missouri was asking admission as a state. His entrance into national politics coincided with the appearance of the slave question as a political issue. The Northerners, wishing to restrict the spread of the slave power, demanded that Missouri abolish slavery within her borders; the South demanded that she enter the Union as a slave state.

As a slave holder, Benton instinctively favored the anti-restriction side, but he believed in the extreme views of neither side. When Congress passed the Missouri Compromise bill, he heartily agreed, announcing that he was "equally opposed to slavery agitation and slavery extension."

Benton's uprightness of character, his delicate sense of honor were shown in two public acts just after his election to the Senate in 1819. As a prominent attorney he was often consulted in land-title disputes. Many of these titles were based on old French and Spanish grants later ratified by Congress under conditions which the Creole holders, usually from ignorance, rarely fulfilled. In taking these claims before the United States Recorder of Titles, the majority of attorneys insisted that the claims be held void. Benton declared it nothing short of criminal to forfeit property on technical grounds. He advocated the confirmation of all honest claims and took many of these titles under his professional charge.

His first act after being elected Senator was to convene his claims-clients and announce that since the successful prosecution of their claims depended upon acts of Congress of which he was now a member, he must be freed from the consulting of any personal private interest. While this decision lost him many large fees, it added immeasurably to the respect in which his constituents held him.

During these years of Benton's swift rise to power, Anne Gooch Benton, sitting among her books and companioned by her favorite granddaughter Sarah, received frequent reports from her son and held many conferences with him. She had watched with interest the events of the first term of the courteous, tactful James Monroe, last President of the House of Virginia. Benton was entering the Senate at the beginning of Monroe's second term in 1820. She bade her son Godspeed as he left for Washington to take his place in the Senate and to bring to happy conclusion his six-year courtship of Elizabeth McDowell of Virginia.

CHAPTER II

"Colonel McDowell's to the Mountain Top"

THE family legend of the McDowells arose in Scotland in the misty ages when, under the cloudberry bush as the badge of their clan, they fought for the overthrow of the right line of the Stuarts. The legend later moved from the hills of Argyleshire to Ireland where, under the protection of Cromwell, the Mc-Dowells lived in peace and furnished their quota of scholars and statesmen to the world. Later still, in 1729, the legend moved to colonial America with the coming of Ephraim McDowell and his family.

The English sailing vessel, the *George and Ann,* which brought the Mc-Dowells, brought also their neighbors, the Campbells, the Calhouns, the Irvines, the McElroys, and the Mitchels. Six other vessels that week brought additional Ulster men, weary of English oppression and hungry for land of their own. Before sailing, these colonists had heard highly romantic stories of the fertile lands and vast waterways of inland America, paradise for trappers, traders, farmers, and herders.

Ephraim McDowell and several of his neighbors had exact information of a prosperous Dutch settlement along a range of the Alleghanies. Within a few weeks after landing, these hardy Scotch-Irish had been welcomed by the Dutch settlers and were soon adapting themselves to a life of freedom of speech and hard work repaid by ample profits.

For eight years Ephraim raised grain and cattle. His son James and his son-in-law James Greenlee floated their cargoes of pelts in canoe and keel boat, and trudged the narrow trails beside their Indian pack ponies in trade with the settlers of the coast region. His son John, a skilled surveyor, was in great demand in the settlement. Mary Greenlee, the daughter, kept house for her widower father, working at cheese and butter making, cooking great joints of beef, baking bread, and teaching her three young children to read and write and recite the catechism.

Returning travelers from the south were by now (1735) bringing romantic tales from the valley of Virginia. James McDowell, well informed and of inquiring mind, decided to investigate these stories. In the spring of 1737, he made a lone journey to the James River. By September he was back again with the glowing reports of a land ranging over wide stretches, "seemly to the eye, of a rich soil, bearing tobacco, rice, and corn, and of a climate that breeds English gentlefolk, fair in person, of good manner and lively spirit."

Among the men James had met in Virginia was John Lewis, who had title to a part of Beverly Manor, a great body of land patented to the Randolphs by the Governor, Sir William Gooch. James had bought a plot of this land from Lewis and now jovially announced himself to his father as James Mc-Dowell of Beverly Manor.

Ephraim McDowell was getting old. Further pioneering did not appeal to him. His farm was successful, his home comfortable. He spoke of his fat cattle, his plans for putting in winter wheat, and the present market for his butter and cheese. He declined to consider the move until one day his daughter Mary, sprightly, strong, and only thirty-one, announced that because of her children's health she would like to move to a warmer climate. She declared that since she had been superintending the cheese and butter making, she felt entitled to enough money to enable her own little family to make the move. This declaration, added to the arguments of James, proved efficacious. Later in the autumn after seeding time, the family lands and such livestock as was not to be taken along were sold to neighbors; and the household goods were packed into the great Conestoga wagons ready for the journey south.

In an eight-family caravan, the party made its slow way through the forests and across the ravines of the hill country along crude wagon roads cut below the Indian trails. The men carried block and tackle to lower the wagons down the steep inclines and to lift them from an occasional muddy morass where the loads almost sank from sight. The women and children rode in the covered wagons when the going was safe, but when it was bad, they rode horseback, seated on a pillion behind a saddle rider. Mary, restless and adventurous, often rode alone, accompanying the outriders who tested streams for fording and sought detours around treacherous marshes, keeping always a sharp lookout for Indians.

Along the James River Valley the party found occasional settlements of other English and Scotch colonists. The sight of church, schoolhouse, and groups of log houses protected by a stockade influenced several families to stop at one or another of these settlements. The McDowells pushed on to a vast and beautiful grant belonging to Benjamin Bordon, upon which he had that year settled one hundred families from Scotland.

The land grants of Governor Gooch were all similarly conditioned: one thousand acres for every family, but within ten years there must be not fewer than one hundred families. When this condition was met, additional land could be had for one shilling per acre. The astute Mr. Bordon, by settling a hundred families in one year, enabled them and himself to enlarge their holdings immediately at this small price. The grant to which Bordon was leading the McDowell family lay midway of the valley, its eastern boundary following the crest of the Blue Ridge for forty miles. Against the far horizon loomed an impressive landmark, a great bridge of natural rock which seemed to command the whole valley.

The caravan now traveled through an autumn wood of oak, elm, and chestnut, glowing richly against the somber greens of pine and cedar. As they drove along the water courses, the air was awhir with myriads of ducks and pigeons. A warm breeze was blowing, and a warm sun shone above them. Here was paradise indeed, a country beautiful and ingratiating. Here the McDowells decided that their land should lie in the shadow of that great natural bridge. Mary, riding her horse at the head of the little procession, was the first white woman to enter the country which was later to be called Rockbridge County and which was to be the seat of the McDowell family for many generations. In exchange for John McDowell's work in surveying the Bordon grant, the family was given additional acreage so that their land patent read "from the intersections of the streams to the tops of all the mountains in sight."

With a keen eye to business, Mary urged her father to write to relatives in England that all the advantages of health and ultimate wealth were to be found in this region. She herself hopefully entrusted many letters to the uncertainties of the newly established post. By another autumn, kindred and coreligionists from England were living on the land now dignified as Rockbridge County Settlement. Ere long the county roster read: Stuart, Patton, Preston, Campbell, Calhoun, and many another, the fruit of whose family trees was to prove nourishing to the body politic.

Ephraim McDowell and his family, strongly imbued with individualistic ideas and aware of the restrictions in the northern colonies, were glad to find themselves in this atmosphere of freedom, in a colony developing a life independent of seaboard and tidewater country. They and their English and Scotch-Irish neighbors practiced the arts of peace in this, the veritable Cradle of Democracy. As time went on, their manner of life, the elements that entered into the working out of their ideals became significant, symbolic of the family history which is the nation's history in the making.

The McDowells, living in their substantial house of brick and cypress, intermarrying with their neighbors of like spiritual and social inheritance, helped to form that older Virginia, the background for the culture which invested later plantation life with the richness and warmth of romance. It was a broad tolerant life, running parallel with the growth of the natural-rights philosophy of France and England.

This significant phase of plantation life was carefully fostered by Sir William Gooch, cultured, shrewd, and kindly, who had presided over Virginia since 1727. Sir William, Thomas Hart, and William Byrd held frequent counsel with Ephraim McDowell and his son John over various projects for the benefit of the colony. The McDowell plantation had become highly developed, and its proprietors renowned for their enterprise. Ephraim built the first road across the Blue Ridge to connect the valley with the tidewater country, affording direct means of egress for the valley products and facilities for securing desirable European goods from tidewater merchants.

Mary, presiding as mistress of Cherry Grove, was typical lady of the manor. She superintended the indoor activities of the household and became renowned among the neighboring plantations for the superior quality of the spinning, dyeing, and weaving operations carried on in the negro quarters. Her children, now numbering seven, were dressed in clothing woven and made on the plantation. They were nourished with vegetables and fruits abounding in garden and orchard. When ailing, they were dosed with rhubarb and quinine. Their education was carried on in a small private school kept by a gentleman from Edinburgh, who added French and Latin to the usual list of subjects taught the Rockbridge County children. Mary's enterprise and practical knowledge were of such wide repute that those who came to confer with the men of her family often asked that she join in their deliberations.

Upon one occasion, in a discussion over increasing land values as lure to prospective colonists, she impressed her visitors by saying:

You do well to praise the richness of the soil and to pity the folk of New England, a country reputed to be of a cold and gloomy spirit and so barren withal that except a herring be put into the hole you set the corn in, it will not come up. But none of you hold of sufficient worth the beauty of this country, its color and warmth, which enter into the spirit of the people and give to each a gracious climate of his own It is this as well as soil and crop which my brother James noted upon his first visit to Virginia.

These conferences were not without their spirited verbal encounters, for Mary was known to encourage the enterprise of other women, even to the extent of slyly defending the girl colonist who, upon finding no land being granted to women, disguised herself in male attire and acquired a fine plantation thereby. "Quite as shrewd and no more dishonest," averred Mary, "than the device of the man who acquired many acres by giving settlers' names to his cattle." She also defended the widely criticized plan, originated by William Byrd, of building towns as trading marts in the vicinity of the plantations. She agreed with her neighbors that town life held no lure, the plantation being a community of itself, but in Mr. Byrd's flourishing town of Richmond one might purchase mirrors and candelabra, fine mahogany furniture, English-wrought silver, and books of French fashions, all of which were held to be essentials of living at Cherry Grove and other prosperous estates.

Mary McDowell was by now twice widowed but still known throughout the colony as Mary McDowell. Although her sons negotiated the sale of crops and improved the breed of their horses, they were often away for long periods, fox hunting, gambling, and indulging in the pleasures of their class. The enterprise which characterized Mary McDowell was directed toward the active management of the vast plantation.

JESSIE BENTON FRÉMONT: a Woman Who Made History

The black man of the late 1700's was considered merely as a domestic servant who produced the crops and worked indoors in return for ample food, clothing, and shelter. At that, he was often held to be a costly luxury. In 1763 a local minister said in addressing the planters:

It would be for every man's interest if there were no slaves, because the labor of a free man, hired and paid for the work he does and only for what he does, is in the end cheaper than the eye service of a slave.

In 1775 Ephraim McDowell died, leaving Mary to carry on the family tradition. As "Aunt Mary" she had long been mentor and friend to a score of younger generation McDowells, many of whose parents she had outlived. So thoroughly had her viewpoint kept pace with the changing times that they heard her refer to the past only in contrast to the more admirable present. And now at seventy she accompanied these relatives on horseback over miles of plantation, advising young men half her age how best to win full cooperation of fellow planters, overseers, and slaves: "In business, give every man his full due, and exact your own dues as fully. Only thus will you hold the respect of others." As to marriage she gave to each the same advice: "Ours is an honorable family. See to it that you marry only one who will bring honor to it."

The family history would indicate her advice to have been well taken, since the McDowell family was later connected by marriage with the distinguished and scholarly Irvine, Paxton, Cloyd, and Lyle families. Mary's son Samuel had rendered signal service as a Colonel in the Revolution. His son James had enlisted as a colonial soldier at sixteen and continued in service until victory crowned the American Army at Yorktown. But it was James McDowell, son of James McDowell and Elizabeth Cloyd, who became Mary's protégé and her favorite among them all, "because of his sense of honor in small things and his thoroughness at any given task." He stood six feet two and was so fine a horseman and swordsman that she predicted great things for him, "should our times ever again bring a man's sword into honorable action against an enemy." Her prediction was verified, for Colonel James McDowell was in command of a regiment in the War of 1812, serving part of the time as flying guard along the coast of the Chesapeake to prevent the landing of British marines.

Jessie Benton Frémont: a Woman Who Made History

Upon his inheritance of Cherry Grove, James' sense of fairness prompted him to divide the lands equally, although he had been born under the law of primogeniture. In this division one-third went to his mother. James McDowell credited Mary with having contributed immeasurably to the development of the younger generation, "because she successfully demonstrated in her own life the practical virtues she extolled." He helped to preserve the classic stories of her fearlessness and wit. A favorite anecdote concerned a lawsuit over the sale of a slave wherein these traits came near getting her involved in a charge of witchcraft. When asked her age, she retorted: "Why do you ask? Do you think I'm in my dotage? I am only ninety-five, sir!" And when she won the case by her accurate memory, her discomfited adversary declared that only a witch could remember so far back in nigger history and that he was tempted to prefer charges against her.

The hundred and four years of Mary McDowell's life covered an epoch in American history. She saw the rise and passing of the wholly self-reliant planter and the rise of the cavalier with his keen sense of civic responsibility. Later when the fast-spreading industrial spirit was seizing all Americans, she encouraged her own restless ones to go westward but herself remained among those other McDowells, solid planters and freeholders whose grants had become great and valuable estates.

Colonel James McDowell, a grandson of Mary's protégé, married Sarah Preston, one of a large family of Lancashire English who had come over in the middle 1700's. She was a daughter of Colonel William Preston and a popular belle. Gentle, light-hearted, and efficient, she presided with ease over the rambling red-brick house with its hospitable spread of wings. She directed a small army of black house servants in the care of the old English plate and the furniture, and trained her three children with loving and whimsical patience. Cherry Grove was scarcely ever free of visitors. Many times in a single week the mahogany dining table was stretched to full capacity of twenty. From it, hot breads, flesh, fowl, and pastries were served three times a day.

Of the three children, Susan, James, and Elizabeth, it was Elizabeth, small, dark, and vivacious, who became the favorite of the household. Her room was the sunniest, its appointments of the best: dressing table with its silver candelabra, four-post mahogany bed with its plump featherbeds, fine linen sheets, and spread of blue damask. Her popularity among the young men and women of the county kept the drawing room filled with gayety. Elizabeth entertained her suitors with the popular ballads of the day and played the pianoforte with skill. At a ball in Richmond she was described as "dancing with dainty grace, her dark beauty set off by a gown of pink brocade over very small hoops, her tiny feet encased in pearl-silk stockings and buckled slippers."

She was a great favorite with her uncle, Governor James Preston, and upon her frequent visits to the Capital, she drove to Richmond accompanied by her own maid and man servant in her own London-built coach of yellow, lined with scarlet morocco. During one of these visits, the Governor introduced his house guest, Thomas Hart Benton of St. Louis. Elizabeth had often heard her uncle speak of his friend Benton as a most admirable young man destined for a future worthy of his unusual talents, but she did not dream that he already considered this man an excellent match for his pretty niece. She saw a tall gentleman with reddish-blond hair, ruddy complexion, and kindly blue eyes looking down at her in respectful admiration. The next day he expressed this admiration to the Governor and to Elizabeth herself in no uncertain terms. The Governor was highly pleased, but to Elizabeth, Thomas Benton was just another in a long line of suitors, not particularly good looking and so openly enamored as to seem tongue-tied and dull among the handsome, eloquent cavaliers of her little court. Moreover, she had learned that he was twelve years her senior.

A few weeks later, Benton became a guest in her own home where both parents fell under the spell of this courtly gentleman in high black-silk stock and double-breasted suit, whose deferential manner, combined with an astonishingly wide knowledge of affairs, made him a welcome visitor indeed. Heretofore, James and Sarah McDowell had not attempted to influence their daughter in her choice of a husband, but now her father declared her quite wrong in thinking Mr. Benton other than brilliant and eloquent. Her mother declared the girl to be equally mistaken in thinking him not handsome, with his English good looks and truly distinguished manner. At this point, more encouraged by the friendliness of her parents than by word or sign from Elizabeth, Benton proposed and was promptly rejected. "Hurt and disheartened," he departed for St. Louis the following day. Elizabeth considered the matter closed, but she reckoned without knowledge of the tenacity of purpose and steadfastness in love which characterized her new suitor.

James McDowell, 1804. Great uncle of Jessie Benton Frémont.

The following year while on business in Washington, Benton again visited the McDowells at Cherry Grove. Again he proposed and was rejected, "gently but with a firmness disconcerting indeed in one so gentle," he remarked to his mother upon his return. The next proposal a year later was by letter, in answer to an encouraging statement from Mrs. McDowell that although Elizabeth had refused him, she had not accepted anyone else. Elizabeth's reply to this proposal was to urge that he seek someone else for his wife. He replied truthfully: "No other woman except my mother has ever fully engaged my affections. There is no one else for me, and I shall not lose hope until I learn you are definitely pledged to another." The fifth proposal came during the Senatorial campaign when Benton was already a nationally known figure. Elizabeth replied to this with candor that matched his own: "Papa and Mamma admire and respect you. I humbly admire and respect you, but I have decided that I could never marry an Army man, a Democrat, or a man with red hair." Benton's reply to this was characteristic:

I cannot alter the color of my hair. I could not be other than a Democrat without violence to principle, but if you become my wife, I shall resign all connection with the Army and shall arrange that you spend as little time in the West as need be, for I, who love home and to whom family ties are very dear, appreciate your sentiments about Cherry Grove and your parents.

Touched by the persistence, loyalty, and tenderness of her lover, Elizabeth accepted this sixth proposal in December, 1820.

In a letter to Governor Preston, Benton apologized for crossing the Alleghanies without visiting him:

But the vortex of business in which I was swallowed up in St. Louis detained me there to the last moment, and when I set out, it was to go by the shortest road to see one whom I find to be inexpressibly dear to me under every circumstance of my life, and thence to this place to attend to my duties.

On March 14 he wrote to his friend Robert Wash of St. Louis:

What I have to say will be both agreeable for me to tell and for my friends to hear. It is no less than that long before the drowsy and heedless postboy shall transport you this scrawl, that is to say, on the twentieth day of this same March your friend Benedick will cease to belong to the order of bachelors.

JESSIE BENTON FRÉMONT: a Woman Who Made History

Time, which puts an end to everything, has put an end to my endless courtship, and in the month of May I shall hope for the happiness of imparting my happiness to all my friends in St. Louis by presenting to them one who is everything to me and who I hope will be something to them. In the meantime I appoint you in conjunction with my well-tried and much-beloved friend Jeremiah Connor Esq. to spread this joyful intelligence when and where it shall behoove me to make it known.

Thine,

THOS. H. BENTON

On his wedding day, March 20, 1821, Benton wrote thus to Governor Preston at Smithfield, Virginia:

I must take a moment on this great day to inform my dear friends at Smith field that I shall be married this evening. It is indeed a great day to me, for I consider it the first day of my life and the beginning of the only existence which is worth having. My dear Elizabeth will set out with me the first week of April, and soon after, be at Smithfield to stay as long as her husband's pressing affairs will permit him to stop, but not so long as her and his wishes would dictate.

Sincerely, truly, and happily yours,

THOMAS H. BENTON

That evening the guests not already staying at Cherry Grove drove through the park of ancient oaks, up the long avenue of cherry trees, and alighted before the house decorated inside and out for the wedding festivities. In the spacious hall they met a cordon of black retainers headed by Colonel McDowell's young body servant Ralph. At eight o'clock, in the candle-lighted drawing room they gathered to witness the marriage of their popular Elizabeth McDowell to Senator Thomas H. Benton of Missouri. Later the Bentons departed in a private coach for Richmond, and after a short visit left for Washington with the special felicitations of Governor Preston, who took full share of credit for the match.

Benton had comfortable quarters in Washington and attempted with true consideration to duplicate as nearly as possible the conveniences, if not the spaciousness, of Cherry Grove. Elizabeth quickly justified her husband's de-

[25]

scriptions of her as "a woman of sense, education, and good breeding." She was soon as much at home in official life in Washington as she had been at Richmond, and in fact, she entered no home that approached in beauty and comfort that fine old colonial mansion built and furnished by the Crown for the Virginia Governors.

From the first, Thomas Benton realized his good fortune in being able to continue his lifelong habit of discussing his problems, public and personal, with a sympathetic and intelligent woman. Elizabeth McDowell Benton was second only to Anne Gooch Benton herself in discriminating judgment upon matters not directly within her province but upon which she desired to be rightly informed. In response to this attitude, Benton conferred with her daily and looked upon his wife as "having really entered public life with him."

Although scholarly and well informed as to conditions throughout the country, Benton stood in awe of the body of forty-eight eminent men which comprised the United States Senate. Long afterward he referred to this as "the period when the national legislature appeared to the greatest advantage . . . when the surviving great men of the first generation were still upon the stage, and the gigantic progeny of the second were mounting to it."

Daniel Webster was not there yet, nor Henry Clay, nor John Calhoun, but the present members were those whose achievements dated to pre-Revolutionary days. John Gaillard of South Carolina was president, while that distinguished old Democrat, Nathaniel Macon, whom Jefferson had called "the last of the Romans," still represented North Carolina. Rufus King, Father of the Senate, aristocrat and stubborn Federalist, was still a man of influence, though his party was in ruins. His youthful colleague was Martin Van Buren, yet to win his spurs. In the House were the brilliant William Lowndes, nearing the end of his long career, the eccentric John Randolph in boots and spurs, and James Buchanan, nearly as new in his career as was Benton.

Nathaniel Macon took a fatherly interest in the Bentons, much to the delight of both. He greatly admired Elizabeth and the ease with which she adapted herself to her position. On Sundays he frequently accompanied the young couple to the Presbyterian Church where Benton, though not himself religious, had taken a pew out of deference to Elizabeth's wishes. So joyously frank was Benton in showing his happiness that his knightly air of protective tenderness to his wife became a matter of comment among his intimates. One unregenerate young man declared it "a sight worth going to church for, to see Benton enter with his wife on his arm, proudly walking up the aisle and placing her in a pew."

So impatient was Benton to present Elizabeth to his family and friends in St. Louis that the close of the session saw them ready to depart from Washington. Anne Benton was anxious to welcome her son and his bride. True, her pride had been flicked by Elizabeth's delayed acceptance of one whom she considered second to no man in America, but being a wise woman, she withheld all critical comment until advised by letter of the impending marriage. Then with a rare touch of irony she remarked to her niece: "Army man, Westerner, Democrat, red hair—these are in fuller force than ever, after six years." But if Elizabeth McDowell's dilatory acceptance had touched Anne Benton's pride, Elizabeth McDowell Benton's tenderly filial letters had touched her heart, and upon the young couple's arrival her greeting to her daughter-in-law was all that the most sensitive bride could wish.

St. Louis society welcomed Senator and Mrs. Benton with all the honors due to their position and in addition showed such whole-hearted friendliness to the bride as to dissipate her last prejudice against the West. In the autumn the Bentons returned to Washington. They spent Christmas at Cherry Grove where Elizabeth was to remain with her parents until after her confinement in February. On February 20, 1822, a daughter was born. She was named Eliza. So delighted with fatherhood was Benton that he began boyishly making plans for her safe travel to St. Louis the coming summer. A letter from the Senate Chamber in Washington on December 28, 1822, to Colonel Preston reads:

We arrived here on the ninth, myself, Elizabeth, and the child. We are very well but had a narrow escape on the road, the carriage being overturned and pitched with violence on its broad side down a rocky hill. Happily no one was hurt but myself. I got a cut of four inches on the head, which is not yet well.

The President inquired very kindly after you. Messrs. Crawford, Clay, and Adams are the persons chiefly spoken of here for the Presidency, and of these three, the two former are deemed to have the best chance by all with whom I converse. Nothing of any moment is as yet done here.

Benton spent much of his leisure during the 1822-1823 session in gaining the friendship of his colleagues. He now had the advantage of Nathaniel Macon as close friend and adviser, and had "broken the ice with King." Robert Hayne, newly elected Senator from South Carolina, was soon to become a close and loyal friend.

Benton had seen very little of Andrew Jackson since their classic encounter in Nashville, echoes of which were kept reverberating by gossip-loving adherents of both. All agreed, however, that "two such iron-strong characters were difficult to speculate about with any certainty." Benton had often rehearsed a possible meeting with Jackson, who still carried Benton's bullet in his shoulder as painful reminder of their old quarrel. He knew that Jackson's recent election as Senator from Tennessee now made the encounter imminent. A few days after Congress opened (December, 1823), Benton was astonished to see Jackson walk deliberately to the empty chair next his own and select it as his seat for the session. Benton wrote thus of the renewal of their friendship, never again to be broken:

General Jackson is now sitting in the seat next to me. There was a vacant one, and he took it for the session. Several Senators saw our situation and offered mediation. I declined it on the ground that what had happened could neither be explained, resented, nor denied. After this, we were put upon the same committee. Facing me one day as we sat in our seats, he said to me: "Colonel, we are on the same committee. I will give you notice when it is necessary to attend!" (He was chairman.) I answered: "General, make the time suit yourself. It will be convenient for me to attend any time." In committee, we did business together just as other persons. After that, he asked me how my wife was, and I asked him how his was. When he called and left his card, "Andrew Jackson, for Colonel Benton and Lady," forthwith I called and left mine: "Colonel Benton for General Jackson and Lady." Since then we have dined together at several places, and yesterday at the President's. I made him the first bow. He held forth his hand and we shook hands. I then introduced him to my wife, and thus civil relations are perfectly established between us. Jackson has gained, since he has been here, by his mild and conciliatory manner.

From Elizabeth's letters to Anne Benton we know that this renewal of friendly relations was a matter of deepest gratification to Benton, for his trust and affection once given, loyalty remained stubborn. Despite Rachel Jackson's crudeness, her staunch nature had its effect upon the discriminating Mrs. Benton, who gained the undying affection of Jackson for her open friendliness to the woman who, as wife of Governor Jackson of Florida, had been the recipient of many slurs and indignities from the official family.

May, 1824, found the Bentons again at Cherry Grove, where Elizabeth awaited her second confinement. The expected child had already been named Thomas in the happy certainty of its being a boy. But when the father was admitted to his wife's room shortly after the infant's arrival, he was informed that the mite whose dark head he saw among the folds of a fluffy pink blanket was another daughter. Instinctive sportsmanship prompted his declaration: "Two daughters are a crown to any household."

The new arrival was at once named Jessie Anne Benton.

CHAPTER III

A Washington Childhood

THE year 1830 found the Benton family established in a commodious brick house on Sixteenth Street, Washington. This house, planned by a Bostonian after the best British tradition, boasted spacious rooms with high ceilings, oak floors, and capacious fireplaces. Among the articles of choice mahogany furniture included in the purchase was a dining table that "stretched" to seat twenty-four. The garden, playground, and coach house were surrounded by a high wall covered with ivy and scarlet trumpet vine. From the drawing-room windows one could see in winter the broad stretch of the Potomac almost to Alexandria. Steamboats puffed importantly past, and sailboats tacked their quiet way. In the street below passed the Blue Safety Coaches with their handsome horses and trappings.

Despite the dignity of the White House and the Capitol and the formal beauty of Pennsylvania Avenue with its triple lanes of Lombardy poplars, Washington still bore the appearance of an overgrown village, but her close neighbors, Alexandria and Georgetown, were already old when George Washington laid the cornerstone of the Capitol in 1793. Since 1780, families of culture had lived in comfortable homes well staffed with servants, and had sent their children to the classical academy. Sir Augustus Foster, British Minister in Jefferson's time, had said: "There is no want of handsome ladies for the balls, especially in Georgetown. I never saw prettier girls anywhere." With these families and the Capital's official family, Washington was already developing a tradition as "the drawing room of the nation." Hospitality stimulated by Southern influence was a deeply rooted custom, blossoming above all difficulties of distance and poor transportation.

The names of Senators were resonant names held in high respect. Thomas and Elizabeth Benton moved at the center of that dignified procession which had marched through the years since 1824, the year they had returned from Cherry Grove with their small daughter Eliza and the new baby, Jessie Anne.

Upon the election of John Quincy Adams, the brilliant inaugural ball made social history. Senator Benton, who liked his wife "set off in pale blue and lace," proudly escorted the beautiful Elizabeth in a gown of azure-blue brocade fashioned over small hoops, with blond lace outlining the deep-pointed bodice, panniers, and train. A corsage of camellias and a single blossom in her dark hair completed the costume.

A high point in that Washington season was the visit of Owen of Lenark, a social reformer, founder of a Utopian community in Indiana. His lecture at the Capital was attended by social Washington headed by Adams and Monroe. The Bentons gave a dinner for Owen at which the Senator declared: "To your credo *education*, I would add, sir: 'Make each man happy on a piece of ground that belongs to him, and he becomes patriotic as well, willing to fight for the land he tills'." Later, Benton smiled at seeing this statement quoted in Owen's Baltimore lecture.

Two acts at this time reveal the strength of character for which Benton was ever famous. Though an ardent Jacksonian Democrat, he refused to join Jackson and Randolph in the hue and cry they raised against Adams for rewarding Henry Clay with the office of Secretary of State. In the Randolph-Clay duel, a consequence of Randolph's having called the Clay-Adams coalition "an alliance of the Blackleg and the Puritan," Benton was on the field as a friend of both parties.

This duel was meat for one of Benton's favorite anecdotes. The diminutive Randolph, clad in a dressing gown, made a ludicrous picture as he faced his tall lanky opponent. Neither contestant was hurt, since Randolph fired into the air, and Clay was no shot at all. As the contestants separated, Benton asked Clay: "Why didn't you kill Randolph?" Clay replied: "I aimed at the part of his gown where I thought he was, but when the bullet go there, he had moved."

In the election of 1828, Benton worked at strengthening the backbone of the Western Democrats, who recognized in Jackson their most eminent representative. Upon Jackson's election to the Presidency, a congratulatory letter sent by the Bentons to the Hermitage found him sitting in speechless grief at the bedside of his wife, who had just died of a heart attack. She was buried on the day a statewide demonstration had been planned; the drums that were to proclaim Jackson's victory rolled her funeral dirge. After she had been laid to rest in the Hermitage garden, Jackson was finally persuaded to take the journey to Washington. Upon arrival, he turned to the Bentons for solace in the overwhelming grief and bitterness born of his belief that his wife had been killed by the scandalous attacks upon him and herself in the opposition press.

Rachel Jackson had been befriended by Elizabeth Benton during one of those brief unhappy stays in Washington, and now Jackson found easement in talking with her and the small girls, Eliza and Jessie. His niece, Mrs. Donelson, who was to preside at the White House, found in Mrs. Benton a wise social adviser and confidante. By an amusing coincidence the name of President Jackson is connected with the first anecdote of Jessie Benton's childhood.

Jessie was a healthy little girl of five, with the red-brown curls, brown eyes, and delicately tinted oval features which already foretold her beauty. Her mother's preoccupation with the ailing Eliza and the infant Randolph released Jessie for long periods to her own devices. To her father she was from the first an enchanting but exasperating child, with dynamic quality, a will to do something about it, a force and fearlessness which marked her as his own. He realized that such a personality must express itself and that certain salient characteristics, even now emerging, must be developed under strong and steady guidance. Although her preference for his companionship over that of her mother and the other children was "frank as fever," there was no danger of its becoming a fixation in so well-balanced a child. However, it aided Benton in directing her activities, for he found that his praise acted upon her as a heady stimulant; his displeasure, as an effective check. Gradually a corner of his library near the fire became Jessie's, and visitors at this time described with amusement the picture of a small girl lying on the floor while she turned the pages of a volume of illustrated travels or history and spelled out the printed matter to herself as best she could until the visitor's departure should release her father for further instruction.

Jessie's first tactical error under this régime came when she was very young, but it had a gracious dénouement, for it pointed up her essential honesty and finesse. For months before Jackson's election she had heard "Hurrah for Jackson" echoed in the street below the library windows, and upon inauguration day she had observed her father's elation over the acclaim of "that monstrous crowd" surging through the city.

Shortly thereafter, Benton finished writing a speech against Senator Foote's bill to remove all public lands from the market except those already taken up by settlers. Carefully placing the finished manuscript on his desk, he allowed a few discarded sheets of the rough draft to drop to the floor, as he departed on an errand. Presently Eliza and Jessie came in to keep an appointment for a walk around Lafayette Square with their father. In new blue velvet pelisses they entered the library only to find it empty. With decorous regard for their new coats and bonnets, they sat quietly for a few moments; then Jessie, looking about for something to interest her, spied the sheets of manuscript. Reaching for the box of crayons, she gave a red one to Eliza, who at once set to work on the sheets nearest her. Jessie, with more initiative, preempted her father's chair and sought the neat pile on the desk.

When Benton entered the room, he found his two daughters working in silence, their velvet clothes powdered with chalk, their mouths besmeared from frequent wetting of the crayons. In sudden anger at the havoc, he demanded: "Who led in this thing?" Eliza burst into tears. Jessie, finding herself in a tight place, sought with instinctive resourcefulness for something to propitiate him. Looking up with a solemn expression on her blue-streaked face, she called out: "A little girl that says Hurrah for Jackson." Disarmed and amused, he forgave the offense, corrected Jessie's grammar, and sent the sisters to clean up for the promised walk. In repeating the incident, he chuckled over the fact that Jessie's blue pencil had scored heaviest on his pet paragraph:

The West is my country, not his. I know it; he does not. It is an injury to the human race to undertake to preserve the magnificent valley of the Mississippi for the haunts of wild beasts instead of making it the abode of liberty and civilization, an asylum for the oppressed of all nations.

Were Thomas Benton to be remembered only for the wisdom and tenderness of his parental attitude, his name should be honored in American history, for he was a man who instinctively lived up to the highest psychological requirements. Elizabeth Benton was a devoted but strict Presbyterian mother who believed firmly in discipline. Benton believed firmly in Mrs. Benton, but he taught her to adjust discipline in each case to the temperament of the child.

There were now five children living: Eliza, Jessie, Randolph, Sarah, and Susan. For them, example loomed large as their father set up in his own daily life the standards by which they were to live. He sought out and developed the peculiar aptitudes of each child, and to that end he listened unwearied to every expression of their active growing minds. His solicitude for his family's physical health was shown in ways both effective and highly original for that day. Study-room and nursery windows remained open winter and summer, and daily breathing exercises were insisted upon. The children's hours with a nursery governess were followed by outdoor play and a daily walk regardless of weather. At meals, the children were allowed meat only twice a week; but plenty of milk, fruit, and simply cooked vegetables was served daily. "Thus only will you meet life on a calm stomach," he insisted.

All this was considered Spartan treatment by relatives and friends whose children shared the rich food and drink under which the tables groaned three times a day. Benton, an indefatigable worker and student, kept his own health built up by morning exercises followed by a frugal breakfast of fruit and coffee. Upon his return from the Senate, he always dressed for dinner before joining the family in the drawing room at fifteen minutes to five o'clock, the fashionable Washington dinner hour.

This master of invective, whose voice on occasion shook the rafters of the Senate chamber, was exceedingly mild and gentle in his own home. One of Jessie's earliest memories was that of the tender and prideful tones which greeted them each in turn and commented upon their appearance. At the dinner table, the children were encouraged to speak of any agreeable or amusing experience, but childish faults of tale bearing or sulkiness were duly punished. Their father decreed, however, that "since the unoffending digestion must go on undisturbed," the child should be allowed to finish his dinner unreproved, but the next evening the culprit found his place laid at a table in an adjoining room where he ate the same food as the others, but ate alone.

After dinner, the family assembled in the long drawing room, Mrs. Benton on one side of the fire with her endless needlework done by the light of fragrant beeswax and myrtle-berry candles, Benton, opposite, reading by the light of his own invention: four spermaceti candles fastened in front of a large sheet of white blotting paper. The children were gathered nearby at a low table with their exercise books. From the example of their parents' mutual consideration in small things, they early derived a sense of beauty of loyalty and graciousness. The few inflexible rules they soon recognized as designed to develop a sense of justice and social obligation within the family circle.

Each day Jessie Benton awoke with a healthy young girl's conception of fun, frolic, and study, against a permanent background of parental love. She looked always for some unique adventure to overtake her, and it usually did, since a lively fancy added glamor to her every experience. The Polish tutor, John Sobieski, who lived in the household and taught the children music, history, and French, was at once fascinated and perplexed by the child. Her fund of general information, gained from daily walks and conversations with her father, was immense and varied, her flair for languages unmistakable, but she quickly grew restive under formal routine and sought by every means to vary it.

One day she interrupted the history lesson to tell about truffles: that the Greeks had thought them produced by thunder because they were black, that they grew like tiny potatoes at the roots of hazel trees in France, and that they were dug up by trained "truffle dogs." The tutor listened patiently, then demanded: "But, Miss Jessie, what has this to do with history?" In surprise she exclaimed: "I was telling you the history of truffles."

On another occasion the tutor accompanied Jessie and her sisters to a benefit concert at the orphanage in Georgetown. When the children marched into the hall singing a hymn, Jessie clutched Sobieski's sleeve and whispered: "Do they have to praise God for making them orphans?" After dinner, while Eliza and Sarah chattered about the refreshments, Jessie sat silent. Later she exclaimed: "Oh, father, I didn't know there were that many orphans in the whole world! Surely there can't be love enough to go round in such a place." Her mother hastened to assure her that the Sisters were very kind. Benton made no comment but sat for some minutes in grave contemplation of his impressionable daughter.

As time went on, Jessie sought every excuse to carry her exercise books to her busy but endlessly patient father in that alluring, red-carpeted, book-lined room where by now a chair awaited her near his own desk chair. She often accompanied him to the Capitol, where under the kindly care of the librarian, Mr. Meehan, she was "pastured" in the Congressional Library. Here she sat before low bookstands where Audubon's *Birds* and collections of illustrated travels kept her occupied until noon, when a servant came to fetch her. In her daily walk with her father, she was encouraged to recount her morning's experience. One day it would be a childish transcript of Audubon: a pair of love birds swaying on a birch twig, a humming bird on a bending grass blade. Another day there would be a lively report of a camel train setting out for the desert. Only to his wife did Benton smile over the strange mixture of fact and fancy contained in these accounts. On one of their walks along the river, Jessie picked up the bleached skeleton of a small bird lying half-buried in the flower-strewn grass. She studied it a moment, then carefully replaced it, saying: "When I die, don't bury me in a box. Lay me in a bed of violets, for I want the flowers to grow up through my bones." Such burial her father solemnly promised her.

Jessie frequently accompanied her father on his visits to the White House. James Parton has rightly said of Jackson's reign: "The White House had no dignity. It had more in common with the marquee of a commander-in-chief than the home of a civilized family." Jackson, that despotic old patriot with his hundreds of implacable enemies, was to Jessie Benton an object of innocent admiration and affection, for she knew his love of children and had often seen him smile and wave his pipe absently at her and the other small visitors when they grew too noisy at play.

On these visits she felt perfectly at home in the family sitting room. Here Mrs. Donelson sat with her daughter and guests, the children busy over picture books, the women occupied with their sewing. Jessie would often leave this circle and go to the far end of the apartment to lean against the knee of Jackson, who sat smoking his reed pipe. While he talked to her father, his long bony fingers would smooth her hair. Occasionally when the discussion waxed earnest, those fingers became entangled and pulled painfully, but no protest came from the victim, for she knew that her father would soon make plausible excuse to release her.

The Capitol and Pennsylvania Avenue, Washington, D.C., 1837.

From Jessie's earliest childhood the Bentons had three homes: the official residence in Washington, Anne Benton's house in St. Louis, and the McDowell estate of Cherry Grove near Lexington, Virginia. The springtime visits to these homes opened new vistas to this lively and intelligent child, vistas which helped to prepare her for the cosmopolitan contacts which were to be a vital part of her whole afterlife. In March at the close of the short session of Congress, the Benton children eagerly awaited the two weeks' journey by Blue Safety Coach and steamboat to St. Louis. The road lay along the Cumberland Highway, built by the Government "to join the Ohio to the Old Thirteen." It stretched from Washington to Wheeling, West Virginia, where it connected with the Ohio River navigation.

This two weeks of posting with change of horses every ten miles and nights spent at wayside taverns was to Jessie a fairy-coach trip through enchanted country. Her father often allowed her to sit on the box between the driver and himself when he chose to take the reins, for he was a lover of horses and often drove the entire day. Jessie thought him a much better driver than weatherbeaten Dan, and was especially proud of his skill at the posting stations when the black stablemen loosed the heads of the four fresh plunging horses and with a shout and a waving of arms sent them bounding away. Later, when the pace grew quieter, Jessie would listen to her father's account of visiting the Bonny Clabber country of the Alleghanies where the Dutch settlers were building these red and blue Conestoga freight wagons, covered with white canvas, which moved like a great patriotic procession along the national highway. The sight of these wagons reminded him of his own boyhood struggle in carrying home his Louisville purchases packed in small barrels three to a horse.

Again he and the driver would exchange tales of snowstorms, upsets, and robbers. Sometimes in the midst of these reminiscences, he would pause suddenly to call Jessie's attention to the beauty of the scene: the dark green of the pine forest, the blue-green of the grass lands, the farms with the waving yellow-green of the early wheat. Sunset found the family at supper in a wayside tavern. Afterward the children left the noisy crowded rooms and went upstairs to the downy fastnesses of the big featherbeds and to dreams conjured by sounds from the barroom: the click of billiard balls, the skirl of the violin, and the rhythmic shuffle of a Virginia hoedown.

Jessie Benton Frémont: a Woman Who Made History

At sunrise after a breakfast of ham steak, hominy cakes, and milk, they continued their journey toward the Belle Riviere (the Ohio). When once she was settled on the *New Orleans,* the strange sounds and colors, the variety of complexions, costumes, and languages heightened Jessie's enchantment. The final stretch of posting carried an exciting sense of homecoming. She eagerly awaited the first sight of the tawny rushing waters of the Mississippi and the strange busy town, fragrant with the blossoms of wild plum and crabapple. She "smelled" before she saw her Grandmother Benton's house, with its wide galleries on both stories, screened by a line of locust trees with their long clusters of vanilla-scented blossoms.

Anne Benton, now in her eighties and an invalid, awaited her son and his family in her rooms at the end of the long gallery. The first moments of greeting always perplexed the lively Jessie, for despite her father's being "so happy at coming home," there were tears in his eyes when he bent to kiss grandmother. When it came Jessie's turn to greet the silent old lady sitting on the couch, she trembled as the white fingers motioned her to draw near, and she felt the touch of leaf-dry lips upon her cheek. Before the dinner hour she came with the other children to pay respects again to the remote old lady in the black dress, a lady who asked anxious questions about their health, and without waiting for reply, kept saying: "Stay out in the sunshine and keep your rosy cheeks." Their signal of release was the appearance of Aunt Nancy, carrying a tray with a bowl of broth, a cup of black coffee, and a single slice of toast. Jessie's feeling was one of sadness that grandmother's dresses were always black and that such meager fare must serve as dinner for a grownup.

Next day, out in the town, a whole new world greeted the lively and curious child, a world whose language, customs, and cookery were predominantly French. Houses with galleries sat amid trees and gardens. The broad shaded main street leading to the Cathedral and Bishop's garden was a veritable procession of priests, Sisters of Charity, old French Army officers in service-worn uniforms, French peasant women in their white caps, sabots, and full red petticoats, yellow kerchiefs crossed over white bodices. Painted and blanketed Indians glided along toward General Clark's headquarters, children danced to school, and on toward Grandmother Benton's house there were always people going to talk to her father, still called *l'ami des Français.*

The day after arrival, it was Benton's custom to establish himself on the

[39]

long gallery of the parlor floor with a settee and a writing table, with a colony of chairs nearby for the visitors. These callers ranged from trappers, hunters, and merchants to friends and political allies come to talk comfortably about the administration. Here came picturesque Mexican merchants in gold-embroidered riding breeches and ringing silver spurs. Waiting under the shade trees in the yard were their horses with silver-mounted saddles and bridles. These horses were often in company with others wearing the military saddles, when the officers from Jefferson Barracks came for consultation.

Occasional black-robed Belgian dignitaries came bringing a missionary priest. Wiry French voyageurs in fringed buckskins sometimes joined the group, and always there were the keen-witted French and Spanish-American citizens, also deeply interested in those new trade routes stretching southwestward to the Sea of Cortés.

All these men came animated by the same purpose, the opening of a safe passage westward for trade and emigration. They spoke freely with Benton, for to them the Colonel was omniscient and well-nigh omnipotent. He whose fight against the salt tax had caused his opponents to complain that their soup was always oversalted at Senatorial dinners, and whose perpetual pounding for gold as against paper currency had gained him the nickname, Old Bullion with his Mintdrops, was the Westerner's ideal of force and honesty. Other officials might come and go, but he was a fixture at the Capitol, the link between their interests and the Government.

Even at these vacation times, Benton had his favorite daughter's education in mind. An old Army officer, Colonel Garnier, gave him and Jessie daily lessons in Spanish, Benton declaring he wanted Jessie to know this "neighbor language" that she might talk over the back fence without fear of the trouble an interpreter might easily foment. A certain Captain Lawless often joined them at the close of the lesson, and the talk would fall upon the Peninsular Wars. Jessie would be sent for a map and a box of pins, beeswax heads for the Spanish troops, red wax for the English, and black for the French. When the discussion flared hot, Mrs. Benton usually sent out a truce of fruit and cakes, though her feeling was unalterably English.

Jessie's sympathies were French. Already proficient in the language, she loved to chatter the Creole patois of her black-eyed, tawny-haired, French-American playmates in whose homes she was a frequent visitor. Restless under the narrow Biblicism of her own training, she frankly envied these children their carefree Sundays, when after mass the day became a family fête day. Her own two-service Sunday began Saturday morning when she and her sisters studied their Sunday-school lesson with their mother, laid out their white Sunday dresses, and reluctantly put away all week-day books and toys. Jessie said that she liked Sunday only for the pleasure of sitting next to her father in the family pew. When he was absent, she always exclaimed: "Alas, my day goes badly."

A serious argument between Jessie and her mother was precipitated by this matter of Sunday observance. One Saturday morning Mrs. Benton was hurriedly called to the bedside of a sick relative. This release from Sunday-school lessons gave Jessie a long-wanted opportunity. Folding a nightgown into a small bundle, she slipped out of the house and ran down the street to the home of a favorite French playmate. There she announced that she had come to stay over Sunday. She was heartily welcomed, permission being taken for granted. Hours of rapturous outdoor play followed, but at sundown the French attendant, Madeleine, whom Jessie had eluded, appeared and escorted her home to a private maternal lecture. Jessie readily expressed contrition over having gone visiting without permission, but her mother, not content with that, demanded severely: "And why did you neglect your Sunday-school lesson?" Jessie replied hotly: "Because I planned to go to mass to learn more about a church that doesn't confine your Sunday reading to one good book. Besides, I hate the Presbyterian church—no flowers, no candle light, no pictures." This declaration rendered Mrs. Benton quite speechless, and Jessie was sent to her room to await the return of her father.

When the sisters were preparing for bed that night, Eliza whispered: "And what did father say?" Jessie paused in brushing her curls and whispered back: "He scolded me for disrespect to mother but not to the Presbyterians."

June of the year following the St. Louis summer would find the Benton family caravan en route to Cherry Grove, Virginia. At Fredericksburg they were met by saddle horses and the London-built family traveling coach. This vehicle, huge, high swung, with many springs, and painted a bright yellow, was called the Pumpkin, and its appearance was hailed with joyous squeals from the younger children. They and the luggage were transferred to the coach, while the parents and the older children finished the journey on horseback, the entire caravan stopping overnight at the homes of relatives along the route to Cherry Grove. At the outer limit of the estate Colonel McDowell accompanied by old Ralph always met them. Despite his being partially crippled from a paralytic stroke, Grandfather McDowell insisted upon sitting his horse and taking one of the children from the carriage to ride in front of him. Through the park with its ancient oaks and up the long pleached alley of cherry trees the gay procession moved, to find little Grandmother McDowell laughing and crying for joy as she tried to hug them all at once.

Cherry Grove was a veritable paradise, the broad lawn dotted with maples and sycamores, the garden a riot of roses and honeysuckle. The big house was filled with relatives, and every evening there was music and dancing. Mrs. McDowell tried valiantly to reconcile Benton's notions of health and education with her own ideas of hospitality. In the conviction that Jessie spent too much time with books, she undertook to instruct the child in the details of managing a house.

Delighted and curious over the great bunch of keys involved in this process, Jessie often accompanied her grandmother on the jaunt to the storeroom where the day's food supply for the family and servants was dealt out. Then on beyond masking hedges of holly, they came to the negro village with its head wagoner stand, blacksmith shop, and the shoemaker's. Just beyond was the dairy under the management of Aunt Chloe, wife of the shoemaker; beyond this was the weaving cabin of Aunt Bek, a tall dignified negress who had remarkable skill in dyeing and weaving the plaid linseys so popular as school dresses for the children. Jessie was sometimes allowed to help with the buzzing wheels, carding wool and winding hanks, and to gather green walnuts for the brown-green dyes, sumac for the red, and to watch fascinated as Aunt Bek handled the minerals for the yellows and blues.

Sensitive to that intangible atmosphere which is the soul of every inhabited place, Jessie sometimes eluded everyone and prowled about the woods and streams, fearless in places held fearsome by local tradition. Sometimes she and her younger sisters sat in the little oak-root house and played Loves 'n' Hates. When allowed two expressions of each, Jessie was often temperamental, but when allowed only one, her love was always "father," and her hate, "saying goodbye to someone you love."

Best of all were the days in early autumn when her father took her quail shooting. She trudged across rough stubble fields and clambered in and out of ravines, proudly carrying the game bag until it became too heavy. Under the convenient shade of a tree they ate their luncheon of biscuits and apples unearthed from the deep pockets of his shooting jacket. Resting there, the breeze whipping an even warmer color into her cheeks and blowing her brown curls about, she leaned against her father while he told her stories of his friend Audubon's life, dwelling upon his perseverance and courage as he struggled through the cane brakes of Kentucky, carrying his knapsack with pencil, colors, and food, scaling mountains to watch the eagles, braving Indians, hunger, thirst, and insects to get the true biography of the birds he studied and sketched. Sometimes Benton brought along a small French edition of Homer's *Odyssée* from which he had her translate. In autumn, "just when the trees were reddest," Jessie complained, the family returned to Washington.

The autumn of 1838 was to make for Jessie Benton the first break away from childhood. She was in her fourteenth year, and in this city of blooming young women she was remarked for her beauty of face and figure and for her grace of bearing. In the course of dinners with relatives and family friends at Georgetown, she had met many personable young men, and her precocious charm had already proved a magnet which resulted in proposals of marriage from two members of the official family. Her parents now held a private consultation and decided that Jessie and Eliza should be placed in Miss English's select academy at Georgetown. During the preliminary interview with the principal, Mrs. Benton remarked: "You will find Eliza a patient Griselda in study."

"And Miss Jessie?"

With a laugh her mother replied: "I fear you will find her a Don Quixote."

To the conventional Eliza, boarding school was an opportunity to be with their best friends, Eleanora Calvert, Georgia Washington, and Mildred Fitzhugh, but Jessie declared leaving home "a great misfortune." She sought her father for a conference in the library. Throwing every coaxing modulation into her flexible, softly penetrating voice, she begged to be allowed to continue her studies with him. To his argument that she needed the daily association of a larger group of young people and the formal discipline of class work, she sat downcast but silent, whereupon her father, thinking the incident closed, dismissed her with a kiss.

That night Jessie scarcely slept for weeping. Next morning after breakfast she slipped away to her room. Soon afterward she looked into the library, and finding her father alone, entered and stood beside his desk. Benton looked up from his work and saw his daughter pale and swollen eyed, her long brown curls cut off close to her neck. At his startled exclamation she announced: "I won't need other groups of girls. I mean to have no more society, just to study here and be my father's companion as Madame de Staël was hers." In the face of this grief and determination, Benton made his difficult choice. His mandate stood, but Jessie's mother came to the rescue with the diversion of selecting new clothes and books. In due time Jessie departed for school somewhat mollified, if not quite happy.

Thrust from the privacy and the large latitude of study in her father's library into this group of one hundred boarders and as many day pupils, among a corps of twenty-five teachers, she was soon frankly miserable. From the first her direct simplicity of manner and speech and the discernment growing out of a natural sensibility were often held against her as offensive precocity. The fact that others didn't do a thing was no deterrent if it seemed good to her. This was held essential insubordination. The petty restrictions and the snobbery among the young daughters of Senators, House members, and Army and Navy officers were distasteful to a mind at once acute and ingenious. Accustomed to "position" and luxury, Jessie could not see why the possession of either should give one girl claim to preference over another less fortunate.

The subjects as taught here, including dancing, music, and deportment, were easily learned, and much of the time allotted to study was spent by her with a charming but unstudious companion perched in the branches of a mulberry tree, listening to accounts of the pranks of this girl's midshipman brothers. Jessie chose as another companion a young day scholar, Harriet Beall Williams, one of the many children of a government clerk.

The first of "Miss Don Quixote's" tilts at windmills came over the selection of a May Queen. It was required that the candidate be the unanimous choice of the student body. At once Jessie began quietly campaigning for Harriet, who was an indifferent student without notable social position or wealth, but who was tall and pretty and a beautiful dancer. When election day came, this girl was triumphant, to the great disappointment of principal and teachers. The next day, to the consternation of the pupils, the principal announced as Queen another girl whom the faculty thought "more worthy of the honor."

Jessie looked about at her silent and abashed schoolmates; then rising in her seat she declared: "This decision is most unjust and unfair to everybody. The first choice was honestly made, and besides the new Queen can't even dance." To this outburst she heard the principal saying calmly: "Miss Jessie, you seem feverish. Doubtless you are not feeling well. Please report to the infirmary for treatment." This treatment consisted of solitary confinement for the day, together with a dose of hot senna tea.

Grief was added to the sense of injustice burning hotly in Jessie's breast when the mother of the displaced candidate came for her daughter's belongings and requested her withdrawal from the school. Ere long, however, there came a startling piece of news. The deposed May Queen was about to be made a Russian countess right before the delighted eyes of her schoolmates and beneath the very noses of the snobbish teachers! And as though to justify fully the recalcitrant Jessie, *she* was chosen as first bridesmaid. Count Alexander de la Bodisco, the sixty-year-old kindly but eccentric Minister from Russia, was well known to all Washington for his elaborate but stately ménage in Georgetown and the flourish with which he drove daily to the Embassy in a snowy barouche drawn by four prancing black horses. Jessie and her friends had once attended a Christmas party given by him at which boxes of white-kid gloves and lace fans had been distributed as favors to the girls.

Bodisco had won the affection of the young bride-to-be by lavish kindness to her and her family. At the announcement of the engagement he settled a comfortable income upon her mother and arranged for a state wedding. When considering the details of the ceremony, he was determined upon having all the bridesmaids young and pretty like the bride, and the groomsmen of age and dignity like himself.

He consulted Mr. Benton as to whether Russia should give first position to England, as represented by Henry Fox, or to the United States, as represented by James Buchanan. Benton made the happy suggestion that both could be first by placing attendants in couples instead of grouping them behind the bride and groom as was the custom. Thus Mr. Fox would stand beside the bride's sister next to the groom, and Mr. Buchanan and Jessie next to the bride.

Bodisco had planned the toilettes of the attendants as well as every detail of the ceremony. The dresses, very long, were of white-silk brocade with blond lace about the neck and sleeves of the deep-pointed bodice and on the full-plaited skirt. Bouquets of white camellias completed the costumes. On the morning of the ceremony, the bride's simple home on the heights of George-town overflowed with guests: President Van Buren, the Diplomatic Corps, Army and Navy officers in full uniform, and ladies in afternoon dress.

When the folding doors were drawn back, this company looked upon a charming picture. In the center beside the groom stood the bride, tall and fair, gowned in white-satin brocade. On her yellow hair rested a diamond coronet, from which a veil of silver lace fell far down the long satin train. Diamonds shone in her ears and about her white throat. To her right was Mr. Buchan-an, tall, silver haired, and distinguished, and beside him the radiant Jessie, only a shade less beautiful than the bride. To the groom's left stood Mr. Fox in court costume of scarlet and gold; next to him the rosy blond sister of the bride. The glistening white dresses, young faces, and flowers were thrown into high relief by the court dress of the men, the dignified Mr. Clay and Bishop Johns in full canonicals giving the last touch to the picture.

After the ceremony, the entire party drove to the home of the groom for the wedding breakfast and reception. A few days later, the President gave a dinner in honor of the distinguished couple. The bridesmaids with white feather fans instead of bouquets were grouped about the bride, whose dress this night was a pale-green velvet with a train embroidered in gold.

The excitement of these festivities ended for Jessie Benton in a violent sick-headache which brought forth the parental edict: "Back to the simple food and early hours of the school girl." However, unknown to her and her parents the swift-moving shuttle of Jessie Benton's life was already busy with the scarlet thread of her own romance.

CHAPTER IV

An Elopement

FTER the Bodisco wedding, Jessie Benton again conferred with her father in an effort to avoid returning to school. Upon this occasion her argument though unsuccessful was salty. She had seen several members of Miss English's staff at the wedding reception and had heard the headmistress herself, between sips of punch and nibbles of cake, proudly proclaiming the beautiful countess as a former beloved pupil. "This conduct," Jessie declared, "is a shameless revulsion of feeling, which makes the thought of going back there most unpleasant." Her father, after a few moments' reflection, gravely announced that she must resign herself, since such an attitude in the teachers, though deplorable, did not interfere with the excellent instruction and discipline.

Somewhat later when Benton asked the principal for a private report upon his daughter's progress, he pondered long over the statement: "Miss Jessie, although extremely intelligent, lacks the docility of a model student. Moreover, she has the objectionable manner of seeming to take our orders and assignments under consideration, to be accepted or disregarded by some standard of her own." Benton filed this report and then proceeded to an important appointment at the home of Secretary of War Joel R. Poinsett. These two men, both scholarly, had much in common and just now were in frequent conference through their mutual interest in Western expansion. These conferences often included Jean Nicholas Nicollet, the French geographer and explorer, noted for his topographical work in the region of the Mississippi. Of late, both Poinsett and Nicollet had spoken with pride of their protégé,

John Charles Frémont. Today they had arranged for Benton to meet the young man with whose history Poinsett had made him familiar.

In 1833 while Poinsett was living in Charleston following his services as American Minister to Chile and Mexico, he was accustomed to assemble at his weekly breakfasts the city's most attractive young men and women. Among these he included a handsome youth of Southern birth, a brilliant but desultory student, who was teaching mathematics in John Wotten's private school. Poinsett was charmed with the boy's good looks and flattered by his eagerness over Poinsett's tales of his wanderings about Europe and his life at the Court of Czar Alexander.

Upon closer acquaintance, Poinsett had found that his twenty-year-old guest, John C. Frémont, had spent three years in college, was familiar with the classics, knew more than a little of astronomy, was an excellent mathematician, and was hoping for a naval or military appointment that would enable him to see the world. A few months later, the sloop-of-war *Natchez* under command of Lieutenant David Farragut was to sail on a cruise to South America. Poinsett had secured for young Frémont a position as instructor of mathematics on this cruise. There had followed two years of monotonous ship routine, enlivened by visits to the colorful South American ports and by the association with David Farragut, the brilliant and kindly young officer in command.

Upon Frémont's return to Charleston, he had joined the United States Topographical Corps under Captain Williams, who was about to survey a railroad route between Charleston and Cincinnati. This adventure into the wilderness was Frémont's first taste of the life for which he felt himself best suited. So well did he acquit himself that Captain Williams chose him as an assistant in military reconnaissance in the mountainous Cherokee country of Georgia, in pursuance of Jackson's plan to move all the Indian tribes beyond the Mississippi. On this expedition, Frémont had shown both cleverness and initiative in the varied arts of sketching streams and mountains, packing in, negotiating steep trails amidst snow and ice, and studying the Indians.

After this experience, he had reported to Poinsett that this was exactly the sort of work he wanted, whereupon his mentor had secured him a commission as second lieutenant in the Topographical Corps and had ordered him to

Washington. Here Nicollet, also much taken with Frémont's good looks, enthusiasm, and charm of manner, had chosen him as a member of the expedition about to explore the plateau country between the Mississippi and Missouri Rivers.

On this expedition Frémont had become as a son to Nicollet, introduced by him into the French-Catholic circles of New Orleans and St. Louis and inspired by him as to the beauties and possibilities of that great Western wilderness. Frémont was introduced to the voyageurs, traders, and soldiers who held sway there. Nicollet had found his protégé fearless in the face of heat, cold, and Indians, quick at learning the scientific procedure of exploration, and accurate in astronomical observation and the detailed study of geology and botany. In their quiet talks about the campfire, he found the young man to be of poetic insight and imagination.

Upon their return to Washington, Nicollet had made his report to Poinsett, and the two had taken Frémont to call upon President Van Buren. Later, Nicollet had arranged for Frémont to live with him and another bachelor, Ferdinand Hassler, superintendent of the coast survey, in Hassler's house on the slope of Capitol Hill. In the survey building they did the map work covering the three years of exploration, and at night they made astronomical calculations in the little observatory Nicollet had built at the top of Hassler's house.

Benton, knowing well the imperious and competent Swiss Hassler and the cultured and even more competent Nicollet, argued there must be something to this young Frémont if they had taken him to live as well as to work with them. Others had met Frémont at dinners, balls, and musicales and had spoken well of him. Benton was frankly curious.

When the two were now introduced in Poinsett's drawing room, each had heard enough of the other to establish friendly terms between them at once. Frémont, just a little awed at first, was amazed at Benton's immense fund of information concerning that northwestern wilderness he had never seen. Frémont soon found himself talking with his usual ardor and enthusiasm, answering rapid-fire questions and fearlessly stating his views to this man of commanding presence, who added to the cold cultivation of the scholar the social amenities of the instinctive gentleman.

Benton in turn was surprised and pleased that so young a man could grasp the full significance of his own dream as to the immense possibilities of the West, a dream which by now had become an obsession, causing his friends to smile and tap their foreheads when he arose in Congress to present yet another measure to help the homesteader. Frémont's capacity for arousing interest and loyalty in men of intellect and accomplishment had already brought him the favor of these two men, Poinsett and Nicollet, eminent in the field of science. This meeting with Thomas Benton brought him the instant favor of a man of national political power.

The following day Benton visited the coast survey office to study the new maps which Frémont explained at length. A few days later he came again and invited Frémont to dinner. The fact that their guest was a Southerner and a friend of the Poinsetts made him welcome to Mrs. Benton and to Mrs. McDowell, who was spending the winter in Washington. His acquaintance with their young friends in New Orleans and St. Louis gave him the favor of the two younger daughters, Sarah and Susan, while his reputation as a traveler among Indians and buffaloes gave him worth in the eyes of the twelve-year-old Randolph.

A week later Frémont again dined with the family and together with other guests listened to Susan's accomplished performance of Chopin and heard Sarah sing English ballads in her rich contralto. He was told that the older sisters, Eliza and Jessie, were in school in Georgetown, and upon his departure that evening he was invited to accompany the family on the following evening to a concert at the school.

Arriving early, they were asked to wait in the visitors' room. They were scarcely seated before Jessie came in, radiant and eager to see the family. She stopped short in her rush toward her father's arms, for standing beside him was a handsome young man in uniform, whose deep-set blue eyes were fixed upon her in open admiration and whose white teeth were flashing in a smile. She heard her mother's murmured "Lieutenant Frémont." Then the dark gentleman bent above her, and she felt the touch of his lips upon her hand. She had a chance for quick appraisal during her sister's more sedate entrance and the formality of her introduction.

During the concert Frémont managed to be seated beside Jessie. Little was said between them, but later that night Jessie confided to Eliza: "At last I've met a handsomer man than Cousin Preston. I'm so glad I wore the pink candy-stripe with the rose sash instead of the dotted muslin with the blue. It made me look much older." Whatever the reason, her choice would seem to have been inspired, in view of the effectiveness of her bright brown hair, warm brown eyes, and creamy skin against the candy-stripes, with the crisp rustle of taffeta as fit accompaniment to her sparkling speech.

That night Frémont reported to Nicollet: "I have fallen in love at first sight. My one thought is how and where I may meet Miss Jessie again."

Their meetings thereafter for a time were limited to an occasional week-end during which Frémont was asked to dinner at the request of Grandmother McDowell, who pronounced him "a highly superior young man." After dinner, friends dropped in, and under cover of music and conversation, Frémont became more hopelessly enamored as he watched Jessie performing her part as hostess to her elders. She listened with graceful, delicate turnings of the head, glances of grave serenity, quick smiles from sensitive lips When asked to sing, she complied modestly but with no air of apology in face of her more gifted sisters' performance. She picked up her guitar and played rippling accompaniment to French and Spanish love songs sung in a soft mezzo-soprano of warm inflections and romantic range.

One evening after an impromptu quadrille in the drawing room, Jessie and Frémont danced through an open doorway into the hall, and in brief whispers arranged for the safe interchange of letters. Next day Frémont spoke thus of her to the sympathetic Nicollet: "She has delicacy and winsomeness, alluring gayety with a hint of fire underneath."

At the inauguration ceremony of President Harrison (March 4, 1841), Lieutenant Frémont, resplendent in a new uniform, was so openly devoted to Jessie as to alarm her parents to action. That evening she was called to the library where both parents awaited her. She stood quietly while her father said: "We all admire Lieutenant Frémont, but with no family, no money, and the prospects of slow promotion in the Army, we think him no proper match for you. And besides, you are too young to think of marriage in any case."

Earlier experiences with the Senatorial tone had taught Jessie discretion; that tone was unmistakable. She knew her mother would side with her father; she always did. Jessie stood silent, with lowered eyes, as he announced in a tone of even greater finality: "You are for a time at least to see Lieutenant Frémont only on rare occasions. We think it best." Next day Jessie learned that a hint to similar effect had been given Frémont, and that he too had taken it calmly.

And now the death of President Harrison just one month after his inauguration threw the city into sadness and mourning. A great public funeral was arranged, for he was the first President to die in office.

During this month the lovers had not met. Frémont now called upon Senator Benton and suggested that since Mr. Hassler's house overlooked Pennsylvania Avenue and the ascent of Capitol Hill, members of the Benton family might like to view the funeral procession from the windows of the workroom on the second floor, where several other friends would be present. The Senator reflected that his and Mrs. Benton's presence would be required elsewhere and that Frémont would be on official duty also. He suggested that perhaps Miss Jessie, chaperoned by Grandmother McDowell, might be pleased to accept this kind offer. They were pleased indeed!

The day was raw and cold. When Jessie and Mrs. McDowell arrived to the strains of the funeral dirges already being played in the streets, they found the large workroom cleared of tables and bright with potted azaleas and geraniums and fragrant with roses. Before the great log fire was a tea table set out with French bonbons, tea, and cakes. Frémont, suffering from a slight cold, had obtained sick-leave and was present to greet his visitors and to seat Mrs. McDowell, the guest of honor.

As the plumed hearse with its six white horses bore the body of the President down the long slope of Capitol Hill, the older guests stood at the windows, struck to silence by the wailing of the funeral march and the solemn tramping of the crowds that followed the hearse. Over by the fire sat Frémont and Jessie, lost to everything but their own happiness. Frémont proposed and was accepted on the condition that they keep their plans an absolute secret for the present. As the strains of music died away in the distance and the tramp of feet grew fainter, the watchers returned from the far end of the room. Frémont replenished the fire, helped serve tea to the elders, and later bade his guests a sedate and soldierly au revoir.

Next morning the potted plants that had decorated the room arrived at the Senator's home with a gracious message for Jessie's mother. When by discreet inquiries the Bentons learned from Nicollet that Frémont, whom they thought on duty with his corps, had suffered from a cold and had been on

Senator Thomas Hart Benton.

sick-leave, they were alarmed to the point of counterplot. Mrs. Benton made a secret call upon Mrs. Poinsett and frankly stated her fears. Poinsett was called and reluctantly agreed to cooperate. Another secret conference took place, this time between Benton and Poinsett.

A few days later Frémont was astounded to receive orders to drop his maps and depart at once to take charge of a surveying party to the Des Moines River country. This was a promotion, but at what a cost! Government orders; no recourse. Nicollet tried to help him by open protest at loss of an efficient aide, but to no avail. Frémont wrote an impassioned farewell letter to Jessie and made ready to depart for a six months' absence.

And now Benton the father triumphed over Benton the Senator; Jessie and her lover were allowed to meet and say goodbye. They were given a half hour of privacy in the library for their farewells, and at the very last, the sight of Jessie's stricken face moved her father to further magnanimity. He announced that if at the end of one year they were still in love, they might marry. Frémont bowed low and gravely thanked him, then bade the family goodbye. As for Jessie, the pronouncement of ten years would have seemed no more final than one.

Torn between pride over her lover's promotion and fears for him out in the wilds where the Sauk and Fox Indians ranged, Jessie spent a miserable two months. Then Mrs. Benton announced that Jessie was to accompany her and Eliza to Virginia to attend the wedding of a relative. This meant new clothes, an exciting journey by boat and carriage, then dinner parties, dancing, and the wedding itself. Such a prospect lifted the volatile Jessie out of the doldrums, and she entered into the plans with such zest that the Senator and Mrs. Benton exchanged triumphant glances behind the back of their ardent seventeen-year-old.

At Cherry Grove they found a wedding house-party of thirty. Jessie's cousin, Preston Johnson, home for his first vacation from West Point and handsomer than ever, danced attendance. He and she staged many impromptu parties. On one occasion in raiding the attic, they came upon a sole-leather trunk containing bundles of letters with crumbling red seals and fragile ribbons that broke at a touch. Thoughtlessly opening a letter, he began to read aloud, "Flower of my heart," whereupon Jessie snatched the envelope, saying: "Would you eavesdrop if those two were here?" Abashed, he answered: "Of course not, but they are dead, long ago." "Love never dies. Let's put it back."

Later the young couple came upon boxes and trunks where the clothes of two generations reposed in lonely grandeur. They fitted the garments to those whom they best suited. That night Cherry Grove beheld a stately and beautiful pageant of happy family ghosts come alive in drawing room, window embrasure, balcony, and garden path.

Next morning Mrs. Benton wrote her husband: "I truly believe our Jessie's childish love affair has quite blown over." Their Jessie was at that moment in her room also writing, composing these verses to a bowl of violets:

> *The violet is my friendly flower,*
> *She lives in quiet places.*
> *She lays no claim to beauty's dower,*
> *Nor flaunts her perfumed graces.*
>
> *She never seeks my love or care,*
> *But when my day goes badly*
> *And I seek hers, with fragrance rare*
> *She soothes and charms me gladly.*

After the departure of the bride and groom and the wedding guests, Mrs. McDowell became ill and within a few days died, happy to have been spared for this wedding of her favorite niece. At the very last she said: "I fear for my descendants when I think how much has been given me. There must come a change for some of them."

One of them, her favorite Jessie, was at that moment lying in the garden hidden behind a row of phlox, weeping her heart out. Eliza, finding her there, took her in her arms and tried to comfort her: "Don't grieve so. Grandmother is old, and hers is an easy death." Between sobs Jessie said: "I'm not grieving for grandmother. She was happy. My heart is breaking for my own unhappy life."

From that moment the quiet Eliza became her sister's avowed champion, and upon their arrival in Washington, defended Jessie's "foolishness" to her mother when that outraged lady discovered on her daughter's desk a lighted candle and a bowl of flowers before a newspaper cut of Frémont, so unflattering as to suggest a bandit rather than a hero.

Shortly afterward the Benton sisters were caught up in the general excitement as the city made preparation for receiving Prince de Joinville, son of King Louis Philippe of France. The previous year the Prince had been sent to St. Helena to bring back the body of Napoleon to Paris. The very name of the Prince was glamorous. His arrival in Washington on September 29, 1841, was therefore a most memorable day for society at the national capital. Invitations to a state dinner in honor of the Prince were issued from the White House.

Jessie was delighted to learn that as one of the young women who spoke French fluently, she was to be assigned to a member of the Prince's staff. The matter of her costume for the state dinner became of supreme importance to her. Her wardrobe had heretofore not transcended the skill of the local mantua maker, Mrs. Abbott, but on this occasion she achieved her first Paris ball-gown, a pale-pink muslin trimmed with frills of real Valenciennes. This creation had been purchased by a cousin for a season at Saratoga, but a death in the family had caused her to dispose of her colored wardrobe to her young cousins.

On the night of this dinner the White House had never held a more brilliant assemblage: the Prince and his suite, Army and Navy officers in dress uniform, the Diplomatic Corps in full court dress, and the ladies in their newest and best. Daniel Webster, Secretary of State, stood near President Tyler, he and Mrs. Webster fully equal in appearance and manner to this great occasion. After the dinner the President led the way to the East room where those chosen took their position for the *quadrille d'honneur.* That ceremony over, the dancing became general.

Jessie Benton was an acknowledged belle of the evening. After the Prince had opened the ball with Miss Tyler, he danced several times with Jessie. This occasion she always recalled as her début, for the next morning her father announced that she need not return to school, but should continue her studies with him. Grateful and happy, she settled to her Latin and Greek, and to impatient waiting for her lover's return.

Near the close of the six months' survey, Frémont received a letter from Nicollet which contained this passage:

Everyone here and in Baltimore inquires after you, even the Benton household, every time I go there. The young girls returned home ten days later than they were expected on account of the grandmother who died at the moment when they were about to set out on their journey to Washington. Everything is going well. She is quite happy and she is impatient to see you.

Immediately upon Frémont's return to Washington, he called upon Senator Benton to pay his respects to the family. As he entered the drawing room, the greeting between the lovers left no doubt in Benton's mind as to the state of their affections. Still opposed to the match, Benton's position became increasingly difficult. That trick of separating the lovers was proving a boomerang, since Frémont's return with full reports of a successful survey had already given him added dignity in the eyes of Washington.

With the whole town talking of her lover, Jessie had hoped her parents would forget to impose the last half year of probation, but when they still held to it, she took fright, her one thought being to forestall another possible "promotion." The occasional meetings at the Benton home were now supplemented by frequent clandestine love trysts at the home of Mrs. Crittenden, wife of the Senator from Kentucky, who had favored the match from the start.

One day in October, Jessie Benton and Bessie Forbes, a niece of Mrs. Crittenden, waited several hours while Nicollet and Frémont visited three Protestant clergymen, each of whom through fear of Benton's wrath refused to perform a secret ceremony. This check proved only temporary. A few days later Mrs. Crittenden met the lovers' plea by going herself to Father Van Horseigh, who promised to perform the marriage.

On October 19, Jessie packed a bag for an overnight stay at the Crittenden home where the family were witnesses to the ceremony performed by Father Van Horseigh. Immediately after the ceremony the couple separated, Jessie promising to report the first propitious moment for breaking the news to her father.

During early November, Frémont visited his superior, Nicollet, who lay ill in Baltimore. Frémont found him nervous and dispirited but working upon the Government report which was to accompany Frémont's completed map. He praised his young lieutenant and declared that he hoped to make the detailed report a clear and adequate accompaniment to the map. To Nicollet's plea that he disclose his marriage soon, Frémont replied: "The sooner the better, but as to that, Mrs. Frémont must decide."

Upon his return, however, he urged Jessie thus: "We have been precipitate but not criminal. Let me go to the Senator and explain at once. This is a matter between men." He received a characteristic reply: "We will explain together. Come to the house tomorrow morning before ten o'clock. I will ask for an early interview."

Next morning Jessie met her husband at the door and accompanied him into the library. As the couple stood before him, Benton looked up and grimly acknowledged their greeting. Lieutenant Frémont, who had been praised by his superiors for courage in the face of prairie fires, stampeding buffaloes, and hostile Indians, alternately paled and flushed as he blurted out the announcement that he and Jessie had been man and wife since October 19.

Jessie was prepared for an angry outburst but was inexpressibly shocked to have her father ignore her completely and bellow at her lover: "Get out of my house and never cross my door again! Jessie shall stay here." Without an instant's hesitation she stepped close to her husband, linked her arm in his, and looking gravely up at him, repeated the pledge of Ruth: "Whither thou goest, I will go. Where thou lodgest, I will lodge. Thy people shall be my people, thy God my God."

Instinct served her well. Here in this room throughout a childhood of unreflecting gayety, gusty griefs, and brief despairs, she had met repeated proofs of the integrity and fidelity of her father's love. Here her eyes had looked into his with serene confidence, and here they now met his stern and hostile glance with resolute courage.

Benton the Senator never acknowledged himself beaten; Benton the father was silent for a moment. Then turning to Frémont, he commanded in a surly tone: "Go collect your belongings and return at once to the house. I will prepare Mrs. Benton." The news, though a disappointment, was no shock to Jessie's mother, and she was soon directing the clearing of a sunny guest suite for use as the young couple's study and bedroom.

Within a few hours Lieutenant Frémont was duly established as a member of the family in whose affections he was already firmly entrenched. Whatever Benton's inner reactions at losing his daughter, he fully realized that it was his training that had rounded the essential contours of her character, strengthened that robust mind ever thirsty for new ideas, and developed that healthy, ardent nature ever hungry for love. His daughter was romantically in love and happy. He was happy to have her remain under his roof.

A few days later he half sheepishly confessed to a friend:"The thought of my own endless courtship, coupled with the picture of my daughter's felicity, impels me to final approval of this marriage."

CHAPTER V

Jessie Frémont, Topographical Reporter

EW Year's Day in 1842 was a momentous day for Jessie Frémont.

During the previous six months Benton, Nicollet, Poinsett, Linn, and others of the expansionist group were busy perfecting plans for that long-contemplated expedition under Nicollet for the purpose of mapping the Oregon Trail and taking further measures to strengthen our hold upon the territory of the Pacific. Increasing British activity in the Northwest warned Washington that delay was politically dangerous. The fact that thousands of adventurous citizens were planning to make their uncertain way over paths marked by the bleaching bones of cattle and the gravestones of unfortunate predecessors made a well-mapped route a necessity.

In these conferences Benton had often bewailed the death of Harrison which had placed in the Presidential chair John Tyler, a Southerner, a man already fearful of a clash with England and greatly influenced by Secretary of the Treasury John Spencer, a fierce anti-expansionist. Harrison, a Westerner and an Army man as far back as 1799 while Congressman from Indiana Territory, had advocated many measures in the interest of the settler. Had he lived, he would have heartily sanctioned this expedition designed to further "America for the Americans."

Benton and Linn now counted upon the diplomacy of Nicollet to win Tyler to a gesture of sanction. As the deliberations of the group progressed, it became apparent that Nicollet's health would forbid his undertaking active leadership. He was ill, dispirited, and fearful. He voiced his doubts openly to

Frémont and Jessie, whom he called *mes enfants,* and he repeatedly urged the expediency of sending Lieutenant Frémont in his stead. When Benton realized that Nicollet was beyond active service, he became open and earnest sponsor for his son-in-law. During December, 1841, when the final plans were being discussed in the Benton library, Jessie was often asked to be present. Seated near her husband, she heard her father praise Lieutenant Frémont for his efficient service in his earlier surveys and for the meticulous care with which his maps and accompanying notes had been made available for study. Benton, expressing regret that he was too old to accompany the expedition, declared his eagerness to have his young son Randolph go in his stead.

As Jessie listened demurely, her heart beat to bursting with pride, and her irrepressible humor allowed her a ripple of reminiscent laughter as she contrasted these warm and gracious tones with that recent bitter and disgruntled order: "Go collect your belongings and return at once to the house."

By New Year's Day, all Washington was aware that the popular Lieutenant Frémont was being openly considered to replace Nicollet in the projected expedition to the Western wilderness. Congratulations poured in upon the young couple from a host of relatives and friends. Mr. Hassler of the coast survey insisted upon the Frémonts' using his carriage for their formal call upon the President. The White House reception as always drew the city's fashionables, and long before the noon hour when the White House was to be thrown open to the public, the streets were crowded with omnibuses, cabs, and private carriages. All approaches to the mansion teemed with a curious crowd come to watch the slow-moving pageant of "dignity and elegance."

Everybody knew the London-built Hassler carriage, and when Lieutenant and Mrs. Frémont alighted from it, a cheer went up and the crowd pressed closer for a better view of the young officer and his bride. Frémont was in dress uniform and Jessie in a formal gown of dark-blue velvet, full straight skirt over narrow hoops, the close-fitting bodice outlined at neck and sleeves with frills of Mechlin lace. A tiny cape of blue velvet, strapped slippers, lemon-colored gloves, and a blue-velvet bonnet adorned with three lemon-colored ostrich tips completed her costume. In her rôle of young matron, she wore her bright brown hair parted in the center and brushed to satin smoothness except at the eartips where a few short curls peeped from beneath her bonnet.

As they entered the White House vestibule where the Marine Band was playing and the greatest crush since Jackson's time was milling about, they were met by Senators King and Linn and escorted to the President. Tyler glanced approvingly at the radiant couple and paused for a few pleasant remarks before turning to the next in line. Later Jessie received further congratulations from officers and dignitaries, and then returned home to assist her parents in receiving many guests who drifted through the Benton drawing room until late afternoon.

At a family dinner that evening, Senator Linn conferred with Benton as to the best way to obtain the modest thirty-thousand-dollar appropriation over which the "antis" were sure to grumble, and to which Spencer would be openly opposed. However, with such a forceful trio as King, Woodbury, and Mouton at his back, Benton's success was assured, and in due time the Topographical Bureau, with the sanction of the Secretary of War, ordered an expedition "to explore the country between the Missouri River and the Rocky Mountains."

During the next three months Jessie Frémont's engagement list extended to fatiguing length, but she was living a romantic idyll and grew prettier than ever under the round of matinées, musicales, and balls of a crowded social season. On every hand, older members of the official family who had known her as a child said gracious things of her twenty-nine-year-old husband, and no day was complete until she had recounted these praises with certain ardent additions of her own.

Their first separation came in March when Frémont went to New York to purchase for the journey essentials not obtainable in Washington. While there he ordered a special American flag made on which the eagle's talons held an Indian peace pipe instead of arrows. This device he believed would be better understood by the Indians as a peaceable symbol. He also ordered to be constructed a collapsible india-rubber boat with airtight compartments, to be used in exploring water courses. The odorless process of preparing rubber being still in the future, the boat maker warned Frémont that at first he might have some unpleasantness from the chemicals, but that the boat would be a certain success for his purpose.

Upon Frémont's return to Washington, he had the huge parcel carried to the upper gallery off the dining room where it could be displayed before dinner. The family gathered about, and when the packings were removed, such an overpowering stench assailed the nostrils that everyone hurried into the house. The boat was hastily removed to the barn, but not before the reek of chemicals had filled the whole house, requiring thorough fumigation with coffee on a hot shovel. For Jessie the memory of those acrid fumes was long to outlive the boat itself, for she was expecting a child, and the severe nausea caused by the combination of chemicals and burning coffee was to prove the only unpleasant symptom of her pregnancy.

May 2, 1842, was the date fixed for the departure of Frémont and young Randolph Benton, and it now became Jessie's duty to act as buffer between her busy husband and the constant stream of visitors: young men hoping to accompany the expedition in some capacity, older men in search of advice before starting westward, and inventors with gadgets they felt necessary to the success of the trip. All these she met and disposed of with patience and tact. She faced the approaching date of departure with dread, but having been warned repeatedly by her elders that fretting was bad for her, she kept calm and cheerful until the very last evening. Then overwhelmed by the thought of separation, she became pale and dejected, falling into a silence which caused looks of solicitude to pass between her husband and her parents. Jessie's "hate" was now upon her: "saying goodbye to one I love."

The mutual ardors, the passionate protestations, the fears, the anguish, the kisses salt with tears—these were of the night. That last morning, whatever of foreboding filled their hearts was concealed beneath tones and gestures of prideful love. Jessie helped her husband adjust his new blue and gold uniform, patting the braid and the buttons, making him blush with the glow of her own pride in his appearance as she bade him look in the mirror at the fine set the tailor had given his collar. She declared that "his young son John Charles would look exactly like his father." By such touching and playful gestures she kept up her courage to the end. She had planned to go to the station, but at the last, Mrs. Benton collapsed over the strain of parting with Randolph, and Jessie was left behind to care for her and the weeping sisters.

At the station it was Benton the Senator who proudly listened to the congratulations of friends and colleagues as the train pulled out carrying the man who he felt would crown with success his own half century of effort. It was Benton the father who returned to his home with red-rimmed eyes and a voice tender with solicitude for his wife and daughter.

After dinner the family sat about the fire discussing the route of the travelers: the train trip to Baltimore, steamboat to Philadelphia, mail coach to Harrisburg, boat again on the Ohio, and a stage coach to the Mississippi, a route familiar and reminiscent of many happy hours. They wondered whether Cousin Sarah Brant would let her son go as companion to Randolph, and Jessie "knew" with what pride Sarah would introduce Frémont to new friends in St. Louis. It was Benton the father who said as he bade Jessie goodnight: "I have a great pressure of work tomorrow. Will you copy some important papers for me in the morning?"

The following morning Jessie found on her desk in the library six new Perry-point steel pens and fifty sheets of satin-finish foolscap. She sat demurely awaiting secretarial orders. She was to copy parts of the treaty of 1818 which had established a joint sovereignty of England and the United States over the Oregon country. After Benton departed for the Senate, she found among notes he had given her a bit of paper on which he had written this excerpt from Marcus Aurelius: "Be not disturbed about the future, for if you ever come to it, you will have the same reason for your guide which preserves you at present." Opening her dress, she pinned the folded paper to her underbody and proceeded with her task, warmed and comforted.

With Benton's prodigious memory it is not likely that the tasks he now set for his daughter were for his own benefit. He knew that she would be happier in concentrating her mind and pen upon that part of the world where her fancy roamed. He declared himself in need of a fuller knowledge of the explorations on the Pacific coast covering the fifty years preceding this year's expedition. He asked her to work three hours daily upon a digest of these explorations. He promised to assist her in gathering elusive data and teach her how to copy maps on a reduced scale.

Jessie was familiar with much of this material, but recalling her father's favorite maxim, "Only exact knowledge of one's subject can act as effective offense and defense," she willingly delved more deeply into this rich exploration lore.

Within a few months her lively fancy was reliving those mythical days when Pope Alexander VI drew a line through the Atlantic Ocean from pole to pole and gave all that lay west of the line to Spain and all that lay east of it to Portugal. She roamed the seas with the Cabots, Balboa, Magellan, Cortés,

De Soto, and all those doughty adventurers seeking to make their dreams reality. She followed Lewis and Clark in crossing the Continental Divide (1804-1806) and read their recounting of the beauty and grandeur of the Columbia River country. Her visits to St. Louis had been highlighted by the stories of Zebulon Pike and his fort on the Rio Grande in 1806. His spectacular capture by the Spaniards, his enforced expedition under guard via El Paso to Chihuahua, and his later return made a tale of high adventure.

From childhood she had known the story of John Jacob Astor, his ship sent around Cape Horn to the Columbia, and his later chain of fur trading posts. These and many others were twice-told tales, but she lingered longer over the exploits of General William Ashley and Jedediah Smith, the Salt Lake trapper whose paths (1826-1828) her husband had now gone forth to mark and map.

She had only to take from the shelves her own marked copies of Henry Schoolcraft's *Expedition to the Upper Mississippi* and Washington Irving's digest of the *Journals of Captain L. E. Bonneville* to recreate those Rocky Mountain scenes soon to be encountered by her husband. For recreational study she spent an occasional hour translating from the Spanish the works of Bernal Diaz.

Benton's strict orders were "only three hours' work and then a long walk." Though solicitous of her health, her father allowed no sentimentalizing of her condition. She pursued her way as any normal young woman expecting her child. In the evening she received visitors, crocheted thread edgings for baby clothes, or prepared garments for the hands of old Emily, the negro seamstress of the family. This routine of stimulating work, rest, and play was finally interrupted by the sudden alarming illness of her mother.

A victim of paralysis, Mrs. Benton lay for three days in a coma from which the doctors feared she would never emerge. For the first time Jessie saw her father quite helpless and incoherent from grief and despair. To her, this prostration of a strong man was in itself a great shock. Refusing to leave his wife's bedside, Benton sat half kneeling, trying to warm her cold hands in his and peering into her pale face for the first sign of returning consciousness. At last it came, a flicker of the eyelid, a smile, and a few broken words. She was soon fully conscious, and next to her husband, she indicated that she wanted Jessie near her. The daughter whose independence and strong will had so often vexed her was now the one upon whose strength she leaned. It was arranged that Eliza take over the ordering of the house and that Jessie remain in the sick-room to see that the negro nurse carried out the doctor's instructions as to her mother's care. The doctor remarked: "We must have cheerful faces and voices here, for she understands everything though she speaks little."

Within a few weeks the invalid could be carried from her bed to a couch by the window where she lay during the day, content as long as Jessie came often to give lively accounts of the household doings or to read from the Bible with its tiny bookmarks placed at favorite psalms. One day in tears Jessie confided to Eliza: "I wish mother liked 'I will lift up my eyes unto the hills.' It takes all my fortitude to read 'Yea though I walk through the valley of the shadow' every morning."

For the Benton household the summer and early autumn passed in concentrated effort to improve the patient's condition. The relation between Jessie and her father was now reversed. She watched him anxiously as he came smiling into the room, lifted his wife from the couch, and sat holding her in his arms, telling her he would soon be carrying her down to dinner and out for a drive in the park. Laying her gently down again, he would go to his room and give way to uncontrollable grief, then return calm and composed to join the family at dinner.

By late October the invalid was able to share in the excitement that gripped the household and the city when word came that the Western exploring party had returned to St. Louis in perfect safety and health and that Frémont was on his way to Washington. During his five months' absence Jessie had often been admonished by her elders "not to fret," and now she awaited his return with ill-concealed impatience. When he arrived, hardened and bronzed, her happiness was "almost unbearable," and when the two were alone, she said gayly: "And Lieutenant Frémont's son John Charles will arrive shortly."

On November 13, 1842, Jessie Frémont became the mother of a six-pound daughter. The bitterness of her disappointment was beyond all concealment. She had spent those past busy months in happy anticipation of the son who would carry on the Frémont name and do honor to so honorable a father. She had fearlessly anticipated and gallantly endured the pangs of childbirth with no other thought than to place Frémont's son in his arms.

Of the many little disappointments she had suffered thus far in an effort

Frémont's Rocky Mountain Flag, Raised on highest peak of Wind River chain, August 15th, 1842.

to make her outer world conform to her pattern, this was the most bitter. She scarcely heard the murmured congratulations of her family, and later confided to Frémont: "This is the first hard blow my pride has ever sustained." All solicitude and tenderness, he was wise enough to refrain from an attempt to comfort her with platitudes. Benton too was wise. He told her how happy he and her mother were that the baby was a girl, and he requested that she be named Elizabeth after Mrs. Benton.

The next day Frémont brought to Jessie's room a faded, wind-whipped flag and laid it across her bed, saying: "This flag which I raised over the highest peak of the Rocky Mountains I have brought to you." Jessie touched its folds reverently and accepted the tribute without further reference to her ironic disappointment.

Within a few weeks this disappointment was seemingly forgotten in the pleasure of sharing with her husband the congratulations that poured in upon them both. The press was filled with praise of the Lieutenant and requests to have in readable form the reports of his experiences in the Western wilderness. It became desirable to expedite these reports, for already more ambitious plans that would take Frémont to the coast were under discussion.

Charles Preuss was to prepare the general map in day-to-day guide-book and atlas form. John Torrey, the botanist, would help to arrange and classify the many botanical and zoological specimens. But the narrative, that account which should be factually correct but not too matter of fact, a narrative to hold the interest of discriminating readers, only Frémont could do.

Jessie was certain that her explorer husband, whose graphic descriptions had held the family spellbound for weeks, would bring forth a story more colorful than those of Lewis Cass, Henry Schoolcraft, or Washington Irving. She helped him arrange his notes and sheaves of data; she set out ink, pens, and paper; she discussed method and form; and she acted as critic of style and literary quality.

Three days of strenuous effort, a sea of waste paper billowing over the basket—and a discouraged author declared himself "quite unable to say anything as he wished it." On the fourth day a severe headache with nosebleed laid him low, whereupon the tactful Jessie mentioned that nothing would so delight her as to have him dictate his story to her. Accustomed to doing secretarial work for her father, she would find the routine easy, and with the baby already in the care of a wet-nurse, her time would be at his command. She overrode her mother's protest that the work would be too fatiguing by declaring that the joy of working for her husband would outweigh all fatigue. She emptied the waste basket, tidied the desk, seated herself, and smilingly awaited his dictation. At the moment, neither she nor Frémont realized that with this act Jessie Frémont "thus slid into her most happy lifework."

And now came into play that salient characteristic of Jessie Frémont's which was to exercise its spell over everyone, old or young, who came in contact with her throughout the seventy-eight years of her life, her power "to make others shine in their qualities." Her familiarity with the writings of other explorers, her knowledge of English, her acquaintance with the classics, and her ability to turn a phrase would have enabled her to transcribe creditably Frémont's dictation as he paced back and forth, contriving his narrative from his sheaves of notes, but she knew that the vividness of his aural and visual memory, his sense of drama, his force and clarity of expression would best be displayed if she assumed the rôle of eager questioner and absorbed listener, and let the narrative style take care of itself.

After a few false starts, Frémont fell into an easy conversational tone and the flow of colorful language which had held her enthralled when he had described earlier adventures. He revisualized his entire experience hour by hour and step by step from the moment the train pulled out from Baltimore on May 2 until daybreak on October 1 when he heard again after five months that augury of civilization, the mellow tinkle of cowbells from farms on the border of Missouri.

Each morning at nine o'clock Jessie began the exciting task of transcribing the adventurous zest, the romance of that journey. Frémont, freed from all self-consciousness, unhampered by the nagging thought of the mechanics of writing, happily recounted the story of his adventures to the woman he loved.

In answer to her eager and adroit questions, he simplified, clarified, and dramatized his experiences. He lived again the artist's thrill over the wild flowers carpeting the prairies, the grandeur of mountain crags, the somber beauty of the forest, the color tones of red granite, foamy quartz, and silvery sands. He reveled in the beauty of early morning with curtains of fog parting to reveal a gilded mountain dome and the opening panorama of trees, streams, and rocks. All the poetry of his nature, all his feeling for color and form crept into the narrative, making more vivid the factual matter without impairing its scientific value.

Transcribed by Jessie's facile pen, Frémont's adventure became a vivid word picture covering a time-canvas of three and a half months. We see him in St. Louis, a guest in the home of his friend Colonel J. B. Brant, whose wife is Jessie's cousin Sarah Benton. There he is introduced to the friends of the Bentons, all curious to meet him as the Senator's son-in-law and Jessie's husband. We see Sarah Brant reluctantly allowing her nineteen-year-old son Henry to accompany the party. We see Frémont consulting with the fur magnates Cyprian and Pierre Chouteau as to completion of equipment and selection of men.

We watch the expedition personnel assembled: Frémont, the commander and chief scientist; Charles Preuss, sketch artist; Lucien Maxwell the frontiersman as game hunter; and the young boys Randolph Benton and Henry Brant as general aides. In addition are nineteen experienced voyageurs, among them the picturesque French Canadians, François Tessier, Honoré Ayot, Baptiste Bernier, and Basil Lajeunesse. All are well armed and mounted except the eight drivers of the stout mules that carry luggage, instruments, and the food supply. Kit Carson, experienced frontiersman, adept at French, Spanish, and the Indian dialects, acts as guide.

The column moves through Kansas woodlands, past Indian farms, and on to the open prairie. At the end of a twenty-eight-mile daily march, they camp at early twilight in order that the fires may be extinguished before dark. Sunset sees their tents pitched within a circular barricade of carts, fires made, and supper of beans, salt meat, bread, and coffee cooking. The horses and mules graze on short tether under the watchful eye of a guard. Supper eaten, the fires are extinguished and the men settle themselves for the night, saddle arranged as pillow and barricade for the head, pistols placed above it, rifle beneath the blanket, protected from damp and ready for instant use. Nine o'clock in the morning finds the party on the march.

After a certain stormy night when they sleep in mud puddles, they have a buffalo hunt and are rewarded by tender roasts cooked on sticks over the fire.

Frémont and Preuss are ever busy with geographical, geological, and botanical observations by day, writing up their notes by twilight, Preuss sketching at night while Frémont makes astronomical observations. The whole company under Carson takes recreation in shooting at targets and learning how to repel Indian attacks.

Frémont's mettle is tested at the beginning when within the stockade of Fort Laramie, Jim Bridger, the frontiersman just returned from the Platte River country, warns them all to remain at the fort because the Sioux, Blackfoot, and Cheyenne tribes are on the warpath and looking for white scalps. Frémont is forced to make his decision in opposition to that of many of his followers, including Carson. He declares that since one purpose of the expedition is the determination of the best points to plant forts for protection against Indians, this is the time to go forth and meet them in the open field. A wagon train is just ahead and may even now be needing help.

Murmurs of dissatisfaction are becoming mutinous. Frémont calls his men together and declares: "I want only those with me who have stomach for a fight. Any others may remain here." In the face of this determination only one "deserter" appears. Frémont now engages Bessonette, a fur trader, to act as Indian interpreter and announces to the amazed and disappointed youths, Benton and Brant, that they are to remain at the fort "until called for."

Early in the morning the march is resumed. The train makes its way up the Kansas River Valley, crossing the Platte and following along its bed into the foothills of the Rockies. They shout in excitement at the first glimpse of the snowy summit of Long's Peak. They struggle up the valley of the Sweetwater to a pass (South Pass in Wyoming) totally unlike the sharp Alleghany gaps, a broad, gradual ascent to a seven-thousand-foot summit.

They march on to the Green River headwaters, which flow into the Colorado. They set out toward the Wind River Range, majestic, snowcapped, and glistening in the August sun. Frémont and five companions begin the ascent of what he considers to be the highest peak of the central Rockies. After some hours of rough climbing, they find themselves along an almost perpendicular granite ridge capped far toward the clouds by a line of jagged peaks. Tortuously they make their way upward with brief glimpses toward the chasm far below aglitter with tiny emerald lakes. Frémont, ahead of the others, works his way along a vertical precipice, reaching the ledge by clinging to the crevices, thence slowly climbing toward the crest.

Finally he springs to the summit where another step would precipitate him into an immense snowfield five hundred feet below. To the edge of this field is a sheer icy precipice. After standing on the narrow crest a few moments, he carefully descends to allow the others one at a time to mount to this precarious point above the abyss; and here occurs the most dramatic incident of the expedition. Frémont and Preuss fix a ramrod in the snow at the summit and unfurl the special flag bearing thirteen stripes but carrying in the white field blue stars and a blue eagle perched on an Indian peace pipe. Here they think themselves beyond the region of animate life, but while one of the men is resting on a rock, a solitary bumblebee comes winging from the eastern valley and lights on his knee. Frémont pleases himself with the fancy that this bee is also a pioneer, first of his species to cross the mountain barrier. The bee is seized and put between the leaves of a book among the flowers which had been collected on the ascent. Later in the afternoon the men return to their cache at the foot of the peak and sleep that night on the rocks.

On the return trip the party divides, some to go overland to an agreed rendezvous, Goat Island, while Frémont and six others, equipping the rubber boat with instruments and supplies, take to the swift current of the Platte River. Between towering walls of dark canyons, amid the thunder of cataracts, they shoot the rapids. As the chasm narrows and the boiling waters grow more treacherous, they tie a fifty-foot rope to the stern, and three men stumble along over slippery rocks, attempting to check the velocity of the boat. Preuss clutches the precious chronometer and clambers out to follow on shore, only to be met after a few hundred feet by sheer precipices to the water's edge. He returns to the boat.

Enclosed in the chasm, amid the deafening roar, the boat safely shoots the last and worst cataract. At the assurance of safety, the weary men burst into shouts in the midst of which the boat strikes a concealed rock and overturns. For a hundred yards food, books, blankets, sextant, circle, and telescope box dance on the boiling surface.

Frémont and Lambert save the two men who cannot swim. The boat is righted, taken farther downstream, and moored in the shallows, while five soaked, battered, and half-naked men search for salvage. The journals, a gun, and the circle are saved. Without food, ammunition, or arms, the men cache the rescued luggage, leave the boat behind, climb the rocks, and struggle on toward the rendezvous. Crossing the narrow winding river and topping the ridges of two canyons, they reach Goat Island late that night to find their companions sitting about a campfire, feasting on buffalo steaks.

This hairbreadth adventure was followed by an incident which showed Frémont's patience and resourcefulness. While crossing a river, the pack horse carrying the barometer stumbled against a rock to the injury of that indispensable instrument. Upon examining the broken tube, although the vacuum chamber was unhurt, the men were sure they had measured their last mountain on this expedition. They watched Frémont patiently work a whole day to repair the tube by using other bits of glass tubing. When that failed, they watched, fascinated, as he took a translucent powder horn, boiled it, stretched it on a piece of wood to the correct diameter, scraped it to the thinness of glass, and with glue made from boiling buffalo tendons fastened it in place on the instrument. He then poured in properly heated mercury, made a pocket of buffalo skin, adjusted the brass cover, and laid the whole aside to dry. Upon tests, the indications of the instruments were exactly its markings before the injury.

Continuing their march, the party reach Grand Island on September 18, and October 1 finds them again at the Missouri border. Young Benton and Brant had been returned to St. Louis by escort. Frémont sells the remaining equipment and leaves for Washington by steamboat, arriving on October 29.

Thus ends the record of the expedition. The credit for the command of forceful English, for the color and quality in that little brochure of one hundred twenty duodecimo pages is Frémont's. The credit for "releasing" the adventurer and poet belongs to his wife. For her he had painted a picture of clear perspective and rich coloring. Pleasing tints of the artist's temperament were revealed in the features he seized upon and emphasized. For her he created "scenes fair or frightening," vignettes of nature that delighted with their alluring quality. These scenes had deeply touched his emotions, even while eye and mind were eagerly fastening upon factual data. In camp at night, those notes on nature's surface, texture, and contour, and her possibility of future contribution to man's practical needs carried with them somehow the sense of nature's unity and splendor. The poet in him realized and admitted that stratum of human sensation lying at the base of human knowledge.

And now, the picture finished, he watched Jessie write the last sentence, then turn to him exclaiming between laughter and tears: "I have not put to paper one half the beauty and truth you have shown me, but I have done the best I could, my darling." By the time the proofs were ready, she had mastered the mechanics of correction.

When the report was finished and filed with the War Department, a motion was passed calling upon the Secretary of War to transmit the report to the Senate. Linn then made a speech surveying the expedition, praising Frémont, and offering a resolution that the report be printed for Congress with one thousand extra copies for public distribution.

The press of the country now seized upon the report, and Jessie found her husband famous for having ascertained elevations of plains and mountains, computing latitudes and longitudes, accurately studying the face of the country, marking routes for travelers, indicating military positions, making large contributions to geology and botany, and including many sketch drawings of maps to make understanding easier. In short, this report illuminated the Oregon Trail to the Rockies.

Though Jessie was fully aware of the importance of the information that the plains between the Missouri and the foothills of the Rockies were not arid and that for hundreds of miles the country was a settlers' paradise of woodland and prairie, nevertheless, the portion of the report which meant most to her covered that dramatic day, August 15, 1842, when Frémont planted the American flag where no flag had ever flown before.

CHAPTER VI

Government Orders in a Sewing Basket

ITH Frémont's report heralded in the papers and now in the hands of an avidly interested public, the expansionists, headed by Benton, Linn, and Young, successfully pressed their plans for a second expedition designed to lengthen those lines of emigrant wagons already stretching along the westward trail toward Oregon. A further bolder plan was involved to examine California, its resources, the attitude of the people, the strength of the Mexican forces, and the extent of British activity on the Pacific coast.

Frémont was eager to connect his own surveys with those of Commander Wilkes. Thus an expedition would cover the lands south of the Columbia downward to the Mexican possession in Alta California. The expansionists hoped that this expedition would eventually lead to making both Oregon and California a part of the United States. A complete scientific survey would correct false reports and demonstrate to prospective settlers the richness and beauty of the Columbia Valley lands and the comparative safety of approach to them.

Jessie Frémont, aglow with the praises lavished upon her husband and convinced that he was the most fearless and resourceful of men, entered eagerly into the plans for this expedition. Since Benton was faced with a season of political fence building in Missouri, it was decided that the Washington home be closed for a time and the Benton-Frémont family proceed to St. Louis. Jessie, whose exuberant health and spirits seemed equal to any task, now sug-

[75]

gested that while Frémont and Preuss were in New York buying instruments, her father should go on alone and that she would arrange for closing the house.

As the married daughter, she assumed command of the family. She knew exactly her invalid mother's requirements and undertook the special plans necessary for her comfort and that of the baby Lily (Elizabeth). Eliza and the younger sisters directed the negro servants in packing for the leisurely two weeks' trip by stage and steamboat to St. Louis.

On the day of departure, a private accommodation coach drew up to the house door. The driver stowed away the luggage needed for the journey and assembled his passengers comfortably. His orders from Jessie were not to travel fast or late in the day. The boat trip from Wheeling by way of Cairo to St. Louis completed the journey. Benton met the party there, and by night they were settled in a wing of the roomy Brant home.

Impatiently awaiting her husband's arrival, Jessie spent the time in ministering to her mother and sharing with a negro nursemaid the care of the baby. Upon Frémont's arrival there followed a brief week of happiness with the family united. Jessie resumed her secretarial duties, opening mail, receiving the dictated replies, and listing for the files all items of the splendid scientific equipment. She also "listed" and interviewed many of the thirty-nine members of the party. These included six from the first expedition, among them the favorites, Basil Lajeunesse and Alexis Ayot. Louis Zindel, a former Prussian artilleryman who had been with Nicollet, was also a valued member. The guide, Thomas Fitzpatrick, was to serve until Carson should be met at Pueblo.

Since Frémont expected to spend much time among the more treacherous Indian tribes and remembered that General William Ashley had once fitted a supply train with a four-pound howitzer, he now applied to Colonel Stephen Kearny for a twelve-pounder. Kearny supplied the gun. All members were well armed with carbines and pistols, and now with two Delaware Indians as hunters, the company was ready. The light wagon with the instruments and the dozen stout mule-drawn carts carrying the packed tents and provisions moved ahead westward toward Kaw Landing.

Jessie gallantly lived through another hated goodbye, but by now the tempo of her marriage had been set to her belief that in a practical modern sense Frémont was "carried of the spirit into the wilderness." Her intense interest in the development of her husband's career kept her calm as she noted his final instructions to open and answer all mail and forward only that relevant to the expedition.

Her popularity among the St. Louis relatives made her an especial object of solicitude during these first difficult days. Before long she had settled with outward cheerfulness to the routine of family duties and the round of visits with occasional hours of reading and writing in an alcove assigned for her desk and sewing basket.

It was a May day in 1843. The city was beautiful in spring green and fragrant with jasmine and locust bloom. Never had Jessie's love of nature meant more to her than now. She returned from a walk along the river and a visit to the cathedral where she had gone on a sudden impulse born of heartache and loneliness at the thought of the four hundred miles even now stretching between her and her beloved. As she approached her desk, she saw lying atop the pile of mail brought by the afternoon boat a long envelope from Washington. Opening it, she read an official order from Colonel John J. Abert directing Frémont to return at once to Washington and explain why he was including a cannon in his equipment for a peaceable scientific survey. Colonel Abert further declared that another officer would be sent meanwhile to take charge of Frémont's men.

Whatever might be the justification real or fancied for such an order, there was none to the shrewd mind of this nineteen-year-old girl. Born and reared in Washington, familiar from childhood with the efforts and ambitions of her father, familiar with every inch of preparatory ground for the first exploration project and for this one, she sensed the pressure brought to bear on the kindly easy-going Chief of Bureau by his envious, discontented son-in-law and one or two Army Regulars who had openly begrudged the laurels of Frémont, this daring intruder from civil life.

Washington was ringing with Frémont's praise for past achievement and hearty sanction of this present undertaking. To let him return to answer questions as to motive, while his picked men were left to the "line and rule control" of a desk officer, was unthinkable. Always sensitive and emotional toward her husband, she now became daring for him. There was nobody at hand to consult, Benton having left on a political canvass of the state. Telling no one of this letter, she sent a messenger to a French Canadian, de Rosier, who expected to join Frémont in a few days. She announced to him:

"I have an important letter for Lieutenant Frémont which must be delivered at once. How long will you need to get ready?"

"The time to get my horse, but two horses travel better. If I take my brother, he will bring back a letter from the Lieutenant."

"Very well. You know how to cut off the bends in the river and can save the time the mail boat loses by lying at anchor on account of the fogs." Thus providing against the mischance of a duplicate letter reaching Frémont ahead of her message, she wrote, urging: "Do not delay another day. But trust and start at once."

Within a week de Rosier's brother returned with the equally brief message: "Goodbye. I trust and go."

This was Jessie's cue for replying to Colonel Abert. She told him exactly what she had done, declaring that this strange order must have been given without knowledge of the facts and that to obey it would break up the expedition for which such thorough and expensive provision had been made, since the delay would lose the animals their best season for grazing and would throw them underfed into the winter. She explained that the Frémont party needed to be well armed, for the country into which the men would venture contained enough to test the courage and endurance of the stoutest hearted. Between the great rivers and the mountains they would encounter the Sioux, the Apache, the Blackfoot, and other fierce Indian tribes who knew nothing of the rights of science but who fought *all* whites. Consequently an expedition of less than fifty members would find a howitzer desirable. Knowing that a military order must be obeyed if received, she had suppressed this one and had urged the expedition onward. No one would know of the order except the Department and herself.

Until this letter was dispatched, she had thought of herself only as saving the imperiled expedition, not as having defied the Government. But now she spent wakeful nights and anxious days awaiting the return of her father. After dinner on the day of Benton's return, she quietly told him of her act and announced herself ready to take the consequences, whatever they might be.

Contrary to her expectation, Benton not only condoned her act of insubordination but was more outraged than she at the Department's attempt to halt an expedition sanctioned by it, already equipped and on its way. He wrote Colonel Abert at once, condemning the order for recall and declaring that he

Last portrait of Andrew Jackson, The Hermitage, 1845.

himself would be responsible for his daughter's act in suppressing it. No reply came to this "defy," and not until several years later did those in Washington whose secret plans were balked find a way to revenge themselves.

Though Benton and Jessie were not with the expedition, they were living at the very core of emigration history that summer of 1843. The house was a rendezvous for those interested in every phase of emigration affairs and a forum for political discussion. St. Louis was more than ever cosmopolitan, a Mecca for westward-moving caravans of every race and creed. Boats arrived hourly, filled with passengers and freight. Grocers, clothiers, wagon makers, and dealers in horses, mules, and oxen did a thriving business.

Jessie and her father walked often to the open country just beyond the town, where the emigrant caravans rested during their final preparations for the westward trek. Jessie talked with the women, a few of them very old, many young and frail looking, but all of them without exception light hearted, facing buoyantly the terrors of hostile Indians, wild beasts, torrid heat, and racking cold for the sake of that new home whose very distance lent glamor to its outline.

In September the Bentons were deeply grieved to learn of the death of Nicollet, who had passed away in his sleep alone in a Washington hotel. Though it had seemed unlikely that he would survive until Frémont's return from this expedition, his sudden death saddened his friends and caused Benton and Jessie to recall his eagerness and pride over Frémont's departure.

Later in the autumn Benton returned to Washington, and about the same time an indirect message came from the expedition that all were in good health and had left the lower Columbia. Jessie devoted herself to the family and continued her habit of writing to her father each evening whether the letters were sent or not. Her state of mind is best shown in the following letter:

This was one of mother's good days. After reading Thanatopsis aloud, I left her and Lily both asleep and took a long walk by the river. In a plot of meadow an emigrant wagon rested. I was attracted by Delaware painted in bright blue on the canvas. No men were about, but seated on an overturned tub near the wagon was a young woman my age, nursing her baby. Her laughing blue eyes peeped up at me from a pink ruffled sunbonnet. A strand of wavy yellow hair, loosed from its coil, lay shimmering on the shoulder of her brown linsey dress. We talked for some time while the baby,"John, named for his father," lay asleep at her breast.

I didn't tell her who I was. Finally she rewarded my interest with,"Wouldn't you and your folks like to come along? There are three wagons of us. Did you know you can get a whole section of good land to yourselves and save your children from a life of wages?" I said,"I can't go because of my sick mother, but how I wish I might." Then I walked away quickly, for I was crying. If it weren't for mother, I would take Lily and go with them. I am strong and not afraid, and waiting grows harder every day.

Upon receipt of this letter, Benton wrote at once, reminding her how necessary she was to the happiness of the family and making tender appeal for her "not to grieve."

Before many weeks he wrote her of the deaths of Hassler and Senator Lewis Linn, that eloquent expansionist apostle and close friend of the family. In the press report of the Senate session of December 12, she read Benton's touching tribute to the character of his colleague.

In December Benton returned to spend the holidays. Christmas was enlivened by a tree for Lily. The custom was not general throughout the country as yet, except among the German population. The yule log, roast goose, plum pudding, and gifts had heretofore been the full procedure.

By the middle of January, Jessie, having received neither letter nor message from her husband since late in September, wrote her father that Lieutenant Frémont must by now have arrived in California and be on his way home by a southern route and that she was expecting him before March at the latest.

If Benton surmised differently, he refrained from voicing his own conjectures. When later a rumor reached him that Frémont had gone into the Sierras after winter closed in, had suffered great privation, and had pushed on and disappeared, he saw that this report was duly censored before passing it on to the family.

In February Jessie began active preparations for her husband's return. During the day her busy needle flew in fashioning new garments for herself and Lily. Her evenings she spent in perfecting her Spanish. By March her house was in order, the new wardrobes ready. Each night a table was set for Frémont's supper and a bed made ready for him. Fresh wood was piled near the fireplace, and a lamp set in the window to burn till morning. Jessie's nights were spent in half-waking awareness of every step on the street, every sound in the house, her imagination fretted with fear. In the morning the evidence of hospitable preparation was removed, and another day of hope and disappointment lived through.

As the summer advanced, though she lost weight alarmingly, she kept cheerful and continued her supper-table and night-lamp vigil which had now stretched to eight months. On the evening of August 6, just as she had arranged the table and lamp, word came that her Cousin Anne's husband, who suffered consumption, was thought to be dying. Gabriel, the negro coachman, drove her to her cousin's to spend the night. She watched beside the sick man until nearly morning, when she retired for an hour's rest.

Scarcely asleep, she was awakened by a messenger who announced that Frémont had arrived in the city. She arose hurriedly and went downstairs to a picture of ironic comedy. Nobody had seen Frémont except Gabriel. He stood trembling in the hall, and in the face of the family's incredulous questioning, wasn't quite sure by now that what had happened in the early dawn wasn't a fantastic dream. He had got as far in his story as "I heard pebbles against the window," when Frémont himself walked in and took Jessie in his arms. He carried her half fainting to a big easy chair, and seating himself beside her, held her close as he told his story to the astonished family.

Two days earlier, he had bade farewell to the members of his party, all of whom were eager to reach their own families. After placing the pack animals in pasturage, he had ridden his horse, Sacramento, to the junction of the Missouri and Mississippi, reaching the boat landing at sunset the night before. When on the boat, he decided he would keep awake until he reached the town. Arriving at three o'clock, he rushed ashore. Since no vehicle was in sight, he ran through the streets to the Benton home. He threw a handful of gravel against the window of Gabriel's room on the upper floor of the carriage house. The negro, quite sure he was talking to a ghost, answered Frémont's question, "Can you let me in without waking anyone?" with "Yes, I can let you in, but Miss Jessie is at Miss Anne's. Her husband is dying, maybe."

With that, Frémont, realizing that his appearance at that hour would be a shock to them all, walked on to a bench in front of the Barnes Hotel and sat waiting for daybreak. A few minutes later, an employee, recognizing him in the darkness, insisted excitedly that he come in and lie down until morning. At first Frémont refused; then the temptation to lay his tired body on a bed for the first time in eighteen months was too great, and he lay down in his clothes.

Meanwhile Gabriel had carried his story to the Bentons, declaring he had seen the Lieutenant "in his uniform and thin as a shadow." The family looked at each other; "either corn whiskey or a ghost." They were inclined to think the former, but in case the story might be true, they sent Gabriel to tell Jessie. But Frémont, awakening after an hour's sleep, had reached the invalid's home almost as soon as the messenger. While he was telling his story, news of his coming had spread over the city, and before breakfast could be served, he and Jessie were the center of an impromptu reception.

Rested and refreshed, Lieutenant Frémont sat beside his wife that night at a family dinner, and the next few weeks they spent in a perpetual reception of citizens who came to do honor to the returned explorer and to hear his story. Jessie's solicitude over her worn and weary warrior was fully matched by his anxiety for her. While arrangements were being perfected for the family's return to Washington, he wrote Benton:

I am alarmed over Jessie's delicate and fragile appearance. While she is vivacious and winsome and touchingly concerned about me, I realize that her anxieties have cruelly robbed her of strength and color. She has little rest or privacy here, and I can but hope that when we are again in Washington, she will be quickly restored.

Jessie's report to her father was characteristically buoyant:

We begin our journey to Washington as soon as possible. The family is well and happy beyond all expressing. Despite his appalling hardships, Lieutenant Frémont is well and handsomer than ever. Lily is as loving to him as though she remembered him. Admiring friends fill the house day and night. As for me, my happiness is at times almost more than my heart can carry.

The journey to Washington was accomplished with ease, and a few days later Jessie wrote to her Cousin Sarah:

We thank you again for all your uncounted kindnesses. Our welcome was a joyous one, father laughing and crying together as he carried mother up the stairs. We had an early home dinner, even Lily at table. As I looked upon our united family group, the picture was all the more beautiful for those background shadows of anxious waiting.

The first official calls made by Benton and Frémont were upon General Scott and Secretary of War Wilkins. The latter was deeply impressed with the lucidity of Frémont's replies to questions concerning his adventures. But he qualified his expressions of amazement at Frémont's youth by saying: "That is a good failing. Youth never sees the obstacles."

Frémont's and Jessie's plan to collaborate on the notes of this second expedition delighted Benton, but it took all his tact to convince his wife that this working partnership "properly managed" would not be too great a strain upon Jessie. Since Frémont's popularity robbed him of all privacy and filled the house with callers and dinner guests, even tentative beginning on the notes was impossible. Jessie finally suggested the plan of renting a two-story cottage within a block of the Benton home to be used as a workshop.

Here Frémont installed young Joseph Hubbard as his astronomical assistant. Hubbard lived on the ground floor and acted as buffer for his superior, since a pathway was soon worn from the street to the cottage. The Frémonts took the upper floor as a workroom with the understanding that Benton was the only person to be allowed above stairs. Each evening Frémont arranged his data and discussed mathematical and astronomical notes with Hubbard. Each morning he arose at dawn, and after a breakfast of coffee and rolls, went to the workshop where Jessie joined him at nine o'clock. From then until one o'clock he labored at painting for her that eighteen months' panorama until gradually every phase of its beauty, every harsh angle, every dark shadow, every charm of perspective emerged as part of a finished whole.

Daily at one o'clock, black Nancy arrived with Lily and a basket luncheon of cold chicken, beaten biscuits, and fruit. Lily was petted and played with, and then taken home while the Frémonts went for a long walk before taking up two hours' labor before dinner.

When necessary to test the accuracy of the sextant by local astronomical observation, Frémont would retire at night with an alarm clock beneath his pillow, and one o'clock would find Hubbard, the negro Jacob, and himself on the flagging in front of a nearby church making observations, Frémont stretched on his back on the large stone carriage step, watching for a certain star to come into position. Their comments and bursts of youthful laughter aroused the curiosity of an old deacon living nearby.

One evening this outraged gentleman appeared at the Bentons' and demanded to see the Senator. He felt it his duty to report that Frémont and two boon companions, one of them a negro, often came home late at night so drunk that Frémont lay on the church steps and could hardly be roused to go home. Benton listened quietly, then sent for Frémont and Jessie, who had just returned from their daily walk. As they appeared, he said politely: "Here are Mr. and Mrs. Frémont. I wish you would repeat to them what you have just told me." The deacon hesitated, but Benton insisted: "Repeat it, sir." His story met with such peals of laughter as to convince him of his error. Benton dismissed the young couple and held the deacon for a ten-minute lecture on his overcuriosity and want of Christian charity.

Every few days Benton visited the workshop to listen while Jessie read aloud and asked for criticism. His delight in the scientific factual narrative was almost equaled by his pride in Jessie's feeling for word values and her sense of the relevant, due to her training at his hands.

Five months of sustained and often grueling effort were spent in the chronicling of those eighteen months. We see Frémont and his party in May, 1843, camped on the bluff at Kaw Landing. Fitzpatrick is making final purchases of animals and swearing over the fact that there are only two kinds of mules: "them as is beat out and them as is balky." Frémont is talking with the leaders of the twelve hundred emigrants bound for Oregon or California. On the eleventh day we see de Rosier riding into camp, delivering Jessie's letter. Frémont reads it in silence, orders food for de Rosier and his brother, and while they eat, orders a fresh horse for the brother and retires to his own tent. He calls Fitzpatrick and gives marching orders.

Next morning finds de Rosier on his way back with Frémont's message, "Goodbye. I trust and go," under seal in his breast pocket. In another hour the entire expedition force is out on the open prairie, Frémont, Fitzpatrick, and Preuss riding in the lead. A cold rain is falling, and the muleteers curse and struggle to bring the green and balky animals into line. Frémont and Preuss are amazed at the long wagon train moving over the Santa Fé Trail, and Fitzpatrick assures them that hundreds of vanguard wagons are on ahead.

The expedition moves far south from the earlier Platte River route in search of a new pass through a gentler country. The men encounter days of travel over arid lands through which the only available water is from shallow, sluggish streams, often putrid from use as buffalo wallows.

By the first of July they are again in sight of the gleaming heights of Long's Peak and its snow-crowned neighbors. We see the party being feasted by the old fur traders at Fort St. Vrain, looking out upon the comfortable farm settlements with vegetable gardens, stock range, and orchard. Frémont makes rapid notes as to every feature of these lands for future colonization and trade.

We see Kit Carson awaiting the party at Pueblo, riding out with a whoop of glee to meet its leader. They ride on to Bent's Fort for more pack animals and foodstuffs. At the central foot of the Rockies, the party divides into two for greater speed and safety, Fitzpatrick with the heavy baggage taking the emigrant road to Fort Hull, Frémont with his picked body of men, Carson, Preuss, Zindel, and Ayot seeking to cut through the mountains to South Pass via Cache de la Poudre River.

We see them surrounded by towering mountains as they ride along the river bottoms through a wilderness of tall white flower stocks which brush their shoulders as they pass. They encamp two hundred miles beyond St. Vrain's Fort after days of struggle through sagebrush and stubble. Here they stop for two days to dry buffalo meat for future use. Another long struggle through almost impassable country is the record of their efforts to find a more southerly route to Oregon. They are finally forced to give up their attempt and turn toward the pass among the rocky peaks of Sweetwater Valley.

Striking trail at Sweetwater River, they ride rapidly on through heat and dust, overtaking an occasional emigrant train or coming upon a single family, rear guard of a larger party ahead. They cross a narrow spur and descend into a valley tributary to the Bear River. Here they find the road along the river dotted with the covers of emigrant wagons collected in groups at different camps. The women are preparing the evening meal at smoking campfires, children are playing about, and cattle are grazing not far off. This valley is a well-known resting place in the long overland trek, a preparation for the hard pull along the rough and sterile banks of the upper Columbia.

Frémont passes train after train, "America on the march." He hurries on toward Salt Lake, supplied by the Shoshone Indians with fresh horses, vegetables, and berries. Later we see the party short of rations, glad of an evening meal of stewed skunk and tea made from wild cherries.

On September 6 we see Frémont standing on a high butte, looking down upon the Great Salt Lake, and later writing his notes descriptive of its bottom lands, soil, grasses, timber, and water. We see the party tormented by hunger and thirst, moving on toward Fort Hull, supping on seagulls shot by Carson, and later eating the meat of a fat young horse which Frémont had given them permission to kill but which he could not muster courage to taste, "feeling as much saddened as though a crime had been committed." Later he shares in a feast of young antelope bought from an Indian.

At Fort Hull they join Fitzpatrick and refit the expedition, purchasing fifty fat oxen. A snowfall on September 19 warns of approaching winter. Frémont calls his men together in the chill of a penetrating rain and warns them of the hardships surely awaiting them throughout the winter of exploration. He begs those wishing to turn back to do so at once. We see him bidding farewell to the eleven who decide to return East, and we follow his party down the Snake Valley in the face of an icy wind. This place he decides must be a future military post to guard the settlements and assist the emigrants who at the end of a 1320-mile journey from Missouri must depend upon the reluctant aid of a British fur post.

Late October finds the expedition standing within sight of the icy cap of Mt. Hood rising in somber isolation against the gray sky. They visit the one-adobe-house mission of Dr. Whitman. They are gratefully received by the sturdy, robust family and given a supply of potatoes in lieu of the bread they had hoped to buy.

In early November they make their difficult way along the shores of the Columbia past the Dalles, and Frémont leaves the main body to make ready for the homeward journey, while he takes Preuss and two others by canoe to Fort Vancouver. This journey connected his survey with that of Captain Wilkes. He adds many independent observations for the benefit of those expansionists awaiting his report in Washington. He returns to camp at the Dalles with three months' supply of dried peas, flour, and tallow. The carts are now abandoned for the augmented number of pack animals, and the cattle for slaughter. The expedition plans its return to the United States.

With rich sheaves of notes and observations on the Oregon Trail and the

Columbia River country, Frémont might well consider the purpose of the expedition fulfilled, but instead he makes clear to his little band of twenty-five men that this scientific survey is to be followed by a journey into an unknown, a foreign country. His object is to explore the Great Basin between the Rockies and the Sierras, that seven hundred square miles of country which had already been covered east to west by Jedediah Smith and Joseph Walker, but whose north and south area lay as yet unexplored.

Frémont again discusses the unknown dangers from winter in the mountains and the known danger from roaming savages. Again he gives opportunity of return to those whose courage fails in face of such prospect. Every man declares himself ready for whatever of peril or privation lies ahead as long as Frémont leads them.

We follow on December 14 as the party, pushing east from the silvery disk of Klamath Lake, flounders through the snow to the headwaters of the Klamath River, the men almost blinded with the glare of the sun on ice, the legs of the pack animals cut by the sharp edges of the crusted snow. We struggle on with them through the somber silence of the pine forest, out upon the verge of a cliff, and down a thousand feet into the valley of the Great Basin with its grass-bordered lake asleep under a tranquil sun. We see them celebrating Christmas Day by the discharge of the howitzer and the serving of brandy, sugar, and coffee.

In middle January (1844) they kill the last of their cattle, and a few weeks later are facing actual hunger when they come upon a lake alive with leaping salmon trout. After a feast they welcome the signal smoke of Indians upon the shore.

Later in camp on the Carson River, we hear Frémont announce his bold determination to cross the Sierras into California. We see him and his men calmly facing the appalling hazards of the High Sierras in January, a prey to death-dealing storms, buried trails, and bleak and frozen wastes, dipping into pine forests dark as midnight. We see them approaching the icy rampart of the central chain. Here they are abandoned by their Indian guide who declares he came to *see* the white man, not to die with him.

For weeks they starve and struggle, camping on heavily wooded mountainsides in freezing winds, Frémont heartening his men with swigs of brandy and stories of the richness of the Sacramento Valley. February 6 finds the men on snowshoes, marching single file to the summit line of barren peaks from which densely wooded slopes drop sleepily to the smiling valley. Kit Carson, pointing toward the coast and its smaller mountain range, shouts: "It's the little mountain. Fifteen years since I saw it, but I'm sure as if I had seen it yesterday."

After heart-breaking struggles over the summit, Frémont, refusing to be defeated when Fitzpatrick declares the animals cannot be got over the pass, leads them with maul and shovel to beat out a path. At last they subsist on dried-pea soup and dog meat.

Victory comes on February 23, when amid rolling thunder they look down into a magnificent valley shadowed with the spring storm, and when the skies clear, they see the waters of the Sacramento flowing toward the broader sheen of San Francisco Bay. That night, watching by their own campfires, they see the flares of the Indians on the Bay eighty miles away.

A week later they are refreshed with food, clothing, and equipment by the largesse of Captain Sutter at his fort near Sacramento. While they remain as guests of Sutter, Frémont gathers important information as to the political situation, learning just how weak is Mexico's hold on California. Refreshed and remounted, the expedition swings down the long sweep of the San Joaquin Valley, dropping into the furnace-like Mojave Desert and on to Los Angeles.

We follow them back across to Salt Lake and hear Frémont tirelessly urging that they do not return by the Oregon Trail but across the Divide. They turn south and reach Pueblo on June 28 and Bent's Fort in July. July 31 finds them at the little town of Kansas on the Missouri River. After eighteen months away from civilization, they are amidst familiar scenes. Frémont arranges to have his travel-worn animals placed in pasturage. A few days later the party has separated, and Frémont is aboard a steamboat on the Missouri. He arrives in St. Louis on the night of August 6, 1844.

The last words of the engrossing record were written by Jessie in late February, 1845, and the next day found her and Frémont excitedly discussing the probability of Congress again ordering one thousand extra copies. Frémont "vexed" her by saying it was not likely since this record had stretched to what the powers might consider a boring length. One day she returned from a drive to find Frémont eagerly waiting to tell her that the Senate resolution on March 3 called for a printing of five thousand extra copies but that

Buchanan had moved and the motion had carried that the number of extra copies be ten thousand.

Jessie's pride reached its height when General Scott made Frémont's services the subject of a special report and recommended that he be given the double brevet of First Lieutenant and Captain "for gallant and highly meritorious services in two expeditions commanded by him." The General declared: "Frémont has returned with a name that goes over Europe and America."

Shortly after this honor was conferred upon Frémont, he and Jessie were invited to dine with Colonel Abert. While dressing, Jessie confided to her husband: "I go into that house with trepidation. Perhaps Colonel Abert hasn't buried the hatchet and is waiting to punish me tonight." She was reassured upon arrival at being treated by the Colonel with courtly consideration and being placed on his right at table.

CHAPTER VII

"All of Which I Saw and Part of Which I Was"

N THE day of James K. Polk's inauguration, Jessie Frémont called at the White House to pay honor to the President and his wife. She remained to share honors with them, for as she and Captain Frémont entered the reception room, they were quickly surrounded by friends and strangers eager to meet the man now widely heralded by the press as a national hero.

Mrs. Polk as the eighteen-year-old-wife of the Congressman from Tennessee had long been a close friend of Jessie's. She was tall and dignified in appearance, a lively conversationalist, and in Jessie's opinion, "a young queen." At the President's reception she congratulated Jessie upon being thoroughly conversant with public affairs and expressed earnestly her respect and admiration for Captain Frémont. A few days later Jessie learned that an appointment had been made for Frémont and Benton to call upon the President. This call would be in reality a conference, and Frémont confessed the hope that he would be able to answer all questions satisfactorily.

Filled with gay assurance as to the outcome of this visit, Jessie awaited his return. The interview had been disappointing. So long as Frémont confined himself to the more dramatic incidents of his travels, Polk was attentive. Encouraged, Frémont had stressed the value of the whole Pacific slope to the United States and had urged the necessity for accurate scientific exploration. He deplored the inaccuracy of reports given the geographers by trappers and travelers, and had cited as an example the "fact and fable map" on the rack in the Library of Congress, showing the Great Salt Lake as connected with the Pacific by three large rivers, one emptying into the Colorado, one into the Gulf of California, and one into San Francisco Bay. The President had listened unimpressed, and like Secretary of War Wilkins, "found him young" and had remarked upon "the impulsiveness of young men." Jessie listened calmly to this report, then replied: "He doubtless believes those rivers are there. He needs a little time, but I wish your report had been made to Mrs. Polk. She is always open to new ideas."

The Frémonts, however, had reason to be encouraged shortly afterward by the President's attitude toward the whole Western problem. The Ashburton Treaty, the conspicuous achievement of the Tyler administration, had been a compromise between the extreme claims of England and the United States as to various boundaries. Polk had been elected on the platform, "fifty-four forty or fight," and in his inaugural address had said: "Our title to Oregon is in question, and our people are preparing to perfect it by occupancy with their families." Secretary of State Buchanan now realized that the forty-ninth parallel as proposed by Calhoun when in Tyler's Cabinet was the logical boundary line, and he advised Polk to accept the offer of compromise now made by the British to withdraw all pretensions to the Columbia River. Benton took the forty-ninth-parallel stand on the Oregon question, and under his lead the proposal for a treaty on this basis was carried through the Senate.

With both England and the United States satisfied in this respect, the way was now clear for the plans of Polk to obtain the entire Southwest. By late spring in 1845, he was in frequent conferences with Benton, Frémont, and other expansionists, notably Baron von Geroldt, former Prussian attaché in Mexico City, and George Bancroft, Secretary of the Navy, whose zeal in regard to our acquisition of California antedated Polk's.

At this time Jessie Frémont had broad knowledge of the complexity of interests involved and the significance of every decision toward that unshaped future looming vast and shadowy before the nation. She sat at dinner at Daniel Webster's and noted his interest in Frémont's colorful descriptions. She heard him agree that San Francisco Bay and other Pacific ports should be made American, declaring them "twenty times as valuable to us as all Texas." Jessie knew that public sentiment was strongly influenced by the opinions of this group, and she eagerly centered her energies on the furtherance of every plan. Her enthusiasm was rewarded by being given an actual task which contributed toward these plans.

Secretary Buchanan, unable to read Spanish and having had reason to distrust a member of his departmental staff, called at the Bentons', and in private conference, asked Jessie to translate a confidential Spanish letter regarding the Mexican situation in California. Within a few days thereafter Jessie was in charge of the translation of all the private Spanish correspondence which came to Buchanan. In this work she was assisted by Eliza. Jessie also acted as interpreter at a secret conference between Buchanan and Señor Almonte, the Mexican Minister. She was close to the successive phases of the proposed joint resolution providing for the annexation of Texas, aware of her father's championship of it and of Almonte's hostile protest, followed by the severance of diplomatic relations between Mexico and the United States.

July, 1845, saw Texas accepting America's terms of annexation. Jessie was now busy translating the highly incendiary articles in the Mexican press and the announcement therein that Mexico was concentrating her troops. Under the watchful eyes of England and France, Washington sat tight, waiting to see whether Mexico would consider Texas a province in rebellion and cross the borders to quell her, or whether Polk's agent, W. S. Parrott, now arrived in Mexico City, would be able to effect peaceful negotiations.

In April Jessie read aloud to her father this article from the British *United Science Journal:*

> *There is no doubt that we, the English, have three powerful rivals in France, Russia, and the United States, but of these three the Americans are the most important on account of their origin, their courage, and their even greater enterprise and activity than our own. They have raw material, working men, and a sufficient merchant navy to arm as men-of-war when called upon to do so.*

To the minds of all concerned in Washington, this was the auspicious time for the third exploratory expedition. The War Department ordered a fund of fifty thousand dollars approved. In secret conference (known to Polk) between Benton as chairman of the Senate Military Committee and George Bancroft, Secretary of the Navy, Frémont's tentative course was mapped. The proposed survey included the Sierras in California and the Cascade Range in Oregon with the purpose of mapping emigration paths through to the Pacific. This was in view of the probable acquisition of the whole Pacific slope by the United States. With war imminent, "the eventualities of war were taken into consideration," and an increased number of men in the Army and Navy was found desirable. Frémont's secret instructions were that if necessary in order to foil England's plan to have her fleet in possession of San Francisco Bay in event of war with Mexico, he was to "carry on" into the territory of California.

Despite Jessie's knowledge of these plans and her certainty that her husband would be away longer than ever before, she said farewell with calm courage and a fortitude at the last greater than Frémont's own. The evening before his departure he sat watching her put the last stitches in a waterproof pocket she had made to carry certain valuable papers. Suddenly he broke down and boyishly lamented the fact that he could not take her with him. She laughed up at him through tears which splashed the pocket; then hastily wiping the new leather, she said: "There! That's properly dedicated, and I must be willing to dedicate you to this service which fits you. You leave us to execute plans my father has worked for all his life. You both are part of me. My work is to let you go cheerfully. Besides," she added archly, "you would soon tire of a repining wife, and surely you wouldn't have me a Mrs. Preuss?"

This question restored them both, for there had been hilarious comment over the ultimatum of Mrs. Preuss: "Choose between your home and family and your instinct to wander." Preuss had been replaced by Edward Kern, a young artist from Philadelphia. Another addition to the party came as a happy surprise to the Frémonts, that of Lieutenant Abert, nephew of Colonel Abert, head of the Topographical Corps. Both Frémont and Jessie were pleased at this evidence of Colonel Abert's continued friendship. The press widely heralded another exploratory expedition. On May 20, 1845, Jessie filed the following item from the *Union:*

Captain Frémont has gone upon his third expedition, determined upon a complete military and scientific exploration of all the vast unknown region between the Rocky Mountains and the Pacific Ocean, and between the Oregon River and the Gulf of California. This expedition is expected to continue near two years, and its successful result is looked to with the highest degree of interest by all the friends of science in America and Europe.

Perhaps no man of his age (thirty-two) in this country has gone through such labor of body and mind as has Captain Frémont. Mathematics is his favorite study, botany his recreation, Greek and Latin came with his schooling, French and Spanish have been added, and German he is acquiring. From the age of twenty, the canopy of heaven has been his covering; the mountains, plains, the lakes and rivers from the Atlantic to the Pacific have been his home. The fruits of his researches are scarcely prepared for publication before he is off on new explorations. His life is a pattern and his success an encouragement to young men of America who aspire to honorable distinction by their own meritorious exertions.

Captain Frémont is very youthful in appearance as well as in fact. Mr. Wilkins, Secretary of War, could hardly believe his ears when in the autumn of 1844 a modest-looking gentleman appeared before him and announced himself as Lieutenant Frémont just returned from the expedition to Oregon and California. To see the leader of such an expedition in the person of such a stripling was a surprise for which the Honorable Secretary could not recover himself until after repeated interrogations.

Jessie filled the weeks following Frémont's departure with the usual domestic routine and a careful study of the war rumors which filled the press. June, 1845, found General Zachary Taylor in command of the Army of the Southwest "to check any Mexican army trying to cross the Rio Grande."

As the Benton family sat at luncheon on June 15, Benton entered with a letter he had received from General Houston telling of the death of Andrew Jackson at the Hermitage on the evening of June 8. The passing of the old hero of New Orleans at seventy-eight was not unexpected, for in an earlier letter to Benton, Jackson had recounted a painful combination of disorders "which will make the pangs of death welcome," but the fact of his passing was to them a personal grief.

On June 29, the citizens of Washington marched through streets lined with crêpe-hung buildings from which flags were flying at half mast. Arriving at Capitol Square, the Benton family joined those seated on the eastern portico to hear the funeral oration delivered by George Bancroft, who paid glowing tribute to Jackson, hero and illustrious patriot.

A letter from Frémont at Bent's Fort on the Arkansas came to Jessie in the middle of August. He reported his sixty men and himself to be in excellent health. Kit Carson and Richard Owens had joined him in response to a message sent to Carson's ranch on the Cimarron. Although settled to farming, Carson had sold his land, left his wife in the care of relatives, and rushed to the call of his leader. Jessie's faith in Carson was only a shade less than her faith in Frémont. If war came, he would be a doughty soldier as well as guide; and with Godey, who was in some respects more fearless even than Carson, she now felt the expedition to be perfect in personnel.

Late in August came the last letter she was to receive for many months. She could now visualize Captain John C. Frémont in command of sixty men, with equipment, two hundred horses, and feed cattle, moving out from Bent's Fort toward the Sierras and to whatever the exigencies of the doubtful diplomatic situation with England and Mexico might bring forth.

In September Jessie made a short visit to Richmond, and while there, met the artist Dodge, who asked to be allowed to paint her miniature. She consented to sit for him on condition that he make her appear very serious. When the miniature was finished, she was pleased, but the artist was disappointed. He said to a friend:

I found it difficult that in order to please my sitter, I had to ignore her most characteristic expression. Though her remarks are sensible, her animation, her flashing eye and smile give her the air of being about to say something charmingly frivolous.

As autumn advanced, Jessie was forced to assume command of the household, owing to the increasing invalidism of Mrs. Benton. Eliza's health was precarious, Sarah was still a school girl, and Susan, now an accomplished pianist, was tied to her practice hours. Benton had refused to attend formal functions after his wife could no longer accompany him, but he delighted to entertain with small dinners at home. Jessie remarked that were she asked her father's most frequent expression, she would reply, "Come out and we'll talk it over at dinner," while her own would be, "Add another leaf and two more plates." The guests at these intimate dinners ranged from fur traders and river-traffic managers to foreign diplomats. One night, Jessie, fatigued to the point of petulance after the departure of the last guest, said: "No wonder I am tired. We had soup in Washington, the entrée in Mexico, and dessert in Belgium."

Early in the summer there had been a dinner to Commander Robert F. Stockton of the *Princeton*. Later Jessie had entertained Samuel F. B. Morse whom the Bentons had championed during his bitter struggle to get his first appropriation, that for the thirty miles of telegraph line between Washington and Baltimore. The night of the dinner Morse was in high spirits; he was leaving soon to make tests in London. He referred to the ridicule with which the majority of the Senators had met his plea for a twenty-five-thousand-dollar appropriation in '43, and he quoted the suggestion of one that the second appropriation be for a line to the moon. "Only my faith," he declared, "kept me insensible to their ridicule, and now I can read you this." He took from his wallet the following *Union* editorial:

As the first suggestion of a telegraph line was from an American Franklin, so is the first practical execution that of another, Morse, and we are glad to hear the most favorable accounts of the rapidity of its extension over the country. Before the next meeting of Congress the line will no doubt be complete from Washington to New York, and the effort is in progress to extend the line to Boston and Buffalo....By the time of the next inaugural address by another President, we have little doubt that every word of it will be read not only at New Orleans and St. Louis but at almost every town of considerable population in the country almost simultaneously with its utterance from the lips of the author.

Later in the autumn at a dinner in honor of Senator and Mrs. Dix, the name of the popular and now deceased Attorney-General Edward Livingstone was mentioned. As a child, Jessie had been fascinated by Mrs. Livingstone, a high-spirited and witty Frenchwoman whose delicious accent made her most heated diatribes amusing. Mrs. Livingstone thought no honor high enough for her husband, and when he came to Washington as Attorney-General under Jackson, she could not reconcile herself to his being at the foot of the Cabinet at dinner. And now Jessie with her inimitable gift of mimicry regaled her guests with the complaint of Mrs. Livingstone, prefacing her story thus: "She did not feel like the Scotch noble that 'where the MacGraegor sits, there is the head of the table.' Instead, 'Madame la Ministre d'État and Madame of ze

Treasuree, even Madame de la Guerre and Madame de la Marine call for precedence over me, but to walk into ze dinner behind Madame Poze-Offeeze! Jamais!' When asked why she had not sought to change this during the four years, she had exclaimed:'Four years! Eet ees not long enough for vangeance or joostice'."

Senator Dix, laughing heartily, declared that as a reward for her story, "Madame Exploreur" should have any favor within his power to grant. Jessie promptly asked: "May I speak to you after dinner?" Later she told him the story of Alexis Ayot, a member of Frémont's first expedition, who had been disabled by a gunshot wound from an Indian but for whom Frémont had been unable to get a pension because Ayot was not an enlisted soldier. Quite helpless and in despair the man had complained to Jessie: *"Je ne sais pas clair, il faut mourir de faim."*

"Can't something be done, Senator?" she pleaded.

"Come to my house tomorrow evening and repeat your story to Mrs. Dix and me. We shall see."

The next evening at the Dix home Jessie met another visitor, Preston King of New York, chairman of the Committee on Pensions. At Senator Dix's request Jessie repeated her story. King said: "Write it briefly as you have told it, and your protégé shall be cared for."

Shortly thereafter a pension with two years' back pay was granted Ayot, and Jessie gave him the news over a glass of sherry in the library. Swaying on his crutches, tears coursing down his cheeks, he cried: "I cannot kneel to you; I have no more legs, but you are my Sainte Madonne. To you I make my prayers."

During the winter a happy addition to the Benton social-political group was Jessie's uncle, James McDowell, former Governor of Virginia, who had just been elected to Congress. In March, 1846, she presided over a dinner at which her uncle shared honors with General Sam Houston, just arrived as Senator from the new state of Texas. Houston, who had been a Corporal under Benton in the War of 1812, proposed a toast, "To my superior officer, Colonel Benton," to which Benton replied, "To the memory of our superior officer, General Jackson."

Among the frequent visitors at the tea hour was John L. Stevens of later Panama railroad fame. His travel books on Arabia and the Holy Land were

George Bancroft, Secretary of the Navy in Polk's Administration.

already popular in the family, and he now had to answer many questions about South America and the projected railroad at Panama. Over the third cup of tea and as many helpings of spice cake, he said: "You must be very good to me, for some day, soon perhaps, I'll be sent to the Isthmus to die." Stevens was an ardent admirer of Jessie and said long afterward:

I carried away with me that day an unforgetable picture of happy family life, the dining room at high tea, candle light playing over the silver service, a blazing wood fire, Mrs. Benton quiet as a shadow, swathed in a blue dressing gown, lying on a sofa, smiling up at the Senator, who had just carried her in from her bedroom and who now stood over her arranging her shawl before seating himself nearby to serve her. Pretty Jessie Frémont, in a wide-skirted dress of silk that made her look like a petunia blossom, sat at the tea urn. The fragrance of potted rose geraniums mingled with the tang of burning sassafras wood, the delicate aroma of China tea and the spiciness of cake. Jacob, the negro butler, paused in his duties to bring Lily, the small Frémont daughter. She kissed her mother and grandmother, curtsied to me, then climbed on the Senator's knee where she sat sedately nibbling cakes as a reward for spelling her own and her father's name correctly.

For Jessie Frémont these social and secretarial duties were interchangeable daily. Besides her solicitude for her own invalid, she kept Frémont's aged mother informed as to family matters and frequently sent her books and periodicals. In April Jessie was translating from the Spanish private advices to her father and to Buchanan concerning the American and English forces in the Pacific. Our new *California* had handled one hundred thousand dollars' worth of oil taken in sixteen months. On the Pacific coast the hide ships carried from twenty to forty thousand hides bought at two dollars each and paid for by general merchandise at a profit of one hundred and fifty per cent. Despite the heavy duty on outgoing cargoes, the business was reported as very profitable. The writer suggested that we as well as the English should have a depot for coal at Panama and that we send two squadrons south with a dispatch vessel attached to each to offset the English whose "mail" steamships between Panama and Peru carried Paixham sixty-eights.

During this month (April) letters came from Frémont at Monterey describing briefly the "far shorter wagon road mapped out to Oregon." His corps was camped near Sutter's settlement. Jessie, importuned by the editor of the *Union* to allow these letters to be printed, copied extracts for his use.

The Mexican war clouds grew blacker, and the varying public sentiment was reflected in the press. Benton, who had studied Mexico in the reports of Humboldt, freely expressed his opinion to President Polk when called in consultation on November 7. Benton advised the taking of Vera Cruz and a later attempt on Mexico City. "It is too late now," he declared, "for a course of masterly inactivity. That policy suited the Spaniard who sat out the Moors seven hundred years in the south of Spain and the Visigoths three hundred in the north of it, and they would certainly outsit us in Mexico." Three days later Benton attended a Cabinet meeting by invitation and urged a more aggressive policy "now that we are in it." As a result Polk made drastic changes in his measure.

One blustery November evening the Bentons received Lieutenant Archibald A. Gillespie of the Marine Corps, come to pay his respects. He announced that he was leaving on the sloop-of-war *Cyane* for the Pacific coast with dispatches from the State Department and that he would gladly carry any letters or messages from the family. It would be many months before these could reach Frémont, and Jessie sat long that night over her own letter which should tell the news and convey all that such letters carry between the lines. The family letters were designed to state the war situation as it appeared in Washington from reports given Secretary of the Navy Bancroft by Thomas O. Larkin, American Consul at Monterey. There were items of information which clearly indicated the imminence of war and the plan of the President in such an event to take possession of California. There were instructions from Secretary Bancroft which changed Frémont's status from that of scientific explorer to that of officer in the Army.

Many weeks later a guarded letter came from Frémont directed to Benton. It announced Frémont and his men to be in good health and spoke of Oregon but not of California. He stated that he could hardly reach the frontier before late September. The Bentons gathered that his stay on the coast awaited the progress of events to a point where he could act.

In her secretarial capacity Jessie made in May, 1846, a press copy of Benton's famous speech on the bill pending to extend the jurisdiction of the United States over all the territory of the Rocky Mountains. He had reluctantly accepted Buchanan's urging to put the bill through the Senate. This speech had been carefully planned as soon as Benton learned that a proposition to settle on the forty-ninth parallel instead of the fiftieth was about to come from the British. His speech would be an unpopular one, but he hoped to win over the opposition by sheer force of logic, as he had so often done before.

The Oregon speech Jessie considered a masterpiece, though neither she nor anyone else could have foretold the epochal value of this exposition which illuminated every dusky corner of the Pacific coast controversy. On May 25 as she walked up the steps of the Capitol with her father, she said: "Should your memory fail, call upon me, for I know every word of it." Benton laughed: "This particular speech would doubtless be more effective if delivered by Captain Frémont's wife than by Jessie Benton's father."

The Senate gallery was filled, and every member in his seat, for it was known that Benton scattered his seeds of information from a well-filled sack. Even his ancient enemies, the militant "fifty-four forties," looked expectant. Standing straight and tall, his thick gray hair brushed back from his high forehead, his ruddy face aglow, his blue eyes clear and piercing, clothed in dark-blue broadcloth with a broad expanse of white-linen vest, a high-standing collar, and black-satin stock, he presented a commanding picture of forcefulness and dignity.

He began: "It is my ungracious task to commence by exposing error at home." He objected to the wording of the Jurisdiction bill as too vague: "Leaving to our agents the solution of questions we find too hard for ourselves, making indefinite extension of authority in a case which requires the utmost precision." With the aid of a map he drew a graphic picture of the Fraser River country. This area, discovered by Sir Alexander MacKenzie in 1793, had been settled by the Northwestern Company in 1806; their establishments covered its length from head to mouth. England's right to this land Benton stoutly defended as follows:

At the time we got it by treaty with Spain, the Fraser had already been occupied twenty-six years by the British, settled by them for twelve years and known by a British name, New Caledonia. No Spaniard has ever made a track along its banks. . . . I think New Caledonia belongs to them, and I shall not ask them for it and much less fight them for it, but the valley of the Columbia is ours by discovery, settlement, and the Treaty of Utrecht. I do not plead our title to that country. I did that twenty years ago when there were few to applaud or repeat what I said....

The line of Utrecht is best for both parties, for the triangle at the head of the Columbia is as necessary to them as the Olympic square is to us. The British could annoy us in the Olympic district, and we could annoy them at the head of the Columbia, but why do it except on the principle of laying eggs to hatch future disputes? Forty-nine was the line proposed by Mr. Jefferson in 1807. It is the line of all American statesmen without exception....

I say, my fellow citizens, through the valley of the Columbia lies the North American road to India. The effect of the arrival of the Caucasian race on the western coast of America opposite the eastern coast of Asia is a benefit not local to us but universal to the human race. Our position and policy will commend us to their hospitable reception. The Caucasian race must wake up and reanimate the torpid body of old Asia. The youngest people and the newest land will become the reviver and regenerator of the oldest....

I have been fighting the battle of Oregon for thirty years when it had but few friends.... For my justification in seeking to make head against so much error, I throw myself upon the equity and intelligence of my countrymen, and never having any fear for myself, I now have none for my country.

This speech stirred his hearers and the press to realization of our dilatory course in regard to the Pacific coast. At the very moment of Benton's ending his speech, dispatches from Great Britain were en route to the British Consul Pakenham, directing him to offer again the compromise on the forty-ninth parallel. When Buchanan was handed the British project on June 6, little yet remained to be done except to sign the pact. Pakenham showed his appreciation of Benton's work by calling formally upon the family. Later Jessie attended a musicale at his bachelor establishment and listened with filial pride to the Consul's praise of her father, which she declared to be sweeter to her ears than the music.

Early in June, 1846, letters and messages bearing upon Frémont's movements in California reached Jessie. The *Union* on June 11 carried letters from Larkin, Consul at Monterey, to Polk, giving an outline of Frémont's movements through the early winter. He reported General Castro's attempt to drive Frémont from the country. The *Union* also quoted Frémont's letter to Larkin:

From the heights where we are encamped, Gavilan Peak, we can see with the glass troops mustering at St. Johns. I would write you at length if I did not fear my letter would be intercepted. We have in no wise done wrong to any of the people, and if we are hemmed in and assaulted, we will die every man of us under the flag of his country.

The effect of this communication upon Jessie Frémont was to increase her anxieties, but she concealed her fears for the sake of her family. In great excitement on the evening of June 17, she helped her father prepare certain reports and documents to be carried by John Magoffin to Frémont in the West. Refusing luncheon the next day when Magoffin was to take the letters and documents, Jessie locked herself in her room to write her own letter:

My dearest husband: A Mr. Magoffin says he will be at Bent's Fort a month from tomorrow and that he will leave a letter for you. So I write, dearest husband, to tell you how happy I have been made by hearing of you up to the thirty-first of March, through Mr. Larkin. Only the day before, I had received the Mexican account of your being besieged by General Castro, and I was much relieved by what Mr. Larkin says: that you could present yourself at Monterey, alone if you wished, and not be harmed. But I hope that as I write, you are rapidly nearing home and that early in September there will be an end to our anxieties. In your dear letter you tell me that le bon temps viendra, and my faith in you is such that I believe it will come! And it will come to all you love, for during your long absence, God has been good to us and kept in health your mother and all you love best. This opportunity of writing only presented itself last night, so that there is not time for a letter from your mother herself, but I had news from her two days ago in which she tells me that during the warm weather she will remain at a place about ten miles from Mount Pleasant. Her stay in the country did her health much good last fall, and indeed it has been good generally throughout the winter. Her heart has been made glad by your brilliant success and your late promotion, although it distressed her to anticipate more separations. You must let me make you my heartiest congratulations. I am sorry that I could not be the first to call you

Colonel. It will please you the more as it was entirely a free-will offering of the President's.

So your merit has advanced you in eight years from an unknown second lieutenant to the most talked-of and admired lieutenant-colonel in the Army. Almost all of the old officers called to congratulate me upon it, the Aberts among them, and I have heard of no envy except from some of the lower order of Whig papers who only see you as Colonel Benton's son-in-law. As for your report, its popularity astonished even me, your most confirmed and oldest worshiper. Lily has it read to her (the stories, of course) as a reward for good behavior.... Father absolutely idolizes Lily. She is so good and intelligent that I do not wonder at it. And then you should see his pride in you!

Mother's health has been worse than ever during the winter, though the force of the disease seems now to have expended itself. That gave me a reason for staying home quietly as I wished, and I have read so much that is improving that you will be very pleased with me. Your mother was kind enough to send me your daguerreotype, and it hangs over the head of my bed and is my guardian angel, for I could not waste time or do anything you did not like with that beloved face looking so earnestly at me. I opened a new history of Louisiana a week or two ago, and it commenced with the Spanish discoveries on the southern part of the continent. I was by myself, Lily asleep, and reading by our lamp. When I came to Ponce de Leon's search for the fountain of youth, I stopped, for it seemed as if pleasant old days had returned. And then I remembered so well what you once wrote to me that I could not help bursting into tears. Do you remember, darling?

It was soon after we were married, and you wrote me: "Fear not for our happiness. If the hope for it is not something wilder than the Spaniard's search for the fountain in Florida, we will find it yet." I remembered it word for word although it was so long since I read it. Dear, dear husband, you do know how proud and grateful I am that you love me. We have found the fountain of perpetual youth for love, and I believe there are few others who can say so. I try very hard to be worthy of your love.

I had meant to tell you of many things which might interest, but it would take a day to choose from the year's accumulation. The road you have discovered is spoken of as giving you more distinction than anything you have yet done. I had to publish almost all your letter, and like everything you write, it has been reprinted all over the country. I have some beautiful poetry to show you on our motto, le bon temps viendra. Editors have written to me for your biography and likeness, but I had no orders from you and then you know it would look odd to leave out your age, and you never told me how old you were yet!

How old are you? You might tell me, now I am a colonel's wife—won't you, old papa? Poor papa, it made tears come to find you had begun to turn gray. You must have suffered much and been very anxious," but all that must pass." I am very sorry you did not get our letters (up to January 24, 1846). Yours gave us so much happiness that I grieved you could not have had as much from ours. You will, of course, come here as soon as you get back. I wanted to go to St. Louis to meet you, but father says I had better not, as it will be very uncomfortable and even dangerous to go out in the worst of the season, and I don't want to be sick, for I am not going to let you write anything but your name when you get home. And then we will probably have to be at Jefferson Barracks during the winter and until the new regiment is ready for the field. Father says you are to accept the appointment as it was given, with the understanding that you were to be kept on scientific duty under the direction of the Senate. Mr. Webster says it would be too great a loss to the science of the country if you were stopped in your onward course. If I begin telling you the sincere compliments from people whose names are known in Europe as well as America, I would need a day.

You must have a few to think of, however. Edward Everett, Mr. Gallatin, Stevens (Central America), Davis, the author of Jack Downing, a Dr. Barrett of Connecticut, a botanist who sent me his herbarium of American grasses (for which he wants the buffalo and bunch grasses) are among the Northern men. The South Carolinians claim you bodily, and Dr. Grayson of Charleston wrote one of the most beautiful of all the notices I saw. Your early and steady friends, Mr. McRady and Mr. Poinsett, were the first to whom I sent well-bound copies of your book. You are ranked with De Foe. They say that as Robinson Crusoe is the most natural and interesting fiction of travel, so Frémont's report is the most romantically truthful. I have a letter from the President of the Royal Geographical Society, Lord Chichester, who says he could not help preparing a paper on your travels to be read at their meeting—and more and more and many more of the same.

Mr. Magoffin has come for the letter and I must stop. I have not had so much pleasure in a very great while as today. The thought that you may hear from me and know that all are well and that I can tell you again how dearly I love you makes me as happy as I can be while you are away....

Farewell, dear, dear husband. In a few months we shall not know what sorrow means. At least, I humbly hope and pray so.

Your own affectionate and devoted wife,

JESSIE B. FRÉMONT

On September 2, 1846, Jessie Frémont was clipping from the *Union* this exciting news:

We have received information on which we place reliance that Commodore Sloat took possession of Monterey July 6 last. On the ninth Commander John B. Montgomery of the Portsmouth summoned the Comandante of Yerba Buena [San Francisco] to surrender. What the result of this summons is, we are not yet informed.

A few days previous to July 6, a detachment of Colonel Frémont's force took possession of a frontier post, called Sonoma, to the north of Yerba Buena.

On September 22 under "Condensed News from California," the *Union* reported:

The inhabitants of California are generally in favor of the Americans retaining possession of the country. The natives seem to look for annexation, though they are somewhat indifferent.

Near the Town of the Angels [Los Angeles] is a large shady plain at the foot of mountains in which [San Fernando] they have discovered gold. A common laborer gets two dollars a day washing the sand in a flat basket. Colonel Stevenson's army has departed for the Pacific coast.

Events of deep significance moved rapidly forward in Washington. On June 15, Secretary Buchanan and the British Minister had signed the treaty partitioning Oregon at the forty-ninth parallel, thus adding to our country the territory of Oregon and the present Washington and Idaho. Benton's Oregon speech, widely quoted in the press, was given full credit for the good feeling everywhere manifested over the treaty.

[107]

Jessie's next filed clipping under the caption, "Frémont," was the *Union* item lauding Frémont in its report that fifteen thousand Mormons were advancing toward the West, using as a guide the published reports of Frémont, and that an army of five thousand volunteers under General Kearny had just left Bent's Fort.

From now on, the press kept the people informed of the Mexican war news, late only a matter of weeks. By the end of autumn, the whole country looked upon Colonel Frémont as an officer acting fearlessly for his country in the conquest of California. During the week of December 1, 1846, Jessie and her sister Eliza were translating for the editor of the *Union* the account of the conquest of the Californians, written by *Comandante-General* Castro for the official Mexican paper, *El Diario del Gobierno*. It reported both provinces lost, all civil and military authorities fled including Governor-General Don Pio Pico. It further stated that Frémont and his men with Commodore Stockton and the Marines were in the City of the Angels, that Colonel Alvarado and other officers were hid in the woods, and that General Castro himself was thirty days out on the road to Sonora, Mexico. A few days later, Jessie "released" to the *Union* editor her translations of Castro's proclamation to the people of California and to the Consuls of France, Spain, and Great Britain, which had arrived via Mexico City.

Christmas was brightened for Jessie by the many personal letters of congratulation from those in touch with national affairs. She answered General Dix, who had affectionately commented on the radiant appearance of the "lonely little Madame Lieutenant-Colonel": "How can I be lonely with all my friends keeping happy vigil with me?" But in a letter to her Cousin Sarah Brant, she said: "How fortunate that we cannot see into the future. Had I known we were to be separated this long, my grief at parting would have been insupportable. I keep myself steady by picturing our happiness when reunited."

In February, 1847, Jessie sat in the gallery while the Senate had under consideration the matter of additional topographical maps and guides for Oregon and California, embodying such notes upon this latest Frémont expedition as were available. So accurate were those notes and so clear the pencil sketches that the topographical maps were considered comparatively easy. Preuss was to be authorized to make the map.

Jessie had copied Benton's speech which now followed, but she thrilled along with the other listeners as he gave a dramatic résumé of excerpts from King's and Frémont's letters and closed thus:

This road map with its two thousand miles of prairies and mountains marks an era in our conception of map making and belongs to a school of which Humboldt is the greatest exponent. The map of Oregon and California will embrace seventeen degrees of latitude. Geography is still in its infancy in that vast region. Under the jealous dominion of Spain and Mexico the greater part of it was a sealed book. Even the labors of the Jesuit Fathers, founders of the missions in Alta California, have been buried in the depots of geographical collections in the City of Mexico. Colonel Frémont at the hazard of life has opened some leaves of this book and revealed a region of violent contrasts, more Asiatic than American in its character.

The materials embodied in these reports were not gathered without great hardship and suffering, but the members of these expeditions did not mutiny against their leader but went where his spirit led, and after conquering nature, had a part in conquering California. A letter from young King said:"I think it likely we will go down through California, peaceably if we can, forcibly if we must." Three months afterward they were in the City of the Angels, and the Mexican Governors of California were on the road to Mexico.

Frémont has claimed no rights of property in anything yet published under his name. He has labored in the interests of science. The episode of the conquest of California had deprived him of a part of his expected honors, but that episode has had the use among other uses of showing that a consummate military leader may be found in a modest lover of science and in the person of a young man who places the honors of science above the fame of arms.

Benton's praises did not seem fulsome nor his prophecies without ground when the report came of Frémont's march south to Los Angeles, the capitulation of Cahuenga, and Frémont's appointment by Stockton on January 16, 1847, as "Governor and Commander-in-Chief of California until the President shall otherwise direct." A few weeks later, Jessie wrote her Cousin Sarah:

I feel that this honor to Colonel Frémont is but honor due for the arduous labors he has performed and for his conspicuous bravery, and it is little enough reward for his incalculable scientific contributions to his country. It is difficult indeed, dear cousin, for me to express my own happiness. Its warmth and light have driven all the chill and dark foreboding from my heart. We will be in St. Louis soon. Later I may join Colonel Frémont, should mother's health improve. In any event my happiness gives me renewed strength and patience.

CHAPTER VIII

Under the Gun of Frémont's Court-Martial

JESSIE Frémont's first intimation that all was not well with her husband in his capacity of Civil Governor of California came as a shock. Seated at her desk one morning in March, 1847, serene in the knowledge that Colonel Frémont had played an important rôle in the conquest of California, confident of his ability to deal adequately with any situation that might arise, and wondering wistfully how long it would be until she might join him, she turned to receive a page from the State Department. He had brought a packet of letters and documents in Spanish to be translated. Telling him to return in the afternoon, she settled at once to her task.

In a lengthy letter from Monterey covering Spanish land-grant queries, she came upon a reference to a clash in authority between Commodore Stockton and General Kearny. The paragraph ended: "This will in all likelihood result in the removal of Colonel Frémont as *Comandante*."

Shocked and incredulous, she made a second copy of this letter before finishing her work. The hours before Benton's return were filled with troubled questioning. She recalled Kearny's friendship for the family, those pleasant talks in St. Louis, Kearny's cooperation in the matter of the howitzer. And Stockton—he had but recently been an honored guest in her home and had expressed admiration for Frémont and his past services. Why this stupid quarrel among the three over authority?

Its implications loomed frighteningly, for she had lived all her life close enough to the whirring wheels of politics to be fully aware of those ignoble impulses that grind sometimes quietly, sometimes noisily about the bestowers and the recipients of honors. When her father came in, she gave him the translation and asked its meaning. Benton's florid face paled under his daughter's accusing glance. Heretofore, he had found it easy to be frank with her. He knew that frankness would have been wiser in this case. Seating himself beside her, he confessed that for some weeks he had known of the situation from letters he had received in St. Louis from Frémont. He had refrained from troubling her in the hope that adjustments would be made on the ground.

The report from California was that General Kearny after his victory at Santa Fé had arrived in California with authority from Washington as of June, 1846. His orders were to assume the Governorship of California, "should he conquer and take possession of California." Kearny considered these orders to hold, even though upon his arrival California had already been "taken." Commodore Stockton had acted under his Washington orders of July 22: "Take and hold California. This will bring with it the necessity of a civil administration. Such a government should be established under your protection." In the ensuing dispute Frémont had naturally declared allegiance to the superior officer who had appointed him.

As Benton finished his recital, Jessie demanded: "But what is the President doing about this? Have you talked to him? Is Colonel Frémont to be made the victim in a quarrel between the Army and the Navy?" Benton answered soothingly: "I have spoken to him. He hopes the disputants will themselves settle the matter."

With this vague assurance Jessie Frémont contented herself as best she might, but the peace of her days was broken. During the following weeks she stifled her fear and entered into preparations for Eliza's coming marriage to William Carey Jones. Her sister had been a confidante in her own stormy courtship, and she was glad that the course of this love affair had run smoothly. William was a gentleman of fine family background and excellent education; moreover, he was romantically in love with the quiet Eliza. There was a simple ceremony in the Benton drawing room, and as the couple drove away to their new lodgings, Benton left for St. Louis. At the door he admonished Jessie: "Look after Lily and your mother, and be of good courage."

Because of a relapse in her mother's illness, Jessie rarely looked at the newspapers during the weeks following. Then one morning in early June she received a letter from a relative in Louisville asking explanation of an article she had seen in the paper. A few days later a similar query came from a relative in St. Louis. Vague fears which had haunted her days and made restless her nights now mounted to panic. If that clash on the coast were a matter of press comment, it was far from settled. As she began a letter to her father, the servant Nancy announced: "Kit Carson to see Miss Jessie."

Hurrying to the drawing room, she was almost overcome at sight of that beloved familiar figure resplendent in a black-broadcloth suit with expanse of gleaming shirt front. His blue eyes smiled out at her from beneath the broad brim of a felt hat which he had forgotten to remove. She led him to a chair, took his hat, and kissed him on the cheek. Drawing a stool near, she sat at his knee, demanding: "Now tell me everything. How is he, the Colonel?" Assured that Frémont was well and busy with his duties in Los Angeles, she repented her haste and said: "Come. You shall meet mother, get settled in a room, and have dinner before we talk."

After dinner, again seated in the drawing room, she closed the door, went to a cabinet, and poured out two glasses of brandy. Then pointing to a chair, she said: "Sit here, light your pipe, and tell me everything. Father keeps things from me for my good, but there is no easement of mind in that."

Carson's affection for Jessie was second only to his love for Frémont. He thought of her always as "plucky and proud." He was aware of the blow to her pride in this account of petty bickering, but he slowly lighted his pipe, took a sip of brandy, and said: "It is best I tell you what I know. I was acting for the Colonel."

He proceeded to paint the picture of Frémont and Andreas Pico signing the peace treaty at Cahuenga Rancho and Frémont leading his bedraggled battalion across the muddy plain and down into the Plaza of Los Angeles. There he had met Commodore Stockton in conference over the steps necessary to a civil government. Stockton had invested Frémont with the title and responsibilities of Governor with a formal commission to follow.

Shortly thereafter, General Kearny had established headquarters nearby on the Plaza and had sent a note to Stockton demanding that he cease all civil government activities, and another note to Frémont ordering him to make no more appointments without his sanction. Stockton countered with a note informing the General that the civil government now in operation would not be disturbed and that Kearny's note would be sent to President Polk with a request for Kearny's recall.

Frémont had written a decisive refusal to obey Kearny and had given it to Carson to copy. Next morning Frémont was summoned to Kearny's headquarters and there Carson brought the note which Frémont promptly signed and handed to Kearny. The note stated that since he had received his commission from Stockton whom he held to be Commander-in-Chief in California, with all deference to Kearny's professional and personal character, he felt constrained to say that until Kearny and Stockton could adjust between themselves the question of rank, he would have to report to and receive orders from the Commodore.

Kearny had advised him to take back the letter and destroy it. Frémont had refused, declaring that Stockton would support him; whereupon Kearny had warned him that such persistence would ruin him. The two had parted as virtual enemies. That very day Frémont's commission from Stockton had arrived. It appointed him "Governor and Commander-in-Chief of California until the President should otherwise direct."

Carson had read the commission and had applauded his chief for holding out against Kearny, who had in his opinion made a cowardly appeal to sentiment in referring to his own obligation to Senator Benton for many favors and his deep affection for Jessie Anne.

Until late March the Southern Californians had recognized Frémont as Governor, and the Northerners had acknowledged Kearny. The latter had established himself at Monterey, had met the new Commodore Shubrick, Stockton's successor as Naval Commander, and had also met Stevenson's New York volunteers. He had been hailed by both Commodore and troops as Chief-in-Authority in California.

A letter from Shubrick came to Frémont shortly thereafter, showing him to be in accord with Kearny, though it held no statement tending to disturb Frémont's sense of security. Carson had seen this letter and believed that with Stockton on duty elsewhere and with Shubrick and Kearny agreed, things did not look promising for Colonel Frémont.

Though unaware of the rapid march of sinister events in California since Carson's departure, Jessie listened to this recital in growing fear. The news was many weeks old. She now exclaimed: "There must be some way to get at the bottom of this. Your story justifies Colonel Frémont in his position. Would you go with me to call on the President tomorrow?"

Carson admitted that he was anxious for the post of dispatch bearer to California and that he would gladly "meet Mr. Polk under her protection." Later that day Jessie received a letter from Frémont, addressed to Benton and inclosed with one from him directing that Frémont's letter be got to the President without delay. Jessie read the letter aloud, flushing with relief and pride as she saw these statements in her husband's handwriting:

When I entered Los Angeles, I was ignorant of the relations existing between these gentlemen, having received from neither any order which might serve as a guide. I therefore waited upon the Commander-in-Chief, Commodore Stockton, and after called upon General Kearny. I soon found them occupying a hostile attitude, each denying the right of the other to assume direction of this country...

The country has been conquered since September last, and General Kearny had been instructed to "conquer the country." Upon its threshold his command had been nearly cut to pieces and but for the relief of Commodore Stockton would have been destroyed.... As to his instructions, how could he organize a government without proceeding to disorganize the present one?...

You are aware that I had contracted relations with Commodore Stockton, and I thought it neither right nor politically honorable to withdraw my support. No reason of interest shall ever compel me to act toward any man in such a way that I should afterward be ashamed to meet him.

Jessie Frémont slept little that night. By the light of a candle she read and reread her husband's letter, then lay waiting until morning. She had early learned from her father to maintain calmness in a crisis by keeping to orderly routine. Carson watched in surprise as she chatted through a leisurely breakfast, settled her mother on a couch, then listened to Lily read a lesson from a French primer before finally retiring to her room to dress. She reappeared in a green cashmere gown with a little green-corded hat atop her brown hair. She turned about slowly to allow her mother to see the new spring costume. Then adjusting the cape about her shoulders, she said: "Mr. Carson and Mrs. Frémont will now have a glass of sherry before going into battle."

When the public office in the White House opened at one o'clock, they were the first to be admitted. The President received them cordially. Carson stated his mission and was assured that he would be given dispatches for the coast if he could depart within two weeks. Then Carson handed the President Frémont's letter. As he finished reading it, Jessie asked eagerly: "Doesn't Colonel Frémont's course seem reasonable in this case?"

An instant's hesitation—and in that instant she knew where Colonel Frémont stood. Polk already held him in the wrong! She scarcely heard his evasive answer: "The misunderstandings may by now be settled, and recriminations ended." No need to prolong this interview. Satin-smooth and smiling, she thanked him for his consideration of her guest and herself and took leave. As she and Carson walked down the steps, she said: "The President is always evasive. Before you leave, we will see him again. If possible, I want Colonel Frémont to have assurances, not evasions from us."

The next visit occurred at the end of a week of suspense. Jessie sought a promise that Frémont should be kept on duty in California. Polk told her that Carson would be carrying orders leaving it to Frémont's option to stay on the coast or rejoin his regiment, the Mounted Rifles, then in Mexico. The letter she wrote the night before Carson's departure was short, and sealed in the packet with it was her miniature made in the winter of '45.

My dear husband: Kit Carson is waiting to take a letter to you. Nothing I can say will express in the littlest degree the love and yearning in my heart— the grief that I cannot be with you. It hurts too much even to write. Besides, I would not make you unhappy by my repining. Kit will tell you everything. I am sending you myself—in miniature. I lay with it over my heart last night. I pray you wear it over yours until le bon temps viendra.

Your devoted wife, JESSIE

Shortly after Carson's departure, Benton returned, and the family made speedy preparations for the summer's stay in St. Louis. Settled once again among old friends, Jessie forgot her anxieties for a time. Then one day Benton asked her to go for a walk, as he wished to discuss matters of importance before returning to Washington on business.

Then came the report of all he had withheld from her: Kearny's perfidy in not sending Frémont a copy of his own orders from Washington, thus causing him to fall into a trap of mutiny and insubordination by continuing in

[116]

Jessie Benton Frémont, 1845. From a miniature painted by Dodge.

office; Kearny's peremptory order that Frémont bring to Monterey all archives, intimating that the explorer need no longer be detained in California; Frémont's refusal to remove the archives, his later determination to have it out with Kearny, his taking Don Jesús Pico and setting out at daybreak on horseback with six loose mounts, each rider lassoing and saddling a fresh mount every twenty-five miles, making the four-hundred-twenty-mile journey to Monterey by the afternoon of the fourth day. All this, Benton said, was followed by a brief and stormy interview with Kearny, who disclosed the information of his recent orders from Washington.

Frémont had at once offered his resignation from the service. Kearny had refused it and repeated his orders that Frémont deliver the archives. Frémont had promised to do so. Then had followed the wild ride home, completing the journey of a thousand miles in the record time of seventy-six riding hours.

Colonel Mason, a harsh disciplinarian, had followed Frémont south to take charge of the district. After enduring weeks of indignity and hectoring, Frémont had asked to be allowed to rejoin his regiment under General Scott. This was refused, as was his request to return to the United States with his own exploring party. Later he had been ordered to hold himself in readiness to start east. In June Kearny had marched eastward at the head of his company and with Frémont and nineteen of his original battalion ordered to march behind them. At Fort Leavenworth Kearny had sent for Frémont and read an order directing him to leave his party, proceed eastward alone, and repair to Washington, considering himself under arrest.

Too stunned for protestation or weeping, Jessie heard her father announce that he was going to Washington to demand a trial by court-martial. "Everything shall come to light," he thundered. "We will have complete vindication out of this. Be of good heart." Faced always with the necessity of sparing her mother and of appearing cheerful before Lily, Jessie saw her father off and awaited his return with outward calm.

Benton reported to her his ultimatum to Polk, calling for an open investigation which would completely vindicate Frémont and make public his services. He bade Jessie cease all foreboding and think only of her husband's coming. She had thought of little else for months, but not of such a homecoming as this!

That night after vainly trying to read, she felt the mounting fears of the past months suddenly overwhelm her, and covering her head to stifle her sobs, she broke into wild weeping. That iron control once loosed, there was no stopping. In the throes of hysteria, she suddenly felt herself lifted bodily in her father's arms, wrapped in a blanket, and carried to a couch where she was held close while her father's voice said soothingly: "Here! Drink this. You are cold and hungry. Drink!" An impulse of childish curiosity broke the hold of hysteria. Obediently she drank the milk and brandy, wondering how it could have appeared so suddenly.

Benton explained that coming up late at night to bed, he had seen a light under her door, and meaning to scold her roundly, had heard her weeping. He had hurried to the kitchen and prepared the hot milk and brandy. Warmed and comforted and grateful for this another evidence of his unfailing solicitude, Jessie rewarded him by soon falling asleep, awakening late next morning to find him gone to Washington.

Eager restlessness now possessed her. She decided to go to Kansas Landing to await her husband's coming, taking her negro maid Nancy with her. Once arrived, she spent the intervening days in long walks and in standing at the log wharf hours on end, gazing out over the water in the direction he must come. The negro wharf hands and roustabouts knew who she was and whom she awaited, and they often remarked to one another at the patience of "the Missy."

Early one morning the steamer *Martha* came in sight through the August haze. Jessie waited until she saw Frémont pushing through the crowd to the gangplank. Then with a choking cry she rushed to his arms. Scarcely was Frémont ashore when a group of villagers came forward carrying a flag which they waved above their hero, cheering and yelling: "Frémont! Frémont!" The Frémonts boarded the *Martha*, which continued downstream to the lusty cheers from the crowds at every river-town wharf. The arrival at St. Louis was a triumphal procession for Frémont. Exaggerated stories had preceded him, and his party now rode into the city on the crest of a wave of public sympathy.

Jessie Frémont's emotions ran the gamut as she watched the demonstration along the river and met the ovation at St. Louis. She found herself nearly carried off her feet by the crowd surging up the gangplank, shouting "Frémont! Frémont!" Before they could proceed, he was compelled to address the crowd. Later the Jefferson City *Inquirer* reported:

Jessie Benton Frémont: a Woman Who Made History

Lieutenant-Colonel Frémont and his lady passed down the river on board the steamer Martha *one day last week and arrived in St. Louis on Saturday the twenty-eighth ult. We learn he is under arrest, growing out of difficulties between him and General Kearny in California.*

Upon their arrival in Washington, Frémont was called to Aiken, South Carolina, to attend the funeral of his mother. But before departing, he wrote Adjutant-General Roger Jones, requesting that he be given a speedy trial and saying that he would ask only one month to bring necessary witnesses from Missouri.

Benton now turned all the force of his powerful intellect and his implacable will toward a speedy and devastating arraignment of everyone connected with "this damnable persecution instigated by petty malice." He shrewdly guessed that Kearny would want the case delayed and then tried quietly at Fortress Monroe on the single charge of mutiny. His witnesses, pressing that point continually, would fix the term in the public consciousness by way of the press.

So great was Benton's influence, so necessary was it that he be conciliated that even the President, reluctant and worried on his own political account, was forced to cooperate with Benton in his demand for a speedy trial. The Benton home now became a law office with the Senator, his son-in-law William Carey Jones, and Frémont outlining procedure, and Jessie, a hard-ridden secretary, copying briefs and writing letters to those called as witnesses.

This labor she called her sanity saver. It steadied her nerves and gave her confidence born of an intimate knowledge of the method by which factual matter was to be marshaled as evidence. Her spirit was like a young juniper tree whose tough little roots grip the earth while the branches bend unbroken in the wind.

While Benton went to Norfolk to summon witnesses, Jessie and Frémont, the lovers, stole a few days' vacation. The day he left for Norfolk, Jessie confided to Eliza: "We are going to mutiny until father returns to whip us back into line. He doesn't realize that though this trial is important, it isn't everything in life." Long afterward Jessie said:

For a week we lived alone together on a happy island surrounded by a sea of troubles. We arose late and had breakfast in our room before the fire. After the mail came, we went for a walk or a visit with friends. We even drove in the moonlight out to the school in Georgetown and looked up at the back window where the Colonel's first love letter had come up hidden in a basket of laundry.

Their idyll ended with Benton's return. From then until the case opened on November 2, Jessie's secretarial pen flew fast. That brief month of delay requested by Frémont had thrown consternation into Kearny's camp. The General, for all his anger at Frémont and his desire to punish him, had a fatherly affection for Frémont's wife and a wholesome respect for the integrity and influence of Benton. Already he perceived that the case was being tried beforehand by the press with every indication of the popular verdict going to the accused, whatever the outcome of the trial. Both sides were scurrying for witnesses to be ready for the opening of this *cause célèbre*, which the Washington dailies called "the most dramatic Army trial since the court-martial of General Wilkinson thirty years before."

Finally the case was ready. The last night, anxious and excited, Jessie slept little. Early the next morning she sat by while Frémont dressed for his drive to the Arsenal Building where court was to be held. He had slept soundly, he assured her, and expressed his perfect confidence in the outcome of his trial. Lying quite as valiantly, she too declared she had slept well and expressed equal confidence in his vindication.

She watched Benton and Frémont depart in the omnibus to call for several witnesses before court opened at noon. Jessie and Eliza dressed carefully for their appearance at the day's ordeal. Jessie chose a wine-colored costume with a bonnet of burgundy velvet. She had vetoed her sister's plan to wear a black gown: "No! This isn't a mourning occasion. Put on your newest dress, the blue one."

General Dix's carriage arrived for the sisters at eleven o'clock, and as they drove down Pennsylvania Avenue, Jessie met many of her friends driving at this fashionable calling hour. She sat self-possessed, bowing to acquaintances as though she too were merely on dress parade, but one ungloved hand clung tightly to her sister's hand. Eliza reported later to Frémont's anxious query: "Her fingers were trembling and ice cold. They weren't warm even when we put on our gloves at the turn toward the Arsenal."

As Jessie heard the house called to order by Brigadier-General George M. Brooke of the Fifth Infantry, her eyes wandered over the array of witnesses on both sides. They were equally impressive, for the picturesque scouts, Carson, Owens, and Godey, were matched by the gold-laced and braided Regulars there to support their superior. Her husband and her father sat calm and imperturbable through the preliminaries. Then a hush fell on the crowded room as Colonel Frémont arose and announced that he would use no technical points of defense and would do all he could to expedite the trial upon the three charges: mutiny from January 17 to May 9, 1847; disobedience of the lawful command of a superior officer; and conduct prejudicial to order and discipline. The trial was on.

Jessie attended throughout the day and the many days stretching into weeks while the trial continued, but her avowed intention not to miss a single session was halted during December by a severe cold and threatened pneumonia. She was expecting a second child the coming summer, and the doctor's warnings finally reduced her to submission, though she insisted upon seeing all press notices, good or bad. More than one space writer grew lyric over the injustice of the picture:

Like Columbus, Colonel Frémont has returned from the hardships and dangers of discovery of a new world beyond the Rockies, a prisoner and in disgrace. Like Columbus, his achievements have aroused sordid minds to jealousy, and like Columbus, instead of being permitted to continue his researches in that region which he first opened to science, he is compelled to return and defend himself against base attack.

These comments were copied by the Western and Southern press with their own laudatory additions. As the trial moved slowly through November and December, it became evident that Kearny's own Army officers were unable to determine the relative ranks of Stockton and Kearny.

Romance was now coloring the formal proceedings of the court-martial, for one of the character witnesses, Richard Taylor Jacob, well known to the Benton family, had fallen in love with Sarah Benton. Jacob was the grandson of Commodore Taylor and "a good match." Though Benton was loath to part with his daughter, he gave his consent to the marriage, which took place on January 7, 1848.

Kit Carson, 1840.

On January 24, Frémont was to sum up his defense, and Jessie was allowed to be present. The room was crowded with spectators, among whom were many of Jessie's warm friends. In the eyes of his adoring wife, Frémont had never appeared more handsome or dignified than when he arose to speak before that distinguished audience of Army officers, Senators, and press representatives from New York, Boston, and St. Louis. She listened proudly while he flung in Kearny's face the charge of perjury, and closed his plea thus:

My acts in California have all been with high motives and a desire for public service. My scientific labors did something to open California to the knowledge of my countrymen. My civil administration was for the public good. I offer California during my administration for comparison with the most tranquil portion of the United States. I offer it in contrast with the condition of New Mexico at the same time. I prevented civil war against Governor Stockton by refusing to join General Kearny against him. I arrested civil war against myself by consenting to be deposed.... I have been brought as a prisoner and a criminal from that country. I could return to it after this trial is over, without rank or guards, and without molestation from the people except to be importuned for the money which the Government owes them. I am now ready to receive the sentence of the court.

There followed three days of cruel suspense for the Benton family while the court deliberated. Then on January 31, 1848, Frémont was found guilty on all three charges. Six of the twelve members recommended him to the clemency of the President because of the defendant's distinguished personal services. This threw the verdict into the Cabinet. After two weeks the members were unanimous that Frémont could be held guilty only on a technicality and that so valuable an officer should not be dismissed from the service.

Buchanan and Attorney-General Clifford recommended that Polk disapprove the sentence, while the "regulars," Secretary of War Marcy, Secretary of Navy Mason, and Postmaster-General Cave Johnson, recommended approval of the technical verdict and a remission of the penalty. Polk made his difficult decision and formally announced his belief in Frémont's innocence of mutiny but his guilt on the other charges. Hence he approved the sentence of the court-martial but canceled the punishment. "Lieutenant-Colonel

Frémont will accordingly be released from arrest, will resume his sword, and report for duty."

Upon hearing this pronouncement, Frémont promptly declared his intention to resign from the service unless completely vindicated. And now Jessie witnessed the first clash between her husband and her father. Benton, though thoroughly enraged, contended that popular sentiment was so entirely with the Colonel that he could far better wreak revenge on his enemies from within the service.

Frémont, amazed at this attitude, declared hotly: "I want justice, not official clemency. Would you have me admit the justice of such a verdict? That is all that concerns me now." Jessie listened, at first bewildered. Perceiving that her father took her agreement with himself for granted and eager to believe him right, she sparred for time, urging them both to consider for a few days before taking this step, so important to her husband's and her own future.

Those few days were illuminating ones for Jessie Frémont; in them she learned that her husband had a strength of purpose and an inflexibility of will quite equal to Benton's own. He too took her agreement with himself for granted. "There is but one honorable course to pursue in face of this dishonorable verdict," he insisted. Though her judgment was still confused, the path of her loyalty lay open before her. She agreed with her husband, and during the argument with Benton that followed, she declared resignation to be the only honorable course. She solaced herself with the Washington press articles which condemned the verdict, and with James Gordon Bennett's *Herald* editorial:

> *During the progress of the assizes we saw, from time to time, evidences of hostility on the part of members of the court against Lieutenant-Colonel Frémont, who held a higher commission and was a greater though a younger man than a majority of his triers; and what we then suspected has this afternoon been presented to us as actual truth.*

Frémont's resignation went to Polk on March 15. The President accepted it. Frémont at thirty-five, having undergone hardships that made a veteran of him and having made contributions in the field of science which would have crowned the brow of a man of sixty, was now returned to private life. Jessie's disappointment was keenest because this retirement shut the Colonel out from the topographical service wherein she felt his greatest talents lay. Her prime object now was to put on record the story of his third expedition, much of which had been recounted to her and in which she saw possibilities for a narrative even more colorful than the preceding ones.

A few days after Polk's acceptance of Frémont's resignation made them private citizens again, Jessie settled herself to making tentative outlines for a geographical memoir to accompany Frémont's map of Oregon and California, which was practically finished. As to this map she was especially proud of the point at San Francisco, marked "Chrysopylae." When Frémont had studied the topography of the Bay, he had named that picturesque opening through which all ships must go and come, the Golden Gate, having in mind both its form and the advantages of the Bay to commerce, Asiatic included.

One day in April, while deep in her work, Jessie looked up to see Frémont with a boyish grin on his face and a twinkle in his eye that made him look ten years younger. "Listen to this, Jessie Anne." A letter from Benton in St. Louis announced that certain influential business men there were interested in a railway route to the Pacific. They were willing to finance Colonel Frémont on an expedition to set forth in early autumn with the purpose of seeking a south-central route which would be practicable in winter. The letter concluded that upon Benton's return details would be forthcoming.

Jessie watched her husband as he read. She saw his shoulders straighten, his hurt pride raise its head again. His eyes were alight with the old eagerness, and her own eyes shone with sympathy and understanding. As he folded the letter, she said: "That means we must hurry. This report must be worthy of you!"

By late May the memoir was complete. On June 5, the Senate ordered twenty thousand copies of the Oregon and California map. One evening while Jessie was at work upon the amplification of further notes of the expedition, she felt the light of the room go suddenly dim. Without looking up, she said: "Don't move the lamp. It makes it too dark." In alarm Frémont sprang to her side as she sank in a prolonged faint. The doctor was called and ordered her put to bed indefinitely. Thus ended her work on the notes. She stopped Frémont's bitter protestations of self-blame, and through the weeks of temporary invalidism she watched him work at what he now called "the curséd memoir."

Upon Benton's return, Jessie entered heartily into all plans for the fourth expedition. At Frémont's ultimatum, "There will be no more long separations," it was arranged that in September she should accompany him to the frontier where six weeks would be required to complete preparations. Then after he had started westward, she would return to Washington and prepare to go with her children to California by way of Panama. Benton delighted her by saying that he himself would accompany her. She faced her confinement in the happy assurance of these plans.

On the morning of July 24, 1848, Jessie Frémont gave birth to a son. She insisted that he be named John Charles, but Frémont objected and suggested that since Lily had been named for Jessie's mother, the first son should be called Benton in honor of her father, to whom they both owed so much. The baby was so named to the gratification of his grandfather.

Upon Jessie's recovery, the Mariposa Rancho plan was completed. In California the previous year Frémont had given Thomas O. Larkin three thousand dollars with which to purchase acreage near the pueblo of San José. A view out to sea made it an ideal site for a home. Before leaving California as Kearny's prisoner, Frémont learned that Larkin had purchased instead forty thousand acres of mountain land in the Mariposa. Angry as Frémont had been at the time, he was in no position to protest. Fit only for grazing and subjected to depredations from Indians, the rancho would be a difficult place to develop. But now Benton and Senator Dix were making him a loan for agricultural implements and milling machinery to be sent on ahead around the Horn.

Jessie's interest in this new project salved her disappointment over the delay in her own departure. She was thankful that she need not say her hated goodbye until she should wave farewell from the farthermost outpost, the Delaware Indian Reservation near Westport Landing on the Missouri River.

On a day in September the little party was at the station awaiting the train to St. Louis: Frémont, Jessie, Lily, and the baby in the arms of his negro nurse. As Benton put them on the train, his parting words to Frémont were: "Promise me on your honor not to let Jessie Anne keep on going westward when you reach the Missouri."

CHAPTER IX

A Forty-Niner via Panama

N THE pleasant deck of the Ohio River steamer *Saratoga*, Jessie Frémont sat with her family about her, happy and at peace once more. After the ordeal of recent months, it was sheer joy to be doing nothing at all. She meant to make the most of these hours of drifting and dreaming, since there would be no privacy once they were in St. Louis. Lily, quiet and old for her years, often bent her solemn little face above her baby brother asleep in his nurse's arms. Her insistent question was:"When will he grow up to play with me?"The arrival in St. Louis was an ovation. At the Brant home the Frémonts had to act as hosts to an informal reception before they could remove their wraps.

Time passed all too quickly as preparations were completed for departure of the expedition. A few days before they were to start, Frémont left the house early. Shortly thereafter the nurse Kitty came to Jessie's door, calling in alarm: "We can't wake the baby." Jessie rushed to the nursery where Lily, shivering in her nightdress, bent over her brother's crib, trying to warm his hands in her own. When the doctor came, he found Jessie sitting with the child wrapped in a blanket in her arms and Lily kneeling beside her. Examination showed the baby to have been dead several hours."Defective heart"was the doctor's verdict."He couldn't have lived long in any case." Apparently uncomprehending, Jessie made no reply and continued holding the child close. Touching her shoulder, the doctor repeated:"The baby is dead, my dear. Let me have him."

As he stooped to take the child from her, she smiled gently up at him without tears and said: "I understand, but I have had him such a little while. Please go away, all of you. We'll wait here together until my husband comes." The doctor sent a messenger for Frémont, and not until he himself took the child from her did the relief of tears come. With the tact born of his great love for her, he made no attempt to comfort her with empty words.

Next day the baby was quietly buried. Lily, who had been spirited away to a neighbor's, was now brought back. When Jessie began to explain the baby's absence, Lily patted her hand and said: "I know, mother. He'll never grow up to play with me." The child was left in the care of relatives, while Frémont and Jessie, accompanied by Kitty as maid, moved on to a Government post. Here they were received by Major Cummins, the veteran Indian agent who had been at this frontier point for thirty years. Jessie stayed with him and his wife in their log cabin while camp was being made under the cottonwoods on the trackless prairie. Then for six weeks she spent her days with Frémont in camp.

The moment of parting came at last, and true to their creed, each sought to lighten it for the other. Jessie stood watching the cavalcade move off until lost in the dusty distance. Major Cummins, who was to put her on the steamer at Westport Landing the following day, waited beside her until Frémont's party was out of sight. Thinking to divert her, he took her along the trail where he hoped to find and destroy a wolf which had been raiding his sheepfold to feed her cubs. They did not find the mother, but to Cummins' delight they found the cubs, which he promptly killed, unaware of the effect of his act upon a human mother who had just buried her child and who could but picture that other mother's return to a ruined lair and her dead cubs. Nor could he realize the effect upon her of the return by way of the deserted camp with the ashes of the morning fire still warm.

That evening while Kitty packed their belongings for the morrow's journey, Jessie sat crouched on a stool before the fire in utter loneliness while the old man rocked back and forth, still complaining of the toothache to which she had ministered. Finally she went to bed and sank into a troubled sleep. At midnight she was awakened by frightening sounds from without. The she-wolf with cries of rage was hunting her cubs, and the hound puppies in the corral had set up an accompanying din. Sleep being impossible, she and

Kitty arose, dressed again, and built up the fire. Then realizing that the fire-light would shine far through the low uncurtained windows, they pinned up their shawls for blinds.

Scarcely was this done when they heard men calling outside and the baying of the older dogs. Suddenly Jessie recognized her husband's voice. He had ridden back the ten miles for another hour with her. While Kitty made tea for them, Mrs. Cummins brought bread and cakes. She then withdrew, and the two were left alone until their second parting at dawn.

On arrival in St. Louis, Jessie was waited upon by a messenger from General Kearny, who was very ill and wished to see her. Perhaps if she had realized that he was on his deathbed, she would have felt different; but with the conviction that her child had been a victim of her own frightful anxieties and with its loss too fresh in mind, she sent word that she was sorry to learn of General Kearny's illness, but that no good could come of an interview, since a little grave lay between them.

Back again in her father's house, Jessie quickly fell into her old habit of talking and working with Benton, whose mind just now was occupied with the serious slavery-agitation aspects of the political situation. Ever since 1835 he had believed that Calhoun and his followers selected slavery as the one subject upon which the South could be held together for the protection of her sectional interests. Thenceforward Benton had drifted away from the South, and during this autumn he explained at length to Jessie his fears that under Calhoun's machinations there were many who might be incited to measures destructive to the Union. These discussions went on while Jessie with characteristic enterprise gathered and filed the remaining botanical notes. On December 8, 1848, she wrote to the botanist, Dr. John Torrey:

My dear Sir: Mr. Frémont left me a list of plants to copy out for you, but until now I have had neither the quiet nor the strength to do it. A few days will bring it to a close, and you may derive fresh interest for examining those from Feather River by reading the accounts of the great wealth of that region. Are there any flowers or plants peculiar to a gold region? One flower (209) which Mr. Frémont supposes may be the cumas *may be belonging to that kind of earth. I have, as you know, very vague botanical ideas. Your daughter would laugh at me, but Mr. Frémont encourages my questionings, and I am a sort of privileged person in the family, which must excuse my questioning you also.*

By some Indians who are to be sent back from Bent's Fort, I shall get letters from Mr. Frémont before the New Year. Then or at any time you wish to know anything I can inform you of, I hope you will let me have the pleasure of doing so. Father reserves for his part the sending of documents. None of any interest are out yet, but Mr. Frémont's memoir is just coming in from the last session and shall be sent to you.

Very respectfully yours,

Jessie Benton Frémont

As she finished these tasks, Jessie Frémont was making her first mental break away from a sense of localized homes— places where as a sensitive child she had absorbed those intangible elements which feed the emotions and develop the character. She had been held by a long and strong chain of association in which the material is tied to states of mind and fluctuations of mood. Now day by day she was reconciling herself to the fact that in a few months she would be cut loose from everything material and geographical that had made her former life. She had no other thought but that her whole future lay out beyond those mountains within whose snowy fastnesses her husband was even now making his adventurous way.

Her father, that frail and shadowy mother, her sisters sweet and talented, her young brother Randolph away at school—all were part of a picture soon to be recaptured only in memory. That background with its wealth of parental love, "always enough to go around," would no longer be hers. Yet she had no fear, since the lover who had never betrayed her trust, never belied by word or act the smallest gesture of tenderness, would fill her future. Her girlish adoration of him had grown up; her faculty of clear efficient thinking was applied to their relationship.

Her dreams now held new and fabulous meaning. She saw paradise ahead, a paradise of this world, achieved through good health, mutual cooperation, and an understanding and abiding love. But only to her sister Eliza did she speak of these things, as they sat sewing together.

A statement in Frémont's letter from Bent's Fort now gave her deep concern:

[131]

Both Indians and whites report the snow to be deeper in the mountains than has for a long time been known so early in the season. They predict a severe winter.... Still I am in no wise discouraged by the prospect, and I believe we shall succeed in forcing our way across. Should we have reasonable success, we shall be in California early in January, where I shall expect to hear from all by steamer.

When Jessie's preparations were complete, her father told her regretfully that because of political complications he would be unable to accompany her to California, and since he could not allow her to go unaccompanied by some male member of the family, he had talked it over with Richard and Sarah. Richard would accompany her, and Sarah, who was expecting a child, would remain behind with the Bentons. Richard had been in California with Frémont and would see her safely in his care before leaving her. Moreover, he had just seen Colonel Aspinwall of the Pacific Mail steamers, who would have one of his employees meet her at Chagres to render every service possible. Jessie masked her disappointment because she knew that solicitude for her mother lay back of her father's decision.

Final arrangements were now complete, another hurdle of goodbyes got over, the highest one mercifully delayed because Benton was accompanying Jessie to New York. When they arrived there, the city was all excitement. The gold rush was on. Hotels and lodging houses were crowded with people awaiting transportation to California on one of the many old boats transformed by coats of paint and bunting streamers advertising "immediate departure by fast route." At the Astor House Jessie found her favorite cousins, the Prestons of Virginia. These young people respected and secretly feared Colonel Benton, and when they found he was allowing their beloved Jessie to start on this wild and perilous journey, they took advantage of his momentary absence from the room to express their vigorous disapproval.

Benton entered unannounced in the midst of this spirited protest. Guessing its purport, he demanded: "Who is making war on Jessie Anne? I won't have her made war on!" Unsilenced now that genuine love and solicitude for their Cousin Jessie gave them courage, they protested: "But she has never been so far away from home."

"There must be a first time in all experience."

[132]

The Harbor of San Francisco, 1849

"But she doesn't know what lies before her."

"Do any of us here know what the next hour holds?" the Senator boomed.

That was begging the question. "Jessie is not strong."

"Not in body, perhaps," their uncle answered, "but she has the kind of strength that counts in this case—a sturdy spirit. We have already seen it tested."

Jessie wrote afterward of this scene:

I was in the position of a nun, carried into the world for the last time before taking the veil: all the pros and cons, old fears renewed, old griefs opened up, the starting made harder than ever. To further complicate matters, the young negro who had expected to marry my maid Harriet reported to a New York abolitionist organization that a free negress was about to be carried out of the country against her will. I was waited upon by an irate official, who demanded an explanation. Harriet, confronted by him, appealed to me in tears to know what she should do. Despite my own dilemma, I could but admire the enterprise of Harriet's sweetheart. I told her she might go, whereupon the happy negress instantly produced a grinning substitute whom she had obligingly secured in anticipation of my verdict.

The disturbing arguments with my relatives lightened my grief at leaving them, but when my father took me in his arms and said, "Goodbye, my brave Jessie, be of good spirit," I felt like a little child being launched literally into an unknown sea, traveling toward an unknown country without even a servant who knew her.

Of her next experience she said:

I went out on deck and leaned against the rail. I had never seen the sea, and no one had told me of the wonderful new life it could bring.... The solitude, the sense of space and freshness, the power and the majesty, these came to me as healing necessities. I hungrily drank in the salt air and sunshine as the boat left the harbor. Richard, wise and kind, spent the day amusing Lily, leaving me to the silent teachings of sea and sky.

The second day out, they struck a storm which made the chances even as to the boat's weathering it or foundering. However, this was followed by quiet days in the blue waters of the Gulf Stream off the coast of Florida, and later on by the heartening sight of a lighthouse on the low-lying coast of the Bahamas.

As they approached the shore of Chagres, the steamer swung dizzily on the ground swell. The sea broke furiously on bar and beach. As the ship rounded to before dropping anchor, she careened crazily, the deck rail nearly touching water. Captain Schenck now came to Jessie, begging that she remain on the steamer and return to New York. He recounted the physical discomforts ahead: boats which must be boarded without gangplanks, often under heavy swells; the crowded, ill-smelling quarters ashore; hard days on muleback over tortuous trails; bad food and the ever-present menace of Chagres fever.

When this recital failed to kill her courage, he took cruel advantage: "I feel responsible to your father and to your husband. Neither of them could imagine what confronts you. I don't wish to be responsible for what I feel certain will be your fate if I put you ashore here with your child." Richard, whose stomach had been sorely tried by the long rollers of the tropical ocean and who was desperately homesick as well, now added his entreaty to the Captain's. But their listener had already won her battle. She thanked them both for their solicitude but declared her determination to proceed.

As the Captain said goodbye, he admonished her: "Don't drink unboiled water. I only hope there's a boat in from Jamaica with sheep, yams, and plantains." Jessie watched Lily being handed down the ladder. Then she followed and took her child from the boatman's hands, holding her steady as they were set on one of the many toy tenders bobbing on the bay. She thus recounted the trip:

At the waterfront I was almost overcome by the stench from stale fish, tar, and cinnamon. There was an indescribable mixture of sounds from the horde of passengers: flowing French patois, soft Spanish, and volleys of Anglo-Saxon oaths from those consumed with impatience to be gone. Crowded into small boats, miscalled deep-water because they carried an engine, we began the river trip.

The banks were low and covered with jungle growth to the water's edge, where white and scarlet flowers rose from the tangled green. The eight miles of deep water were soon covered. Then the tiny boats, stopped by the shallows, discharged their passengers to the tender mercies of canoes.

When I saw these ten narrow dugouts, each manned with naked yelling negroes and Indians, I was almost as frightened as Lily, who clung trembling to my hand.... But as I looked uncertainly about, I saw coming toward me Captain Tucker, of whom Colonel Aspinwall had spoken. He said that he was expecting me and that I was to go up the river in the steamship company's boat. I would be the only woman aboard but would be safe since this crew was reliable and had often taken his own wife to company headquarters.

Then followed three days of slow poling against the heavy current, sometimes in midstream, sometimes gliding lazily under arching trees and canopies of flowering vines. Occasionally balked by overnight growth of jungle creeper, we would have to alight while the Jamaica negro crew cut a pathway with long knives, jumping on and off the boat, shouting a laughing jargon, half song, half speech, as they worked. The sense of novelty and comparative safety set my spirits rising. I forgot my discomfort, dismissed my fears, keeping in mind the fact that along this highway the buccaneers and revolutionists urged their cayugas, by it the despoilers of Peru carried their loot to the Atlantic on their way to Spain, and that now I was among these other Argonauts upon its waters seeking the Golden Fleece.

At Gorgona they were met by another employee of Aspinwall's. With his first glance at Richard he said: "You have had a touch of sun atop of seasickness." Richard admitted that he had felt ill for several days. Within an hour he was put to bed in the company's lodging house and ordered to stay there until able to take a return steamer. Again he entreated Jessie to remain and return with him. But as soon as she learned that he was in no danger and would be cared for until he could get passage home, she declared that she must go on. When Mrs. Gray, a fellow passenger, pitied her for this abandonment, she laughed and said: "Poor Richard has been ill from homesickness all along. He has never been a tonic for my courage, and he has now become a pull on my patience."

The *Alcalde* of Gorgona came to meet Jessie and invite her little party to his home for breakfast. Of this experience she said:

The stilted house with its wattled sides, thatched roof, and inside walls of unbleached sheeting looked more like a magnified vegetable crate than a human habitation. At breakfast the chief dishes were baked ringtail monkey and boiled iguana, a large lizard. Both dishes were tasty, once you forgot the monkey's resemblance to a child burned to death. As I ate, I was reminded of Sam Weller's, "Weal pie ware a good thing when you knew it waren't made of kittens."

After breakfast the *Alcalde* took them to the place where the muletrack to Panama confronted them. Since the Indian porters had no system about baggage, Jessie saw part of hers placed on a mule and the rest on a cow far ahead in the baggage procession. Jessie begged that Lily be set on a mule immediately in front of hers and the animal kept there. The baggageman laughed: "He'll stay dere, lady! No place to go else." This muletrack followed the face of the country to the top of the hills and down again. Sometimes the "mule steps" down a mountainside were but four feet wide, slanting perilously. Alder and mangrove trees were checkered on either side with towering palm and coconut trees. An occasional ray of sunlight lingered aloft in their dark branches; then swiftly without warning it darkened again, and there was the crackle and splash of raindrops. There were no bridges across the narrow streams, and when the mule gathered his feet together and jumped, the rider either kept his seat or got a fall and a wetting, with incidental bruises. At night the travelers slept in tents or Indian huts.

One day the party climbed for an hour among the débris of broken baggage shed by a cow that had measured her horns against a narrow opening through a defile and had dumped her cargo of books, bags, clothing, and tinware, and continued her journey unhampered. Innocent Lily found laughter for a day in this mishap, a sorry joke in which Jessie could but pretend to join. Her one compensation was the sunrise. Of this she later said:

From the mountain top we looked down upon an undulating sea of unknown blossoms sending clouds of strange perfume into the freshness of the morning. And from the last of the peaks we saw, as Balboa before us had seen, the Pacific at our feet. We felt at home with the Pizarro of Prescott's history—those family readings!—in a time that seemed so far back now, for it lay before this date which would hereafter mark all things.

At Panama she and Lily were carried through the water and over the reef

[137]

on the back of an Indian. Her first sight of the walled city with its ancient cathedral, the roof and spire of which were inlaid with mother-of-pearl, was as of something unreal, out of a dream. But even more fantastic was the sight of several thousand gold-seeking campers, raging and complaining at the non-return of the *California*. This ship, which had preceded them, was the first being sent around the Horn. If it did not return, they must await the arrival of the *Panama*.

Meanwhile the Isthmus mail steamer had come in with packets of money and letters addressed to many of those detained here, but because the bags bore the stamp, "San Francisco," the Consul refused to release them. This problem was met in true Yankee fashion by a committee of two custom-house officers and an American export commissioner, who were authorized to open and distribute the mail.

While this was in progress, Jessie was taken to lodgings kept by a Madame Arcé. Here in a balconied, red-tiled house with a garden, she and Lily had their first taste of comfort in many weeks. Added to clean beds and tasty food was the luxury of a bath, a primitive tiled "shower bathhouse" without light but with slats near the top for ventilation. On its slanting floor stood a series of jars ranging from small vase-like containers holding a quart to large ones three feet tall. The bath attendant poured over the bather the contents of the smallest jar first in order to accustom him to the shock from tropical heat to cold. After the final deluge from the large jar, the bather dried himself in the sun of a sheltered court, towels being non-existent.

The gallery of Madame Arcé's house overlooked the square of the Catholic cathedral and convent. Here Jessie sat long hours reading to Lily, who nibbled the delicious *dulces,* a confection of native fruits held together with sugar. After the reading they would watch for the mail, letters passed up to them on the split end of sugar cane. One day there came a fat envelope forwarded from Washington. Jessie read:

Taos, New Mexico, January 27, 1849

My very dear wife: I write to you from the house of our good friend Carson. This morning a cup of chocolate was brought to me while in bed. To an overworn, much fatigued, and starving traveler, these little luxuries of the world offer an interest which in your comfortable home it is not possible for *you to conceive.* While in the enjoyment of this luxury, then, I pleased my-self in imagining how gratified you would be in picturing me here in Kit's care, whom you will fancy constantly occupied and constantly uneasy in endeavoring to make me comfortable. How little could you have dreamed of this while he was enjoying the pleasant hospitality of your father's house. The farthest thing then from your mind was that he would ever repay it to me here. But I have now the unpleasant task of telling you how I came here. . . .*

Former letters have made you acquainted with our journey so far as Bent's Fort. . . . We left that place about November 25, with upward of a hundred good mules and one hundred thirty bushels of shelled corn, intended to sup-port our animals across the snow of the high mountains and down to the lower parts of the Grand River tributaries, where usually the snow forms no obstacle to winter traveling. At the Pueblo I had engaged as a guide an old trapper well known as Bill Williams, who had spent some twenty-five years of his life in trapping various parts of the Rocky Mountains. The error of our journey was committed in engaging this man. . . .

Then followed the shocking account of the sufferings and privations of that unhappy expedition. To the tortures of desert heat and mountain cold had been added guide treachery and Indian treachery, the deaths of ten men from starvation in the frozen fastnesses of the Rockies, and Frémont's own departure thence with Preuss, Godey, and Saunders, searching for help at Red River settlement, which was reached after ten days of agonizing struggle on starvation rations. The rescue party found those twenty-three remaining men tottering skeletons with bloodless faces, who cried like children as they were lifted onto mules and taken into camp at Taos. This letter glossed no de-tails, and Jessie did not spare herself a second and a third reading. But at the end were these heartening words:

The survey has been uninterrupted. . . . As soon as possible after reaching California, I will go on with the survey of the coast and coast country. I shall then be able to draw up a map and report on the whole country, agreeable to our previous anticipations.

---

*Frémont was at this time in bed because of a badly frozen leg, which caused him much suf-fering then and later.

When I think of you all, I feel a warm glow at my heart which renovates like good medicine.... We shall yet, dearest wife, enjoy quiet and happiness together. I make pictures of the happy home we are to have, and oftenest and among the pleasantest of all I see our library with its bright fire in the rainy, stormy days, and the large windows looking out upon the sea....

La Harpe says there are two gods which are very dear to us, Hope and Sleep. My homage shall be equally divided; both make the time pass lightly until I see you. So I go now to pay a willing tribute to one, with my heart full of the other.

Your loving husband, J. C. F.

With her defenselessness against her love and with her capacity for suffering, this letter held for Jessie Frémont every element of torture, but from out the anguish shone one clear gleam of comfort: her husband had survived and would be waiting at Monterey to meet her. She must hold to that and let the future adjust itself. Her determination to hope for the best did not lessen, even though in a Washington paper later brought to her, she read her father's report of the disastrous expedition with all it connoted of hardship and sorrow to the man she loved.

In her extremity instinct and habit served her well. She took long walks, studying the picturesque particolored natives and watching the crews of San Blas Indians unload their schooner-rigged cayugas from the Bahamas. And always she remembered that behind her on the hills those crowds of impatient campers waited like herself for the steamer that did not come.

Seven weeks had passed when one night Jessie was awakened by a sudden uproar in the streets, following the signal gun of a steamer. She arose and stood at the window watching as men rushed wildly about hugging one another in frantic joy and shouting: "We're off for California."

Madame Arcé came running to tell her that two steamers were in the harbor. The *Panama* had rounded the Horn, and the *California* had come down from San Francisco with a shanghaied crew. Before Jessie could dress herself and Lily, the Captain of the *Panama* himself appeared, accompanied by Lieutenant Fitzhugh Beale, who had often been a guest at Jessie's home. The exuberant Lieutenant exclaimed as he looked about: "God! What a crib for a lady!" Whereupon Jessie rebuked him gently: "This has been my home for seven weeks. Here I have learned the genuineness of the Spanish saying, *La casa y todo que tien es á su disposición."*

After hasty goodbyes, Jessie and Lily, jostled by the frantically happy crowds, took their turn at being hoisted aboard the *Panama* from the small boat by the customary route, a tub at the end of a boom. As Jessie looked about at the hundreds of fellow passengers, she exclaimed in consternation: "Where will all of us stay?" An officer replied: "I don't know, madame, but we dare not refuse anyone as long as there is standing room."

When the count was taken, Jessie found herself on a boat which had comfortable quarters for eighty passengers but which now harbored nearly four hundred. The decks were soon parceled out for sleeping quarters, and Jessie allowed Mrs. Gray to share her and Lily's tent room, made by throwing the folds of a large American flag across the spanker boom. Here they slept on iron cots padded with blankets.

The efficient discipline on the steamer, combined with the happy exuberance of the passengers, made the trip far from unpleasant, and Jessie Frémont made heroic effort to rise to the situation. By now everyone had learned who she was, and she was conscious of the unspoken sympathy of these strangers who had read of her husband's hardships.

Just before reaching San Diego, a heavy rain caused her to take cold, and after a slight warning cough, she suffered a hemorrhage of the lungs followed by a fever. The Captain managed to get her a private cabin, surrendered by a sympathetic passenger. Here, tended by Mrs. Gray, she lay gathering her strength for whatever news might await her. When the boat reached San Diego and everyone rushed on deck, a sudden impulse made her lock her cabin door even against Lily, for she wanted no one to see her if the news should be bad. Mrs. Gray took charge of the child and promised to bring whatever news there might be.

As Jessie lay on her bunk listening to the shouts of the passengers who were landing here, someone pounded on her door, and a man's voice shouted: "Mrs. Frémont, the Colonel's safe, riding up to San Francisco to meet you. He didn't lose his leg, only a bad frostbite." At this she opened her door, and in describing the scene afterward, she said: "I think every man on the ship came to tell me and say a choking word of joy for me." With this news as tonic, she rested quietly until the ship neared San Francisco. For hours she schooled herself against the possible disappointment of not finding Frémont awaiting her.

At last on the morning of June 4, 1849, the steamer moved through the Golden Gate. The *Panama's* gun announced their arrival. Thrilled and silent, she stood watching the forests of masts and the dark hulls of the United States Government boats past which the steamer glided. On the hills rising steeply out of the water rose tier upon tier of flimsy tents and shacks of canvas and unpainted planks. From the wharf a dozen boats crept out to them. She heard the signal to drop anchor. Her long voyage was over.

Through the high-running surf, the sailors of the small boats carried the women and children to shore. Among the hundreds milling about, Frémont was nowhere to be seen. A fog was rolling in over the town; its chill was making her cough again. Mrs. Gray insisted that since Colonel Frémont had not yet arrived, Jessie should go to the Parker House at once and to bed. Mrs. Gray's husband had met her and was now eager to give Mrs. Frémont all possible aid. She was soon settled in an upper room of the flimsy hotel on Portsmouth Square.

The next day she was called upon by W. D. M. Howard, a friend of Frémont's and one of the few well-to-do tradesmen who were wisely gleaning their gold over the counter. He too offered his services and told her that Frémont was on his way up from Monterey.

Ten days after her arrival Jessie was sitting listlessly in her drab little room before a fire of brushwood fagots. No word had come, and she was fast giving way to morbid fancies when she heard a voice shouting outside the window: "Your wife's inside the house, Colonel." Before she could reach the door, she found herself half smothered in her husband's arms. It was long before either spoke. All the hardships they had endured were ended, and all the anxious waiting. There were no words in any language for the joy of that moment. She was led to a chair, and her husband knelt there beside her, too overcome even to speak. Later she described the scene:

Then we both spoke at once, each wanting the other to begin at the moment we had parted over a stirrup-cup of tea that morning on the Missouri. Suddenly he looked at me closely with fear in his eyes. "You have been ill, you are ill now, my darling." I was about to deny it when Lily came in, released at

Portsmouth Square (Plaza) showing Parker House, 1849.

the door by Mrs. Gray. She looked at her father gravely as he knelt beside me. As he rose and hugged her, then drew a chair up close, and took her on his knee, she said bluntly:"You didn't come. Mother almost died. A lady downstairs says she will die."

There was nothing to say in refutation, but I answered his stricken look: "In her innocence she is partly right. Being away from you is a kind of death. Only with you am I fully alive and well."

That night while an icy wind blew in from the Bay, rattling the windows and shaking the flimsy building, Jessie sat beside the smoking fire, wrapped in blankets and listening to the outlines of the Colonel's last exciting weeks. Reference to the preceding horrors was shunned by both. At Taos his old friends, Kit Carson, Lieutenant Beale, and others had lent him money to purchase animals and continue his journey. Telling his remaining followers that he would equip any who wished to accompany him to the Pacific, he was gratified that most of them volunteered to go. His company of twenty-five men and sixteen horses traveled to the Rio Grande by way of Gila River and followed down the south bank. Here he met a caravan of shouting, hurrahing men and women with pack mules, old wagons, and carts in a wild, disorganized march westward. To his question, "Where are you going?" they answered, "Alta California." When he asked, "Why such a crowd?" they yelled, "Gold, gold!"

This was his first news of the discovery which by now was known around the world. If gold were at Sutter's, it would certainly be found at the Mariposa, he reasoned. That forty thousand acres, mostly up and down, a hundred miles from an ocean view, that seventy square miles for which he had cursed Larkin more than once, might mean a fortune! He had promptly engaged twenty-five Mexicans who were at Mariposa ready to work on grubstake terms. He was now expecting the farm and mill equipment any day.

Despite Jessie's declaration that she was strong enough to go direct to the Mariposa and live as he would have to live, Frémont insisted she must have a home in San Francisco. He announced that he had a surprise awaiting her, a six-seated surrey which he had ordered built for her in New Jersey long before leaving on the last expedition. This carriage, the first in California, now awaited her in a nearby warehouse. The vehicle had many conveniences suggested to him by Colonel Aspinwall: a large boot and compartments for storage, reversible seats to make a bed, Spanish leather upholstered cushions. Moreover, it was guaranteed by the builder to ride as smooth as a boat.

"You must have a house from which to step into such a luxurious equipage," he declared. She went the next day to see this wonder and found it all that had been claimed. Happy as a boy presenting a gift to his sweetheart, Frémont made her examine the compartments and sit to try the cushions.

Frémont now secured rental of a well-built adobe house which had been occupied by the late Vice Consul Leidesdorff. When Jessie saw the comfortable furniture and walked out into the unkempt but gay little garden, the only one in all this higgledy-piggledy place, she exclaimed:"This is my home!" Since no servants were available, Mrs. Gray again came to the rescue, saying she would cook and wash for them all, as laundry elsewhere was twelve dollars a dozen.

In the next few weeks the Frémonts were visited by Alfred Robinson, representative of the Pacific Mail Company, and by Frémont's admirers, Lieutenant Beale and Major John Derby. Everywhere lay proofs of the fabulous tales their guests recounted. Since January,'49, a steady stream of every kind of craft had discharged passengers from every port on earth, some to go to the mines, hoping to return home as soon as a fortune could be piled up, others to remain in the town, planning to carry on their chosen business or profession. Jessie was assured that all sorts of merchandise could be found in the planked and canvas stores on the Plaza, while fish and fresh vegetables were available even in winter.

Jessie remained in the Leidesdorff house with Mrs. Gray as companion while Frémont made several trips to the Mariposa. Though her happiness was complete, it could not conquer the persistent cough which kept her weak and ailing. Upon Frémont's return, Mrs. Gray took him aside one day and said:"Your wife can never stand these fogs and winds in her condition. Can't you get her down to the peninsula where it is warm?" While she spoke, Frémont sat dejected, his head bowed in his hands. Then he exclaimed:"It's worth a trial. I'll talk to Beale." He hurried out and soon returned, accompanied by Lieutenant Beale. Jessie, sitting in the garden, looked up to see these two bronzed and serious young men bowing before her. Frémont announced:

Madame, we have come to entreat you to make a long leisurely journey overland in your carriage with Lieutenant Beale and myself as outriders and with a few minions and scullions for making camp. If they desert us for the mines, we will turn minion and scullion. My friend Beale makes excellent pot au feu when it hasn't too much pepper in it, while I can make a bed of your surrey cushions that will tempt you to sweet slumber. What is your pleasure? The carriage waits without, practically.

Assuming the grand manner, Jessie replied: "Gentlemen, your offer intrigues me. Pray, let us be off at once." In recounting this scene long afterward, she said:

As I listened, I felt like a fond mother letting herself be deceived by her boys. I preferred to stay quietly here, as by now all movement had become an effort, but I knew this journey was a desperate remedial measure, and I wanted so much to live.

CHAPTER X

In Search of Health

THE little camping party that moved along the rough but well-traveled road toward the pueblo of San José resembled a gypsy caravan from an Italian opera rather than the sanitarium that it was. The native Californians in their heavy-wheeled, ox-drawn *carretas* noted at the head of the caravan the familiar figure of Old Knight the guide; following him were the equally familiar gayly dressed Indians, Juan and Gregorio, leading two pack mules. One mule was half hidden under leather panniers bulging with clothing; the other rattled along under the clank of cooking vessels set atop a roll of grass hammocks. The mules too were familiar, but what followed immediately behind made drivers and *carreta* occupants stare in astonishment.

A strange black vehicle, high-swung and shining, drawn by two stout little mules, moved slowly along. Its rolled-up curtains revealed red-leather cushioned seats occupied by a pale dark-eyed young woman closely enveloped in a blue Army cape. Beside her sat a red-cheeked little girl of seven. Alongside the carriage rode two young men; one was tall, of military bearing, who sat his saddle very straight; the other, slightly shorter, wiry in build, his black hair well sprinkled with gray, his hawk-like eyes looking out from a lean bronzed face with furrowed cheeks. They all hailed him smilingly as Don Flémon'. Surmising his relationship to the woman and child within the strange equipage, the natives included them also in friendly greeting.

The passerby failed to note the apprehensive look in the eyes of the lady as she watched the animals that drew the carriage. Jessie Frémont had lived through another thrilling experience during the efforts of Lieutenant Beale and her husband to secure a safe team. Frémont had suggested a pair of stout mules, but the dashing Lieutenant had insisted upon horses as more befitting the equipage of a lady. He took on trial an Oregon mare warranted gentle and a California riding horse supposedly tamed by time and work. Beale felt he could drill these into carriage horses. They stood quiet while being harnessed and while the carriage was being loaded. When Jessie and Lily were seated, Beale took the reins. The team moved off sedately for some distance. Beale was triumphant. Suddenly the mare rose straight on her hind legs and pranced sidewise while the horse stopped short, then started backing. This move arrested the antics of the other, and she too joined in retreat, sending the carriage briskly backward down the slope and across the grass hummocks. By a miracle of horsemanship Beale saved the carriage from overturning as he whipped the animals into forward motion.

Once on the ground again, Jessie declared for mules, whereupon Frémont secured a stout pair from a passing caravan of miners. The larger mule, white, slow, and patient, Jessie promptly named Job, while the other, a brisk little brown fellow, she dubbed Picayune. The only fault of these animals was their considering the harness a badly balanced pack which they tried occasionally to shift. Under tutelage, however, they soon submitted to Beale's outrider driving, and all went well.

This spring season was the most delightful of the year in Alta California—no rains, no heavy fogs. The great fields of wild oats softened the contours of the hillsides. Evergreen oaks, under which wild cattle grazed, so reminded Jessie of the apple trees at home that she half expected to find fruit under them. During the day the sky was deep blue and clear, but at sunset the distant hilltops became deep azure, glowing beneath softly moving clouds.

The camping route followed the ridden horse trails among the trees, and when the ground grew perilously sloping, the Indians swung *riatas* around the carriage and held it steady until it reached level ground again. The party made long noon halts and sought to camp at night beside a stream. Warmly enveloped in her Army cape, Jessie walked about at twilight, watching the men make camp. Gregorio had charge of the larder, a great supply of Spanish onions, half a sheep, and a spray of sweet red pepper. Soon savory odors of *guisado* arose from the soup kettle swung over the fire on its tripod of stout sticks. When Jessie fretted that she was not allowed to help with the meal,

Frémont sternly said: "Your work, madame, has to do with the results of ours: to eat with all the appetite you can muster."

On those feverish coughing days "that went badly" she found this task more difficult than to have prepared the food. Her seat at table was a couch of carriage cushions arranged atop a folded grass hammock. After the supper which duplicated breakfast, the campfire lighted the gay gypsy scene about them.

For the entertainment of the invalid, Beale and Frémont regaled her and Lily with sea stories, Indian tales, and accounts of hunting trips. Occasionally they spoke of politics and the coming convention at Monterey. Then Jessie would surprise them by quotations from her father's enthusiastic speeches in 1848 on the subject of California's admission as a free-soil state. Discussion ensued because of her hearers' doubt whether admission on these terms could ever be brought about.

Nine o'clock was sanitarium bedtime. The carriage seats were turned and placed together for Jessie's bed, while Lily slept in the capacious boot, its apron drawn above her when chilling winds blew in from the sea. The men slept in the open. By nine thirty all was quiet; no sound save the crackling log fire and the slow munching of the animals at their feed.

At sunrise a cup of hot tea was brought to the patient. Then Frémont lifted her down into her dressing tent made from a pair of blankets. With a jug of hot water, a barber's tin basin, a cake of French soap, and towels rough but clean, Jessie declared she fared far better than the goddess Diana.

After two months of this idyllic outdoor life, her condition showed such marked improvement that Frémont's face lost its careworn look, and Beale protested himself entitled to an M. D. One night, however, a heavy shower presaged early autumn rains, and next morning Jessie's amateur physicians exchanged anxious glances over the huskiness of their patient's voice. In consultation they decided that since returning to San Francisco might undo all present gains, Jessie and Lily should be lodged for a few weeks with a Californian family in San José while Frémont made arrangements for their moving to permanent lodgings in Monterey.

This plan delighted the patient, who had begun to feel that camp life had definite limitations. Besides, as she afterward said in writing of those months: "I welcomed the opportunity of staying in a real Californian household." Frémont secured rooms in the home of a member of the Peralta family. The graciousness and dignity of Madame Peralta and the beauty of the young daughters fascinated Jessie, and they in turn were touched by her frail appearance and were desirous of offering every aid to her recovery. Later in speaking of this happy interlude, Jessie said:

The roomy long one-story house with its courtyard and high-walled garden made the boundary of the women's lives. Here they overlooked diligently their Indian servant girls, baptized and Christian, whom they trained in sewing and cooking. These Spanish housewives were amused that I should so much admire the fine needlework which decorated their wearing and household linen. Like their cooking, it was a survival of Spanish convent training become household tradition.

There was fashion even here. It was de modo to wear on fine occasions a full petticoat of scarlet broadcloth with green silk stitched beautifully point upward as a border around the bottom. Over this a gown of dull-toned damasked Chinese satin. Madame, our hostess, wore the scarlet cloth petticoat, and her gown of olive satin was pulled through the pocket holes on either side, making a Watteau effect. A small crêpe shawl of many soft colors was crossed over the breast and the ends tightly tucked back. Sunburned and naturally dark, she had still much of the rich color of the young women near her. Her brilliant black eyes were large and steady; the thick white hair made a puff as it turned back from the face and coiled in a large plait at the neck.

As she introduced her three daughters, each came forward gracefully bowing in smiling welcome. We were soon settled comfortably in our rooms. The next day while Lily rode with the daughters out along the three-mile double row of willows connecting the pueblo with the San José Mission, I lay in my hammock under the open gallery of the house, listening to the servants singing at their work, songs similar to those I had heard in Panama, alluring, melodious, strange, and sad. At night when the family gathered in the court with their guitars and violins, I contributed my own selections, old French and English ballads, and to their delight, a Spanish serenade they had never heard.

Though used to the Castilian nicety of pronunciation, I learned and quickly taught Lily the colloquial Spanish with its hard d and c and an occasional dropping of an s as the Cockney does his h. We were aided in this by constant

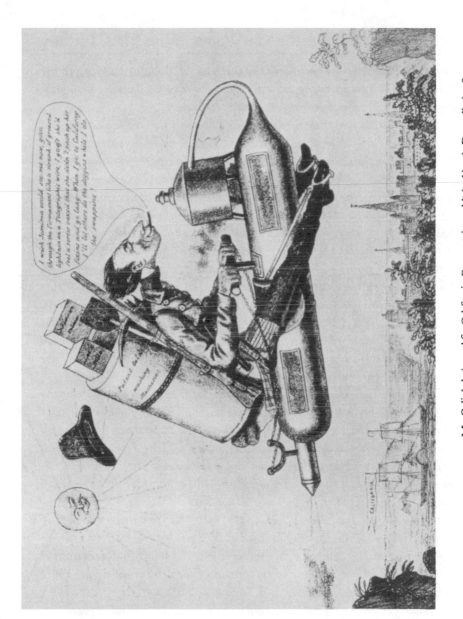

Mr. Golightly bound for California. From a print published by A. Donnelly in 1849.

opportunity to speak in gratifying the curiosity of Madame Peralta and her family as to the manners and customs of our country, while we in turn profited by observing the charming customs of their own.

During our stay my hammock became a box seat for viewing a three-day vaquero wedding celebration. On the first day the wedding party passed to the church for the religious ceremony and returned for the wedding breakfast served under a flower-decked ramada. The second day a formal parade was staged. Three hundred beautiful horses, perfectly caparisoned and superbly ridden, marked the parade. The girl sat in front on the saddle, the man behind holding the reins. The riders rode eight abreast. The musicians followed, also on horseback, playing as calmly as though in a hall. The bride now appeared, riding alone under an arch of flowers and ribbons carried by two groomsmen, the ends of the arch resting on their saddles. On either side of the groomsmen rode the bridesmaids. The groom followed, riding alone.

The whole was a glittering picture of gold lace, flashing beads, flowers, and ribbons. The girls were in satin dresses and slippers; the men in Californian dress, short velvet jackets covered with braid, velvet trousers open to the knee over full white drawers, and strings of tiny bells down the trouser seams.

The manner of the wedding party was decorous in the extreme. Even the horses were so perfectly trained that they paid no attention to the noise and sparks of firecrackers exploded beneath their feet. They stood proudly still with arched necks and fiery eyes, occasionally making feints of progress without moving forward. The crowd along the pueblo street now contributed songs with local allusions that brought trills of laughter from the bridal procession as it came to final halt and disbanded.

On the third day we were driven out into the plain to witness the feats of skill in horsemanship: the rush forward as though shot from a bow, to bring up standing as still as an English horseguard; the whirl in circles until it would seem that both horse and rider would fall to the ground from sheer dizziness; the mounting of a vicious, screaming horse with the quiet agility of a cat and the clinging with the hold of a panther. At the end of these performances, Lily and I decided laughingly never to refer to our having been called excellent horsewomen.

Upon Frémont's return, the little party left the Peralta home and made their last camp on the Salinas River, then proceeded to Monterey. Jessie's first impression of this place from which she had received so many documents and letters for translation was one of astonishment that so beautiful a spot had not become a developed little city of character and charm.

Back of the village rose the pine-covered slopes; below were rocky inlets and the far expanse of silver-crested bay. Seagulls flew in and out, the under side of their wings gleaming white in the sun. Sandpipers and other tiny unknown birds flew low about her head. The sea that had wrought spiritual healing when she had looked down upon it from a steamer deck now broke bright with promise upon the long low beach at her feet.

Turning to Frémont, who stood watching her anxiously, she said: "Let us make permanent camp here, anywhere within sight and sound of this beauty." Pointing to a long low adobe house built in the usual fashion around three sides of a court, he said: "Our home for the present is to be here. Madame Castro, wife of the Mexican General, holds no enmity toward me, although her husband is still exiled in Mexico. She lives here with her little daughter Modesta. She will give us two large rooms for our own home."

Deeply touched by such courtesy and grace from one of whom understandable hostility might have been expected, Jessie went at once to pay her respects to Madame Castro. Within a few days the Frémonts were settled on temporary cots and chairs, and Jessie began the struggle to make a home of these two rooms.

The urgent matter of laundry and cooking was one calling for all her diplomacy and skill. Out of thin air a negro girl appeared, saying she was willing to leave the family who had brought her from the East if Jessie would buy her. Jessie refused this offer and took Frémont's suggestion that they keep Gregorio on as cook, to tend the wood fires in their two-room lodgings, and to broil quail and make the nourishing if monotonous *guisado* over an open fire in the courtyard.

Overjoyed at being allowed to remain with the family, Gregorio proceeded to find a laundress, an Indian woman, who carried the linen away and brought it back white and fresh smelling. Though it had been merely soaked in cold water, pounded on stones with soap bark, and rough dried, Jessie wore it gratefully.

With the exception of rice and beans, only canned foods were available.

There were no fowls, eggs, butter, potatoes, or other vegetables. The thousands of gold seekers had swept the land locust clean, and nobody was left to plant garden plots or care for domestic animals.

This young housewife, used to every luxury, now set her ingenuity to work upon concocting wholesome dishes without other staples than flour, rice, meal, and sugar. She made a shopping list embodying such household furnishings as she could recall having seen displayed in those strange shops around the San Francisco Plaza. When she learned that fire had destroyed the warehouse in which her family clothing was stored, she wept a little, then dried her eyes, and added to the shopping list "any material you can find for women's underwear and dresses."

Frémont returned from San Francisco with a weirdly assorted but practical list of merchandise: a bale of Chinese matting for floor covering, a pair of New England bedsteads with numbers of sheets and blankets, East Indian wicker chairs, gayly colored china, white curtain material, and a large teakwood table. In lieu of wash basins were two English-china punch bowls. A gross of tall spermaceti candles and many tin candlesticks completed the homemaking elements. These had possibilities, but the material for clothing quite discouraged Jessie. Bright cotton-backed satins, harsh merinos, and thick muslins had been recommended to the Colonel as "very durable for a lady's winter clothes."

Through daily exercise Jessie Frémont's adaptability was rapidly developing into genius. Within a week her two rooms had become a home, far more comfortable than the harassed housewife had anticipated.

After a few days' rest, this ailing girl, whose heaviest sewing tasks had been to roll hems for delicate frillings and to embroider flowers in petit point, now began single handed the task of constructing a winter wardrobe for herself and seven-year-old Lily. She carefully ripped up her one remaining set of cambric underclothes to use as patterns for them both. One faithful black-silk dress remained of all the Washington wardrobe. This too she carefully ripped apart as a guide and attempted to copy its lines in these new and strangely intractable stuffs. Laying fabrics and patterns on the floor, she pinned, measured, and remeasured herself and them before daring to put scissors to cloth.

She had grown so thin since the black silk had been made that the first fitting disclosed necessity for expert alteration. Again she tried, with results still discouraging. Then she recalled the story of the old lady at home who never shaped stockings. She knitted them straight to the heel, saying: "It's a mighty poor leg that can't shape its own stocking." Jessie now built her wardrobe on this plan with more easement to her mind if not more skill to her hand. Her greatest achievement was one soft warm dress got by cutting off the extra length of a navy-blue riding habit.

She rested from her labors by reading books borrowed from an acquaintance of Madame Castro's, a flour merchant who had inherited a few volumes which he declared himself too busy to investigate. These treasures, five bound volumes of the *London Times,* an unabridged Byron, and a collection of *Merchants' Magazines,* made choice reading in the lonely evenings when Frémont was at the mine being developed on the Mariposa property, a hundred twenty-five miles away. As her birthday gift Frémont had found in San Francisco a copy of Lane's translation of *The Arabian Nights.* This she called her "Sunday dessert," parceling it out to last as long as possible. A rare treat was the arrival of a packet of clippings from *London Punch* with her father's notations on the margin. Beneath the Mr. Golightly cartoon he had scribbled: "This is the way I shall travel. Look for me."

Monterey was a village of only fifteen hundred people, including the officers and their families at the Army post. General Riley, who had followed Colonel Mason as commander, was in charge of the post, and his wife and the wife of Major Canby now came to Jessie's rescue, bringing a sense of the familiar amid all this strangeness. The gracious Madame Castro brought her friend, the *grande dame* Doña Angustias de la Guerra, widely known and beloved among the Californians for her charities. Of her Jessie said: "She was magnificent. To me she combined the wisdom of an Isabella with the tact of that Duchess of Alba who was famed for enchanting wallflowers into belles at her balls."

One Sunday morning Jessie received a very much depressed visitor who introduced himself as Samuel H. Willey, a Dartmouth graduate and a minister, who had just opened a school at Colton Town Hall in the village. He had found to his consternation that not one of his sixty pupils knew a word of English, and since he knew no Spanish, he was in despair. He would be expected soon to report to the missionary society which had sent him out. What could he say? Jessie heard him through, then said: "This is easily remedied. I will teach you Spanish, and if you do well, you can honestly report, 'I am making progress here'."

Overjoyed, Willey exclaimed: "When shall we begin?"

"At once," she replied. "Dry those dishes for me as we study." The first two words his smiling teacher taught him were the significant ones, *persistencia* and *fidelidad*.

While Jessie Frémont was making her adjustments to primitive living, Frémont worked feverishly at the mines, often returning home exhausted and depressed. But one day in early autumn he came riding down in a blinding rainstorm to show her specimens of gold quartz from a vein two feet thick at the surface and growing even wider and richer below. This specimen he was taking to San Francisco to show to men whom he wished to interest in developing the mine on a large scale. He reported later having had dinner with Bayard Taylor at the United States Hotel and showing the quartz to old prospectors who were greatly excited over it.

The news of this rich vein on the Frémont property spread fast, bringing a rush of prospectors and squatters. Already Frémont foresaw trouble over his title to the mineral rights, but he kept doggedly on, sending the buckskin bags of the precious metal down to be stored in an adobe building behind the Castro house.

When congratulated by Mrs. Riley over the Colonel's growing riches, Jessie made characteristic reply: "Gold isn't much as an end, is it? It can't conjure comforts nor an ounce of brain rations. I'm simply famishing for the taste of a good book."

Jessie herself was far more excited over the political situation rapidly developing about her than over those buckskin bags of gold dust for which her husband toiled. She had eagerly devoured the lengthy letters from Benton which had outlined the situation in Washington. The separatist and disunion elements within the Democratic party were growing bolder. The slavery question was rapidly dwarfing all others in national politics and was now having its day in the matter of the admission of California.

Benton's stand here was one of the most courageous acts of his career, for he knew that in opposing the growing slave faction of Missouri Democracy, he was preparing his own death notice as their leader in the Senate. The new administration having inherited the most momentous problems springing from the war with Mexico, Benton was delighted to find in President Taylor a Union Southerner as fearless as himself. He wrote Jessie at this time:

The Whigs elected Taylor on the popular "soldier" platform. They're finding he has more soldierly qualities than they counted on. He can put up a fight. He agrees with me against Clay's trying to cloud the question of California's admission with other measures relating to the fugitive-slave laws and slave trade. The disunionists are trying to dig a slave tunnel through to the coast. Watch out for that.

When Frémont was home, the little band of officers and their wives from the barracks made Jessie's living room a rendezvous and a round-table for political discussion. Among these habitués was young Captain William T. Sherman, frail and suffering from weak lungs. Jessie mothered him and gave him many sensible suggestions for conserving his health. One day when prospective callers, intent on political discussion, expressed regret to General Riley that Frémont was away, the General assured them: "If you want the real Washington situation with well-thought-out opinions on it, ask Miss Jessie."

When these callers arrived, they expressed surprise at the "achievement of such comfort in this queer place." Jessie, suspecting irony, looked critically about the room as if seeing it for the first time. She noted the windows, curtained with Chinese brocade, the whitewashed adobe walls adorned with a color print of St. Francis, the inlaid teakwood table on which was a two-year-old copy of the *London Punch*, a bronze Buddha, and a Martha Washington sewing basket. Her glance fell to the grizzly bearskin on the floor, his glass eyes gleaming in the firelight. Raising her voice to lecture pitch, she said: "Ladies and gentlemen, at first glance you might think this room incongruous, but having made close study of it, I find it true to the period, Pioneer Forty-Nine, worthy elements from all over the world, guarded by a California grizzly." Weeks later when the bear was placed on the state seal, General Riley reminded Jessie of this statement and credited her with the gift of prophecy.

Late in August, Riley recounted to an appreciative group at the Frémonts' his struggles to organize a state government and quoted the declaration of the *Alta:* "It takes a fire to pull the Californians into concerted action." But the election of August 1 was now past, and the elected provisional officials

[157]

and the thirty-seven delegates to the general conference were ready to convene on September 1 for the purpose of formulating a state constitution.

Just before the convention date, Jessie learned that her brother-in-law, William Carey Jones, was en route to California. He had been appointed by Secretary of the Interior as confidential agent to report upon land titles and to examine the archives at Monterey. In telling this news to Mrs. Riley, Jessie declared: "I realize now just how bitter has been my battle against longing for home. The very thought of direct news of my father makes me strong and well again." At the end of her first interview with William, he remarked: "This has been good practice for my later report to Washington. In two hours I have given you a six months' digest of the Benton and McDowell history."

Jessie walked abroad, noting the progress of the town's preparations for the convention. The wonted quiet of the village was now broken by the echoes of hammers and the shouts of workmen trying to complete the one hotel. It still stood without a roof. The owner hoped to complete it but declared: "They come horseback mostly, and if the weather holds good, they can roll up in their *serapes* and sleep under the pine trees."

Colton Hall school was being closed, and the two-story building with an assembly room fifty by sixty would accommodate the delegates and visitors, but their housing was a problem to tax the hospitable citizenry. Thomas O. Larkin and Doña Angustias were prepared to house a few and to feed many. When Jessie Frémont deplored the fact that she herself was living on the house-room charity of Madame Castro, General Riley declared: "There's more to a convention than food and sleep. Never fear, Jessie Frémont's home will be the scene of more than one star-chamber session."

This remark proved prophetic, for with the first arrivals on horseback came John A. Sutter, who sought her house at once and was her guest for supper. William M. Gwin, who had come out on the *Panama,* dined there a few evenings later. Jessie declared she could smell Washington air as the delegates began to assemble. She planned meals ahead and enlarged her dining table by laying thin planks on top. For a company tablecloth she used strips of unbleached muslin briarstitched together with red thread. Her most successful dessert was steamed spice pudding which she had evolved after much seeking for a new way to cook the inevitable rice.

At the invitation of the committee, Jessie attended the opening session of

Monterey, California, showing Convention Hall, 1849.

the statehood convention, September 3, 1849. She watched with interest the American and Californian delegates sitting in dignified silence as Robert Semple arose to preside. She stared in astonishment as he drew himself up to his full six feet six on the rostrum, above him an American flag, behind him a "somewhat startling" chromo of George Washington. Turning to a friend, Jessie said: "Now if they have someone here who can make the rafters ring, I shall feel perfectly at home."

The circumstances of this convention did not, however, lend themselves to rafter ringing. Of the thirty-seven delegates assembled, ranging in age from twenty-five to fifty-three, twenty had come originally from free states; seventeen from slave states. The nearest approach to rafter ringing came when the interpreter reported William M. Gwin's statement that it was *not* for the native Californians the convention was making a constitution, but for the great American population, comprising four-fifths of the country. José Antonio Carrillo took this as a fling at the Californians and had the interpreter say for him that he considered himself as much an American as the gentleman from Iowa; whereupon Gwin explained the matter and peace was restored.

Jessie, present on this occasion, remarked: "What a pity all the delegates haven't father's neighborly back-fence idea of Spanish. Washington especially should speak many languages."

With the constitutions of Iowa and New York as a basis, the convention made speedy progress. The press reports indicated no lengthy debates on the subject of the admission of California as a slave state. The final votes reflected the conclusions without indicating the many warm slavery and state-boundary discussions held in those adobe quarters of the Frémonts.

From the first, the Southerners sought to make the state boundary so large that it would need to be divided. In such case with an east and west dividing line, all south of thirty-six thirty (extending to the ocean slightly south of Monterey) might be made a slave state. These plans had no chance to reach the floor of the convention. They were talked over and disposed of at the Frémonts' round-table.

Long before the discussion of slavery had reached the floor, Morton M. McCarver had declared in one of these informal meetings that he expected to propose that free negroes should be excluded and that slave owners be forbidden to bring negroes into the state for the purpose of freeing them. He and Henry W. Halleck argued that California was the most valuable territory acquired as a result of the war and that to exclude slavery might defeat its admission to the Union. This argument influenced many already concerned by the extreme slowness of Congress to act in the matter of admission. Another strong pro-slavery argument was that Government patronage was on the side of slavery; another, that slave owners and speculators were eagerly waiting to bring their slaves in droves overland, and that with the more rapid opening up of the mineral wealth of the country, those acquiring wealth would want servants.

Colonel Frémont's mine was now producing even more heavily. Great piles of hundred-pound buckskin sacks of gold dust were already stored in the shed behind the Frémont house. Frémont's steady-going Sonorans had advantage over the swarms of squatters; yet he could now use ten times as many helpers as were available from any source. Jessie envisioned her permanent home here. She could picture the placers worked by negroes, whom both she and Frémont understood and under whose labor a leisured and ordered domestic life would be opened for her and for all future residents of the state; yet amidst the confusing flight of pros and cons, one point stood clear. Slave labor would shut off opportunity from those thousands of families even now on their way, those who, like that young pink-sunbonneted mother she had talked with in St. Louis, had only their labor to depend upon for ultimate security and comfort.

One evening when the pro-slavery leaders, headed by William Steuart, enlarged upon the glories of vast plantation holdings for those who had plenty of slaves, Jessie said:

Then you also plan for thousands of poor whites. Must we have them here? Mr. Frémont has called this the Italy of America. It is an ideal place for small homes and well-tended acreage. If we keep slave labor out, we will have the wealthy and comfortable middle class, but no poor. Surely we should abandon this selfish cause and keep the spirit of liberty in this land which now breathes that spirit.

"Fine sentiment, Mrs. Frémont," answered Steuart, "but the aristocracy will always have slaves."

"But why not an aristocracy of emancipators?" she continued. "We Bentons could qualify for that. We freed our slaves long ago at voluntary sacrifice of money. Mr. Frémont and I have refused two legacies of slaves."

On another occasion Jessie helped convince a wavering one with this argument:

It isn't a pretty sight in a free country for a child to see and hear chain gangs clanking through the streets or to watch officers chasing a fugitive slave and putting him in irons. Nor does such an advertisement as I recall make good juvenile reading: "Sale of twenty-six valuable negroes, tobacco, and provender from the Mendell estate," or "Fifty dollars' reward for the return of a black girl Nancy, five feet tall, thick built, and strong."

"But," argued McCarver, "what if the South says to Congress, 'Unless a man have a right to take his own slave property to California, *no vote.*' We can't get on without it."

"They may have to get on," she answered, "to make shift like the commercial traveler who left an article of his wardrobe in an inn in Dublin. He wrote to the chambermaid to have it sent on by coach. He got this reply:

I hope, dear sir, you'll not feel hurt;
I'll frankly tell you all about it.
I've made a shift of your old shirt,
And you must now make shift without it."

With a general laugh the party broke up, and the next morning J. M. Jones of San Joaquin, the youngest member, returned to congratulate her upon her frankness and to confer upon the Frémont maps and memoirs from which he expected to make his boundary argument.

Jessie was present in convention when his proposal carried the day. She stood with the crowds in the street on the morning when the last signature to the constitution had been set and the flag from the balcony of Colton Hall unfurled to the breeze. The first gun in the harbor boomed out, and gun followed gun until, at the thirtieth, the village rocked with the shout: "That's for California."

Laughing and crying with the others, and little dreaming what awaited her so soon under this new régime, Jessie Frémont returned to the house to prepare for the ball toward which each delegate had contributed and at which all guests were requested to appear in some semblance of "full dress." Ruefully she recalled her Washington ballgowns of tulle and satins as she donned her red-brocade basque and the navy-blue skirt made from the tail of her riding habit, but it was "all hers," as she declared later when she read Bayard Taylor's facetious description of the ball:

The dress of the dancers was as varied as their features and complexions. Scarcely a single dress that seemed to belong entirely to the wearer, and I thought if the clothes had the power to leap severally back to their respective owners, some dancers would have been in a state of utter destitution.

Taylor himself would in such case have become garbless, since he, not a large man, danced all evening in a pair of pinned-over pantaloons lent him by an officer who weighed two hundred pounds.

CHAPTER XI

Wife of the First Senator from California

IMMEDIATELY upon the adjournment of the constitutional convention, General Riley called an election for November 13 to choose a Governor and state officers. There being as yet no party machinery, any man aspiring to office was free to present his name as candidate. William M. Gwin had early made known his ambitions toward the Senate. Quite as early, however, the name of Frémont had been suggested for the Senate. Captain Halleck let it be known that he aspired to the same honor, while the editor Robert Semple, unwinding his six feet six of length, announced: "Newspaper folk are good to have in the Senate because in a controversy their gun is always loaded."

A self-appointed committee approached Frémont. They argued that he was the logical candidate since his explorations had made him a popular hero, his maps and memoirs were even now guiding those long lines of emigrant wagons westward, and his dignity under the injustice of his court-martial had made him a popular idol, while his reputation for wealth, born of those hundred-pound buckskin bags of gold coming out of the Mariposa, gave a last touch to popular fame. The reason for his local popularity lay in his fearless avowal of attitude toward statehood itself and toward boundary lines with their possible bearing on the pro-slavery ambitions of certain of the delegates.

It was argued that as a Democrat and a free-soiler, he would properly represent the new state, and there was a bit of poetic as well as political justice in thus honoring the man whose services had helped secure California and whose sense of beauty and fitness had named that entrance through which the whole world seemed to be pouring, the Golden Gate.

[164]

On the morning of December 14, Jessie opened the door to her husband, whose return from San Francisco she had not expected for several days. With restrained eagerness she listened as he told her of the committee's request that he enter the Senatorial contest along with William M. Gwin, T. Butler King, John W. Geary, Henry W. Halleck, and Robert Semple. With a simple dignity that matched his own, she said: "It is an honor you deserve. And you can be of great service."

Now as often before, she restrained a tendency to express the bitterness and recrimination that lay in her heart. Frémont's habitual restraint made such expressions seem unworthy, but she was too much her father's daughter not to harbor secret desires for vengeance against injustice. Her husband's election to the Senate would connote much more to Jessie Frémont than an honor earned by his past services to California. Her pride had been crucified by the indignities he had suffered here at the hands of General Kearny. She still writhed under the lashing memory of the court-martial and the defection of President Polk. Her sanguine temperament had saved her from useless brooding, but it had not weakened her sense of the cruel injustice her husband had suffered. For him to sail through the Golden Gate as one of the first Senators from the state out of which he had ridden two years before as a virtual prisoner eating the dust of Kearny's cavalrymen would be a well-earned honor to him and the final bit of healing salve to her own hurts suffered for him.

These thoughts sent her spirit soaring above all doubts as to the election of her candidate. She knew that each had his popular following and that each, her own included, would have a few detractors snapping at his heels. She was not surprised, therefore, when those of Frémont's caught up with him at San Francisco early in December. He received a letter from one of the local party leaders, Jacob R. Snyder, asking him to state clearly his political views and the nature of his controversy over his mineral rights in the Mariposa and requesting him to clarify certain points relative to his civil governorship in California.

These queries Frémont answered, declaring himself "a Democrat by association, principle, and education and a member of the party's free-soil wing." He expressed belief in the feasibility of a national railroad to the Pacific and averred that if elected, he would work for its immediate construction, his judgment being backed by his years of exploration along a great part of the way such a road would pass. He gave full history of his title to the Mariposa. He was willing to await decision of the courts as to the validity of his claims to sole mineral rights, meanwhile leaving the gold free to all who had the industry to collect it. He reviewed his acts as Governor in brief and trenchant terms. This frank letter turned the dogs toward some other candidates' worried heels and promptly made Colonel Frémont the most popular Senatorial candidate of the seven.

While Frémont traveled between the mines and San Francisco, Jessie sat in her lonely two rooms, shut in by the violent rains which were to make the winter of '49 memorable for the hardships they created throughout Alta California. Already the storms had worked havoc at the placers, leaving them without food supplies by making the trails impassable to man and beast and driving the miners to seek the scarcely less uncomfortable quarters available in the mud-bogged streets of the towns.

The windows of Jessie's living room looked out on the bay with its crescent-shaped sweep toward Santa Cruz. As she went about her household tasks, the boom of the breakers was with her day and night. Like the long roll of drums, it called her to action, but its call was to the spirit alone, to the courage that companioned lonely hours, to the valor that faced daily battle against homesickness and fear for her husband's safety on treacherous mountain trails and gully-scarred plains.

At the end of a dark December day when the rain dashed ceaselessly against the windows and the pounding surf was like the roar of many guns, Jessie lighted the row of candles in their flat tin holders and then sat before the fire, showing Lily the pictures from an old copy of the *Illustrated London Times*. Suddenly the door opened, letting in a shower of icy raindrops borne on the gusty wind. Startled, she turned to see her husband standing against the now closed door, too drenched and dripping to move forward into the room. Laughing, he called out: "I couldn't wait. I've ridden from San José to be first to greet Jessie Frémont, Senator's lady from the state of California."

He had ridden the seventy miles over steep hills and across gloomy valleys to tell his wife of their good fortune. Gregorio brought dry clothing, and later over a supper of cold beef, biscuits, and coffee, the Frémonts sat far into the night discussing this yet another incredible event in their careers.

To Jessie's "It will be a happy day for me when I see you in Washington,"

John Charles Frémont. First United States Senator from California, 1850.

he countered: "I am unalterably opposed to slavery, but it will be a happy day for me when I see old black Nancy serving you your morning tea in bed." At daybreak under clearing skies, Jessie saw him off again for the seventy-mile ride back to San José. A few days later she read from the *San Francisco Alta:* "Senators Gwin and Frémont will be setting out on the steamer, New Year's day."

As Christmas approached, Jessie planned a special feast and a Christmas tree for Lily. The tree itself was easy to achieve, a shapely little evergreen cut on the hill by Gregorio, but the trimming was a problem until Jessie hit upon the plan of rolling tinfoil into balls soft enough to be stuck on the ends of the tree spines. When Gregorio opened cans of sardines, she had him cut the shining tin into disks and pierce each near the top. When she recalled having seen shavings of scrap tin left from roofing the new hotel, Gregorio salvaged this treasure from the corners of the carpenter shop. Touching up a few of these with red paint, she completed her Christmas color scheme. The little tree now stood glistening in the firelight, awaiting Santa Claus.

Colonel Frémont returned from San Francisco with an assortment of gifts: a red cashmere shawl for Jessie, a china doll for Lily, and a great package of excellent candy he had bought on the Plaza from a man named Winn, who peddled his wares from the lid of a trunk suspended from his neck. Frémont regaled Lily with an imitation of Winn's musical voice, calling: "Here is your California candy. It neither came round the Horn nor across the Isthmus. None but Winn can make it. Buy it, taste it, try it."

Christmas week was spent by Jessie in packing their few belongings, while Frémont arranged to leave affairs at the mine in the hands of agents. The excitement of departure was increased one day when Captain Sherman came running all the way from headquarters to report that he too was sailing with them. While Jessie was expressing her joy over this news, Doña Angustias also came in to tell her that "Don Sherman, *un gran joven gallardo,*" was taking her sons Antonio and Porfirio East to place them in Georgetown College. She was eager to know whether two bags of gold dust would be sufficient for their passage.

Jessie did her last packing while in the clutches of a cold, but when Frémont became alarmed, she said: "Never fear. It changes the climate and checks a cold to have the ship's prow turned the way you want it to go."

When the ship's gun went off on New Year's night, the rain was falling in torrents and the streets were running brooks. While Gregorio carried Lily to the wharf, Frémont carried Jessie. Then they all climbed into a large rowboat, Frémont holding Jessie in his arms and Gregorio holding Lily, while another Indian rowed the boat. Jessie declared later that Gregorio's weeping at parting with the family fairly waterlogged the boat by the time the steamer was reached and that only their promise to send for him later finally quieted his sobbing.

Once aboard ship, they settled to enjoy the voyage. At the first stop, Mazatlán, Jessie found to her delight a solid stone pier with steps. An English man-of-war stood at anchor, and suddenly she heard its guns boom forth in salute. The officers had learned that the newly elected Senators were aboard. She was lowered into the Captain's gig to be taken ashore, but the tide being out, the boat couldn't quite reach the steps, and the sailors jumped into the water and laid oars into a compact bridge from the bow of the boat to the steps. On shore the officers from the barracks stood with the English Consul-General to greet them.

At the barracks dinner that night Jessie began for the first time to distrust her Monterey clothes. The night was hot, and the only cool garment she could unearth was a white ruffled morning sack to wear atop her rough merino skirt. "Is it too dreadful?" she asked Frémont. He solaced her as always with promptness and tact. "It looks cool and you look happy. What more can the Consul ask?"

As the boat neared Panama, Jessie noticed that her husband limped badly. He confessed that the leg injured from frostbite had been troubling him for many weeks and that the tropic weather aggravated the condition. A few days later Jessie's cold, which had refused to yield, sent her to bed. At Panama, too weak to walk, they were both taken ashore on stretchers, bidding reluctant goodbye to their fellow passengers.

Again did the generous Madame Arcé place her house at Jessie's disposal. She put the patients to bed in adjoining rooms and bade Lily "be one of ours." John L. Stevens, now vice president of the Panama Railroad Company, hurried to their rescue with a doctor, and Sisters sent volunteer nurses. Frémont's recovery was rapid, but Jessie lingered in the grip of an intermittent fever which reduced her to a shadow. Greatly perturbed, Stevens exclaimed to Frémont: "Pioneering is hell on women. That child is all eyes and grit. Nothing else left."

Jessie's reaction to Stevens was: "He who had been called a beneficent gargoyle, with his short squat body, unshapely head, long arms, and beardless wrinkled face looked to me like a god of the celestial regions from which I had been banished." Stevens, himself ill and soon to die, came each day to sit beside her, saying: "I've come over to have my chill with you."

Jessie later declared that the most vivid memory of these wretched, clouded weeks was that of an opiate-conjured white horse with a vampire bat on his back fanning the horse with its wide wings as it sucked his blood.

The problem of getting Jessie across the Isthmus was solved by Frémont: a palanquin made of a ship's cot swung on two poles carried by four men. A top and awning curtains which rolled up provided a measure of privacy. The four trusty bearers were of the Arcé household.

Leavetaking from her compassionate hostess and the nuns who had nursed her left Jessie much shaken, and to make matters worse, she overheard a villager say in Spanish: "Colonel Frémont will live, but this poor young thing! To die so far from home and country!" But stimulated by quinine and coffee, Jessie survived, and when she found the steamer north to be in command of the son of Admiral Porter, an old family friend, her spirits rose to the point that sustained her more slowly rising health.

Upon their arrival in New York, they dispatched a wire to Benton and then drove to the Irving House. The proprietor, quite flustered over his distinguished visitors, told Jessie he had reserved the suite just vacated by Jennie Lind, now on tour. When the door closed behind him, she turned about to find herself in a room fragrant with great bowls of roses and violets sent by friends who knew her taste in flowers.

She bent to catch more of the old friendly fragrance, and as she raised her head, her eyes met an apparition in the long French mirror. There stood the Senator's lady from the Golden West, a sunken-eyed emaciated young woman whose pale skin was made a jaundiced yellow by the brown-satin basque below which a dark-blue skirt hung straight and shapeless to her ankles. Her feet were encased in rusty black-satin slippers, and on her head was a leghorn hat held down by a china-crêpe scarf.

Beside her stood a fat red-cheeked child fairly bursting from a dress of brown merino whose too-short skirt revealed ruffled panties of unbleached muslin. Her shoes were buckskin, a gift from Gregorio. This emigrant-child picture was completed by a head wrapped in a black-silk handkerchief, her hat having blown overboard. Two days of rest and replenishment of wardrobe, however, fitted the Frémonts for Benton's greeting. Of her homecoming Jessie said:

No person living understands better than I the term "speechless with joy." Father, mother, all the others in the old home greeting us, our old rooms with their heavenly smells of rose geraniums, old friends greeting us, the whole city greeting us! I took sedate little walks down Pennsylvania Avenue and across the Common in the spring twilight, but I wanted to run and shout, to hug the tree trunks, to drop down on the ground and lay my cheek against the new grass, to kiss the crocuses and wild violets, and to float away upon that misty gray-green cloud of young leaves above me.

Renewed health came fast in the wake of such ecstasy. Before many days Jessie was having tea with Madame Bodisco, returning formal visits, and going the round of dinner parties arranged in honor of Senators Frémont and Gwin. Old black Nancy coddled her charge and fussed endlessly over the lace frillings and soft brocades of Jessie's dinner gowns. To Mayor Seaton himself we are indebted for this picture of the Senator and Jessie at a dinner where she sat on Seaton's right:

Colonel Frémont in his correct dinner clothes was of an arresting dignity, but he looked worn and thin. His black hair, heavily streaked with gray, gave distinction to his weather-worn features. His eyes shone youthfully as he answered questions as to the possibilities of the coast under a railroad project. He listened with grave deference to whoever was speaking, but under cover of general conversation he lapsed into frequent silences, his glance resting with scarcely veiled admiration on his wife as she spoke and laughed with all the sparkle of a carefree school girl. When Jessie caught his glance upon her, there was an exchange which I can only describe as a mental wink, a flash of eye, a fleeting smile, discreet flirtation throughout the long dinner.

Shortly after this dinner Jessie had an amusing anecdote to tell of Mayor Seaton. Alexander Bodisco, the Russian Consul at whose wedding Jessie had been bridesmaid, had just died, leaving a will in which he bequeathed his fortune to his wife with the unusual request that she soon marry someone who might make her as happy as she had made him. The funeral was largely attended, but there being no priest of the orthodox Russian church in Washington, those in charge of arrangements had made the blunder of engaging an old-fashioned Baptist minister, a tactless cleric who spoke of the errors of the creed in which the departed had been trained. The preacher admitted, however, that the Count had been a good man of large philanthropies. Glancing over the audience, the minister smiled and said: "If our departed brother's spirit could look down upon this distinguished throng—" Seaton quickly whispered to Jessie: "He would say, 'What a bad manage' ceremony'."

Jessie's days were not all given over to society, for soon after her return the old conferences in the Benton library were resumed, and soon both Frémont and Jessie were filled with concern over the questions now harassing Benton and other old party leaders. With all Benton's foresight in others matters, he had been singularly loath to admit that the South was actually headed for disunion. Now he confessed to being in a state of panic over the outlook. "How long," he asked sadly, "can the gathering forces of sectionalism be held back by compromise?"

For the Frémonts' benefit he graphically pictured that first meeting of the Thirty-first Congress on December 3, 1849, with those members talking seriously of the dissolution of the Union who a year before would have considered the thought treason. Henry Clay, old and infirm, had come out once more after eight years of retirement. Webster too was there, on the decline. Calhoun was nearing death. Everybody was deeply moved seeing him sitting there too weak to speak while his speech was read by Mason of Virginia. Calhoun and Clay had settled their differences, and Benton joined them in their concern over the culmination of the disintegrating work of the past decade, every step of which they could now see clearly in retrospect.

There had been a long and disappointing session with California entitled to come in but committed to anti-slavery. Clay had reported a bill to which so much had been tacked besides admission that President Taylor had dubbed it the Omnibus bill. Benton had fought this bitterly, declaring California should come in on her merits alone. His labors had finally got the bill trimmed, and he had predicted that California would soon be in. His prediction proved right. On August 13, 1850, the bill was presented; it passed the House on September 7 and received the President's approval on September 9. The waiting Senators and House members from the new state of California were admitted to their seats as representatives of the thirty-first state.

Jessie sat proudly in the gallery on September 10 when the California Senators presented themselves. Senator Barnwell of South Carolina, a family friend of long standing, declared it well known that he entertained the strongest constitutional objection to the admission of California to the Union, but Congress having passed the act, Mr. Frémont's admission could not be other than acceptable. Immediately afterward, the Senators ascertained by lot the length of term of the respective Congressmen. The short term expiring in March, '51, was drawn by Frémont. This gave him little time to accomplish all he hoped to do for California, but with his usual promptness he very soon asked leave to present certain bills he had already prepared.

Later Jessie attended a dinner at which Senator Barnwell said: "I must admit that the Colonel showed statesmanlike qualities in so prompt and clear a presentation of bills covering the immediate needs of his infant charge." Jessie could well agree, for she had done the final copying of these and the thirteen others she knew he would present as soon as allowed.

At this time there came an especially sweet morsel for Jessie's wifely pride. She had often worried secretly over the haste with which the last maps and memoirs had been prepared, but there came from friends in Europe press clippings and marked periodicals which indicated that Frémont was receiving recognition from scientific societies in England, France, and Germany. The botanical memoir, edited by Dr. Torrey and published by the Smithsonian Institution, had further added to Frémont's fame abroad.

One morning as they sat over their mail, Frémont opened a letter from Abbott Lawrence, now Minister to England, announcing that Frémont had been awarded the Founder's Medal of the Royal Geographical Society. Scarcely were they through congratulating each other when a messenger brought a letter from John Clayton, Secretary of State, inclosing the medal itself. Soon thereafter came a letter from Baron von Humboldt written at Sans Souci, saying:

You are a worthy holder of this honor. You have displayed noble courage in distant expeditions, braved all the dangers of cold and famine, enriched all branches of the natural sciences and illustrated a vast country which was unknown to us.

In telling of this incident Jessie said:

Mr. Frémont wore his laurels with becoming dignity, but I allowed myself several mental skips and jumps as I laid away the beautiful medal with the head of Frederick William on the one side and Apollo traversing the zodiac on the other.

At the close of the session she and the Colonel were receiving grateful letters from the California constituents for his success in having passed laws which covered matters of land titles, customs duties, provision for a university and an insane asylum, the relinquishment of certain lands in San Francisco no longer needed for public purposes, an Indian agent bill, and one for the opening of a road across the continent.

Jessie and Frémont now went into close conference over immediate future plans. Living in Washington with all its heartening sense of security and peace was happiness, but letters from California showed that the Mariposa was suffering from Frémont's absence. Squatter troubles were increasing to the point of menace. Also friends had written disquieting news of the political prospects in California. The pro-slavery wing of the Democratic party was waxing stronger. If Frémont expected to succeed himself for the new term, he had better look to his California fences.

The sensible and obvious course was for Frémont to return at once to California. Jessie was expecting a child the coming April, and she declared she was happy to return since she wanted her next child born in California. When Frémont protested the trip as too dangerous, she said: "No! I've thought it all out: reliable stretcher bearers with a chair instead of a cot for the land trip, proper foods which we take along, tea equipment, and plenty of quinine. And awaiting us there will be the faithful Gregorio."

Family protests were weaker than the conditions seemed to warrant, but the family had learned by now when not to interfere. They trusted to improved conditions of travel for the safe journey of the member they called "the Colonel's chief-of-staff."

The journey, by now a routine matter to the Frémonts, was made with less than the usual discomfort. Upon arrival they found a new San Francisco: countless indications of orderly growth, a thriving newspaper, improved business organization, better shops, but still an alarming dearth of houses, though there was the never-ceasing sound of hammers at work upon shelter for the families arriving from every country on the globe. They agreed to the pleas of Dr. Turner and other Eastern friends who urged them to remain in the city from which Frémont could commute to the mines.

In search of comparative quiet, the Frémonts found a two-room house in Happy Valley, the site of the present Palace Hotel. The structure had been brought from China and had been put together with pegs. It insured privacy with the customary thick cotton-cloth partitions. After a few weeks of this half-camp life with Gregorio again established as major domo, they bought an ugly but comfortable furnished house on Stockton Street high on a hill side overlooking the Plaza. Jessie set about with characteristic energy and taste to make the place homelike. Gregorio, however, objected to cooking his mistress' meats in a black iron box and expressed his contempt of the cook-stove by banging its doors and muttering *carambas*.

Word now came from Washington that the efforts of the pro-slavery faction headed by Senator Gwin had been successful and that in the legislative ballots Frémont had been defeated of reelection. No choice had been made of his successor. The Frémonts were not surprised nor greatly disappointed, for the tangled Mariposa affairs were demanding all the owner's time and energy.

On April 19, attended by Dr. Turner, Jessie gave birth to a son who was named John Charles. When the doctor called their attention to the child's remarkably sturdy build, Jessie said: "He is strong as a native son should be, and as a son of Colonel Frémont he is already well traveled." Lily stood studying her young brother, then looked gravely up and asked: "Can you promise he won't leave me?" They promised, hopefully. The nurse being available for a week only, Gregorio announced: "When she goes, I will take care of Doña Flémon' and the baby. My mother had ten. I know everything to do."

When the baby was fifteen days old, Jessie was startled by shouts in the street and the acrid smell of smoke. Gregorio reported a paint shop afire on the south side of the Plaza. In a few moments Frémont rushed in with a grass hammock and blankets. He told her to lie quiet and ordered Gregorio to stand guard for further orders. As the houses lower down the hill caught fire, the neighbors helped Frémont hang water-soaked carpets, blankets, and canvas over the sides of the house. This procedure and a shift of wind saved their house and the one above it, and Jessie avowed herself no worse for the excitement. The toll of this fire was estimated at ten million dollars, but such was the unconquerable spirit of the townspeople that new buildings were begun upon the smouldering ruins of the old, and homeless families cheerfully took to tent life, pending rebuilding of their houses.

The Frémonts' homely but comfortable shelter now settled to routine with a girl cousin of Gregorio's established as nursemaid. Frémont, relieved of anxiety over Jessie, returned to the Mariposa after exacting a promise from Gregorio that Jessie should never be left alone in the house.

On a bright Sunday morning (June 22) again the firebell clanged danger, and the frantic people came rushing across the Plaza. Jessie and Lily stood in the window watching the firemen work as only San Francisco firemen could work, helping the citizens blow up buildings in the path of the flames and tearing down flimsy shacks. Suddenly a veering wind sent showers of sparks toward Stockton Street. Jessie turned to see the nurse Anita hurrying downstairs carrying the baby and calling to Lily to follow. Jessie felt herself lifted bodily in Gregorio's arms. At the door stood a neighbor to help them up the hill to his house. Here seated with the baby in her arms, she watched her house burn to the ground. In a daze she allowed herself to be cared for through the night.

The next morning Gregorio announced that he had found a good house a short distance away among the sand dunes, and thither he carried her bodily while Anita followed with the children, and the neighbor himself came bringing extra cots and bedding. Here a few days later Frémont, frantic with anxiety, found the family unharmed, and Gregorio proudly cooking his soup in a kettle over a tripod.

A few days passed and Jessie looked out of the window to see half a dozen brawny young men and women coming over the dunes carrying a variety of boxes and bundles in pushcarts. Their spokesman, doffing his cap, explained that when they saw the Frémont house doomed, they had run to offer their services, and finding the family flown, had rescued much of the household goods. Jessie's astonished eyes beheld certain treasured books, china, furniture, and linen restored to her. Before she could find words of thanks, another spokesman untied a red-silk handkerchief, displaying a heap of gold and silver and saying: "We know the master is from home and a young babby in the house. So we brought a quarter's rent in advance." He then explained that he and the others were from a little English colony to whom the Colonel had leased a tract of city land where they now had a brewery and workmen's cottages.

Such acts of neighborliness were everyday matters in this fabulous community of practical heroes, and they were rewarded in this case by a sturdy practical gratitude. Frémont heretofore had been unwilling to sell the property on lease to the colony, but the good-hearted lessees were told they might buy for a very small sum and on their own terms as to payment.

The Frémonts were now faced with the question whether to continue camping in those primitive but comfortable quarters or rebuild on the old site. During these discussions Frémont confided that unforeseen conditions had developed at the mines and carried ever-increasing worry and care. He and all other owners of land on which gold had been found were put to the humiliation of fighting for their titles, since Congress had passed an act refusing confirmation of titles without written proofs of ownership. In many cases these proofs had gone up in fire; other titles were nailed up in various repositories and could not be produced to wave in the faces of an ever-advancing line of squatters and claim jumpers. Owners could only file a statement of their claims, and if necessary, appeal to a higher court.

Between Frémont's own Mexican labor and these squatters, the placers at the Mariposa were being rapidly worked out. To mine the gold-bearing quartz veins would require large capital. Since differences had arisen between his agents, David Hoffman and Thomas Sargent, over the organization of mining companies on a basis of leases, Frémont had decided to suspend further transactions in the Mariposa pending settlement of his claim, which would reach the Supreme Court in the spring of the new year (1852).

One evening in December as he watched Jessie preparing for another makeshift Christmas, he asked suddenly: "How would you like a trip to Paris as a New Year's gift?"

"Splendid," she replied, looking up from her sewing. "Let's also give Charley a closer peep at the man in the moon."

Whereupon her husband took from his wallet and handed to her a brightly colored packet: steamer tickets reading from "San Francisco to Chagres, thence direct to France." To her excited response, "It will be your first vacation and rest," he replied, "And yours—well earned. The first rest since you spoke those fateful words, 'Whither thou goest, I will go'."

CHAPTER XII

A Guest at the Courts of England and France

OR Jessie Frémont, the planning of a trip to Europe this year of 1852 was but the planning of a visit to another official family. She would renew acquaintances with Sir Henry and Lady Bulwer, who had been of the Embassy at Washington in 1849. Mary Caton of Baltimore, now the Marchioness of Wellesley, was an old friend, and Kitty Lawrence, daughter of Abbott Lawrence, United States Minister to Great Britain, would be waiting to welcome her. She felt secure in the thought that these friends would be her sponsors in any unfamiliar situation growing out of those ceremonials she knew to be awaiting her husband.

The prospect was wholly enchanting. The problems involved in steamer and train travel with two children could not daunt one whose family tradition extended to prairie caravans and who as a child had been one of a brood of six on those annual journeys by stage coach, river steamer, and saddle horse. In reply to the solicitude of the chivalrous Lieutenant Beale, she said: "I already lean on Lily. She isn't a child; she's a protectorate."

Late February, 1852, saw the Frémonts aboard the boat for Chagres, thence to France. Upon discovery that Jessie was the only woman aboard, the Captain offered her the use of the ladies' cabin for herself and the baby, since the staterooms were small and the bunks narrow. Two sofas were lashed together, making a wide bed. Here she rested with Charley for two nights.

On the third night she was awakened by a tugging at the covering about her feet. Sitting up, she saw a dark object scurrying away in the dim candle light. Next morning she reported having been disturbed by a playful kitten.

Frémont and the steward exchanged glances, and the steward said: "We'll give you a watchman tonight. I guess those rats expected the ladies' cabin to be empty."

To Jessie's horror he explained that even the newest steamers had to wage continual fight against the Norwegian rats, large as kittens, which came aboard ship at the wharves, as did cockroaches which despite all efforts infested the boat. He promised she should be duly protected from both.

That night there appeared an old seaman whom she had noticed about the deck. He announced that he had been detailed as a special watchman to "flap 'em off." He referred to the cockroaches, which she later declared resembled fat dates with legs on them. The last sound she heard at night was the rhythmic swish of a palmleaf fan wielded by her cavalier. Thus protected, she and the baby traveled in comfort throughout the easy voyage to Panama.

During this voyage Jessie observed her "protectorate" with tenderness touched at times with perplexity, for that tactless relative of long ago had been right. Lily was *not* Jessie's child. Physically the girl had gained neither beauty nor grace with her growth. As accompaniment to her plain features and practical intelligence was a stolid literalness, no flights of fancy, no discursive speech; only uninspired repetition of the factual in her experience. Her sturdy health and her air of insouciance gave her a certain attractiveness, and the occasional terrifyingly truthful observations issuing from her lips caused her elders to regard her with due respect. She had the easy obedience of the unoriginal and unresourceful child.

Ironically enough, it was Lily's worshipful deference to her mother that most often attracted favorable comment to herself. From infancy she had come close beneath the spell of her mother's special charms: a low softly modulated voice, a captivating smile, a demonstrative warmth. The child noticed that visitors, men and women alike, were attracted by her mother's beauty and instinctive grace.

Undemonstrative and unimaginative herself, Lily could yet sense her father's love which enfolded her mother as with a bright garment. She had observed her father's characteristic gestures of tenderness. Inarticulate herself as comforter, when she noted her mother's sadness over even their brief separations, she imitated and then adopted as her own those gestures, calling Jessie "darling," kissing her hand, brushing her forehead lightly with her lips, or smoothing her hair as they sat together before the fire. Deeply touched, Jessie lived gratefully under this "protectorate."

On the morning the Frémonts went ashore in Panama expecting to board the *Amazon* of the West India Mail Line, the message came that the *Amazon* had burned at sea but that if they hurried, they could catch the American steamer soon to leave for New York from Chagres.

An Indian runner who had been one of Jessie's bearers now offered safe convoy for the year-old Charley, declaring that he often took babies across the Isthmus and that his mother would care for Charley at Gorgona pending the arrival of the rest of the party. A hammock made from a tablecloth was slung about the Indian's neck. A bottle of boiled water and a packet of dried figs were provided for food. A cotton blanket and a length of mosquito netting completed the equipment. Just before setting off, the runner insisted that Charley be given a chicken bone to suck. This was provided, and the runner started ahead of the muleback cavalcade.

When Jessie next saw her sturdy little son, he was sitting naked in an earthen bowl, squealing with delight as an old woman poured water over him from a tin cup. His clothes, laundered Indian fashion, were drying on a near-by bush.

The river trip was safely made, and the party were soon aboard a steamer from which they transshipped at Havana, arriving in New York on March 6. There they secured passage on the Cunard sidewheeler *Africa*. With four days remaining before sailing, Jessie at once wired Washington only to find that the Bentons were all in St. Louis. Chilled and disappointed, she wrote her father at length before setting out to shop for proper traveling clothes and to engage a nurse for the children.

On the rolling old *Africa* Jessie again found herself the only woman passenger. The Captain promptly offered her the ladies' cabin as a family sitting room. Later in speaking of this voyage she said:

This was to be our first vacation trip, and when I looked at that clean and cosy room with an open fire burning brightly behind its brass netting, walls lined with books, plenty of good light for reading, and a table piled with English periodicals and New York papers, and when I realized we were safe at last from rats, roaches, and fear of Chagres fever, I thanked the Captain with

what dignity I could muster, but when he was gone, I sank into Colonel Fré-
mont's arms in a burst of foolish happy tears.

So calm was the weather, so right the wind during the entire voyage that
the fire behind its brass screen was never put out. Every comfort available on
a British steamer of that day was Jessie's to enjoy: tea, long hours of quiet on
deck, long evenings for reading, and nights of unbroken rest. She saw the
marks of weariness smoothed from her husband's face, the anxious look in
his eyes changed to one of contentment. This fact alone enabled every ebul-
lient quality of her volatile nature to reassert itself. The past became for the
time but a shadowy background for the land of enchantment she was about
to enter.

At Southampton they were met by a messenger sent to escort them to the
Hotel Clarendon in London where the Marchioness of Wellesley had engaged a suite for them. Before they were unpacked, Abbott Lawrence and
his daughter Kitty arrived. Jessie confided her sartorial problems, and Kitty
offered to superintend all costume requirements for what Jessie termed "a
terrifying program," since they were to meet London society at the height of
the season. Under the kindly aid of the Lawrences, correct wardrobes were
soon acquired for all the functions scheduled.

The first of these was their Court presentation at St. James' Palace. Kitty
Lawrence, Jessie's mentor and inseparable companion, arranged for her to
join a group being trained in presentation etiquette by a former member of
the Queen's household. Next in importance to the curtsy was the costume.

Since white was the exclusive right of débutantes and brides, Kitty suggested for Jessie a gown of pale-pink moiré over a petticoat of deeper-pink
satin with the traditional length of train and a corsage of French roses. When
the costume arrived at the Frémont suite, Jessie allowed Lily to remove the
boxlid and lift the gown from its tissue wrappings. As the shimmering folds
of satin came to view, Lily sighed and said: "We'll have to send it back. We've
got the Queen's dress by mistake." Her father patted her shoulder. "We have
the Queen's dress, my dear, but there's been no mistake."

On the Court morning Jessie resembled a figure in a French print, as in
full costume she sat before the mirror. Behind her a thin little French hair-
dresser exclaimed, "*Quelle belle chevelure!*" as he arranged her wealth of red-

brown hair in the accepted puffs and curls. Later, her dark eyes shining, her cheeks aglow, she paraded slowly before Mrs. Lawrence and Kitty, come for a last critical survey of their charge. As she made the final curtsy and stood awaiting their verdict, Mrs. Lawrence turned to Frémont, who was also looking distinguished in his new and proper habiliments, and asked:

"Colonel Frémont, did you ever see your wife as beautiful as now?"

With a low bow he replied: "Yes, madame, the first time I ever saw her."

"But you can't possibly recall what she wore then!"

"Yes, quite possibly! She called it a pink candy-stripe. In this gown she reminds me very much of herself at that time."

Whereupon Jessie extended her gloved fingers and said: "For that, monsieur, you may kiss your lady's hand and pray she doesn't fall fainting among the folds of her train when she curtsies to the Queen."

On the day of the presentation the Frémonts, accompanied by Ambassador and Mrs. Lawrence, made their way out a side entrance of the hotel to their carriages and joined the procession moving along the crowded streets. The foot passengers along the curb peered into the windows of each carriage as it passed, making frank comments upon the candidates.

In the waiting room of St. James' Palace, Jessie met Lady Clarendon, who led her to a window overlooking the entrance and pointed out the notables as they arrived. As Jessie watched the Queen alight, she felt a touch on her shoulder, the signal to take her place in line. Then the doors of the throne room opened. In describing the scene later she said:

When I beheld the Queen and the Prince Consort, Albert Edward, at her side the picture of devotion, I lost all nervousness. I felt myself not a Democrat bowing the knee to royalty but an American paying homage to a figure of womanly goodness and power.

First passed the Ambassadress of France, and after her Russia and Germany; America came fourth. Mrs. Lawrence made her curtsy, then presented Mrs. Frémont. She was not to look openly at the Queen save to notice the bend of the head in return of her own low curtsy; another curtsy less low as she passed before Prince Albert, and another to the Queen's mother and to her cousin, the Princess May, completed the formalities of presentation. These curtsies performed, Jessie took her place beside her sponsor in the line of Diplomatic ladies. Here she stood watching the dreamlike procession of women gliding, advancing, curtsying, and backing in unbroken silence. Of this scene Jessie said:

The Queen made a beautiful picture standing above the level against the red-velvet and gold hangings of the throne. Her gown of white satin and lace made her appear taller, while the very long red-velvet train, disposed in folds to the step below, added to her air of majesty. The broad blue ribbon of the Garter crossed her breast. Diamonds flashed from neck and arms, and gave out their light from the crown upon her small and graceful head. Prince Albert in a white and gold uniform completed this truly royal picture.

Among the guests on this day was the Duke of Wellington. The stooped old man walked slowly back and forth across the room, a privilege indeed, since no one was supposed to move about in the presence of the Queen.

This fleeting panorama over, Mrs. Lawrence expressed her approval of Jessie's performance and heartened her for future ordeals by telling her that Lady Clarendon had called her "a young woman of beauty, natural charm, and grace." From the drawing room the Frémonts went to have tea with the Duchess of Bedford, and that night, though weak from excitement and fatigue, Jessie refused to retire until she had written to her father. Frémont added an enthusiastic postscript to her letter. His too had been an exciting day, for he had early found himself the center of a group of Englishmen who expressed their pleasure in having read his reports and who were eager to hear further of America.

A dinner at the Embassy as guests of the Lawrences soon followed, and here Jessie's memory and her sense of humor served her well. A belligerent gentleman, having had several verbal encounters with guests, now turned upon Jessie. Referring to Harriet Martineau's caustic comments in her *Society in America,* he asked Jessie whether she considered those comments to be just. "But perhaps," he added, "as an American you wouldn't admit the truth of adverse criticism."

"Yes, I would admit it if the criticism were made by way of a disinterested characterization and not as a vent for ill humor due to the discomforts of travel in a strange new country."

"Very good!" he exclaimed. "If I could remember well enough to quote what she said about the Yankees, I'd put you to the test."

Glancing up demurely, Jessie said: "It's rather long, but I recall it. You shall be punished by having to listen:

It is by no means rare to meet elsewhere in this workaday world of ours people who push acuteness to the verge of honesty or a bit beyond, but I believe the Yankee is the only one who will be found to boast of doing so. It is by no means easy to give a clear and just idea of a Yankee. If you hear his character from a Virginian, you will believe him a devil; if you listen to it from himself, you might call him a good though a tricky one—Mercury turned righteous and notable.

I expect, calculate, guess is only the shell; there is an immense deal within both bitter and sweet. In acuteness, caution, industry, and perseverance he resembles the Scotch; in habits of frugal neatness he resembles the Dutch; in love of lucre he doth greatly resemble the sons of Abraham; but in frank admission and super-admiration of his own peculiarities, he is like nothing on earth but himself.

The laugh went against the baiter, and Jessie finished her dessert in peace.

During their stay in London the Frémonts were the guests of many distinguished men and women, but Jessie's most thrilling experience was her meeting with the Duke of Wellington. Of this she wrote her father:

You have often smiled over my "What more can I ask of life." But you will not smile when I say it now! I have told you how we dine and breakfast and drive in the park with personages it is a delight as well as an honor to know. I have told you how Colonel Frémont's reputation makes all our introductions personal and kindly; how Kitty has got me all into gay-colored gowns, saying I must keep away from my favorite violet and gray, for I am too fragile. (You know I am not.) But I have not told you that your little daughter's eager but undistinguished hand has lain in that of the Duke of Wellington. What more can I ask of life?

We were dining at Sion House, seat of the Dukes of Northumberland. The Duchess looked tall and stately and impersonal. It was good to see Lady Bulwer's kind face there beside her! Mrs. Lawrence introduced me, and as always, her tact turned each meeting into a friendly one. Lady Bulwer then took me on a tour of the rooms while other guests were assembling. Moving about by himself, silent and abstracted, was the Duke of Wellington. Lady Bulwer whispered:"There is my uncle. He is eighty-four and very feeble. Come, I'll present you." Going to him and taking his hand, she spoke my name distinctly. He peered at me, bowed, then said slowly:"I know that name, a distinguished name." Taking my hand, he pressed it and smiled. It is well that only a smile was demanded of me!

To Frémont a deeply appreciated honor was the dinner given him by Sir Roderick Murchison, president of the Royal Geographical Society. At this dinner were men from the uttermost corners of the earth, to whom danger in the service of science was familiar. They talked with unreserve and were frank in their expressions of admiration of Frémont.

Jessie's happiest memory of this dinner was her meeting with Landseer. She wrote her father:"I had a good dog-and-deer talk with him." The only embarrassing moment for Jessie was sight of the expression on the face of the Duchess of Sutherland when Lady Bulwer called out:"Oh, Susan, come and meet Mrs. Frémont from North America." Jessie explained later:"From her startled look I knew the Duchess expected to see the red skin, straight black hair, and multicolored garments of a squaw."

At the end of the London season the Frémonts made joyous preparation for going to Paris. But the fateful weaver of Jessie Frémont's life pattern was ready with another dark strand of grief. Word came of the sudden death of her brother Randolph. The shock of this news was the greater because that very day she had received a letter from Benton expressing his pride that Ran at twenty-one had been chosen to deliver the address of welcome to the exile Kossuth in St. Louis. Young Benton had delivered that speech in German with such eloquence as to call forth general press comment. Shortly thereafter he had been seized with a malarial infection which proved fatal within a few days. After the first helpless grief had subsided, Jessie wrote comforting letters to her father, and with characteristic consideration for her family, complied with Frémont's request"not to wear that grief-reminder, black."

She entered into the plans her husband now made to divert her. She soon found herself the owner of a brougham and a pair of beautiful chestnut carriage horses driven by an Irish coachman. She also became mistress of a romantic house on the Champs Élysées, owned by Lady Dundonald, who had allowed the "exquisite" Count d'Orsay to furnish it. Here crowned heads and the darlings of French society had dined, but perhaps not one of them had appreciated the beauty of the fabrics, the paintings, and the tapestries as did its American mistress, Jessie Frémont.

This twenty-eight-year-old girl who three years earlier had bathed from a barber's basin in a blanket dressing tent now saw her bath water flow from the beaks of gilded swans into a marble tub. She dried her skin with satin-damask towels and made her leisurely toilet in a mirror-lined dressing room. She who had transformed adobe quarters into a salon now received her callers in a tapestry-hung drawing room. But it was of other things than these that she wrote her father from Paris:

In London my spirit felt at home with the spirits of my English ancestry. Here, my heart feels even more warmly at home with the spirits of the Frémont ancestors. French history, literature, and language seem somehow my own. At dinners, the playful teasing banter, the epigrammatic wit are a happy challenge, while the Englishman's pronouncements are more often a thrust.

Yet she had the English to thank for the following press notice sent her by Mrs. Lawrence:

Mrs. Frémont is a graceful, distinguished woman sharing the renown of her husband, the American explorer and recent medalist of the Royal Geographical Society. In the faultless taste of Court dress, she was a gratification to the most critical eye.

Jessie Frémont's capacity for making enduring friendships had carried her safely through a London season. This capacity now made a loyal friend and sponsor of that grand seigneur, the Comte de la Garde, a member of the Bonaparte family, cousin of Eugène and Hortense Beauharnais, and leader of the French inner circle. After meeting the Frémonts at a British Embassy ball, the Comte declared that while he admired and respected the explorer, only his rheumatic knees prevented his kneeling in passionate adoration to the explorer's wife. Jessie became *ma petite* to him, and the Frémonts were placed by him on the *liste intime* for the French fêtes and balls of the season.

Jessie had to submit to Frémont's teasing over the devotion of her seventy-year-old admirer when almost daily the Comte appeared for a visit of an hour on his way to his airing in the Bois. Delighted with her knowledge of French literature and art as well as her ease with the French idiom, he declared Jessie a perfect companion, and for her he relived his part in the drama of France as the son of a minister in the last cabinet of Louis XVI. In recounting the cruel scenes of the French Revolution he said: "My mother and all the women I knew remain with me as visions of tears and prayers, of tender consolation to each other."

One morning the Comte announced: "You must see my silent sulky Louis Napoleon. Tomorrow there is a *thé dansant* at St. Cloud in honor of the Prince President. You shall go, *ma petite*, and I invite the friends to go with you." In referring to this occasion Jessie said:

Once arrived, the Comte's sad comments on the absence of noble names among that brilliant throng failed to spoil the picture for me. The mirrored room repeated the beauty of the women in their pinks and blues and buffs, drifting like butterflies toward the tea tables inlaid with Sèvres plaques and set with Sèvres tea service.

As Louis Napoleon entered alone, the guests arranged themselves in two lines, but there were no formal presentations as he walked between them down the long salon, followed by his suite, the gentlemen brilliant in dress uniform, the women in brocades. The tea and dancing then proceeded to its stately conclusion, but before we left, the Comte took us to a corner of the terrace to enjoy the moonlight view, the Seine flowing far below the steep hill, the shadowy haze above the Bois lying between the river and Paris. The drive homeward was pure enchantment.

In the early autumn of '52 the Frémont drawing room became a salon. Friends returned with them for supper after evenings at the opera, and those who came to dinner came again informally to luncheon or tea, delighted with the quiet dignity of the host and the personal charm of the hostess.

From her own balcony Jessie and her friends witnessed the official entrance of Napoleon III, as the procession coming into Paris from St. Cloud passed down the Champs Élysées to the Tuileries. As a counterdemonstration was feared, the sheer courage of the Prince riding alone, not a single officer within forty feet of him, won the shouts of approval from the crowds which packed the streets. Jessie declared this picture to be etched in memory, not to be blurred by criticisms of the Emperor.

The Christmas season and the month of January were spent quietly by the Frémont family, as Jessie was awaiting confinement. On February 1 she gave birth to a daughter whom she promptly named Anne Beverly in honor of Frémont's mother. A dainty and fragile infant, she was called by the Comte *petite Parisienne.* Since Jessie made a rapid recovery, she was soon receiving the gifts and congratulations of her French friends and was writing her father of the marriage of the Emperor and her impressions of the bridal procession which she had watched from her balcony two days before her confinement. In this letter she said:

Nothing in that glittering pageant interested me so much as the bridal coach which had drawn Marie Antoinette and Marie Louise. The coach looked like a great bonbonnière *with its high-swung length, its glass construction, white-satin linings, and the gilded supports topped by a gold crown.*

All eyes were on the Empress, who sat tight lipped beside the Emperor, who with half-closed eyes also sat rigidly upright in his dress uniform profusely decorated with orders. Already gossip was busy with the Empress' deplorable lack of tact in having refused to wear the French satin gown and veil which the lace makers at Alençon had prepared for the bride of the French throne. Instead, she was swathed in a gorgeous dress of white uncut velvet; on her gleaming yellow hair, an English point lace veil. As I noted these things, Comte de la Garde turned to me and remarked: "That fatal want of tact will cost her dear. You, ma petite, would have worn a gown of French manufacture, though it made you look as ugly as your American squaws, for you have the chief requisite for a queen—heart understanding." I told the Comte that his faith in me was beautiful, but I hoped such sartorial loyalty need never be put to test.

Jessie had occasion to recall the Comte's tribute on the day she herself fell into tactical error. On her husband's fortieth birthday she invited guests to dinner and herself decorated dining room and drawing room with his favorite flowers, heliotrope and white roses. In the midst of her preparations she was waited upon by the nurse, who announced that the servants below stairs were packing to leave at once, for "they are legitimists and cannot remain in a house that is celebrating the death of Louis XVI." After Jessie had patiently explained that she was celebrating her husband's birthday and was not to blame because it happened to fall upon the anniversary of the death of Louis XVI, they consented to stay.

The Frémonts' plan to remain longer in Paris was now changed by disquieting news from America. Frémont's claim to the exclusive mineral rights on his estate had not been definitely settled, and the debts incurred while he was Governor of California had not yet been paid by the Government as promised. Another tentative promise that Frémont should lead the first party sent to report upon the best railroad route to the Pacific had been disregarded. A letter from Benton disclosed that Secretary of War Jefferson Davis was planning to name as leaders certain West Pointers with little experience in the West. Benton suggested that Frémont head an independent survey equipped by himself.

As in all crises, Frémont and Jessie went into conference, with the result that they surprised their friends by announcing an immediate return to the United States. The Comte protested, and Jessie's intimates pleaded with her to "remain and let Monsieur come to you here." When the Paris household was broken up, the French maid and the governess refused to be dismissed. "Who will dress Madame?" and "Who will teach the children?" they wailed. Jessie kept them on, and when she arrived in Washington and settled herself in a house near her father, these maids announced to him that they had "adopted Madame Frémon' for her life."

While Frémont outfitted his expedition to which Benton and several Missouri admirers were largely contributing, Jessie set the house in order and took up her usual round of social duties. Until now the baby Anne, though fragile in appearance, had been in good health, but the hot weather affected her and she showed symptoms of the digestive ailment that had already proved fatal to several children in the city. Jessie took her at once to the Francis Blair estate at Silver Springs, Maryland, where she had often visited her relatives.

On July 11, almost at the moment the physician was reassuring Jessie, the child died in her arms. Frémont hurried to her side, and together they brought the baby home for burial. When Benton remarked upon Jessie's calmness through this ordeal, Frémont replied: "It was she who remained dry eyed to comfort me, for I was unmanned over the cruelty of this bereavement. Her calm stoicism, so superior to mere resignation, soon shamed me into control."

As plans for the expedition neared completion, Jessie was happy to learn that the artist and daguerreotypist, S. N. Carvalho, was to accompany the party. He would be the first to bring the use of photography into Western exploration. She little dreamed when expressing her pleasure to Carvalho that from his pen would later come a lasting tribute to the character of Frémont under stress.

The journey was to be a retracing of the route beyond the point where the guide had misled the party in 1848-1849. Frémont was certain that this route when properly covered would prove the most practicable of all for a railroad.

"Yet another hated goodbye," Jessie declared, but with a wealth of happy memories and future hopes to sustain her. In August she saw Frémont depart for St. Louis to meet the others of his party of twenty-two members, ten of whom were to be trusty Delaware Indians. A reassuring letter from him at Westport Landing relieved her mind of anxiety.

This winter of 1853-1854 carried much of responsibility for Jessie Frémont. In addition to active correspondence with friends in London and Paris and discharge of social obligations, she resumed her happy custom of performing secretarial duties for her father. Benton was at work upon his *Thirty Years' View*, a digest of his lengthy career in the Senate, and it became Jessie's duty to transcribe and verify notes by frequent recourse to Congressional files.

The evenings found Jessie and her father entertaining certain younger members of both houses of Congress who came to confer informally with Benton, whom they regarded as a father. These conversations were full of the color of past days. Benton made live again old Rufus King of New York, a model of courtly refinement in his full dress of short small clothes, silk stockings, and low shoes. He portrayed the gentle Nathaniel Macon in his Revolutionary suit with cambric stock and fine fur hat, and John Randolph, booted and spurred, calling for his small beer in the midst of a speech. Benton's little audience caught intimate glimpses of the great triumvirate, Clay, Calhoun, and Webster.

Soon to leave this stage forever, Benton sought to impress his hearers with the characters of Andrew Jackson and Sam Houston, who like himself were imbued with a burning love for the Union. That love had made Jackson suffer; it was now preparing heartbreak for Benton and Houston. Refusal to compromise on the slavery question had lost Benton his seat in the Senate, and as a member of the lower house and on the Committee of Military Affairs, he often voiced his fears for the future of the Union.

Benton looked forward eagerly to the return of Frémont with his reports on the railroad survey. Jessie waited with foreboding, since no good news had come of him and she feared for his safety through a winter in the mountains. As months passed with no word, she became possessed with the unshakable conviction that Frémont and his party were starving in some mountain fastness or dying of thirst in the desert. As she was expecting a child in May, the family considered her overanxiety as due to her health, but neither their assurances nor their remonstrances resolved her gloomy certainty. Only her father realized that she whose being was ever sensitized to tactile and visual memory of her lover might now have an awareness of his peril. He allowed her to dwell freely upon her fears and did not chide her hysterical complaints at "the criminal abundance of food and drink here, while her husband and his companions were starving."

Nights of wakeful brooding were beginning to tell upon her health when, on the evening of February 6, Susie and a young cousin, returning from a wedding, came to spend the night with her. Finding her reading beside the fire, they doffed their party dresses, put on wrappers, and proceeded to tell her of the wedding. The fire needing replenishment, Jessie went to an adjoining room for a piece of wood. As she stooped to balance a stick on her arm, she felt a touch on her shoulder and heard Frémont's laughing whisper: "Jessie, Susie." No other sound came, but she got the impression that on this as on other family evenings, Frémont intended teasing Susie by some practical joke. She felt an instant lightening of the heart, a sense of peace. Hurrying into the other room, she found Susie in a half-fainting condition. She could give no explanation except an impression of a presence, which frightened her. Though at the time the whole incident was taken lightly by the family, it served to restore Jessie's spirits completely.

In early May, Frémont returned, and now came to light the story of his hardships culminating in actual starvation over a period of days. Jessie reported her strange psychic revelation, and Frémont with his exactitude as to details, unearthed his notebooks and began to study them. By allowing for difference in time, he concluded that at the very hour of Jessie's revelation he had just landed his party at the Mormon hamlet of Parowan, after taking them over a maze of slopes and canyon defiles where the deviation of a single mile would have caused the starving party to miss the village and perish miserably. They had been without food for forty-eight hours, and he declared that his elation at having got relief had so winged his spirit that after a bit of food he had written up his notes, indulging meanwhile in a happy daydream of Jessie and home and a gay family party about the open fire.

To Benton's skeptical question as to his interpretation of the experience which had so quickly restored his wife, Frémont said: "It doesn't seem strange to me. With each so much a part of the other's thoughts and feelings at all times, a crisis with either might cause these thoughts to materialize into a sense of actual physical presence."

Frémont's anxiety to reach home before Jessie's confinement had caused him to decline a public demonstration in his honor at San Francisco. He now anxiously awaited the arrival of the child who, he secretly hoped, would be another daughter. On May 17 Jessie gave birth to a son whom she named Frank Preston in honor of a favorite cousin. To her intense joy this baby showed the same sturdy physical quality as Lily and Charley.

During her convalescence Frémont often came to sit beside her while he opened sheaves of letters from editors begging him for reports of his journey and statements as to the advantages of his easy central route to the Pacific. These articles he prepared throughout the summer.

Early in September Benton was feeling ill and decided to ride into the country for a few days' rest. On the tenth Jessie was alone with her mother, who seemed no more frail than usual. She asked Jessie to help her walk into the library, a long walk for the shadowy invalid. Once in the book-lined room she gazed fondly about. Stooping, she touched the surface of Benton's desk and chair and then asked to be led back to her couch. Here she fell into a deep sleep from which she did not awake.

For ten years this beloved and patient invalid had been the special care of Thomas Benton; yet so free of complaint had been his service that his children had taken it as a matter of course. They now saw him broken and incoherent with self-reproach that he should have been absent from her in that last hour. Later they learned from many letters of condolence that his unselfish devotion had become a thirty-year tradition in Washington, a classic among friends and enemies alike. The family rallied about him, and his Christmas holidays were lightened by visits from children and grandchildren.

On a day in February while Benton was at the Capitol and Jessie at the home of her cousin Mrs. Preston, word came that the Benton house was afire. Hurrying home, they stood together in the street watching while the firemen struggled uselessly, and half the town ran about calling out suggestions and trying to assist. Eliza, the elder sister, was the heroine of this catastrophe, for she had risked her life in an attempt to save valuable papers, including the manuscript for the second volume of *Thirty Years' View*.

That night the family gathered under Jessie's roof and took stock of salvage. A box of Jessie's letters to her father marked "most precious" had been saved, and many of his letters to her had been taken earlier for reference. These were to remain a partial record of their rich and happy association.

Benton confessed to the family that the political bitterness and the death of his wife had made Washington hateful to him, and now the loss of his home had matured a plan long in his mind. He would accept the offer from a lecture bureau to travel through New England and the West, speaking on political matters touching the imminent sectional crisis. Jessie also confessed a long-cherished plan for making a home in New York.

Reverberations of forensic cannonading at the Capitol had reached Jessie's sick-room in '54. By the spring of '55 relatives and friends in the South were expressing the boldest secession sentiments and ending their letters to her with: "Are you and Colonel Frémont with *us,* or are you following your father's views, so *strange* for a Southerner?" To these letters Jessie replied with frank avowal of her own pro-union and anti-slavery convictions, but she said to her guest, Mrs. Dix: "Another secession letter! We shall move to New York near you very soon. I already feel the ground swell here. This is no longer my place."

Squatter troubles at the mine called Frémont again to California. Awaiting his return, Jessie, influenced by concern for her children's health, decided to spend the summer at Siasconset, Nantucket. July found her settled with the devoted nurse Marie and the children. Here for a time she forgot all care and became a boat maker, sand-castle builder, and teller of sea stories and island folklore to a family audience augmented by several neighbor children.

One day Lily came running to report:"Charley said two'damns'when the castle tower fell.Young Sears taught him. Shall I send him home?"

"No. Bring them both here," Jessie commanded. Then smiling at the abashed culprit, she asked:"If you like to swear, Johnny, why don't you swear as these Quakers do? Come, I'll teach you and Charley."Then frowning, she shook her finger at young Sears and said crossly:"Thee's a little *thee!* Thou!" Amused with this oddity, the small boys practiced this "oath," soon to become a family classic. To Lily's blunt question, "And what about those damns?" Jessie whispered, "Let's forget them."

Another classic grew out of the Quaker custom of calling the days of the week by their number. Lily's joy in running errands for her mother had given her the nickname My Girl Friday. She now became My Girl Sixth Day.

As they studied the weather on gusty mornings, Jessie taught them the fishermen's couplets:

> *First the rain and then the wind,*
> *Topsail sheets and halyards mind.*
> *First the wind and then the rain,*
> *Hoist your topsails up again.*

In August these idle days were interrupted for Jessie by the arrival of S. N. Carvalho and his notebooks. He came to discuss with her his own forthcoming book, which would be the first to be illustrated with daguerreotype views of an unknown country.

Although Frémont had written articles for the press and his full reports were embodied in Government documents, *this* report, Carvalho declared, was to be a personal one, based upon his experiences under Frémont's leadership.

To me Colonel Frémont is a hero in the highest sense. I want to tell clearly and candidly the incidents in our experience where in that long gamut of hardship and suffering his heroic quality sang above the minor jangle of despair. I know why his old followers and the scouts, Carson and Godey, rally to him as their hero. Personal courage and skill he showed at all times, and his high qualities of fairness to subordinates. Through every vicissitude his self-

control, his endurance of spirit against obstacles won from us a kind of wor-
shipful loyalty. The Colonel's worst enemies grant him personal courage. We
can prove all our claims from actual suffering with him.

Carvalho read to Jessie many pages of his manuscript, and then he said:
"This book is but a poor tribute to so noble a character, but I feel it will gain
in value if I may dedicate it to Jessie Frémont." He received permission and
the promise that she would find a room in her New York home where he and
Mr. Brady might develop the daguerreos with which his book was to be
illustrated.

Frémont was now on his way East, and Jessie awaited his coming, all unaware of what the fateful year 1856 held in store for her and her hero.

CHAPTER XIII

"Our Jessie," the Toast of the Nation

ESSIE Frémont, resting with her children on the sands of Siasconset, was happily unaware of that fast-moving shuttle all set to weave yet another colorful strand into the fabric of her life.

The previous winter while at work on *Thirty Years' View*, Benton had poured into his daughter's understanding ear his lamentations over the pro-slavery determinism in high places and his fears for the condition of the country. He sadly recalled the utterances of John Q. Adams in '43: "I am satisfied slavery will not go down until it goes down in blood." In the winter of '54 Benton had said to Jessie: "I feel I must go like Peter the Hermit and cry aloud a crusade to arouse the North to its danger. The South already sees its slavery horizon stretching from Maine to Lower California."

This summer at Siasconset he had visited Jessie and announced his bookings for lectures in New York and Boston. This man who had dominated the Democratic party for thirty years, who had been the "right arm" of more than one President, now declared: "With this nullification treason among us, we Union Democrats have become the victims of our loyalties. If the Democrats don't unite, they will have plenty to fear from those rag-tags now trying to form new parties." Benton's pronouncement proved prophetic, for the Congress which met in December held within it all the elements of farce: free-soil Democrats, pro-slavery Whigs, and fence sitters, waiting to see where self-interest would land them. After a few polls it became clear that the majority were against the Pierce administration.

By the spring of '55 the most progressive among the opposition had crystallized into a Republican party. This infant party combined some of the best elements of the country, for the most part enthusiastic young men full of sanguine courage. Its platform stated that Congress had no power over slavery in the states, that slavery should not be permitted in the territories of the United States, that Government officials should be chosen by direct vote, and that officers selected must support their platform. The party's next problem was to find a candidate so popular that he could win over many doubtful ones from all parties.

Just returned from California, Frémont now reported to Jessie his frequent discussions with various groups of influential Southerners seeking an alliance between the Democrats and the Native American group. His frankly stated views so impressed these men that Edward Carrington, fusionist leader, went to the fusion conference in New York determined to urge Frémont as candidate for the Presidential nomination.

Later Frémont was summoned to a three-day conference at the old St. Nicholas Hotel. Here he was offered the Democratic nomination with two strings to it: the endorsement of the Kansas-Nebraska act and the fugitive-slave law. He refused to consider this proposition. Next day the overtures were earnestly renewed, and Frémont declared he would take the matter under advisement. The parting shot of young Carrington, who knew Jessie, was: "We Democrats are sure to win, and no woman can refuse the Presidency."

As Frémont approached the cottage at Siasconset, he paused unobserved to enjoy the picture on the terrace. Jessie, in a light-blue gown with a ribbon around her head, sat at the tea table, serving the children. Lily held in her lap the pink-cheeked chubby Frank; Charley stood leaning against his mother's knee as she told the Nantucket whaling story, which on demand had stretched to a summer serial. As Jessie saw Frémont coming, she waved her hand and called for fresh tea.

Afterward, in recounting this scene, Frémont said: "As I watched that family picture, I longed for the power to make it the symbol of my Jessie's future, but already I had come to impart disturbing knowledge." Late in the evening he asked Jessie to put on a wrap for a long walk to Lighthouse Hill. Here they sat hand in hand as she listened to his dramatic account of that three-day conference. He ended his recital with: "Carrington said no woman can refuse the Presidency, but with those strings to the nomination we must refuse. It isn't likely they will be loosened, for the fugitive-slave law was clearly specified."

With her ability to face facts, to visualize and dramatize their implications, Jessie was confronted with a difficult decision on her own account. These implications had loomed large as her husband thought aloud to the one listener from whom he had no secrets. Her deep family feeling had made her keenly sensitive to that disturbing ground swell in Washington. Frémont's acceptance of the Democratic nomination would restore her to the favor of the disaffected relatives and friends whose letters had practically accused her of family treason.

The possibility of return to the settled order of the old Washington life held happiness, but to return as mistress of the White House! She recalled herself a six-year-old, clinging to her father's hand as they walked through the great rooms with myriads of candles shedding their soft light over the camellias and laurustine, banked row on row. She saw herself peeping into the state dining room, marveling at the table loaded with glittering pastries, at either end a monster salmon resting on waves of meat jelly. She saw herself, appeased with a packet of cakes, driving home with the coachman, who would later take her parents to the party. And the White House sitting room on a sunny morning! Herself leaning against an old man's knee, his long fingers smoothing her hair as he talked to her father.

But only for a moment was she swayed by these memories. Even as she listened, she knew that traitorous compromise awaited the free-soil Democrat who accepted this nomination. Frémont himself had often denounced the Kansas-Nebraska act and the fugitive-slave law as infamous and disruptive to the nation. Jessie later described the scene thus:

There was no shadow of doubt in our minds. At the foot of the bluff on which the lighthouse stood were the remains of a ship embedded in the sands, the seas washing her ribs. Above, steady and brilliant, flashed out the recurring light. Here was symbol of a choice between a wreck of dishonor or a kindly light on its mission of good. With clasped hands we made our decision and turned homeward with the kindly beacon at our back.

By late autumn the Frémonts were settled in New York in a roomy house at 56 Ninth Street. Here Jessie turned the north drawing room into a studio for the use of the artist Carvalho, who with the photographer Brady was to develop the daguerreotypes. Another artist, Hamilton, a pupil of Turner's, had asked permission to reproduce several of them in oil. During the winter Jessie presided over a veritable art salon, for many visiting painters and engravers came to study the work. When their discussions carried over to the dinner hour, extra places were set, and the artists joined their hosts in discussions of the exciting political trends.

The Republican party was growing prodigiously, and now William H. Seward, the great New York leader, was followed by all his Whigs when he declared: "The party's principles are equal and exact justice, its speech open, decided, and frank, its banner untorn in earlier battles and unsullied by past errors. That is the party for us."

In February, 1856, this party, dubbed Black Republicans and Negro Worshipers by the South, held its convention in Pittsburgh. The delegates stated their anti-slavery platform and set the date June 17 for the nominating convention at Philadelphia. Long before this date, Republican leaders began considering Frémont as a candidate. Already a national figure, unconnected with political quarrels, and known for his uncompromising anti-slavery principles, he would have a large personal following. Francis P. Blair, the Washington editor, a close friend of the family, called upon the Frémonts and announced that he, his son Frank, and Nathaniel P. Banks were all for Frémont as leader. John Bigelow of the *New York Evening Post* came also. Would the Colonel accept the nomination?

Again were Frémont and Jessie faced with a difficult decision. Though it involved no question of political principle, since both heartily endorsed the Republican credo, their decision threatened harsh personal reactions not easy to reckon with. The hospitable family doors in Virginia and St. Louis would be closed and double locked against them. Those democratic aristocratic friends abroad with whom Jessie was even now in lively correspondence would never understand when those opprobrious epithets nigger lover and rag-tag were boiled down into cartoons and spread over the European press.

And her father? At this point Jessie's resolution faltered. Could he be influenced to look upon Frémont as a standard bearer of freedom, or would he violently oppose his son-in-law's alliance with what he termed "a motley mixture of malcontents with no real desire in any of them to save the Union?"

"Frémont and Our Jessie." Republican cartoon, campaign, 1856.

Her love for her seventy-four-year-old father had in it full measure of reverence; to anger him was to worry and hurt herself. She sadly voiced these doubts.

Frémont's reply was characteristic: "This is a matter of principle for us alone to decide. Your father will be compelled to respect the honesty of our decision, though he will never agree to the wisdom of it." With that declaration Jessie Frémont saw her way clearly. In a conference of free-soil leaders at the home of John Bigelow, hearty private endorsement of Frémont was expressed by Edwin Miller, Edwin P. Morgan, Francis P. Blair, and Samuel Tilden. Plans were made for a publicity program, Blair promising Jessie to secure Benton's endorsement of Frémont. In accepting the invitation to a large meeting in New York, Frémont said:

I am opposed to slavery in the abstract and upon principle sustained and made habitual by long-settled conviction. While I feel inflexible in the belief that it ought not to be interfered with where it exists under the shield of state sovereignty, I am as inflexibly opposed to its extension on this continent beyond its present limits.

Between April and June the Frémonts had a clear picture of the current of popular sentiment setting in toward Frémont as the Republican candidate. Though this current was strongest in the West, it also swept swiftly through the central states. The *Cleveland Herald,* the *New York Tribune,* and the *Post* were all open in their sponsorship. The *Herald of Freedom,* the organ of the Emigrant Aid Society, was the first of many publications to place his name at its masthead: "Our candidate, John C. Frémont."

Before June it became apparent that the other possible Republican candidates were being eliminated as unavailable. William H. Seward and Salmon P. Chase were too conspicuously labeled abolitionists. John M. McLean of Ohio was past seventy, too old to father a young party. On the other hand, Frémont, only forty-three, a gallant and glamorous national figure, was held eminently as a knight to lead this young party on a crusade against slavery.

We know of but one interview between Jessie and her father at this time. Jessie's sister, Sarah Jacob, had sent to her excerpts from a letter written to Colonel Jacob, in which Benton had declared:

It has been a great mortification to us all that Frémont has allowed himself to be got hold of by the fusionists. I did what I could to prevent it but in vain, telling him that my opposition would have to become public. I was not able to stop it, but I think it will die out. Those who started counted upon the support of my name.... I think he will be got out of it yet.

Jessie wept in secret over this letter, but realizing that Frémont had withheld the knowledge of that interview from her to save her feelings, she now concealed the letter and awaited her father's arrival on his way from a speaking tour through Missouri. There was no quarrel when he came. These two understood each other perfectly. Benton could not question her allegiance; she could not question his stubborn adherence to lifelong principle.

He greeted the children, watching them open the packets of sweets he had brought. Then Jessie dismissed them and devoted herself to lively accounts of their behavior. She then took him to meet Carvalho and to examine the work being done in the studio room. Benton kissed his daughter tenderly as he started down the steps to the bus which would take him to the evening train. He had refused to wait for the carriage, and Jessie humored him, knowing he wished to avoid a meeting with Frémont. As he waved to her from the bus window, she waved back, blinded with tears but not too unhappy, for somehow beneath the harsh judgment of the Senator mind, she felt the approval of the father heart.

On June 17 she saw her husband off to attend the Republican convention assembled in Philadelphia at Music Fund Hall. Before the doors were opened, Frémont's nomination was spoken of by the *Tribune* correspondent as "already inevitable." Robert Emmet of New York acted as chairman and Colonel Henry S. Lane of Indiana as president of the convention. The platform was read by David Wilmot before a room filled with crusading delegates of every profession, from every free state in the Union and from the territories of Kansas, Nebraska, and Minnesota and from the slave states of Virginia, Missouri, Kentucky, and Delaware. The nine resolutions were read amidst applause "hearty but dignified," as one of the seventy press men reported, for this convention was fervid and exalted in spirit as befitting an assemblage launching a campaign for free men, free speech, and free thought.

The third day's balloting went forward with a swift clearing of the way for

Frémont. Seward, McLean, and Chase were duly withdrawn by the proper delegates. The veteran politician Blair, who had Frémont's letter of authority in his pocket, expected to announce him when Thaddeus Stevens asked that the Pennsylvania delegates be allowed to confer, since McLean, the only one who could carry the state, had been eliminated. The recess was granted and also Stevens' appeal to have McLean replaced.

At the reopening the formal ballot gave Frémont three hundred fifty-nine votes, McLean one hundred ninety-six, Sumner two, and Seward one. At Wilmot's plea for unanimity all but thirty-eight votes were cast for Frémont. At this announcement the delegates rose in a body with a shouting and waving of arms, hats, and handkerchiefs. The band struck up a military march, a flag with Frémont's name waved above the platform, and across the width of the hall stretched a banner inscribed: "John C. Frémont for President." The reporters rushed to wire their papers. The crowds in the street took up the cry: "Frémont for President! Frémont!"

Over the name of the Vice President, Blair and Frémont had hot argument. Frémont held that the only way to wage a real fight against Buchanan in Pennsylvania was to name the popular Simon Cameron. However, Blair and Cameron being personal enemies, Blair stood pat for W. L. Dayton, to Frémont's anger and Blair's later regret. Dayton was nominated. Thus Frémont and Dayton for the Republicans were opposed by Buchanan and Breckenridge for the Democrats and Millard Fillmore and Andrew Donelson for the Whigs.

In the library of the Ninth Street home Jessie received the news calmly. Not at all certain of the nomination and fully aware of the precariousness of the cause they had espoused, she held herself in readiness for whatever might come. Frémont too was calm as they read together the letter that announced his nomination. She kept this for the files along with his letter of acceptance.

Francis P. Blair now assumed active management of Frémont's campaign while Frémont's personal headquarters were at 34 Broadway in the office of John Howard, his friend and business associate. The Ninth Street house soon became branch office, mail station, press clipping bureau, and buffet lunchroom, with meals obtainable throughout eighteen of the twenty-four hours of each day. Here was sung the first Republican campaign song to the tune of the *Marseillaise*. It ended with this alliterative appeal:

Jessie Benton Frémont: a Woman Who Made History

Arise, arise, ye brave!
And let our warcry be
Free Speech, Free Press, Free Soil, Free Men,
Frémont and Victory!

Among the first visitors was Henry Ward Beecher, come to outline a series of campaign speeches he intended making.

The ratification meeting, held in New York on the evening of June 25, crowded the Tabernacle to the doors. At its close practically the entire audience followed the torchlight procession as it moved up Broadway to the curb before the Frémont house. After the candidate's speech from the steps, the crowd shouted, "Jessie Frémont, Jessie Benton," and the candidate's wife presented herself and acknowledged the roars of the excited mob.

After the publication of Frémont's speech of acceptance, Jessie was gratified to receive a letter from Lady Bulwer, inclosing a clipping from the *London Times* which commented approvingly upon the passage in his speech declaring opposition to aggressions against the domain of other nations.

The wife of the Republican candidate expected to keep open house for those directly interested in Frémont's election. To this end, like a true general she promptly organized her household staff, but she was totally unprepared for the sudden flow of callers, both men and women, demanding interviews with her upon religion, marriage, divorce, phases of the political situation abroad, and other subjects she considered quite outside her province. She now faced the disturbing fact that a curious public had critical and often belligerent interest in her opinions and beliefs. To offend one of them was to make an enemy for her husband. With characteristic tact and patience she girded herself for these difficult encounters. One of her first callers gave her needed practice in parrying impertinent and cruel questions. This guest was a militant-looking woman in a blue-bombazine cloak and a terrifying helmet-shaped bonnet. As Jessie entered the drawing room, the visitor nodded briefly but ignored her extended hand. Jessie waited in embarrassed silence while the woman consulted a fat notebook. Peering closely at her hostess, she finally announced: "You're not as sensible looking as the cartoons make you out. Are you prepared to speak truthfully about the slaves you had in Washington as body servants and about the girl you tried to entice to California?"

Jessie gave an account of the freed slaves who stayed on happily with the family and who, when too old to work, were pensioned off with their relatives in the South. She described the negress left behind in New York to marry her sweetheart in a new red-silk dress given her by Jessie.

While she spoke, the visitor checked off items, then began again. Jessie answered questions as to whether she read profane literature on Sunday, whether her children were obedient, how many she had lost, and what they had died of. On the arrival of tea, she turned with relief to the neat maid with the tray. But her ordeal was not yet over.

"I see you ape the English by serving tea and cake between meals."

Jessie admitted it. "I *am* English in the tea-hour tradition. I find it a comforting break in my full and often wearying day."

"But you serve it by a French maid," she added with scorn.

"Yes," Jessie whispered, "but between us, I think I make better tea myself. I had no maid in Monterey. I heated the water in a long-handled iron saucepan over a smoky fire. Instead of French cakes, I lifted a sardine from his crowded can and gave him decent burial between two soda crackers."

Disarmed, her tormentor laughed and proceeded to drink her tea, then departed.

When Jessie reported this call to Frémont, he demanded: "Why did you endure such treatment? Why didn't you show her out?"

"Ah, my dear, you didn't *see* her. I would as soon think of snubbing Napoleon's aide." Later Jessie's tact was rewarded by seeing an article in a woman's paper, extolling the Republican candidate's wife as a good woman and a housekeeper who could cook over a campfire.

Her worst encounter was with a sharp-nosed gentleman who resembled John Knox. He began by denouncing all Protestant denominations in turn, then demanded to know how she stood on "popery and the rest." Already aware of the acrimonious turn the campaign was taking toward Frémont, she trod warily:

If a creed is a formulated expression of our search for God, don't you believe that there may be something in each that is worthy, since it gives comfort in sorrow and help in temptation to its followers? For that reason I hesitate to condemn any creed.

[206]

The Mustang Team. Democratic cartoon, Presidential campaign, 1856.

Her inquisitor looked annoyed, then admitted that he was an agnostic who had hoped to get a contribution for his lectures, but he "opined" that for a young mother, this gentle attitude toward orthodox religion might be more fitting.

These incidents were interludes in Jessie's chief labor of the campaign. John Bigelow, editor of the *New York Evening Post*, had asked her to assemble the factual biographical material for his campaign *Life of Frémont*. It was to be printed by Derby and Jackson and sold at a dollar a copy. At her request it was dedicated to Alexander von Humboldt: "This memoir of one whose genius he was among the first to discover and acknowledge."

In the preparation of this material Jessie Frémont faced the most difficult task of her life. It must be so presented as to overcome the prejudices of many thousand well-meaning but narrow-minded readers regarding divorce and illegitimacy. Frémont's opponents were already hinting at his being ineligible "because of his being a Catholic and of questionable parentage." His backers were urging him to make a public statement.

This was the Victorian era. A divorced woman, however innocent of wrongdoing, was ever on the defensive. For a child born out of wedlock, no extenuating circumstances could lighten the color of the brand. In the family background of Frémont's mother, Anne Whiting Frémont, there was much material for honest pride. But would the fact that her father, member of the Virginia House of Burgesses, had held the infant George Washington in his arms count in his daughter's favor in face of her act of independence when she tired of a family-ordained and childless marriage to a man forty-five years her senior and fell in love with a handsome but penniless French schoolmaster? She had been honest with her husband, but upon his refusal to allow her a divorce, she had eloped with her lover, living with him until a year and a half later when her husband consented to a divorce in order himself to remarry.

Would the enduring devotion of the Frémonts thereafter condone the fact that their son John Charles was nearly three months old before they were free to marry? How many voters would place the honorable career of John C. Frémont in the balance against the bar sinister?

Jessie Frémont was pondering these points more than seventy years before the pronouncement of the Pacific coast jurist, Judge Leon Yankwich: "There are no illegitimate children, only illegitimate parents." In personal argument

Jessie Frémont could modify resentment with all the skill of a diplomat in a tight place. How could she handle the thousands of strangers into whose hostile hands she must place these delicate controversial facts at a dollar a volume?

This book must speak for a candidate who refused to speak for himself, since Frémont declared he had made public utterances covering all points that concerned the public. He held that the circumstances of his birth concerned only himself and his immediate family, that a man's religion was between himself and his God, and that though he was not a Catholic, he would make no declaration of it as a virtue.

With Jessie Frémont courage had become automatic. She steered her dangerous course between the Scylla of censure-evoking factual incident and the Charybdis of censure-evoking evasion. The result may not have been great biography, but it was a masterpiece in its handling of this stormy material. Frémont's mother, Anne Beverly Whiting, as a young orphan under the control of her uncle, Mr. Cary, was thus described by her daughter-in-law, Jessie Frémont:

Anne, being the youngest, was most defenseless in the hands of Mr. Cary, and instead of being an heiress she found herself at an early age almost dispossessed of a large proportion of the ample heritage which had been left her. When she had reached the age of seventeen, her sister, Mrs. Lowry, desiring to provide for her against what in those days and in that circle was deemed the greatest of all calamities, poverty, arranged a marriage for her with Major Pryor, also of Gloucester County, who was very rich and very gouty and sixty-two years of age; just forty-five years her senior.

Aside from the fatal disparity of years, Major Pryor lacked refinement and sensibility and was in every respect repulsive to the young creature who was sacrificed to him. Anne resisted the importunities of her sister as long as she could, but finally overcome by a sense of her homeless and dependent condition which was constantly pressed upon her consideration, the despairing orphan yielded to her venerable suitor and became Mrs. Major Pryor. Marriage only increased her regret for the sacrifice to which she had submitted. She became melancholy, shunned the gay society and habits of life to which her husband was addicted, and thus dragged out twelve long years of wed-

ded misery. By this time, as they were childless, both had become convinced that the happiness of neither would be promoted by continuing to live longer together, and they separated. As both had influential friends, the legislature of the state sanctioned their separation by passing an act of divorce. Not long after, both married again, Mrs. Pryor to Mr. Frémont, and Major Pryor, in the seventy-sixth year of his age, to his housekeeper.

Bigelow was delighted with Jessie's work and soon had the book on the press.

Meanwhile the orators, Horace Greeley, Charles Sumner, Salmon P. Chase, and Edward E. Hale, were holding audiences spellbound with their eloquence over "Free Speech, Free Soil, and Frémont." Beecher made a widely quoted speech which declared Frémont not a Catholic but added:

Like a true lover and a gallant man, Frémont said he didn't care who married him, so it was done quick and tight. If we had been in Colonel Frémont's place, we would have been married if it had required us to walk through a row of priests and bishops as long as from Washington to Rome, ending up with the Pope himself.

While Faneuil Hall was resounding with the speeches of Judge Hoar and Hannibal Hamlin, and the Tabernacle in New York City rocked in applause over Charles A. Dana, the campaign song writers were busy with stanzas, shouting the praises of "Our Jessie," and the Republican press artists were drawing friendly cartoons to offset the opposition screeds. Processions miles in length headed by blaring bands bore transparencies emblazoned "Frémont and Our Jessie" and "A Toast to Our Jessie." The glee singers, dressed in white, chanted their favorite:

The choice made by Jessie is ours;
We want the brave man she did wed.
He crowned her with gay bridal flowers,
And she is a crown to his head.

She shall be our Liberty's queen,
And he shall rule over the state
From mountains of granite and green
To the land of the Golden Gate.

Another popular ditty ended with the lines:

> And Freedom's star shall brightly shine,
> And Plenty's horn shall bless ye
> When in the White House we enshrine
> Frémont and gentle Jessie.

But the verses which the song writers deemed fit to be especially embossed and sent to Jessie were:

> The sun has gone down o'er the homes of the freemen
> And left but dark clouds brooding over the West;
> Our hope bids us look for a happier morning
> When we gaze on sweet Jessie, our loveliest and best.
>
> Oh, dear are the maids of the far western prairie,
> And ever beloved will the Yankee girls be,
> But close to our hearts as our own fireside fairy
> Is our lovely Jessie, the pride of the free.
>
> Sing on, lovely bird, sing of dawn from our darkness;
> Thou art dear to the hearts of all patriot men,
> And whom shall we toast for the Queen of the White House?
> We'll give them "Our Jessie" again and again.

Though touched by these evidences of popularity, Jessie was too anxious over the coming appearance of Bigelow's *Life of Colonel Frémont* to enjoy any personal triumph. When the book appeared, it met with instant success, many thousand copies being sold and many Frémont votes due to it.

And now began the working of the Jessie Anne Frémont legend. Wherever she went, she met young women in violet-colored muslins, others in white with her favorite flower at their belts. Beecher reported that half the women of his congregation were copying her hair dress, her manner of speech, and her walk. Sketches of her life, often highly colored, appeared in the press. Letters came revealing that the storks flying over American homes were delivering Jessie Annes to every state in the Union. Deeply touched by the tenor of these letters, Jessie fought off fatigue to sit far into the night answering them.

A second life of Frémont had been written by Charles Upham and published by Ticknor and Fields. Horace Greeley of the *Tribune* had written a pamphlet life, but the Bigelow biography was outselling them all. One wag on a Cleveland paper declared that the Bigelow book had replaced the family album on half the parlor tables of the country and that "Jessie Anne" had replaced half the family names.

One day while she was busy teaching Lily how to clip and file properly, Jessie was handed a packet of eulogistic poems from the Carey sisters. Scarcely were these read and acknowledged when there came "with the compliments of John G. Whittier" a manuscript copy of his *The Pass of the Sierra*, with its lines:

> *Rise up, Frémont, and go before;*
> *The Hour must have its Man;*
> *Put on the hunting shirt once more,*
> *And lead in Freedom's van!*

Jessie had not yet met the Quaker poet, and as she wrote her letter of acknowledgment, she little dreamed that the resultant friendship would enable Whittier to help her in the most critical decision of her afterlife.

Thus far the campaign had not degenerated into the vituperative and mud-slinging stage; but these waves of Frémont acclaim had to be turned back in some way and soon, lest they engulf both Democrats and the already tottering Whigs. A costly but effective coast-to-coast propaganda was begun on the only possible grounds of attack. These were the ones the Republican leaders had at first anticipated, but since their own canvass had made no attack upon Buchanan's private character, they had trusted too far. Without warning the most scurrilous charges were hurled at the Republican candidate and his wife from every quarter.

Added to accusations of Frémont's repudiating his being a Catholic were the statements that he had carved a cross upon a mountain rock, that he was often seen coming from the cathedral, and that his niece and ward Nina was at school in a convent. By the end of July the Catholic press was against him, and many Protestant publications repudiated him.

The slave-holding gossip was directed against Jessie. Women in abolitionist households read that she had been suckled by a slave mammy, washed and dressed by slaves, and that she owned them now and had watched them beaten. The accounts of Frémont's political and financial transactions were garbled beyond all semblance of truth. Scandalous lies kept well ahead of all denials. These things were no surprise to Frémont or to Jessie, but that the story of his parentage should now be so badly garbled, turned into an ale-house anecdote, crucified her spirit and nearly broke her heart. Character-istically she tried to hide from Frémont these blasphemous screeds such as: "Do you want to see a Frenchman's bastard enter the White House, carrying a nigger-worshiper banner?" And it was characteristic of Frémont that he let her believe she succeeded.

The elements now contributing most to Jessie's inner hurt were the pub-lic utterances of Benton, who declared the whole Republican movement a menace to the Union, since it was a sectional movement, accentuating sec-tional hostility. Said he: "Do the people believe the South will submit to such a President as Frémont? We are treading on a volcano that is liable at any mo-ment to break forth and overthrow the nation." Though the stout fiber of the love between Jessie and her father stretched, it did not break. She still wrote him of his grandchildren, and he replied with admonitions about her health and thanks for her solicitude over his own.

As the campaign waxed more virulent, it became evident that the efforts of such champions as Wendell Phillips, Carl Schurz, Schuyler Colfax, and Abra-ham Lincoln would not avail against the array of equally eloquent orators working on slave-holders' fears and secessionist ambitions. A month before election day, both Frémont and Jessie gave up hope of his election. Those who later commented upon the quiet dignity exhibited by both as the results came in did not know that in this as in earlier crises, these two faced the cold hard facts together and were already balancing their losses of old-time friends with their gains: the loyalty of such constituents as William M. Evarts, Charles Dana, President Felton of Harvard, President Silliman of Yale, Washington Irving, Emerson, and Whittier.

Jessie reminded Frémont that losing the election would not lose them these friends and that due to his honorable course throughout this "trial by mud," even his enemies must concede him some strength of character. Thus fortified they faced election day with calmness.

The election results showed, as such results often do, how a little more vigilance here, a little better organization there, might have saved the day. Frémont's vote in New York State was prodigious. The same popularity was attested in Ohio, Michigan, Wisconsin, and Iowa. Even in Pennsylvania, Illinois, and Indiana he had polled a large popular vote, but the Whig votes cast for Buchanan and Fillmore had turned the trick for the Democrats. These votes were cast to kill a sectional party and to clamp the ever-increasing number of tongues loudly threatening secession. Of the thirty-one states, Buchanan carried nineteen, Frémont eleven, and Fillmore one. Buchanan got one hundred seventy-four electoral votes, Frémont one hundred fourteen, and Fillmore eight.

The Frémonts, Francis Blair, and John Bigelow spent election night at headquarters, then returned to the house for coffee. Calmly the defeated candidate and his wife ate their breakfast. When they spoke of the poll in Missouri, Jessie said without rancor: "Colonel Benton, I perceive, has the best of this family argument." Frémont smiled appreciatively, but old Francis Blair declared in a voice choked with tears: "Tom Benton's stubborn stand cost us many a vote outside Missouri."

At this unashamed breakdown of a grownup, thirteen-year-old Lily, with her hopes of living in the White House blasted, laid her head on her arms and burst into violent weeping. Jessie quietly left the room and brought Lily's hat, coat, and veil. Lifting the sobbing girl to her feet, she gently wiped her eyes, put on the coat and hat, swathed her in the veil; then giving her a gentle push, she said: "Go take a walk, a long walk.

> First the wind and then the rain,
> Hoist your topsail up again."

At this sally Blair blew his nose vociferously and got up: "That will do for me too, Jessie Anne. Come, Colonel, let's go to headquarters."

Within a week there was recovered much salvage from the wreck of the Republican Presidential hopes. The infant party itself had grown to stalwart proportions with every prospect of becoming the dominant party in the North, for this campaign had sounded the death knell of the Whigs.

Frémont's personal popularity was already moving the *Herald* to suggest his nomination for the campaign of 1860. Jessie Frémont filed these cheerful items in the family archives together with the cartoons and the campaign songs. A hint of what had deeply touched her in this experience is indicated by her laughing reply to Mrs. Bigelow, who came to condole with her: "I'm very glad that all my little Jessie Annes are too young to weep over the discovery that they are *not* the namesakes of a President's wife."

CHAPTER XIV

Life at Mariposa and Black Point

JESSIE Frémont quickly readjusted herself and her household to the comfortable pre-campaign status. Viewed in perspective, her husband's defeat had in it much for encouragement. Within a week Blair and Bigelow had salvaged from the wreck many heartening facts which they promptly heralded in the press. The returns from the Democratic stronghold states had been a rebuke to their leaders. The Whig party, having spent its dying gasp on Fillmore's campaign, would be no check to the Republicans in 1860 when they planned to make Frémont their candidate. William Cullen Bryant in the *Post* proclaimed: "The cause is not going back; it is going rapidly forward. . . . If we look back to '48, where we then counted our thousands, we now count our millions, in the ranks of politics, church, college, and the homes."

Here was compensation indeed for the wife of the defeated Republican candidate. Removed from the merciless glare of publicity, she returned to wonted tasks, among them the supervision of the children's education. She read German with Lily and urged the governess to "smooth down the child's fuzzy French and see that Master Charley hewed closer to the copybook line."

Though she had been hostess to a wide variety of guests in her brief and crowded thirty-two years, she now prepared for the most singular dinner party of her life. Sagundai, one of Frémont's picturesque Delaware hunters, had visited Washington with the braves, John Grass and American Horse, on a mission for his people. That accomplished, he had come to New York to see his friend Colonel Frémont. With him was a young warrior as interpreter.

[216]

During Sagundai's visit in Frémont's office, he asked to see the White Chief's son, and was promptly invited to dinner the following day.

In discussing the menu, Frémont cautioned: "You must not serve made dishes of any kind. He will think them scraps. Serve large pieces of meat. Have Charley at the table. You and Lily dress as you would for any dinner guest." Six-year-old Charley was sternly warned to keep silent, for though the Indians loved children, they wanted them quiet before their elders. Jessie ordered a ten-pound beef roast and a twenty-pound turkey. Lengthy explanations touched with authority were necessary before the butler would consent to put these both on the table at the same time.

While the family awaited the arrival of Frémont with his guests, Jessie described to the children that semi-circle of Indian hunters and guides at the far-away camp of Westport Landing, the firelight playing over their handsome faces and naked bronze torsos, only their lower limbs being blanketed. "They will probably be in buckskins and high boots tonight," she added regretfully. Even as she spoke, the guests were ushered in. Silently all three acknowledged the introduction, but had Charley been less well coached, he would have voiced his childish disappointment at the appearance of the two braves. The magnificent lines of Sagundai's six feet three inches of muscle and sinew were hidden behind a stiffly starched white shirt front and an ill-fitting black-broadcloth suit which gave him a look of bulk.

His manner was composed, as was that of the smaller brave, equally badly dressed, who accompanied him. Both spoke a mixture of French patois and English, easily understood. The interpreter tactfully confided to Jessie that Sagundai liked Frémont because he wasn't afraid of "wild animals, rapids, high mountains, or black canyons."

Sagundai sat holding Charley's hand as the child stood against his knee, and when dinner was announced, he stalked solemnly to the dining room and seated the boy on his right. He cast a casual glance over the dinner table as though quite at home with shining linen, silver, and ladies in dinner gowns.

Charley nearly exploded at the size of the helpings his father served the guests. Sagundai fell to at once with an air of frowning concentration so intense that the others felt they would need a flag of truce before daring to distract him. With Charley's inquisitiveness throttled to big-eyed attention, Jessie rested easy.

All went well until the dessert came on, a pink frozen pudding. Having chosen his utensils at random, Sagundai was left with a tablespoon. He scooped it full of the frozen pudding and filled his mouth. Indian fortitude alone enabled him to bear the shock to the nerves of defective teeth. His face contorted with sudden paralyzing pain, but he uttered no sound. Frémont hastily poured a glass of brandy. Sagundai drank it gratefully, and presently his face relaxed. Pushing the offending dish aside, he finished the meal with many small cakes and a second glass of brandy. The other Indian, "catching on," took his ice cream in sips from a small spoon, with evident relish. Only their excellent training carried Lily and Charley through this episode, but after the departure of the Indians, they were allowed hilarious comment.

The winter passed for Jessie with the usual social round and renewed correspondence with friends in London and Paris. As spring advanced, Frémont's Mariposa interests, which had suffered from his long absence, now demanded his presence in California. Since the small boys were making slow recoveries from illness, it was decided that Jessie remain with them and later take the children to visit her sister Susan in Paris. Susan's husband, Comte Boileau, was soon to be sent as attaché at the French Embassy in Calcutta. Frémont jokingly remarked that what really won Jessie to this plan was a pleading letter from her devoted ancient, the Comte de la Garde, who bewailed her neglect of him and begged that since five of the ten years of life he had allotted himself were already gone, she would now fulfill her solemn promise to return to Paris. There was another hated goodbye as Frémont left for California. Shortly thereafter Jessie wrote to her sister to secure small lodgings in the country, and in May she closed her New York house, and with the children and faithful Marie, sailed for France.

A quaint little house had been found for her in St. Germain-en-Laye, and here for several months Jessie and the children lived an idyllic life. At the roadside near the house was a votive tree where the brightly dressed peasants often dismounted on their way to market to present offerings and petitions to the Virgin. A bunch of grapes with a written prayer attached would beseech a good harvest. One day when the children returned from a donkey ride, Charley reported that they too had made their petition: "*Sainte Vierge, rendez-vous la santé.*" Jessie smiled and said: "Very good! The election is over. You will not be held to account."

Of these Paris days Jessie wrote her father that her "most prideful" experience was that of hearing Susan play at one of Rossini's Sunday musicales. The family pride in Susan's skill as a pianist was fully justified, for Rossini often declared that Madame Boileau played Beethoven better than any other of his pupils. So great was his respect for her performance that on the Sunday Jessie and the Comte de la Garde attended, he sent his wife among the guests to announce: "Madame Boileau is going to play. Those who wish to talk may retire."

Mail from home brought Carvalho's book to Jessie, and as she read it, she wept at the homage paid her husband by the man who had seen him under the greatest hardships of his career.

Though occupied with her friends and sharing the social life of Madame Boileau, Jessie's true state of mind at this time is revealed in a letter to Frémont, dated September 23:

Your letter from Aspinwall came to me a day before the usual mail, my darling, and gave me the pleasure of knowing you so far well on the way. You must not look for a good letter from me this time. . . . Susie sails from Trieste the twenty-fifth. It keeps me thinking of her. Until she is past hearing from, India dwells in my mind. But as somebody says: Les malheurs prevues n'arrivent.

My darling, I want to see you more than you can think. I am well, but I am such a great fool I want to be still beside you, with nothing to think or do but sit and wait for a kind word from you—Sirius by the dear master. I am trying to make the sun go from west to east, that is, trying to look young and pretty. Je deviens coquette dans mon vieux temps pour te plaire. *I walk like Queen Caroline did, and I eat when I don't want, and I try generally to follow all the rules for that sort of thing, but one affectionate look from you will give me more life than all the rules. You see, I have nothing to tell, sweetheart, much to wish and hope and, my darling, so much to thank you for.*

We are all well and all look to your coming for the only real happiness we know. Most of all, darling, I love you and want you.   *Your* JESSIE

When Jessie returned to New York, Benton was with her husband at the pier to meet her. Shocked at her father's thinness and pallor, she questioned him anxiously. He declared himself well, but on the way uptown he confessed great longing for the children. He urged that instead of reopening their home, the Frémonts come to Washington for the season and take a furnished house near Eliza with whom he was living. Jessie gladly met this plea, and November found her renewing her daily visits with her father.

Benton's lifelong tenderness toward his children was heroically shown during this time. The previous year he had pledged his doctors to secrecy as to the cancer that was killing him: "My daughters are young mothers; they shall not be subjected to the prolonged anxiety and grief over my illness."

With iron hand he held himself grimly to his literary task. He was now engaged upon *A Digest of Congressional Debates*. As he gained rest at night by the use of opiates, he was able to show himself in good spirits. When February came and Frémont found it necessary to return to California, Benton, knowing he wished to take his family, staged a "remarkable improvement." He forced himself to drive and to receive guests at dinner.

On the day of the Frémonts' departure, he bade them hearty farewell and promised to join them in June. The last effort of will and waning vitality had been used to deceive his beloved Jessie and to send her away with peace of mind. The day the Frémont party set sail, Thomas Benton took to his bed never to leave it again.

When the *Moses Taylor* steamed out of New York harbor on a crisp February morning, it carried the Frémont family, Frémont's young niece Nina, his business associate John Howard and his son John, and two mining engineers, Dr. Festus Adelbery and young Charles Fox. Seasoned sailors all, they christened the narrow-built boat the *Rolling Moses,* as she pitched and rolled fore and aft to every heave of the Atlantic swells. At Panama they embarked on the *Golden Age* for California, and after an uneventful voyage, arrived in San Francisco.

They lingered in the town only long enough for Jessie to order household equipment for the mining-camp cottage in the Mariposa. Her mental adjustment to another struggle with pioneer conditions had been made weeks before when she went to New York to dismantle the Ninth Street house. She had insisted upon going alone, telling Eliza that she wanted no one to witness her foolish tears at seeing her treasures carted off to a warehouse. And now in these heterogeneous San Francisco shops, her pioneer experience served her well.

BRET HARTE IN 1861

What looks like a "little bill" in the hands, is a glove — the position one assumed unconsciously in expostulating with the artist who wished me to have as a background the Pyramids of Cheops — with of course "40 Centuries looking down on me."

Bret Harte in 1861. From original given to Mrs. Frémont by Bret Harte.

Within two days her party and equipment were aboard a steamboat making its easy course up the river to Sacramento. Spring wagons took the party across the plains into the Sierra Nevada foothills and on to the village in Bear Valley, Mariposa County. The little mining town with its single street lined with a double row of saloons looked desolate enough, but the sheeting-partitioned bedrooms of the one hotel were clean and comfortable, and the supper of corned beef and flapjacks palatable.

Next morning as Frémont led Jessie up the hill toward the cottage they were to occupy, he was apologetic, remarking that the closer they approached, the smaller it seemed to become. This adobe cottage standing among the oaks was a challenge to any housewife's grit and resourcefulness, but Jessie Frémont, past mistress in facing contemporary experience full front, surveyed it calmly.

The large unpainted storehouse looked promising, but Frémont warned her that the smaller room must suffice for household supplies, the other having been preempted by Biddle Boggs. This lanky Pennsylvanian, whose services as handyman and watchman were invaluable, had a genial nature, proof against everything but trespass on his quarters. Jessie pondered long, her ears assailed by the unceasing hammering of stamps at the ore mill in the valley. She concluded that though the cottage had possibilities, their development must depend upon the cooperation of Mr. Boggs.

Later in the day as she sat on a log in perplexed study of her housing problem, she heard a low whistle, and upon looking up, saw the odd figure of a man standing before her. With his stooped shoulders, sparse yellow hair and beard, and deep-wrinkled skin, he might easily have arisen from beneath the dried-grass hummock near her. But his pale-blue eyes twinkled pleasantly, and he spoke in a comfortable drawl.

"I take it you're the Colonel's lady. I'm Biddle Boggs. Me mother was a Biddle and me father a Boggs, and there you have it. Do you reckon on me keepin' my quarters?"

With the aid of Boggs, Jessie soon transformed the cottage. Declaring that her lungs would fight back if she made them live with an airtight stove, she persuaded Boggs to build a fireplace in the dining room. She purchased a rose-trellised wallpaper to cover the canvas partitions which separated the floor space into bedrooms, and directed Boggs in the building of a lean-to kitchen.

After the cottage had been given a fresh coat of whitewash, Jessie promptly christened it the "White House," to the delight of the family and the mystification of Boggs, who opined: "Anybody can see it's white."

Once more Jessie was faced with the old Monterey problem of catering for a family with neither fresh meat nor fresh vegetables. Again with canned goods, rice, and beans, she was able to set palatable food before her family.

Jessie found the valley settlers' stories of the stealing of household supplies by the Indians highly exaggerated. A friendly attitude proved the best weapon against these practices. A group of squaws were wont to gather at noon under a tall pine which stood between the cottage and the storeroom. Here in the pause of fagot gathering, they solemnly awaited their daily handout. From one of them who spoke Spanish, Jessie learned that their favorite luncheon was a sandwich made of warm bread, suet, and turnip peelings. These dainties she faithfully provided.

Jessie now acquired a stout and highly temperamental Irish cook who came and went at pleasure, timing her days off to coincide with the dances in the neighboring mining towns. Dinner hour at the "White House" always found the family group augmented by the Howards and Charles Fox. On these evenings after violin, guitar, and voices had given her a musical treat, she confided to Frémont that this group of young people was highly exceptional for intelligence and gayety, and would be so considered anywhere.

While Jessie Frémont was gallantly adjusting herself to this return to pioneer living conditions, there awaited her a supreme test of fortitude. She thus related the experience:

One day Mr. Frémont's lawyer and his wife rode out to the ranch house. He left her sitting on her horse outside the gate and I went out to speak some polite word. She surprised me by saying that she was glad to see me in colors and cheerful again.

"Why not?" I asked. "I am very well now."

"Oh, so soon after your father's death —"

Mr. Frémont was beside me at once. "Is my father dead?" I asked. For answer he gathered me in his arms, and as I asked, "When?" I saw his tears.

Word had come to Frémont of Senator Benton's death on April 10 in a letter delivered to him at the mine a few days before. He had been trying to gather courage to break the news to Jessie, and now he reproached himself bitterly for this cowardice, adding: "I wish you need *never* have learned it."

Inured as Jessie was to shocks and grief, she found this final separation from her father a heart-breaking experience. Frémont's never-failing tact and tenderness supported her as always through the first bitter hour with its cries: "We've never been really separated before. It's the finality that kills me." When Eliza's letter came, revealing the sacrificing love back of that last smiling farewell, Jessie exclaimed: "His memory is for me to worship, not to weep over."

While Jessie was making her difficult adjustments, Frémont was working from dawn to dark at every kind of mine and mill labor and keeping a smiling courage under the constant menace of squatters' threats. Soon, however, the safety of the whole family was endangered by an outbreak at the mine. Early one morning there came a knock at the bedroom window and the words: "Colonel, the Hornitas League has jumped the Black Drift."

"What does that mean?" asked Jessie.

"Only mining work. You'd better go back to sleep." She promptly did so, having been spared knowledge of their real danger.

Ever since the confirmation of Frémont's land titles in '55, his original tract had been overrun by hordes of squatters who had used it as their own, tapping its gold veins, cutting its timber, using its forage for their animals, and making no offer of compensation, though the taxes on this property were running twenty thousand dollars annually.

The Black Drift, one of the richest veins, had that day been seized by a crowd of eager squatters who had bribed the night watchman to stay away from the open shaft long enough for them to enter and take possession under the new ruling as to the right of entering and holding an unoccupied claim. The entrances to two other mining shafts nearby were held by the mob. These mines, high on the mountainside, reached by narrow roads dropping down to the Merced River, were now an embattled scene.

Jessie bade the young people stay safely within the house until further word came from the mine, but Charles Fox slipped quietly out, saddled Lily's horse Ayah, dashed away over the hills, and found messengers who would ride to Stockton. From there the Governor himself sent militiamen who reached the mine to find Frémont and his little force of twenty men waiting for the first shot from the enemy. Under the leveled guns of the militiamen, the rabble dispersed. All this Jessie heard after a twenty-four hours' wait.

A few quiet weeks intervened; then a later siege was directed against the family. In Frémont's absence an eviction order signed "Dinis O'Brient, Prisident," came to Jessie, giving her twenty-four hours to move off the premises.

Leaving Boggs to act as watchman, Jessie called old Isaac, the hired man, to drive her and Lily to the Bear Valley inn. There she showed the landlord the eviction order and asked him to deliver the message to O'Brian that she would remain on her property, and if the house were burned, she would proceed to camp on the grounds. The innkeeper, impressed with her pluck, insisted that "Tom Benton's daughter" join him in a glass of wine before returning home.

That night the occupants of the "White House" slept under the guard of Biddle Boggs, their slumber broken by the detonations of exploding bombs made by powder in tin cans. After the trouble quieted, a committee of women living along the valley came riding in to thank the Colonel's wife for her courage in staying: "If you had been driven out, our hills would have run blood."

Lily and Nina were amused at the strange appearance of these women, all wearing their best dresses and hats, their hoopskirts lifted over the pommels of their saddles. Jessie, however, rebuked the girls for their want of understanding: "They did not care to wear dusty riding habits into a strange woman's parlor. You observed how pretty they looked as they sat talking."

With the mines working peacefully again, Jessie took renewed interest in plans for the development of the village, the building of a storage dam on the Merced, and the establishment of a smelting works.

Jessie's tenure of the "White House" held two memorable visits, both of which called out all her reserves as hostess. Early in '59 Horace Greeley came to California, and upon his arrival in San Francisco, sought out the Frémonts. Greeley had been a guest at many a dinner presided over by Jessie Frémont. Now with but three days' notice of his arrival, she replenished the larder, ordered a fresh supply of fragrant pine cones for the fireplace, then turned to a critical survey of the family wardrobe.

The better parts of two cashmere dresses, rather the worse for wear, served to make one for herself. Several white jaconet underskirts were combined to make new dresses for Lily and Nina. A linen dress shirt of Frémont's was cut down for Charley, who protested hotly at not being allowed to keep on his red-flannel shirt and overalls "for the *Tribune*." Three days of flying needles produced new and prideful garments.

These efforts met due reward from the observant *Tribune* editor. As Greeley sat beside the fire that first evening, listening to the young quartette sing Spanish love songs to the soft strumming of guitars, he turned to his host, saying:

I was prepared for your enormous development here and seeing you in good health from successful work, but I expected to see Jessie Anne a worn, if not a resigned little recluse, living on bacon and greens. What I see is French frills and blue sash ribbons, and what I eat is good rolls and French made-dishes.

The ever-blunt Lily's word of explanation was stopped in midflight by a look from her mother, whose smile still held the eye of the speaker as he ejaculated: "Well, you have executive faculty. My wife has none." After his departure, Jessie explained to the puzzled and offended Lily: "It is sufficient, my dear, that others see the results. The process of an achievement in economy is likely to prove boring to all but the one who accomplishes it." Later when a marked copy of the *Tribune* arrived with Greeley's reference to Frémont and his tribute to Jessie, she said: "You see, my girls, our petticoat contrivances would have looked foolish spread over the pages of the *Tribune*."

The visit of Richard H. Dana was another red-letter day over which to dream when the young people were off on the mountain trails and Jessie sat alone. This young explorer was at the time collecting material which appeared in a subsequent and enlarged edition of his *Two Years Before the Mast*. Jessie was amused at Dana's remark: "This country is full of Colonels, but when people speak of *the* Colonel, they mean Frémont."

Cleverly as she continued to embroider the dull days of her exile, happily as she entered into the carefree life of the young people, Jessie failed to deceive her husband as to the irksomeness of this complete isolation from her wonted mode of life. Though Frémont was apparently absorbed with hard work in the open, his daily fare made piquant with the spice of danger, yet he noted

Thomas Starr King. Preacher and patriot, 1861.

his wife's pallor, her restlessness, and the abstraction of her gaze when she thought herself unobserved.

He resolved to act upon a plan long forming in his mind. One morning after a solid week of dust storms when the wind blew a hot blast that forced the closing of windows and blinds against it, when the thud of the stamp mill seemed to fall directly on one's brain, Frémont asked Jessie to go with him to San Francisco.

They drove to Stockton, and from there went by steamboat to the city. Dreaming of the cool breeze off the Bay, Jessie endured the blistering heat and suffocating dust of the mountain drive. Upon arrival in San Francisco, she exclaimed as always at "the tonic quality of the air" and regretted that they were not staying a week. "How would you consider a lifetime, madame?" Frémont demanded. Then he told her of his recent purchase, subject to her approval, of a homesite to which he pointed as he spoke, a small headland jutting out into the channel entrance of the harbor, in fact, directly opposite the Golden Gate, affording an unbroken view westward to the Pacific and eastward toward the mountains of Contra Costa.

Within an hour the two stood on this hundred-foot bluff, called Black Point because of its dense growth of mountain laurel. Below its summit sat a rambling house, protected from the wind but not cheated of the view to east or west. A short mile off lay the Island of Alcatraz with its revolving lights and its battery of Columbiads. Frémont explained:

Here are the three things we have always held as requirements for a home: the sound of the sea, a view, and a gentle climate. I can get the twelve acres from Mark Brumagim, the banker, for forty-two thousand dollars. It shall be in your name to have and to hold for your heirs forever.

In describing this scene later, Jessie said:

So swift moving is Fancy's brush that even as he spoke, I saw myself walking along the glassed-in corridor connecting the house Virginia fashion with the outside kitchen and the servants' quarters and glancing out at the La Marque roses already climbing its roof.

While Frémont concluded the details of the purchase, they stayed at the Union Hotel, and here Jessie remained while her husband superintended the family's move from Bear Valley. Within a month of its purchase, the house at Black Point was scarcely recognizable, so swift were the changes under Jessie's executive genius. She had even achieved a "sunset bench" overlooking the water and protected from the wind by a vine-covered trellis. In referring to the little estate, she said:

The flapping of sails, the swearing of ship captains came in our quiet parlor as distinctly as the lapping of the waves, for the channel is narrow and strong between our point and the Island of Alcatraz only a mile off. The revolving light made my night light. I loved this sea home so much that I had joy even in the tolling of the fogbell.

She who had seen Washington but a small town, St. Louis a French village, and San Francisco only barren hills could take this spot and here set her roots happily. She yielded her weary body to the comforts of her home and her mind to the stimulating contacts of friends old and new.

Her first callers were her neighbors, Leonidas Haskell and his wife. They had sailed from Gloucester, Massachusetts, in '49 on the clipper ship *Morning Light*, which also brought their small yacht the *Restless*. Jessie found Mrs. Haskell, with her cultured manner and her knowledge of music, a rare companion, but her greatest pleasure came from the ten-year-old daughter Nellie, a shy sensitive child to whom she was drawn from the hour they met and exchanged ideas on gardening.

One morning Nellie came and asked to hear the story of *Il Trovatore*. "I want to think about it tonight while you and mother are hearing it." Then bursting into tears, she said: "The seats are full, but I'm not very big. Couldn't I sit on the floor by you?"

The Frémonts had a box at the opera house for that night's all-star performance. Lily, who had shown little interest, now remarked that she would rather sit at home than in a stuffy theater. Whereupon Jessie wrote a note and sent her visitor home with it. That night Nellie Haskell sat close beside Mrs. Frémont. When Manrico sang to Lenore,

Now with my life fulfilling
Love's fervent vows to thee,

Nellie gazed up adoringly at the author of her happiness.

[229]

As Jessie watched that eager young face, glad to have given pleasure to a music-loving child, she little dreamed that here was being formed one of the closest and most enduring relationships of her life. As Nellie said goodnight, she whispered: "Will Miss Lily care if I love you as much as I like?" Upon being reassured, she trotted happily home with her mother.

Nellie Haskell soon joined the schoolroom group which studied four hours daily under Mrs. Frémont's tutelage. Jessie taught her new songs and opened to her realms of poetry and the classics, even as she catered to the fact-seeking literalness of eighteen-year-old Lily. Her comment to her husband was: "Lily assimilates only the tiniest bites of verse; the rest remains an undigested mass in her memory." Of Nellie she averred: "She absorbs poetry, and her reading of it becomes a picture in sound."

One Sunday morning the Frémonts went to hear the new Unitarian minister, Thomas Starr King, just out from the Hollis Street Church in Boston. Jessie was not at all impressed with the frail beardless youth, whose painful thinness was scarcely disguised by his ministerial robe and whose lank yellow hair hung nearly to his shoulders. But once under the spell of those dark luminous eyes and a voice singularly deep and rich, she forgot everything but his eloquence as he pleaded for a liberal Christianity as a positive faith. After service she expressed her appreciation and asked the Kings to dinner the following evening.

This she later described as "an enchanting evening." She took her guests to the sunset bench, and as King looked off over the Bay, he said: "You must call your house the Porter's Lodge near the Golden Gate your husband named."

"Thus you have christened it," she replied.

At dinner Starr King confessed his reasons for having come West:

I thought it unfaithful to huddle so closely round the cozy stove of Blessed Boston, and I wished to go out into the cold and see if I were good for anything. I do feel, however, that my size tells against me here in a land of big trees, big waterfalls, and big vegetables.

This cultured and eloquent youth, who in Boston had been called the only rival of Theodore Parker, embodied the type of Jessie's own broad humanitarian religion. Already charmed with his earnestness, she was now delighted with his humor when he said: "Before our friendship progresses farther, let me ask: Do you think it sacrilegious for a man constitutionally hilarious to become a minister?" From the first they disagreed upon many things hilariously, among them the physical aspects of the city. To her declaration, "I love its every sand dune," he exclaimed: "What a vast struggle of houses over these hills! And the streets simply bilious with Chinamen." Upon returning from a lecture tour through the mining camps, he reported: "I never knew the exhilaration of public speaking until I faced a front row of revolvers and bowie knives."

Since his popularity robbed him of all privacy at home, he soon preempted a quiet corner at the far end of the Frémont grounds. Here he came to work in solitude upon those eloquent appeals for the preservation of the Union and the abolition of slavery, which made his later fame. At noon Jessie would send a servant out to him with a bowl of broth and a few biscuits. When the lecture was finished, he would consent to share the tea hour with Jessie, and then she became his dress-rehearsal audience.

So pleased was King with her services as reader and critic that he asked permission to bring out a young man, Bret Harte, who wrote well but who was greatly discouraged about his writing ability. The next Sunday after church, King appeared with young Harte in tow. Tall, handsome, with regular features and a firm well-rounded chin, he made instant impression on the Frémonts.

Under the interested questioning of Jessie, Harte recounted his experiences in California. He had learned the printer's trade in the office of the *Humboldt Times* and was now setting type in the office of the *Golden Era*. Under Jessie's encouragement, Harte later brought her a sheaf of his writings. He admitted he was thoroughly discouraged over his literary future. Sensing his need of a sympathetic audience, Jessie had him read aloud to her and King. From the wealth of her own background she gave generously of a wise and sometimes sharp criticism. She told him he had two dangerous gifts, grotesquerie and irony. "Don't ride them too hard. It will tell on your heart."

In reporting this to King, Harte said: "Sometimes her comments cut like a lash, but her praise is sincere and freely given. To know her is a liberal education."

Frémont said of these meetings: "When we heard the two talking together, their low well-modulated voices rising and falling, it was beautiful. When

[231]

to them was added the deep and vibrant tone of King's voice, it was a trio as good as music."

The Frémonts' house became a second home to Harte. He talked horses to Lily, and when she bought a beautiful Californian mare, Harte promptly suggested the name Chiquita, "little sweetheart," much to the owner's delight. She little dreamed that her beautiful horse would later become celebrated in Harte's poem *Chiquita*.

One Sunday morning Harte appeared in a state of such dejection that Jessie insisted upon knowing the cause. He was badly in need of money; yet he declared that he longed to live like Nebuchadnezzar on grass and write as he wished. "But alas!" he added. "I write so slowly and with such prodigious labor that mealtime would come before I could earn even that, I fear."

Falling in with his mood, she replied: "I can see how succulent grass spread with buttercups might be good spring food for a poet, but your genius must be sustained by a diet of security. Come tomorrow. Perhaps I'll have news for you."

She was expecting a visit from her old friend, Fitzhugh Beale, now a General and head of the coast survey. When he heard her plea, he said: "So you think a young poet who obviously hates business will make a good Government employee?"

"No, General, but I think a poet's mind quite capable of applying itself to earning its freedom. If Mr. Harte takes a Government position, he will fill it creditably, never fear." This declaration of faith was effective, for on the following Sunday Jessie's melancholy young visitor was told of his appointment to a minor position in the Federal Surveyor's office. Too overcome to do more than murmur his thanks, he applied himself to his dinner and afterward brought out new sketches for her criticism.

The next day she received this note from him addressed "Fairy Godmother": "Though I doubt not that spring grass spread with buttercups would be satisfying food at your hands, this appointment enables me to bite into the good wheaten loaf of independence." Thereafter Bret Harte always referred to Mrs. Frémont as Fairy Godmother. Later when a change of administration threatened his security and Jessie again intervened, he wrote:

I shall no longer disquiet myself about changes in administration or any-

thing else, for I believe that if I were cast upon a desert island, a savage would come to me next morning and hand me a three-cornered note to say that I had been appointed Governor at Mrs. Frémont's request at twenty-four hundred dollars a year.

With the war clouds gathering between the North and the South, the Sunday discussions soon became a political round-table, with Leonidas Haskell, Senator Edward D. Baker of Oregon, and Joe Lawrence of the *Golden Era* present. Of these conferences Harte said: "Politics was their meat. I sat back and listened to Mrs. Frémont's stories of Benton and the old Washington that were better than a play."

For weeks King had been working over his lecture of *The Union*. In listening to parts of it, Jessie had suggested: "No quarter when touching secession!" On the night of King's lecture, Platt's Hall, which seated a thousand hearers, was packed to the doors, with hundreds turned away. For two hours King's golden voice and inspired face swayed the throng as he wished. "Secession, concession, and Calhoun" he flayed alive. He pledged California to "a Northern republic, to a flag that should have no treacherous threads of cotton in its warp." The audience applauded to the echo and pledged themselves to support the Union.

In the autumn of 1860 Senator Baker on a hurried trip out from Washington reported to the Frémonts a conference with President-elect Lincoln and William H. Seward, whom he had chosen for Secretary of State. Seward had suggested Frémont for Secretary of War, and Lincoln was considering him as Minister to France. These official intimations failed to excite Frémont. His career in politics had carried many whiplash stings; his Army service had involved the broadside of a court-martial. He had no desire to return to political life. Moreover, his mines were in need of further development, having reached the "inevitable" stage where the amount poured into them about equaled the amount taken out.

Turning to Jessie, he asked: "And what do you wish?"

"Above all, to stay here where I have taken root along with my rose bushes; otherwise, to do what you think best."

With that pronouncement, Frémont asked the Senator to report to Lincoln that in the event of war he was willing to serve wherever placed. It is needless to speculate as to the result if Frémont had secured either of the posts contemplated, but there can be little doubt as to the manner in which Jessie Frémont would have graced her position as wife of the American Minister to France. Her disciplined mind, the tact born of a kind heart, her graciousness, her gayety and good humor, all these qualities would have shone at their best among the French whom she instinctively understood and loved. Jessie Frémont had presided over a salon in a two-room adobe lighted by tapers in tin holders, and at a whitewashed cabin within the sound of a thudding stamp mill. In view of her later sorrows it seems an essentially cruel fate that refused her this respite to exercise her special qualities within a worthy setting.

She was now told of Frémont's financial problem and his decision to dispose of half the mining property in order to secure funds to develop the remainder. He and his attorney, Frederick Billings, planned a quick trip to Paris to negotiate a sale. He insisted that Jessie accompany him, but she was destined to remain behind.

One Sunday morning her horses bolted on Russian Hill, the pole of the carriage broke, and she and Lily were thrown out. Since her injuries, though not serious, would delay departure, she begged Frémont to hasten on without her and return the sooner. Reluctantly he departed, leaving her to the care of efficient Lily and the small devotee, Nellie Haskell.

Jessie was touched by the notes and flowers with which Bret Harte announced his visits. One day at the hour she expected him, there came instead a packet containing his photograph. On it was written:

What looks like a little bill in the hands is a glove.... The position, one assumed unconsciously in expostulating with the artist, who wished me to have as background the Pyramids of Cheops with, of course,"forty centuries looking down on me."

Late in February Jessie received a letter from Frémont recounting an interview with Lincoln at the Astor House. The President-elect was on his way to Washington and seemed to have no doubt that war would be averted. Frémont added a postscript: "With the inflammatory press and inflammatory conversation on every hand, I am convinced that actual war is not far off."

On April 13, 1861, the storm burst with the bombardment of Fort Sumter in Charleston harbor and the hauling down of the flag in surrender to seceding rebels. When the echoes reached California and all hope of preserving peace had fled from the most optimistic minds, Jessie waited daily for whatever disquieting message might follow. It came soon. Postmaster-General Montgomery Blair had suggested that with Frémont's Southern birth and Western popularity, he should be appointed a Major-General of the regular Army and assigned to command of the Western Division with headquarters at St. Louis. Blair had said to Lincoln: "There is an elevation in his character that will endear him to the Army and the people."

Jessie was informed of the appointment and requested to meet her husband in New York. Upon inquiry she found she had just twelve days to complete plans for sailing. She rented her Black Point house to General Beale, dismissed the servants, and packed for the journey. She took her last walk through the garden alone. About to pluck a bouquet of her friendly violets, she decided they would not want to die at sea away from the sweet air and sandy soil. From her bench on the bluff she watched the sun drop behind the Golden Gate, little dreaming that she would never sit here again.

On the boat next day Starr King was the last to leave her. He stood at the door of her cabin, his arms filled with long-stemmed English violets from his own garden. He gave her these and a copy of Emerson's *Essays*, saying: "Smell, read, and rest."

Upon arrival in New York the family were met by Frémont and taken to Irving House. During hasty preparations for the move to St. Louis headquarters, Jessie was called upon by Dr. Bellows, president of the United States Sanitary Commission, to whom she and King had been sending money for hospital equipment.

Not until long afterward, when he and Mrs. Frémont had become friends and coworkers did Dr. Bellows show her the letter of King's, which read:

Have you met Mrs. Frémont? I hope so. Her husband I am very little acquainted with, but she is sublime, and carries guns enough to be formidable to a whole Cabinet; a she-Merrimac, thoroughly sheathed and carrying fire in the genuine Benton furnaces.

CHAPTER XV
Civil War Duty, Western Department

ESSIE Frémont's preparations for the removal to St. Louis were high-lighted by her husband's report of his interview with Lincoln. The President had carefully reviewed Frémont's plan of campaign, the clearance of rebels from Missouri, and a later movement down the Mississippi on Memphis. He had accompanied his guest to the White House steps, and upon Frémont's parting question as to instructions, he had said: "No, I have given you *carte blanche*. You must use your own judgment and do the best you can. I doubt if the states will ever come back."

On July 20, the day before the Frémonts departed for St. Louis, Jessie wrote a letter to Starr King:

My dear Mr. King: I wrote you a long letter two days ago and tore it up bodily—too much in it to run the risk of Missouri railroad riots or even the Gulf pirates. We will be on our way in another twenty-four hours. Lily and the boys and the silent bewildered Ellen, who has heretofore lived decently. Her breath leaves her at my pace and contempt for bonnet boxes. Everybody thinks we are going by Buffalo, but we take the only six-foot track in that line of travel (through Pennsylvania) and so will have a quiet travel all to ourselves. We have hardly had speech with each other; sometimes a word, sometimes only a look, but after the hungry yearning of far-off Black Point, it is enough....

On the journey westward Jessie learned that Leonidas Haskell was on his way overland to join Frémont's staff and that the Haskell family were en route by way of Panama for the old home in Gloucester, Massachusetts. Upon hearing this she exclaimed:

Now I can keep my promise to Nellie! With Charley weeping to be left on the Restless *with Eric, Nellie weeping to come with me, and Lily weeping into Chiquita's mane until Mr. Harte declared it ruined, I wept too and promised many things.*

As the train entered St. Louis, the sadly changed picture sent her into a chill of panic. Steamboats swung idly at their wharves, the streets were practically deserted, a Confederate flag flew from secessionist headquarters, and business houses stood gloomily behind their iron shutters. She who had so often "smelled" her beloved home before she caught sight of it, now looked out upon a frowning, hostile city, the old Missouri friends gone secessionward. As they drove to the Brant home, their horses' hoofs rang loud and harsh along the quiet streets.

Jessie's feeling of forlornness was lightened when she was met at the door by the old negro butler, Uncle Vincent. He conveyed Mrs. Brant's instructions, sent from Paris, that Frémont was to use the place as he saw fit. This house, standing within spacious grounds, bounded by three wide streets, was ideal for staff headquarters.

After a night's rest, Jessie established the family in a far suite on the third floor with private access to the grounds. She directed the removal of unnecessary furnishings from the second-floor rooms, which were turned into officers' quarters. Soon the French tapestry carpets were covered with canvas, and family portraits gave way to maps and reports; with the help of young John Howard, jubilant over his opportunity to serve Frémont as secretary, the office equipment was soon in place.

Far down the hall in a window embrasure was her own desk, and here she instructed young Howard: "Bring me any work you think within my capacity to do." And work there was in plenty, for Frémont had arrived in St. Louis to face conditions so critical as to appall the stoutest hearted and to stagger the keenest executive mind.

Governor Claiborne Jackson of Missouri and his official following were in full control of the state's Southern-bred and Southern-sympathizing population. Opposed to the Governor was the doughty Union-element leader,

Frank P. Blair Jr. While Blair and Captain Nathaniel Lyon had prevented the rebels from seizing the St. Louis arsenal and had later met Governor Jackson's Confederate militia at Booneville and put them to flight, they were now in fear of a growing force of bold Confederates who might sweep Southern Missouri, seize the key point Cairo, and carry already wavering Kentucky into the Confederacy.

Upon Frémont's arrival he found rebel camps already honeycombing the state and hundreds of young pro-slavery men aligned with the Confederate forces. There had been a skirmish at Carthage between these rebels under General Price and the Federal forces under General Franz Sigel.

The battle of Bull Run had strengthened local Confederate numbers and fired Confederate hopes. Before Frémont could properly survey the situation, he was faced with the challenging task of turning river boats into gunboats, collecting an army, and distributing munitions, clothing, and general equipment. Proper requisitions of blankets, tents, uniforms, and shoes became a major problem, because the administration a thousand miles away was desperately trying to equip the armies of Virginia where the principal fighting danger lay. In the training of recruits Frémont was aided by loyal German and Hungarian cavalry officers, among them Major Charles Zagonyi, who formed a battalion called the Zagonyi Guard, mustered in for three years of service. Frémont had as efficient chief-of-staff General Alexander Asboth, a Hungarian patriot of distinguished service in the Revolt of '48; as topographical engineer Colonel John Fiala; and as Judge-Advocate of the Department R. R. Corwin, a distinguished lawyer from Cincinnati.

Jessie Frémont also faced disheartening problems. The Sanitary Commission, recently organized, had not begun to function this far west, and upon her first visit to the hospital at Jefferson Barracks, she found the patients suffering shocking neglect from lack of proper equipment and from the inadequate number of nurses and orderlies. She went personally to solicit food and clothing in hostile shops. Sometimes she was spoken to roughly, but more often she was given supplies with the grudging comment that they were given to Tom Benton's daughter and not to the wife of the Yankee General.

Now came a letter from the philanthropist and social worker, Miss Dorothy Dix, who had just been appointed Superintendent of Women Nurses. Miss Dix's qualifications for this task lay in her international success in establishing almshouses and hospitals for the indigent insane in this country and England.

Upon Miss Dix's arrival in St. Louis, Jessie arranged for her to lodge near headquarters, and together these two attacked the local hospital problem. At Jefferson Barracks they found the overworked orderlies passing among the fever patients and putting the bread, coffee cup, and slice of salt pork on the chests of those too weak to help themselves. Jessie showed Miss Dix the windows, shaded with blue blinds which she herself had supplied but a few days before to shut out the sun that blazed down into the eyes of sick and dying men.

Under Miss Dix's authority, proper supplies were ordered, and Jessie was set to organizing circles for knitting, scraping of lint, and the countless other tasks done in the homes by the women of that war. Jessie's greatest difficulty was to find housewives willing to open their homes for Union service, but patriotic Germans set the pace, carrying their knitting with them openly in the street.

Lily joined one of these circles, and Jessie tried valiantly to teach her to knit, expecting improvement under the stimulus of patriotic fervor. Having watched her daughter's cramped and roughened fingers awkwardly handling the needles, she hadn't the heart to criticize the result when Lily appeared with a dozen pairs of socks neatly stacked for delivery to the matron in charge of forwarding supplies to soldiers. Nor did she smile when Lily reported the matron's remark that the socks would have to be sent to the hospital for use of men who had lost a leg, since no two socks were alike in size or length.

Yet another facet of Jessie Frémont's character came to view in the argument with Miss Dix over the matter of volunteer nurses. Miss Dix was a spinster nearing sixty, and her plan to accept only "settled and moral" women as nurses caused her to reject the proffered services of many a young woman Jessie thought highly suitable. One day when half a dozen strong and pretty girls had been turned away after questions which Jessie thought irrelevant, she protested: "Since our need is so great, why do you refuse these young women?"

Miss Dix replied tartly: "Would you have *no* moral standards, Mrs. Frémont?"

[239]

"Standards, yes," Jessie replied with spirit, "but surely in this crisis strong hands and a desire to serve make up for a lack of experience. And as to morals, you and I have both observed that the hand of female virtue often has chilly fingertips."

For an instant only did Miss Dix hesitate. Then with a grudging "Perhaps you are right," the incident was closed. The effect was noticeable, however, in a more generous attitude toward the young applicants who appeared before Miss Dix's departure for Washington.

The variety of burdensome duties that fell upon Jessie Frémont's shoulders would have crushed a less buoyant spirit. These duties ranged from the care of hospital patients to the collecting of food and uniforms for the struggling bands of Union volunteers arriving daily. She directed the packing of extra supplies to be sent to the sick in the forces of General Lyon at Springfield and to General Prentiss at Cairo, many of whose men were dying of fever and dysentery.

In answer to appeals for reinforcements from both these Generals, Frémont, aware of the week's march to reach Springfield, had ordered General Lyon to fall back on his base. He himself chartered steamboats and went down the river with a force of four thousand men to the relief of General Prentiss. At what labor this feat of raising and transporting the troops was accomplished, no one knew better than Jessie Frémont, who saw her husband retire after midnight and arise at five each morning. On the day of his departure he went to his desk at four thirty in the morning where he worked steadily until time for the flotilla to leave at three in the afternoon.

Meanwhile General Lyon had not retreated to base but had moved to attack a Confederate force of twice his numbers. In a fierce battle in which he acted with conspicuous bravery, General Lyon fell with a bullet in his breast. Soon thereafter his surviving officers ordered a retreat. Lyon's body was sent to St. Louis, and it became Mrs. Frémont's duty to superintend the arrangements for the body to lie at headquarters before being shipped home by boat. She had a side porch draped with flags, and she herself placed the flowers that covered the casket as it lay in state. A squadron of cavalry formed an escort for the body to the boat. As Jessie stood pale and red eyed, she answered young Howard's pitying protest at her exhaustion: "No, I am glad to have done a small service in this 'soldiers' farewell' to a good soldier."

Jessie Benton Frémont, 1861.

The next evening she returned from the barracks hospital and announced: "I wrote six letters today to break the hearts of mothers. On top of yesterday it has thrown me into a panic. I could never condemn a deserter to death, for I know too well that impulse."

Frémont had arrived in Cairo in the nick of time. He had not only saved the day there but had rescued many a dying soldier by having him transferred to the ship deck, thus inaugurating the use of flotilla hospitals.

The first brutally unfair criticism of Frémont was that he should have sent relief to General Lyon instead of ordering his retreat. Other criticisms were that he had a foreign guard, though loyal foreigners were in regiments all over the East, and that he placed a reception officer before his door for the weeding-out and warding-off service. This precaution was a matter of course in the East, but here the doughty descendants of Colonel Benton's porch-crowded conferences resented having to state their business as "an aristocratic barrier," and they complained that upon gaining entrance, they found a harassed and preoccupied General.

These complaints and the reports of extravagance in reorganization and enlargement of the city reserve corps were avidly seized upon by secessionist correspondents to the Eastern press, especially after Frémont had stopped Confederate recruiting, which had been openly carried on at the Berthold mansion. Another telling item for the secessionist correspondents was that Frémont's headquarters were luxurious, with rich carpets and furniture. The reporters ignored the fact that the furniture and carpets were covered with brown drilling and that the practicality of the large rooms lay in their ability to house the Departmental activities under one roof.

Whether or not an officer of the highest executive ability, which General Frémont admittedly was not, could have successfully coped with the difficulties that beset him is a question for debate. The evaluation of men and events, seen in perspective, is comparatively simple. The quality of imagination necessary to visualize the struggling actor and his problems is rare, and when found, is not likely to foster harsh judgment.

Missouri was a hotbed of secession, and only ten thousand men were under arms. The problem of raising and equipping an army was complicated by the chaotic conditions at Eastern supply points. The extent of the Western Department delayed the issuance and the execution of orders. Mistakes of subordinates were popularly credited to the General and his immediate staff.

With the horrors of Bull Run in immediate memory, Frémont had taken command fully determined not to move forward until properly equipped. The clamor of criticism with its catchwords, "delayed preparedness, extravagance, and irregularity in letting contracts," now grew louder, for to it was added the disappointed cry of the profiteers in mules, horses, and beef, with whom Leonidas Haskell of the Commissary refused to deal. General Frémont, aware of but undeterred by this clamor which extended to the Capitol itself, drove his steel-braced frame twenty hours a day and worked his helpers, including Jessie, into a coma of exhaustion.

Frémont's own moments of discouragement were not lightened by the foreknowledge that his "extravagant" gunboat flotilla with Captain Foote as commander would later do splendid service for Grant at Fort Donelson and at Fort Henry on the Mississippi, nor that the "extravagance" of placing forts at St. Louis and other important points to be held by a small garrison, releasing forces for field work, would later become a military policy from St. Louis to the Eastern seaboard. Nor could he foresee that his "extravagant" Union station at the river bank, insuring safe and rapid convoy for countless troops, would later in the war become a matter of approval in official circles. The "extravagant display" of marching and countermarching a small force of thirty-eight hundred men through the streets before embarking, which spread the report ahead that his force approaching Cairo was ten thousand, was later to be generally practiced as good tactics.

The descendants of Frémont's most violent detractors were later to approve the act which above all others was to work his undoing on that fatal Western front. With forty thousand Missouri rebels overrunning the countryside, seizing horses, food, and clothing from Union citizens; with rebel guerrillas burning bridges, wrecking trains, and attacking exposed Union units; with loyal families forced to become penniless refugees in Illinois and Iowa, drastic measures for control of the state became necessary.

The measure decided upon was not taken without due consultation with both the radical and the conservative wings of the Union party. There can be no question that Frémont's own love of the Union and his hatred of slavery inclined him to listen more closely to the radicals who said:

The South has seceded. The secessionist has forfeited his right to protection for his home or property. The local secessionists are responsible for the wiping out of peaceful Union homes and the killing of peaceable Union citizens in guerrilla outbreaks. Only the stern measure, confiscation of the property of men in arms against the Union, will serve in this crisis.

On August 28, Frémont called Jessie in consultation with the staff officers, John A. Gurley and Owen Lovejoy, on the matter of a proposed proclamation. This would place Missouri under martial law, so that secessionists under arms would be arrested and the property of all persons taking active part with the enemies in the field would be confiscated to public use, and their slaves, if any, declared free men. Frémont said that he wanted his wife to understand fully the background for this decision and its dangerous implications. He reviewed the entire situation, then left further discussion to Gurley and Lovejoy. The result of this conference, Jessie afterward said, was "the conviction of us all that no other course was possible in Missouri under existing conditions."

At daybreak two days later (August 30, 1861) Jessie was called and requested to meet Frémont at his desk. There she also met Edward Davis of Philadelphia. Turning to them, Frémont said: "I want you two, but no others." Then he read to them the first emancipation order that gave freedom to the slaves of rebels.

Davis said: "Mr. Seward will never allow this. He intends to wear down the South by steady pressure, not by blows, and then make himself the arbitrator." To this Frémont replied:

It is for the North to say what it will or will not allow, and whether it will arbitrate or whether it will fight. The time has come for decisive action. This is a war measure, and as such I make it. I have been given full power to crush rebellion in this Department, and I will bring the penalties of rebellion home to every man striving against the Union.

The proclamation was published at once and was followed by such shouts of acclaim from the anti-slavery elements of the nation as to drown the ominous roar of the approaching storm from Washington. So right did this proclamation procedure seem to Jessie Frémont that she went calmly about her duties, hearing only occasional reports from young Howard busy with the drawing up of papers for the commission for taking evidence. He reported to her that one especially turbulent secessionist had been tried and his two slaves given manumission papers.

Far-seeing Northerners had for long been demanding the freeing of the slaves. The abolitionists had even predicted in open letters that if the President would proclaim the liberation of the slaves, the war would end in thirty days. The *Tribune* had boldly announced that "handling traitors with kid gloves is not the way to subdue them."

To the General's wife the "subduing" of rebel Missourians was now a possibility. Among the sheaves of approving telegrams, the most encouraging came from Secretary of War Simon Cameron, who, ill at home, declared himself ready with his endorsement as soon as he could return to his desk.

This act, soon to be the chief cause of Frémont's removal, sounded the keynote to which the whole North and later the nation were attuned by the strain of unsuccessful war. While Frémont's name was ringing as the great anti-slavery crusader, President Lincoln, patiently thinking things out in Washington, was grieved at the applause from his own state and shocked at this precipitation so likely to alienate hopelessly the wavering Kentuckians. Lincoln wrote an earnest plea for modification of the slave-freeing clause and sent it to Frémont by personal messenger.

Shortly after the issuance of the proclamation, Jessie Frémont was called to welcome John Hay, just arrived from Washington. This bright-eyed, ruddy-cheeked youth, one of Lincoln's private secretaries, had brought to Frémont Lincoln's plea, a kindly letter asking him to modify that part of the proclamation touching the freeing of slaves. The note ended thus: "This letter is written in a spirit of caution, not of censure. I send it by special messenger in order that it may certainly and speedily reach you."

While Jessie Frémont had no part in the reply which Frémont sent to Lincoln, refusing to modify the slave-freeing clause, no one understood better than she his reasons for refusal. She herself had witnessed the almost instant effect of the proclamation in restoring a semblance of order and decency among the secessionist population of the city. While the beleaguered Union citizens applauded and held up their heads again, the Southern sympathizers with their property endangered became far less noisy in declaring their "principles." Furthermore she had seen a brief ironing out of those lines cutting deeper daily into the thin cheeks of her husband. Before Hay's departure she made a copy of Frémont's reply to Lincoln, which read:

If upon reflection your better judgment still decides that I am wrong in the article respecting the liberation of the slaves, I have to ask that you open-ly direct me to make the correction. The implied censure will be received as a soldier always should receive the reprimand of his chief. If I were to retract of my own accord, it would imply that I myself thought it wrong and that I had acted without the reflection which the gravity of the point demanded. But I did not. I acted with full deliberation and upon the certain conviction that it was a measure right and necessary, and I think so still.

The delivery of Frémont's letter to the President, Lincoln's open order for modification, Frémont's break with the Blairs due to Frank's desire to keep his hand on the helm in Missouri, Blair's garbled reports to Lincoln concerning conditions he was supposed to have surveyed—all these elements entered into the later removal of General Frémont from his command in the West and his being pocketed in Virginia.

Jessie Frémont's intimate part in these stressful and humiliating experiences was due to her lifelong close relationship with the Blairs and to her certainty that the long course of blocking which thwarted Frémont at every point was the direct result of their machinations. Like many aggressive families, the Blairs often clashed among themselves but stood as one against an enemy. In the South Jessie had often heard it said of them: "When the Blairs go in for a fight, they go in for a funeral." They considered Missouri their political meat in Frank Blair's Presidential plans, and they intended that no one should be in power independent of them. They had often told Jessie they favored the appointment of Frémont as "being in the family."

Jessie Frémont blamed herself for not having realized in those Frémont-Blair conferences upon her arrival in St. Louis that Frank as a political power in Missouri and Montgomery as Postmaster-General in Washington had expected the Western Department headquarters to be Blair headquarters, where any move inimical to immediate Blair interests might be checked at the source. At first Frank had been practically helpful in stating the need for money and equipment this long way from Washington. He had been wittily critical of Secretary of the Treasury Chase in his dilatory methods of granting

General John C. Frémont, 1861.

money, saying: "He has more horror of seeing treasury notes below par than of seeing soldiers killed."

The first break with the Blairs had come when Frémont objected to giving the contracts for supplies almost exclusively to friends of Frank Blair, who was busy building political fences while Frémont was building his army. Frank had appealed to Jessie to influence Frémont to relet a cancelled contract. She refused, saying that while she knew of her husband's activities, she had no hand in directing them. It was during this argument that Frank intimated that Frémont had best appreciate his indebtedness to the Blair influence. When Mr. Blair Sr., whom Jessie really loved, sent a letter exhorting Frémont to use his influence to have Frank made Militia-General of Missouri, Frémont was forced to refuse this bold request. From then on, it had been that worst of all feuds, a family feud.

Political ambition became a strongly myopic lens to investigating eyes when Montgomery Blair was sent to report on the Western Department and to advise with Frémont. Here again Frémont could not know that the perspective of time no later than 1864 would so disclose the character of the Blairs as to justify their own party leaders in calling them a menace and in having Montgomery removed from his seat in the Cabinet. Meanwhile amidst the turmoil of charge and countercharge, Frémont traversed his difficult course, even reading and filing without comment Montgomery Blair's harsh arraignment of him "for making emancipation a pivotal term."

Among General Frémont's many significant though unapproved acts was the appointment of the unknown Brigadier-General Ulysses S. Grant to command the troops of southeastern Illinois and Missouri. The appointment was against the earnest advice of local regulars who urged that General John Pope be sent to the danger zone at Cairo. Frémont argued that as a West Pointer who had seen service in the Mexican War, and as a Captain who had been chosen by the Illinois delegation in Congress for the position of Brigadier-General, Grant was highly suitable for the post. The appointment stood, with all its later justification in Grant's Cairo victory.

Meanwhile Frémont wrote a letter to President Lincoln with a statement of the situation and an outline of his future plan. The problem was to get it safely into the President's hands. With Jessie's first-hand knowledge of the bitterness of the Blairs and of the present implications of speedy disaster to

Frémont, she was prompted to take the only course which seemed possible. She proposed going herself to Washington to deliver in person the letter upon which so much was at stake.

To her such an enterprise held no unusual features. Washington was her home; the White House the home of a man who had showed himself a wise and kindly friend. Lincoln had lent his ear to the shrewd and designing Blairs, Frémont's enemies still posing as friends "fearful of his failure." As one closely familiar with the acts of these men, she believed herself a suitable as well as a trustworthy messenger. To feel the essential rightness of her position was to act, thinking of herself not as the wife of an ill-treated officer approaching the President to protest in his behalf, but as messenger from a man of unimpeachable integrity, laboring under intolerable conditions, whose letter was written to the only man to whom he could speak.

On September 8, Jessie Frémont arose early, made her hospital rounds, packed a bag, and took the train for Washington, accompanied by her maid. For two days and nights she sat up in an overcrowded car, subsisting on tea and biscuits.

Arriving in Washington at eight thirty in the evening, she went direct to Willard's Hotel where by prearrangement she was to meet Frémont's friend, Judge Edward Coles of New York. She had intended greeting him and then retiring for a bath and a night's rest, but realizing there would be no rest for her until an appointment was made with the President, she sent a messenger to the White House, asking when she might deliver a letter to Mr. Lincoln. The messenger returned with a card upon which was written: "Now, at once. A. Lincoln." Though it was nearly nine o'clock, she went, accompanied by Judge Coles. In reporting this meeting, she said:

We were asked into the usual receiving room, the Red Room....After some little waiting, the President came in from the dining room by the farther door, leaving the door partly open. As he crossed the room, that door was a little more widely set open.

I introduced Judge Coles, who then stepped into the doorway leading to the Blue Room—we were just by it—and there he remained, walking to and fro, keeping in sight and hearing, just within range of the doorway. For he was struck at once as I was by the President's manner, which was hard, and the tones of his voice were repelling. Nor did he offer me a seat. He talked standing, and both voice and manner made the impression that I was to be got rid of briefly.

I afterward told over this interview to friends. It was clear to Judge Coles as to myself that the President's mind was made up against General Frémont and decidedly against me.

Briefly in answer to his "Well," I explained that the General wished so much to have his attention to the letter sent that I had brought it to make sure it would reach him.

He answered not to that, but to the subject his own mind was upon. "That it was war for a great national idea the Union, and that General Frémont should not have dragged the negro into it, that he never would if he had consulted with Frank Blair. I put Frank Blair there to advise him." *The words quoted are exactly those of the President. He first mentioned the Blairs in this astonishing connection.*

It was a parti-pris, *and as we walked back, Judge Coles, who had heard everything, said to me:* "This ends Frémont's part in the war. Seward and Montgomery Blair will see to that, and Lincoln does not seem to see the injustice, the wrong of receiving secret reports against him made by a man authorized to do so, but as everyone knows, with a mind often clouded by drink and always governed by personal motives."

The President said he would send me his answer the next day. The next day passed and nothing came from him. But Mr. Blair Sr. came and told me many things. I had known him always and liked him though Mr. Frémont did not. He was very angry with me for coming at all, for not letting Montgomery "manage things." He talked angrily and freely, as was natural, to one who had grown up to defer to him, and in his excitement uncovered the intentions of the administration regarding the protection of slavery.

That caused me to write note no. 2 to the President. The originals of these must have been in possession of the secretaries. I have copies which I kept for General Frémont. I confined my requests to asking for the promised letter no. 1 and for copies 2 of the charges against Mr. Frémont. In the President's answer he says: "Not hearing from me he had sent the answer by mail, and declined to give letters without the consent of the owners." *Yet he acted on them injuriously to the reputation of General Frémont.*

Jessie Benton Frémont: a Woman Who Made History

I did not risk a direct telegram to General Frémont, but through my English maid I sent a cipher telegram in her name to an operator at headquarters, a man we could trust, and in that way the General was fully warned against being trapped into any plans arrived at by a show of friendship from Postmaster Blair.

I returned immediately to St. Louis and found him [Frank] working to "modify" and reshape the General's course, but he had been "listened to only." My arrival ended all their attempts at concealing their real conduct.

There was no written record of that interview, nor was it referred to by President Lincoln himself for more than two years afterward. But the careful record made in pencil by Mrs. Frémont, along with copies of the notes exchanged between them, became a part of the family archives so that later garbled reports were merely absurd.

One comical version circulated by the Blairs intimated that in her rage Jessie had called the President "Abraham" and had "threatened and stamped her foot like a virago." This version is particularly amusing in view of the fact that even informally she referred to her father as Mr. Benton or Senator Benton and to her husband as Mr. Frémont, and that up to this the thirty-ninth year of her life she had never failed to address officials "native" and foreign by their proper titles. Certainly this occasion would not have prompted the first display of such vulgarities of speech or act as were reported.

After her return, harried and sleepless, Jessie worked with dogged persistence at the daily grind of helping distressed men, women, and children who expected miracles of the wife of the General.

On September 26 when she saw Frémont depart for the South, her mind held one sustaining thought: he would perform his duty as he saw it. Of the cumulative causes which shortly led Lincoln to decide upon Frémont's removal, she had but dim knowledge, but with the same courage which had supported her in other disasters, she faced that disclosed by Frémont's note from Tipton Camp, November 2:

I have just received the order relieving me of my command, directing me to turn it over to General Hunter. Get quietly ready for immediate departure from St. Louis. I shall leave this place forthwith for St. Louis.

J.C.F.

Through all Jessie Frémont's anguish over the humiliation connected with this brief note, she had a glimmer of relief. She knew that despite official bitterness and recrimination, the people at large held Frémont in the greatest trust and affection. This fact was to be speedily proved. While the family awaited his arrival, they watched the citizens putting flags at half mast and shouting anathemas against "the Blairs and all their works." On November 8, the city met General Frémont as one family, cheering wildly and welcoming him with bands of music. Again did Jessie see her husband "condemned" officially, only to be hailed as a hero by a united populace.

While those acquainted with the valuable side of Frémont's services in Missouri were denouncing the injustice of his removal, the North was proclaiming him as the first man to make the abolition of slavery a "practical" object of the war. The press reprinted Ben Wade's October letter to Frémont:

All your enemies have yet been able to do has not in the least shaken the unbounded confidence which the people have ever had in you. No greater misfortune could befall the country than that you should retire at this period.

Jessie filed this letter along with the manuscript poem sent to her by Whittier:

Thy error, Frémont, simply was to act
A brave man's part, without the statesman's tact,
And taking counsel but of common sense,
To strike at cause as well as consequence.
Oh, never yet since Roland wound his horn
At Roncesvalles has a blast been blown
Far-heard, wide-echoing, startling as thine own,
Heard from the van of Freedom's hope forlorn.

But Jessie Frémont needed no public acclaim, no stirring lines from a militant poet to sustain her faith. The hundred days in Missouri had left her with undaunted spirit, bearing as a crown upon her head the masses of gray hair which were the physical price of her own "hundred days."

Upon the Frémonts' return to New York, their apartments at the Astor House became open forum for the scores of prominent visitors who called to protest in person. Professor Stowe of Andover, William M. Evarts, and Henry Ward Beecher stayed talking far into the night. On the occasion of a Frémont mass meeting at Cooper Institute in November, the same men accompanied by Schuyler Colfax and the orator of the evening, Charles Sumner, returned to the Frémont rooms to "continue the mass meeting until morning dawned."

December saw the Frémonts in Washington, where the General was aiding the Western Department investigation, the findings of which were later to exonerate him. Jessie's friends rallied about her, commenting in private upon her "startling" gray hair and marveling at the good humor with which she met questions and comments. Among these friends was Dorothy Dix, who declared: "The name Jessie Frémont is held in love and reverence everywhere in the West."

When Judge Coles called upon Jessie and referred to her unfortunate experience at the White House, she remarked dryly: "Strange, isn't it, that when a man expresses a conviction fearlessly, he is reported as having made a trenchant and forceful statement, but when a woman speaks thus earnestly, she is reported as a lady who has lost her temper."

Her reaction toward further White House visits was soon to be tested, for in February she was invited to a ball at the Executive Mansion. In speaking of this experience later, she said:

It was announced officially that on account of the illness in the house, there would be no dancing, but the Marine Band at the foot of the steps filled the house with music while the boy lay dying above. A sadder face than that of the President I have rarely seen. He was receiving at the large door of the East Room, speaking to the people as they came but feeling so deeply that he spoke of what he felt and thought instead of welcoming the guests.

To General Frémont he at once said that his son was very ill and that he feared for the result. On seeing his sad face and grieved appearance, the feeling with which we had gone gave way to pity, and after expressing our hope for the lad's recovery, we passed on to make our respects to the President's wife. The ball was becoming a ghastly failure....

So many criticized the conduct of the war and regretted that the effort of four years before had not been successful, and there was so much feeeling of sorrow that General Frémont's policy of emancipation was not to be carried out, that it became embarrassing, and we left. I had hardly got my wraps on before we were recalled by Mr. Sumner, who came with a message from the President, saying that he wanted us to return, that he especially wanted General Frémont. As we crossed the long East Room, the President came forward to meet the General and took him by the arm, leading him to General McClellan, who was at the upper end of the room. He introduced them to each other, then introduced Mrs. McClellan and myself. We bowed, but as each seemed to wait for the other, neither of us spoke a single word. One look showed me she was dressed in the secession colors. A band of scarlet velvet crossed her white dress from shoulder to waist, and in her hair were three feathers of scarlet and white. If this was intentional, it was unpardonable in the wife of the Commander-in-Chief of the Union Armies, and yet it seemed impossible to have been quite an accident. After a few minutes' talk between the President, General McClellan, and General Frémont, we left.

Jessie now sent to her loyal friend, Starr King, the extra sheet of the *Tribune* with full text of Frémont's defense before the committee and their vote approving his administration of the Western Department and also an editorial declaring that no other commander in the war had been hectored and pursued with such malevolence. Her accompanying letter reveals the inner workings of her mind:

My dear Mr. King: You can fully realize my reactions as you read the inclosure, for you know how my very life depends upon him about whom every fiber of my being is entwined. To see him maligned, discouraged, and humiliated is to be struck down into the torment of utter darkness. My only prayer is that I escape the clouded vision and warped thinking that would render me useless to him. I do try to forgive our enemies but would find it easier to forget them! And I try above all not to brood, that outstanding vice of good women.

Be not solicitous for my health, dear friend. After all this sweating in rebellious agony, a sanguine vitality responds to my will. In that I am my father's daughter. You will recall that he lay within an hour of death, dictating from papers propped upon his chest.

As long as I can serve my Chief, I shall not die.

J.B.F.

CHAPTER XVI

"There Is a Time to Do and a Time to Stand Aside"

URING the early months of 1862, the same official critics who had flayed Frémont for his inability to raise an army of twenty thousand men, to feed and train it without supplies or arms, and then to march it to victory without adequate transportation, turned on Lincoln himself for being unable to produce out of a hat munitions for half a million men and to conjure up an adequate commissary. Badgered and burdened, "Down with Lincoln" ringing in his ears, the President struggled on, collecting arms and ammunition abroad. He swallowed his natural dislike of the irascible Edwin Stanton by making him Secretary of War in the hope that he could stir the snail-like Commander-in-Chief McClellan to action.

General Frémont had established his family in a cottage at Nahant, Massachusetts, and there he and Jessie awaited his promised commission, which came in March, 1862. He was ordered to the Mountain Department of West Virginia, and on March 29 he arrived at Wheeling to relieve General Rosecrans.

Jessie Frémont now moved the family into New York and continued her work on the Sanitary Commission. In some swift, mysterious fashion her resiliency of spirit became quickly restored. Though often weary in body, she never bore the air of being beaten down in spirit. It was due to her attitude that in her family there grew up no collective bitterness. Her inner enemy faced, her inner battles fought, she regained a calm control and surrounded her children with an atmosphere of confidence and security.

Nellie Haskell, now fourteen and a pupil at Miss Haines' School not far from the Frémont home, spent many week-ends with them. She declared long afterward that through these "upsetting" months in the life of her beloved *marraine* she saw Mrs. Frémont only as gay and affectionate with them all.

Jessie received heartening letters from Mr. King and money especially collected by him for her use in the Western Department hospitals where her keenest interest still lay. In one of her letters to him, she thus refers to having been placed on a committee with Mrs. McClellan: "Now let the lion and the lamb lie down together."

Through Jessie's personal popularity and practical experience, she was able to collect many small sums from an indifferent public and to coax larger sums from reluctant friends by her understanding attitude toward their grievances. In reply to a reluctant one who asked, "Isn't the head of your hospital a secessionist in a rather ill-fitting abolitionist coat?" she replied, "Perhaps, but we must draw the line at partisan terms somewhere, and I draw mine at a hospital bed. Even Jefferson Davis must believe in the abolition of human suffering. But if you prefer to send your subscription for sick children only, I will so use it and make a direct accounting to you." This rebuke brought a check for twenty-five hundred dollars "without strings."

Though Jessie Frémont successfully masked her resentment, she was no Minerva, "faultlessly wise." To her loyal friend, Starr King, she gave vent to the smouldering fires that lay beneath that calm exterior:

Such real loving friendship as our little circle had for each other is not dependent on the chance of mail and travel. Especially was I sure you were truer than ever when "Stone him" was the cry of the slavery party. You have heard enough of that in your time, and it is an honored few among whom Mr. Frémont has been received. For himself he thinks he did right, and is willing for the personal results. He is not willing to be reconciled to see the cause muddled away and betrayed by those elected to uphold and promote it.

Mr. Lincoln would be in Springfield today and Mr. Seward in Albany if the voters of last November could have seen the record of this November. Now that we are in the dust before England and the rebels feel that they have Europe with them, it will become more than ever evident that we were strong from ideas as well as from strength of numbers. The Germans are chilled and nearly alienated by the treatment to the Missouri Germans, Sigel, and Mr.

Frémont, and the repudiation of Liberty and Free Labor. The Irish are almost in mutiny on the Potomac at the yielding to England. How Northern men feel, you can imagine.

Of course you saw Wendell Phillips's speech? He is to repeat it in Philadelphia and Washington. The officers of the Potomac Army are generally subservient and silent, the men loudly for emancipation. Burnside's expedition, intended to attack Fredericksburg, Virginia, while McClellan attacks at Centreville, has hung fire for weeks. It is promised now for early January. If they win a great victory, the administration can stand. If they keep still or are beaten, then all the malcontents give tongue....Only an overwhelming victory on the Potomac can delay their fate. Wellington used to say a battle was always uncertain until ended, and the rebels have numbers, skill, and fanatical enthusiasm on their side. We have only principle on ours. The prestige of success is with them, and they are about sure of recognition from Europe. All this could have been averted by two words, "Be free," but they are not allowed to be spoken....

You ought to have a summer's furlough to bring Mrs. King home for her health. Let that congregation know by your absence! They will call for you fiercely. I did not fully realize your gifts as a lecturer until I measured you by Mr. Phillips. I do not like a lecture with the chill on. Your voice and gestures are greatly beyond his, and you have magnetic power much greater. Mrs. King knows that I was surprised by you into emotions and enthusiasms, and it takes an uncommon kind of fuse to touch off this grim siege piece in my left side. To Mrs. King every kind remembrance, and may the opening year bring you health and keep you happy.

JESSIE FRÉMONT

Before Frémont's departure in March, he had left many commissions in Jessie's hands, among them the writing of a letter of introduction to Mr. King for James Hayes, a man of influence who was taking an interest in the Mariposa mines. She begged that the Kings keep him from growing homesick while he looked after the mining property. In this letter thus early do we find refutation of later mistaken reports that along with Jessie Frémont's intimate knowledge of political moves was a like knowledge of business transactions over which Frémont and his partners were later censured. In this letter of introduction she says:

More of the financial part you can have from him and from those who do not realize the poet Burns' feeling about business so keenly as I do:"As for me I loathe, detest, and swoon at the very word business." I want Mr. Hayes to see that"all the decency"is not necessarily unprincipled. He said,"What a set they must be in San Francisco,"to which I opposed you and many others, and asked,"Would you like all New York to be judged by the aldermen and the common council?"...Friend is not the next thing to angel; it is Minister of Grace that you were in the days when we were safe on Ararat, but as yet no good thing has come to us out of the boiling waters....Lily has been happy since October with a dear horse, a gray mare that follows her voice, but Chiquita still has a golden halo that no other horse can attain.

Cavalry and infantry send you their heartiest love and good wishes.

J.B.F.

The events that caused Frémont ultimately to resign his commission and return to New York were in line with the highly controversial happenings involving differences between the Generals themselves and between Lincoln and the Generals. When Frémont took command of the small and badly equipped force in Virginia, Lincoln expected him to march over the mountains into eastern Tennessee and seize the railroad at Knoxville. The plan was one which Lincoln believed practicable, and in that belief he promised that an adequate force for this attempt would be forthcoming. A few months, however, were to prove this and Lincoln's whole West Virginia alignment of forces to be mistaken, for the skill of three Generals, including Frémont, was put in question by the redoubtable Stonewall Jackson's troops, who made spectacular raids at the scattered points where Banks, Frémont, and Irwin McDowell were stationed.

After the defeats of Banks, Schenck, and McDowell and the successful eluding of Frémont by Jackson, Lincoln sent Carl Schurz to make a critical survey and a confidential report. His findings exonerated Frémont of blame for his failure to arrest Jackson's flight at Strasburg. Later when Lincoln consolidated the forces of Frémont, Banks, and McDowell into the Army of Virginia under the command of General John Pope, the way was open in Frémont's mind to resign and avoid serving under a General whom he felt to have been disloyal and insubordinate. With his usual courage and promptness when he felt himself in the right, he asked to be relieved of his command and later retired with his personal staff to New York. Though inwardly resentful, Frémont refused to take any part in the anti-administration talk that filled the air in every place where men foregathered. He gave himself entirely to his private business pursuits.

Jessie's conviction about her husband's resignation was that the President was still under the domination of the Blairs where Frémont was concerned and that time alone could loosen that hold or show up the flagrant unfitness and incompetency of General Pope.

The issuance of the Emancipation Proclamation, January 1, 1863, had softened Jessie's resentment toward the harassed President, and her conviction deepened that he would soon weary of the machinations of Montgomery Blair, who was even now endangering his Cabinet position by openly advocating "easy and quick restoration of all rights for the South by full reimbursement for freed slaves." Jessie's last letter to her sister Eliza before the latter's death in 1863 discloses prophetic insight:

Well, my dear Eliza, the Emancipation Proclamation has brought England to our side, and emancipation has proved a pivotal term after all. A few of us felt this in '61. War-politics — hyphenated heartache. My one hope is to see the end of both in our lives. At fifty the General is gray, worn, and in poor health. At thirty-nine my heart, played upon by joy and bereavement, pride and humiliation, longs only for the privacy of a real home again. . . . I am no prophet, though the daughter of one, but I foresee the fall of the House of Blair. I still have filial affection for father Blair, but Frank and Montgomery will soon betray to the long-suffering President that the Blair soul is with the South. Mr. Greeley, Mr. Sumner, and Mr. Chase know that already. When I talked with Mr. Lincoln, what a pity he could not consider my analysis of the Blairs à bon entendeur salut.

This letter proved indeed prophetic, for when Congress convened in December, the Committee for the Conduct of the War was in the hands of the radicals, and the President was struggling against the selfishness, the jealousies, and the personal ambitions of his Congress and Cabinet. And *Blair* was the bitterest drop in Lincoln's bitter cup of 1864, for Frank had resigned his commission as Major-General so that he could return to Congress. His first act was to start a bloc against Secretary of the Treasury Salmon P. Chase, whose personal ambitions for the Presidency might endanger his own plans. With the same virulence and disregard for truth as he had used against Frémont, he now turned upon Chase, whom he accused of conniving with his son-in-law on a cotton deal in the South by which he would make two million dollars.

In annoyance over this charge, Lincoln said: "The man has kicked over another beehive." And so it proved, for Lincoln was accused by the radicals of siding with the Blairs in this and other vicious attacks instigated by them.

After Jessie's return from St. Louis, she began looking up the families of the Zagonyi Guards who had fallen in the Springfield and other engagements while the Guard was in service with Frémont. The maimed survivors and their families were receiving no relief, and for months she had been supporting the most destitute cases herself. Her sense of justice had been shocked over the disbanding of the Guard, and she felt that the incidents of their personal bravery should be made public. She wrote to the publisher, Mr. Fields of Ticknor and Fields, concerning a book manuscript which would set forth the services of the Guard:

> *It seems to me as much an obligation of feeling and honor to do them justice, and heal the hurts to their just pride, as it would be to visit them in the hospital, had they been wounded bodily in the discharge of their duty near the General in the field....*

Mr. Fields replied that they would take the manuscript for publication and would give her an initial payment of six hundred dollars when the rough draft was in their hands. Telling her family that she should neither eat nor sleep until *The Story of the Guard* was complete, she shut herself in her bedroom and set to work with feverish haste. Just twelve days after Mr. Fields had made his promise to her, she walked into his office with a practically completed manuscript and asked the astonished publisher for the advance payment. She got it, but the publication was delayed when it seemed likely that the Guard would be restored to service under Frémont's new command. When this relief failed, she wrote:

> *Again disappointed for them, I have no restraining motive, but launch it*

SAGUNDAI.

Sagundai, Delaware Indian. Hunter and guide for General Frémont.

now, taking shame to myself for deferring for any cause a right act. For in this as well as in great matters, I do not believe that there is any specially appointed "more convenient season."

The manuscript was published in October, 1863. This little volume, among the first to recount Civil War stories of heroism in action, met with instant success. It sold well in the United States and was translated into German. To Starr King, Jessie wrote in happy mood over its success, calling it her "bookling" and declaring that though many had spoken in praise of it, she cared only for a "kind word from the Chief, Mr. Harte, and himself."

About this time Jessie received the startling news from Washington that the Government had commandeered the entire Black Point area in San Francisco for defense purposes against possible trouble with France. Her patriotism gallantly withstood the shock of learning that her house and garden, laurel thicket, rose walks, and even the sightly summit of the bluff, had been leveled for earthworks. The narrow harbor entrance, only two miles off, and the Island of Alcatraz in range with the entrance had also been fully fortified. The former site of the Haskell and the Frémont homes had been selected for earthworks and a light battery.

As a dispossessed and unpaid property owner, Jessie was sore at heart, but in full expectation of being reimbursed on her forty-two-thousand-dollar investment, she tried to forget the lovely secluded spot within sight and sound of the sea where she had hoped to dwell in peace and maintain a heritage for her children. After the first pangs, she set about looking for another home site, this time along the Hudson River Valley where her friends, the George Peabodys, the Aspinwalls, and Mrs. J. G. Phelps, already owned estates.

It was at this time while thinking sadly of the loss of her California home that she received news of the death of Thomas Starr King. Already in grief at the passing of her sister Eliza, this was an added blow that struck deep. King, that eloquent, diminutive preacher, the patriot who had held California firm for Lincoln and who had been collecting and forwarding war funds at the rate of twenty-five thousand dollars a month, had broken under the strain. He had refused to cease work when he contracted a severe cold. Diphtheria quickly developed, and after a brief illness the end came. Jessie wrote to Mrs. King: "Put violets for me above our dear friend who rests."

Shortly thereafter Jessie received a letter from Bret Harte, describing King's funeral and expressing his gratitude for her having persuaded Charles Warren Stoddard to accept his story, *The Legend of Monte del Diablo*, for publication in the *Atlantic*. He inclosed in his letter the manuscript of his poem, *Relieving Guard*, in honor of Starr King:

> Came the relief. "What, sentry, ho!
> How passed the night through thy long waking?"
> "Cold, cheerless, dark—as may befit
> The hour before the dawn is breaking."
>
> "No sight? No sound?" "No; nothing save
> The plover from the marshes calling,
> And in yon western sky, about
> An hour ago, a star was falling."
>
> "A star? There's nothing strange in that."
> "No, nothing; but above the thicket,
> Somehow it seemed to me that God
> Somewhere had just relieved a picket."

As Jessie Frémont read, she wept bitterly at thought of those departed Black Point days. That evening she said to Frémont: "I've a certain conviction that when I have a garden again, I'll meet Mr. King walking there."

Jessie was immersed in hospital work, and Frémont deep in a railroad project for the opening of the great trans-Mississippi region. For a year they had played no active part in political discussions, though they were aware of the highly incendiary sentiment reflected through the press of the country. From the opening of Congress, the anti-administration radicals were in the saddle. The Speaker, Schuyler Colfax, was a close friend of Frémont's and actively opposed to Lincoln's policies. Leaders in both the Senate and the House were loudly demanding: "Less dilatory policies! On with the war."

Such men as Charles Sumner, Lyman Trumbull, Benjamin Wade, George Julian, and James A. Garfield were openly hostile and ready for any lineup that might defeat Lincoln's reelection. The harassed President was now almost an alien in his own Cabinet. Edwin M. Stanton, Salmon P. Chase, and Lyman Trumbull all had Presidential ambitions, of which Lincoln was aware.

Almost within his hearing Henry Davis of Maryland and Senator Samuel C. Pomeroy planned the forming of the Republican National Committee designed to push the Chase candidacy. The Blairs, with their loud denunciations of the attitudes of the radicals, had become anathema to this organization, and its members now united in plans for weeding out the Blairs, root and branch.

While Congress was disaffected and the Cabinet seethed with personal ambitions, the press was purveyor of column after column of anti-Lincoln propaganda. Without exception the important newspapers, James Gordon Bennett's *Herald*, William Cullen Bryant's *Evening Post*, and Horace Greeley's *Tribune*, were opposed to Lincoln's renomination on the ground that the burdens and horrors of the war would be but prolonged under his dilatory policies.

Frémont was aware through letters and private conversations that he had been suggested for various important posts, among them that of Military Governor of North Carolina or one of the other reconquered states. And now with Chase openly a candidate and Greeley announcing that Chase, Frémont, Butler, and Grant were all good timber, Frémont's friends laid active plans for his candidacy. Greeley came out openly for Frémont, referring in glowing terms to the "energy, large financial experience, and indomitable will" of the General, who with Samuel Hallett was planning a railroad line connecting the East with Missouri River points.

General Frémont was now faced with the most important and far-reaching decision of his life. In late March the abolitionists and the radicals were planning a Frémont demonstration in Cooper Union, and the library of the Frémont home where Jessie was directing war-work groups became a scene of political conference.

For a year the Frémonts had taken no part whatever in either personal or political machinations against the administration. Frémont had buried his personal resentment in absorbing private business affairs and had paid no heed to letters repeatedly reminding him of his popularity among the people at large. At this point, with health impaired, he had no intention of giving up his freedom for return to the old strain and stress of political activity.

Jessie's drawing room, turned into a Sanitary Commission volunteers' workroom, rang with the rumors of plots and counterplots. Jessie served luncheon to the workers and listened unperturbed to their declarations: "Of course, the *Tribune* referred to the General when it spoke of calling another and better leader than Lincoln to the helm," and "Mr. Beecher most certainly meant the General when he said that great men are few in any country, but few as they are, we must make diligent search to find one for the next President."

The wife of a Boston clergyman stopped running the new chain-stitch machine on which she was sewing to ask: "Mrs. Frémont, whom of the possible Republican candidates would *you* rather vote for?" Jessie promptly answered: "None of them. I should like to bring out an independent candidate, influenced by neither political nor military ambition—John Greenleaf Whittier."

Thus did she avoid partisan declarations while stating a personal preference. Her acquaintance with the poet had followed upon his publication of the Frémont poems and his letter to her in praise of *The Story of the Guard*. Whittier had later called upon her when passing through New York.

Aware of the strong current setting toward Frémont, Jessie listened with distaste to a conference between Samuel Hallett, Frémont, and a trio of German-Americans from St. Louis. During dinner they surveyed the entire political field, declaring the sentiment of the West to be against Chase, Butler, and Grant, provided Frémont allowed his name to be used. Whatever the temptation may have been, Frémont gave his pleaders no satisfaction at this conference.

Jessie's attention was next called to the desires of Frémont's old constituents when the candidacy of Salmon P. Chase, which had begun so propitiously, fell through. Benjamin Butler's name had also been set aside. The Republican National Committee, meeting in Washington, were practically unanimous for the renomination of Lincoln and called the Republican convention for June at Baltimore.

The backers of Chase now joined the hue and cry for Frémont, and without consulting him, staged a meeting at Cooper Union. Greeley was reported as suggesting that all nominations wait upon Grant's summer campaign. He declared: "The people of New York are in favor of putting down the rebellion and its cause, and sustaining Freedom, and I believe that John C. Frémont will carry out such views." However, the general opinion was that Lincoln's nomination was assured for June, whatever might be his chances of election in November.

With James A. Garfield's declaration, "Lincoln will be nominated and a copperhead will be elected," began the effort to arouse enthusiasm for a third ticket. Jessie believed that with a clear field against the Democratic nominee, Frémont's personal popularity would bring victory, and that elected, he would carry the war to a speedy end. Thus far she saw no reason for anxiety. Her father had once said: "Too early and anxious a contemplation of disastrous possibilities only weakens us for combating them." She would wait.

Frémont had discussed with her the rather doubtful possibility that his supporters could turn the tide sufficiently to prevent Lincoln's nomination, but further than that the talk had not gone. Frémont was full of enthusiasm over the Western Railroad development, and did not talk seriously of the political future as it might affect him.

Her first real anxiety came when the third-ticket enthusiasts planned to anticipate the Republican convention by calling for a mass convention in Cleveland on May 31. Shortly before the opening of this convention, David Dudley Field called upon the Frémonts and assured them both: "The stage is set! Your nomination will be unanimous, and your popularity will cause you to outdistance any and all rivals." Wendell Phillips had also made a point of calling upon Frémont as well as speaking and writing in his praise.

With mixed feelings of pride and concern, Jessie saw her husband depart for Cleveland. She awaited his return with anxious eagerness. He was neither elated nor indifferent as he reported that he had been unanimously nominated and that General John Cochran of New York had been named for Vice President. He said he had accepted because of the planks calling for the uncompromising prosecution of the war, for the constitutional prohibition of slavery, and for leaving reconstruction policies to Congress.

Jessie Frémont felt that her husband knew the doubts that assailed her when at the Republican convention in June, Lincoln was renominated with such shouts of acclaim as left no doubt of his popularity with the real backbone of his party. This left Frémont's position highly equivocal in Jessie's eyes. Sitting together reading the press reports of the convention week, they could but approve the action of the Committee on Credentials in excluding the Blairs, and the coup of the anti-Blair delegates in passing a resolution for the reorganization of the Cabinet, which would mean the certain removal of Montgomery Blair.

[266]

MCCLELLAN AND LINCOLN IN THE CAMPAIGN OF 1864

The legend below this cartoon makes McClellan as Hamlet say: "I knew him, Horatio; a fellow of infinite jest . . .
Where be your jibes now?"

Lincoln and McClellan cartoon.

JESSIE BENTON FRÉMONT: a Woman Who Made History

Jessie planned for the family to spend the summer at Nahant, while she commuted between the cottage there and the house in town, since the services of the Sanitary Commission members were in heavy demand. The terrible losses at Cold Harbor and the Wilderness had filled the hospitals with the wounded. Bad news came that Grant had been checked near Petersburg, and the reports sped as to the weakened condition of the Army of the Potomac. When the raid of General Early had actually endangered the Capitol itself, the country gave way to panic, and national sentiment again swerved away from Lincoln. With greenbacks at forty cents on the dollar and confidence in the administration thoroughly shaken, it looked like clear sailing for the Democrats in November.

At this crisis an open letter was published in Boston proposing that Lincoln and Frémont both withdraw in favor of a compromise candidate. Frémont replied favorably to this, "provided Lincoln also withdraw," but he soon learned that instead of advising Lincoln's withdrawal, the strong party leaders, such as Senator Harlan and Zachariah Chandler, were in anxious conference as to methods of strengthening Lincoln's candidacy. This fact Frémont reported to Jessie without comment on the eve of his departure on a business trip to St. Louis.

Jessie Frémont was now suffering from that condition most disastrous to her peace of mind, indecision. She hated cloudy issues and involvement in questionable situations of any sort. Quite as much did she dread facing her husband with a suggestion as to his conduct. Never in her knowledge of him had there been occasion for her to differ with him as to a point of honor in either his public or his private life. The danger of fatal error lay in the fact that his unwonted reticence was open to misconstruction by her as well as by others.

Might not he too be considering his withdrawal from the race as the only honorable procedure? Or might he be so overestimating his own support as to feel himself capable of sweeping the country? Various groups of dissatisfied Republicans were already quarreling among themselves. With shrewd insight she knew that many who now spoke loudly in favor of Frémont were of the vacillating type to be swayed easily by the fanatical last cries of the campaign.

She reasoned that while Lincoln's plan of reconstruction was obnoxious to the radicals in Congress, since it stopped short of abolishing slavery in Louisiana, Frémont's avowed program of uncompromising emancipation would prove equally obnoxious to the conservatives who wanted the recalcitrant states whipped back into the Union but who would stop short of confiscation of slave property. She knew that many issues which now loomed large, such as that between the President and Congress over the limitation of negro suffrage, might easily be sunk in a few major issues favorable to Lincoln.

She reasoned that unless Frémont could ride openly to victory on the votes created by the radical Republicans, the war Democrats, and the Unionist Germans, he would be acting only as a tool to undermine Lincoln. She remembered her father's rage and disappointment over his party split in '44 when the majority of intelligent and high-minded voters in the country stood behind Clay while Polk was backed by the most rabid of Southern extensionists. Polk's victory had been given him by a third-party candidate, James Birney, who polled but sixty thousand votes, enough, however, to weaken Clay and elect Polk, thus playing directly into the hands of the extreme slavery men. Benton had called this running of Birney a political crime, a treasonable act within the party, from which only evil could come. If the wise and earnest Republican party leaders were seeking ways to strengthen Lincoln's support, how could it be other than a treasonable act within the party for Frémont and his backers to go on opposing him?

As to Jessie's personal reaction toward the President, though her resentment over that unhappy interview had gone deep, she had later shared his sorrow over the loss of his son. She understood his daily harassments, his struggles under vituperative criticism more bitter than had attacked Frémont, since a victorious battle brought him public acclaim and a battle lost overwhelmed him with savage malediction. At Monterey in '49 she had pleaded with her hearers to abandon the selfish cause. Whatever decision Frémont made now, she felt, must be made in the service of the larger cause.

Later in speaking of this conviction, she said: "Never since my father's passing had I so longed for him. Yet even as I grieved, it was as though he had spoken, for I thought of that other man of clear vision and courage, John Whittier."

The staff of her own courage, needed for approach to the poet, was supplied by a cartoon in the Democratic press. McClellan as Hamlet stood holding the skull of Lincoln and saying: "I knew him, Horatio, a fellow of infinite jest....Where are your jibes now?" Shocked into full realization of the crisis, Jessie wrote a confidential letter to Whittier declaring it most important that she see him and begging that she be allowed to consult him privately in his own home. Years later in describing this visit, she said:

We reviewed the devious paths this country had taken since 1856, the great influence of his poems, articles, and speeches in the cause of freedom, and the part his translation of the song, Ein Feste Burg Ist Unser Gott, *had played in Lincoln's decision to issue the Emancipation Proclamation. I laid my questionings, my perplexities, my convictions open to those earnest, kindly eyes. He agreed with me and promised to come to Nahant, and if possible, not betraying our previous consultation, to lay before Mr. Frémont his own convictions as to the best course to follow. He agreed to come when I should give the signal.*

Upon Frémont's return, Whittier came to the Nahant cottage as guest overnight. Frémont, profoundly grateful for past loyalty, received him as a patriot and a prophet. In a quiet talk among the three, Frémont declared to Whittier: "Although I am not gratified at contemplating myself as an opponent of Mr. Lincoln, I feel wholly committed to the course which I have begun. However, I welcome frank expression from you." Whittier then replied that while he had been in heartiest accord with every move the General had made up to now, he believed that Frémont would best serve his country at the present crisis by withdrawing in Lincoln's favor. He ended with: "There is a time to do and a time to stand aside."

Only now did Jessie feel herself justified in expressing the same conviction. When the discussion ended, she knew that Frémont's mind was definitely made up to the same conclusion, unless unforeseen events should change the whole political scene.

Not long after this interview, Frémont was waited upon in his New York office by his attorney, David Dudley Field, and Zachariah Chandler. Field, who had been his trusted political adviser as well, now declared it to be in the interest of party unity that the General withdraw. Chandler then added his plea: Lincoln would not withdraw, but would be defeated if Frémont, with his great popularity in the doubtful states, remained in the field. In such an event, McClellan was certain of election.

Then the wily Chandler presented his political sop: if Frémont would consent to withdraw, he would be given a high command in the Army, and his enemies the Blairs, already made innocuous, would be completely wiped off the official map. Frémont announced his willingness to withdraw from the race for the benefit of the party and took these offers of preferment under a week's advisement.

During this week he reviewed with Jessie his own business situation, which was deeply involved. He discussed with her their plans for the purchase of a home on the Hudson. He mentioned the Blairs, taking no mean satisfaction in their downfall and regretting that such superior abilities as Frank's should have been put to such low uses. In referring to these talks later, Jessie said: "With a feeling of joy akin to ecstasy I heard his decision to remain in private life."

A week later Frémont met Chandler and Field in conference and gave them his answer. He later made this trenchant statement: "Offered patronage to my friends and disfavor to my enemies, I refused both. My only consideration was the welfare of the Republican party." His withdrawal was published on September 22. Thereafter for a month his office in town and the cottage at Nahant were besieged by protesting radicals and friends, including Wendell Phillips, who declared Frémont's act "a great mistake and not likely to effect its purpose." To these protests Jessie replied: "The General and I think alike in this matter."

The good effect of Frémont's withdrawal was felt immediately throughout the Union party. Dissenting factions came together, providing powerful support to the President. Lincoln received a majority of nearly half a million votes at the polls and two hundred twelve of the two hundred twenty-four votes cast by the Presidential electors, among whom was John Greenleaf Whittier, the Bard of Freedom. Jessie Frémont was loyally content over the result. The secret of that confidential visit to Whittier was not disclosed by her for many years. In a letter to the poet written a quarter of a century after this crucial period, she thus refers to his Nahant visit:

Los Angeles, California, November 19, 1889

Dear Mr. Whittier: You would have had many letters from me if I had written each time you were brought up in my mind, for thoughts of yours have become part of my ruling motives. This time I write because I know it will try even your inborn and controlled patience to hear the injustice to the Emperor of Brazil, a man who has felt and lived up to the claims of humanity in all forms. And see his reward! "Oh, Republic, what crimes are committed in thy name."

Among the words I remember from you are: "There is a time to do and a time to stand aside." *I never forget your saying this to me at our Nahant cottage in 1864 when you had come to say them to Mr. Frémont. Wendell Phillips, who saw the do more clearly than the stand aside, insisted I had dreamed your visit.* "Whittier goes nowhere. He never visits. His health does not let him," *and laughing arguments against your wise and necessary view of what the time demanded of Mr. Frémont—to renounce self for the good of the greater number. Do you not remember it too? It was a deciding word, coming from you.*

And how we have outlived all of that time! Here on this far shore where the serene climate gentles even hard memories, I seem to look back into another life, its strifes ended, only its results in good cherished. I have my daughter with me. My other children and the dear young grandchildren I have not seen for two years. It is much that they are well and write me fully and often, but your Angel of Patience is more than ever part of my life....

I am writing by an open window, a La Marque rose wreathing all the gallery in deep green foliage and white roses kept well trimmed back to pillars and balustrade to let in the sweet sweet sunshine.... We are established here.... We have many pleasant friends and take our part in some of the good works of the town, for there are many uprooted families here.... And I write, hoping often that I too may find place in some tired heart and lead to new courage....

With our affectionate regards to you and your household, I am

Your always remembering friend,

JESSIE BENTON FRÉMONT

CHAPTER XVII

Pocaho Salon

THE Frémonts were in Washington that memorable May 23, 1865, as part of the vast loyal throng who witnessed the review of the triumphant Union Armies. When the pageantry of waving flags, thrilling music, and the long blue columns marching was ended, the volunteers became civilians again, joining those other civilians in plans to restore their country's interrupted life.

As Mrs. Frémont returned to her New York house and removed the sewing machines and wartime worktables, she was conscious of having contributed her full quota of service to her country. Her life now entered upon a new and happy phase wherein her ideals of family and social well-being were to be realized under almost perfect conditions. In attempt to still her grieving over the loss of the Black Point estate, she had taken many drives along the Hudson River seeking some spot for a home that would enter into the family and possess it as her homes had possessed her, training the mind, developing the character, and feeding the affections.

Uncomplainingly she had led the harried life of a city dweller during the war, but the monotony of dull streets and cluttered squares grew oppressive to one whose eyes had feasted on far Pacific horizons. The bits of gardens seemed but floral samples to her whose rich tapestries had spread down Black Point hill to the fringes of wild strawberries at the foot. The drooping heads of flower-stall violets exposed in tin cans made her ache for the friendly blue-bonneted blossoms of Black Point. She longed for a place that would give her the same sense of strange unearthly beauty as had those luminous distances and spectral island forms of San Francisco Bay under a full moon.

[273]

Aware of her feelings, Frémont declared: "We must soon find something to cure this Black Point nostalgia, for it can prove as destructive to your health as an organic disease." "I know," she replied. "I'll speak to Hannah."

Hannah Lawrence was the sister of Joe Lawrence of San Francisco, and the family estate was one of the most beautiful in the region of Sleepy Hollow. Hannah had often enlarged upon the desirability of the Hudson River estates, and now when appealed to by Jessie, she suggested that they inspect the General Webb place, which was for sale.

Driving far along the headlands, Jessie was enchanted with their endearing quality of landscape, the river quiet itself but flowing toward the city, the friendly hills, the comely estates. Upon her return she said: "The whole scene is a blur of beauty in my mind. I must go back again."

Next day she drove along to the Webb place about two miles north of Tarrytown. The estate looked down on Tappan Zee, that expansion of the Hudson where early Dutch navigators shortened sail and implored the protection of St. Nicholas before they crossed. From the windows of a commodious house of rough gray stone she studied the scene: rugged mountain summits in the distance, the far expanse of water with its fleet of sloops and schooners, nearby the gentle wooded slopes and cheerful orchards of neighboring estates. She recalled what Henry Ward Beecher had said when he purchased his farm at Peekskill: "It was the aptitude of the place for eye-crops that caught my fancy."

She returned to New York resolved to be first to share this beauty with the family. Later, when she walked through the house with Frémont, she pointed out the room that should be his alone, sacred to his precious maps, his histories, his digests of wars, his trophies, and mementos.

The family agreed that the local Indian name, "Pocaho," should be given the estate, and soon after its purchase Jessie wrote Nellie Haskell:

You shall come on Sunday to see this home which combines all our homes! The sweetness of honey locust and elms combines St. Louis and Washington. The bluebells and wild grapevine, the thickly wooded glens where the eye travels from the fern carpet at one's feet to the blue upland trails—that is Cherry Grove. And the fresh breeze off the water when Little Mountain wraps her fog ruff about her neck is our own beloved Black Point.

Jessie spent long happy days superintending the planting and general improvements, striving to keep her scheme simple so as to involve a minimum of aftercare. When someone suggested an elaborate water garden, she said: "No, my friend N. P. Willis said that the only rule for perfect independence in the country is to make no improvement that requires more attention than the making."

Warned by her neighbors that watchdogs were a necessity, Jessie procured a pair of fine Scotch staghounds from Marcy Martin, a friend and neighbor. The parents of these hounds had been sent to the Martins by the actress Charlotte Cushman, who had found them in Edinburgh. Mr. Martin offered a pair from the first litter to Jessie, who promptly named the puppies Thor and Sheila from *Lorna Doone,* which she had just finished reading.

The boys were delighted with the dogs, and upon seeing them for the first time, Frank proclaimed: "Thor likes me best of all! I know." This prophetic remark was often recalled by the family since from the first Frank became Thor's god. Before his door the dog slept each night, curled up on Frank's old school overcoat, and only at his god's voice did he allow anyone to enter.

While Jessie was superintending improvements on the estate, the family remained in town, the children content with frequent visits to the grounds and with sailing trips on the river. But their mother was impatient to have her family "settled once for all."

Jessie Frémont was intensely proud of her three children. The daughter Lily, now in her early twenties, possessed what her mother called "a frank, endearing good-nature that is a staff to my tired mind." Charley was a slim, dark-eyed, high-strung boy, still grieving over the *Restless* and San Francisco Bay. When promised a sailboat, he declared: "Even if it is built by Sears like the *Restless,* it won't have gone round the Horn in the clipper *Morning Light.*" When laughed at by Lily for declaring he meant to be an admiral, he said: "Why not? The sea is the only life for a man, and the sea is the life for me." The younger brother Frank was a studious, dreamy child, whose idea of pleasure was the piano, "to play it whenever I like." With his perfect ear and good memory, he was the despair of Lily, who agonized over every selection and remained thereafter tied to the score. Of her family Jessie wrote to a friend:

My children's differing dispositions are an unending source of wonder.

[275]

The only thing comparable is watching the sea. The human-nature elements remain the same, but there is constant variety of temperamental movement.

Jessie applied her father's large and generous program of child education, expecting each to develop along the line of his own special tastes. In moving permanently to the estate she said:

I want each child to absorb that especial atmosphere which best nourishes him. Lil shall make her own bridle paths; Charley shall drink up Tappan Zee; Frank shall play his piano when he likes, if I have to put it in a tree house.

When the family had moved from the city, Mrs. Frémont wrote Nellie Haskell:

The children are all settled to their own life here. I want you, Nell, for the life you and I like best—the garden and fixing the house. Mary Martin sent me some of the deep Russian violets which are hardy....They are planted at the angle made by the parlor wall and at the feet of the ivy which was in the city house schoolroom in the jardinières. As it had lived so long in the house, it will grow better for remaining where it can see the family often and hear the piano.... Sometime soon you are coming up. Whenever you please is always the right time to me.

Nineteen-year-old Nellie Haskell found the house inside and out a matter of wonderment, and while Lily took the boys on long excursions through the hills, she helped Mrs. Frémont arrange furniture and decide where pictures should be hung. Long afterward in describing their hours together, Nellie Haskell said:

Throughout my entire eighty-four years of life, these hours with my beloved marraine stand as purely golden hours. An incident the first day was to set the keynote to our whole future relationship.

I was unpacking a box of photographs of Charley, Lil, and Frank, together with one of my own. On the back of Charley's was written in Mrs. Frémont's handwriting: "Adorable restive little beastie." The back of Frank's read: "Ward of St. Cecilia." Lily's bore: "Precious, unshakable as Bunker Hill." And under my own undistinguished features topped by a sailor hat, I read:

Jessie Benton Frémont, 1868. From original by Fagnani and painted at Pocaho.

"Nellie, daughter-in-love." From that moment I belonged to Mrs. Frémont, body and mind.

Mr. Frémont had bought the Humboldt library after Humboldt's death in '59, and it was my happy lot that day to help place the books. Shelves ran to the ceiling, with a three-step ladder to reach the highest. This work went slowly because of Mrs. Frémont's desire to have me fully appreciate the beauty of the typography and the hand-tooled bindings. When we came to the Audubon books in color, she sat beside me on the floor, pointing out the very pictures that had absorbed her as a child in the Congressional Library. She told me of meeting Audubon with Humboldt in Washington. She made me see Audubon as a real person, his high serene forehead, his deep gray eyes, straight nose, and the cluster of white locks falling to his shoulders. Mrs. Frémont also told me of the Comte de la Garde, and showed me the precious collection of Napoleonic souvenirs he had willed to her. Among them was an ivory miniature of Napoleon by Isabey, watercolor portraits of Josephine and of Queen Hortense, and autograph letters of great personages.

After we got the books arranged, I watched the big room grow into a home under her direction. On the floor was spread a moss-green carpet with a rich border. The well-spaced windows were hung with green and cream fabric, the glass of the French doors to the terrace left clear for the view.

On one side of the fireplace she set the General's easy chair; beside it, a stout oak table with a reading lamp. Opposite was her own chair and table with its now historic Martha Washington sewing basket. Closer to the General's chair she set a hassock "for my use when we are alone and the fireplace opening separates us too far," she said. Couches and easy chairs completed this room, except for the tea table with tiny wheels on its feet, which she had bought in France.

Next day we arranged the music room: piano, cabinet, guitars, and a violin. Here she had a couch placed in a quite dark corner. To Lil's objection that nobody would want to sit there, her mother said: "I want one in shadow, for music is a tonic to be taken sometimes in repose and darkness. Nell here needs it thus."

Regretfully Nellie Haskell left the newly arranged house to return to school, but with the promise that the saddle horse Jessie had bought for her use should always be waiting for her beside Lily's gray mare and the boys' ponies. One of Jessie's first letters to her pictured the activities at Pocaho and touched upon a youthful school sorrow of Nell's:

Dear Nell: I'm glad you changed your room at school. Coming into places where you have been bothered brings up everything. I know there is a street in New York where as I cross its head, I feel a damp blast of old memories that makes me shudder and hurry on. This dear lovely Pocaho has brought change and healing both to me. I absolutely continue to come down dressed by seven thirty or eight. If the General is here, by seven thirty. Frank comes in at ten and works with Miss Crowly till one. Then we have a light luncheon and we dine at eight thirty and by eleven are up for the night. I am busy with my violets off and on all day. They are best quality and will last a few years. Then a change is needed.... Some things don't change, however, dear Nell. You are a steadfast little soul, and for that I love you.

Jessie's protective attitude toward Nell is further shown in the following letter. At school Nell often agonized over her duty. Just now she was going through a religious conflict as to joining the church. Jessie, an inner non-conformist herself, thus got round the question of conviction of sin:

My dear, don't think you need to feel that you are wicked! If you feel sure you want to be better than you are, and you feel very sure you can't keep yourself up to what you ought to be, then it is a great pleasure to bind yourself openly to the outer as well as the inner laws of the church. Church membership is like marriage; it not only binds you to do certain things for another, but it gives you the friendship and protection of that other. You set yourself apart from other loves and thus double your capacity for this one. The highest honor and good breeding are just the highest religion. And our best goodness is so poor that it will not do to wait to be good enough. Just as I am, remember....

While writing this letter, she picked up Nell's photograph and studied the sensitive face with its frame of curly brown hair, then remarked to her husband: "Poor darling! Her troubles come from an excess of virtue. She is in for much rainy weather. I must save her from developing a talent for sacrifice."

Jessie Frémont was soon to realize that this child was temperamentally more her child than the forthright Lily. Spirited, keen to sense atmosphere, and just quick tempered enough to add zest to her makeup, she was a lively acquisition to the family circle. To her Mrs. Frémont gave encouragement, reproof, and healing sympathy out of the wealth of an infinite understanding.

The house at Pocaho was filled with an almost continuous stream of visitors, young nieces and nephews, friends old and new, and men of note from other countries come to pay respect to a fellow scientist and explorer. Because of these visitors the guest-room suite soon became known as the Foreign Department.

The painter Bierstadt, just in from a sketching tour of the Rockies, was a welcome and "exciting" guest. Later, his beautiful painting of the Golden Gate, with the sun setting behind it, hung above the library mantel. When Jessie saw it in place, she exclaimed to Nell: "If I should never enter that gate again, this will keep me from grieving too much. I must never part with it."

After his first visit, Bierstadt told Mr. Beecher: "Madame Frémont has *courtoisie de coeur*. She makes one feel himself a contributor." Beecher replied with a laugh: "How she makes us pleased with ourselves! Being unorthodox, she lets us all speak freely. We sometimes quarrel among ourselves and with her, and she lets each think the sparkle and wisdom all his."

When the scientist Louis Agassiz visited Pocaho before his trip to the coast, Jessie was struck with his six feet of height, his noble countenance, and the clear gaze which so recalled her father to memory. She told him at parting that she would like her house to merit in time what a student had said of his: "One has less need of an overcoat in passing Agassiz' house than any other in Cambridge."

Her modesty forbade the thought that even now her house was thus remembered. On one occasion when Collis P. Huntington was asked to stay with a friend at his New York club, he said: "I've already accepted an invitation to Pocaho. I always find it such a happy house, filled with gay and pleasant people."

The most surprising of the younger Frémont guests were always brought by Charley. Any boy who professed a love of the sea was welcome to share Charley's bed and board. He was now a midshipman at Annapolis and delighted in having his classmates up home for vacations. On one occasion when the house was overflowing, he appeared with a tall and very odd-looking youth in tow. Annoyed, Lily demanded: "Why didn't you ask mother first?" Quite unperturbed, he replied: "I didn't need to. Baker just saved a young seaman's life. I know mother will love to meet a hero."

A vignette of Pocaho life is furnished us by Nellie Haskell:

The General was often away in the West on his railroad business, but when home he usually read quietly or took evening walks with Mrs. Frémont or long rides through the woods and along the post road with the boys, Lil, and myself. He loved to listen to what he called home-made music. He went occasionally to the theater when Mrs. Frémont asked him, which was seldom because she knew he preferred to play chess or to chat with the neighbors, the Phelpses, Schuylers, Aspinwalls, or Beechers, who dropped in often. As to formal dinners he attended them only when Mrs. Frémont said. "You really must go this time." She attended many such functions when he was West on business, going to Washington for dinners and musicales. She was present at Mrs. Grant's first White House reception, and at a famous dinner given in honor of Robert Schenck, Minister to Great Britain. But when Mr. Frémont was home, she tried to have only the sort of guests in the house agreeable to him.

One evening an observant house guest noticed that her host was taciturn and restless until Mrs. Frémont appeared. As she approached them dressed in a pale-lilac gown, her wavy white hair in neat bands, the guest was moved to compliment her attractive appearance. With a smile Frémont answered simply: "She contents the eye."

His remark was justified, for in this frilly era Jessie Frémont wore her clothes in such a manner as to give character to those tucks and ruffles that on so many women became merely bits of sartorial futility. On one occasion she wrote Nell to order a pair of boudoir slippers from a woman dealer in New York. "But you select the trimming. Her taste is fuzzy."

The matter of taste in dress was a sore point between Jessie and a visiting relative. This young girl "refused to be bothered" when urged to take an interest in her clothes, but when on occasion she did choose her own, she showed a capacity little short of genius for selecting unbecoming fabrics and colors. One day Nellie Haskell, surprising Mrs. Frémont in a moment of exasperation over an expensive "horror" just home from the dressmaker, said: "How unfortunate that she has such poor taste in dress." "Oh, if she only had," Jessie exclaimed. "Poor taste can be improved, but no taste at all! *Jamais!*"

The family tea hour inside the house or on the terrace always meant easy chairs, good talk, and what Jessie called "a general feeling of *bien aise.*" On one occasion, however, a clever but rude young man in from the West on a business call was asked to remain and have tea later with the young people. He declined, then launched into a diatribe against the time wasted by busy people in useless chat over a tea table. Highly amused, the General waited to hear how Jessie would handle him. "It does take time," she smilingly admitted, "but I agree with the learned Abbé Raynal that the use of tea has contributed more to the sobriety of the Chinese than the severest laws, the most eloquent discussions, or the best treatises on morality. It makes every man a gentleman one hour each day." The discomfited youth took hasty departure, leaving behind him a hostess sorrowing "because so fine a man couldn't have had better home training."

Among the guests Jessie called "treasured" were the portrait painter Fagnani and his wife. This Italian artist, trained in Paris and Vienna, was a source of great pleasure to the family during the weeks Jessie sat to him for her portrait. He had just finished the portraits of the nine most beautiful women in New York under the title the Nine Muses, and declared he was tempted to invent a tenth in order to include Madame Frémont. Though Jessie herself was pleased with the result, the artist said he felt he had failed to portray the "reality" of his subject.

The year 1868 was the fullest of the busy Pocaho era of Jessie Frémont's life, and in its type of experience, the happiest. Her proudest hour was that one in St. Louis on May 28 when before an immense and distinguished audience she unveiled a bronze statue of Senator Thomas Hart Benton. This statue of heroic size was placed in Lafayette Park to commemorate the man who in life had been called "a grand old Roman" and who in death was still a victor, for his written and spoken words had been the potent element that held Missouri in the Union against all efforts to drive her into secession. And now ten years afterward this tribute was ready for dedication.

The General and Jessie went to St. Louis for the unveiling ceremony. To Nellie Haskell she recounted this experience:

Hans Christian Andersen, 1869. Given to Jessie Benton Frémont by
Hans Christian Andersen, 1869, in Denmark.

Dear Nell: I had a wonderful travel to St. Louis and back. The General and I were alone and nothing to do but be happy for eight whole days. Of course, I did not get tired. The statue is superb, and everybody was so glad the General had come, and all were very nice to him and to me.

As the General and I entered the Park, Ralph [the old body servant] *dropped behind servant fashion, but I felt he belonged in front of us all, bought in and freed by the family.*

There were more than forty thousand people in the Park, hundreds of public school children, both boys and girls, dressed in white and carrying bunches of red roses, father's favorite flower. The children were grouped around the base of the slight rise on which the statue had been placed. Toward the valley below, the trees and shrubbery had been cleared, leaving an open view of the line of the Pacific Railroad. The band played inspiring music. As I drew the cord and the white drapery fell away from the statue, its bronze was gilded by the warm sunshine, and the children threw the roses at its base. At the same moment the outgoing train to San Francisco halted and saluted with whistles and flags. When the speaker of the day dwelt on the public schools, the homestead laws, and other cherished measures of my father's, all hearers knew he deserved these words of praise. Though the sun shone bright, I looked through a mist of tears at the bronze image of my father facing westward with the words carved below: "There is the East. There lies the road to India."

While Jessie Frémont was in truth the mistress of a salon, she was no less eagerly sought for her practical advice to young people and her good offices in securing preferment for them. Here she used such discrimination as to the subjects themselves, worded her recommendations so happily, and made her plea with so trusting an air that she was seldom refused. In most cases her confidence was proven justified.

After the death of her sister Eliza, her nephew Benton Jones wished to make a start in California. He appeared at Pocaho with the confidence of youth but with no fixed plans. Jessie gave him a letter to Governor Leland Stanford, and in due time Benton wrote Lily:

Dear Cousin: Please give my thanks to Aunt Jessie for writing to Governor Stanford about me. He answered her letter by giving me two letters, one to the chief engineer and one to the secretary, for me to take my choice. I was given a place in the Engineer Corps of the Western Pacific Railroad....

Although Jessie's greatest pleasure was in affording opportunity to youth, she gave of herself and her fortune to those in pecuniary distress. How much of her large income went for private assistance to old friends and their children will never be known, but at the opening of a certain school term, when her rheumatic wrist compelled her to press Nellie Haskell into secretarial service, a part of Nell's duties was the listing of eight young men's names with notations attached to each for "strictly anonymous" tuition payments. The schools listed were Harvard College, The Gunnery, and the University of Virginia, as well as the Peekskill Boys' School. A similar list of twelve girls was made for "anonymous tuition" in seminaries at St. Louis, Richmond, and Washington.

During these years when her husband was rated a millionaire, she served whoever came to her in need. She besought assistance or preferment for each, and discussed with no one the details of her uncounted charities. In a day of excess in food and display in jewels and clothes, Jessie's personal habits were almost as Spartan as Frémont's own. Her guests praised her hospitality, not in the abundance and variety of food, but in the taste and distinction of service. She bought no jewels, nor allowed Frémont to buy them for her. Her only indulgence lay in the quality of the fabrics and laces that went into the gowns suitable for the functions which as a social personage she must attend. Her own taste was for simple dinners and music which she could enjoy from a couch or an easy chair. In a letter to a friend she spoke thus of an afternoon at the home of Sally Anderson, who was later to become Charley's wife:

Bella Berenger and Sally Anderson gave me a glorious musical matinée Saturday. Sally sang most beautifully Gounod's Ave Maria, *Mendelssohn's* Barcarolle, *and lovely unknown things that were like tender Greuze faces with tears on them, or bunches of pale roses with wild flowers....Then Bella began with her* Rapsodie Hongroise *which Esipoff plays, then a Chopin* Polonaise *and* Nocturne.

I just had a thorough musical bath. I sat on a sofa with my feet up, Berenger mère *in a sack and petticoat, I in my holique, Bella in a cambric morning*

[285]

suit, and the songstress in a little short gray gown made for Hudson River traveling, as she is with her aunt at Sing Sing.

Jessie Frémont's appreciation of music made her peculiarly sympathetic to her son Frank's temperamental bias. He was a light sleeper, and often came down late at night to play softly behind closed doors the melodies that he declared kept him awake. Jessie had placed the piano where this playing disturbed no one. However, when a somewhat critical relative, visiting Pocaho, learned of this habit of Frank's, she called it "most peculiar" and urged Jessie to put a stop to it.

"Did his playing disturb you?" Jessie asked.

"No," the guest admitted, "but you should stop it."

Jessie pondered a moment and then said: "Frank has good and sufficient reason for liking his music late at night."

"Well, what is it?" interrupted the relative curiously.

Fixing her with a look, Jessie said: "I don't know. I've never asked him."

The relative departed a few days later and reported her Cousin Jessie "a ruinously indulgent mother." A part of this ruinous indulgence lay in long walks with the young people and talks before the fire on stormy winter nights. While strolling one morning in the woods, a visiting child came suddenly upon a tiny spring. Stooping quickly, she drank, then ran back to announce herself as "the first who had ever drunk from it."

"Nonsense!" Nell laughed. "Many people before you have drunk of that water."

Later, Mrs. Frémont took Nell gently to task. "Her own discovery of the world is all important to her. Let her have the joy of it. You will discover love some day and believe yourself to be the very first to have tasted it to the full."

Long afterward when Pocaho days were but a happy memory, the young people declared that their keenest delight had been those winter evenings when, seated on the floor before the library fire, munching cakes and apples, they listened to the romantic and true stories of the South, of French St. Louis, of Spanish San José, and most romantic of all, Black Point and the Golden Gate.

"Never mind, my dears," she would say, looking up at the Bierstadt painting. "I shall some day carry you all through that Golden Gate again."

About this time the serious illness of Charley gave Jessie grave concern. She rarely left his bedside until the crisis was past and he was well on the road to recovery. She then wrote to Nell:

Since it is over, I feel the strain and have not been well. I get so weary I almost fall asleep standing. My twenty-fifth-year ring slipped off my hand today and fell upon my plate. In the three years I've worn it, my hand hasn't been thinned enough for that. Charley is back at school and doing so well he was made first officer of the day. He is in the right place and all safe and right. It is a great peace for me.

Since business was taking Frémont to Europe again, it was decided that Jessie and the children should accompany him to Paris and visit Susan, whose husband, Comte Boileau, was in the Government service there. Leaving a caretaker at Pocaho, the family sailed on the *Java* for France. Before embarking, however, Jessie went to Annapolis for a visit to Admiral Porter's family. While discussing tentative plans for the summer practice cruise, Jessie enlarged upon the advantages of France over the accustomed South America or Madeira. The Admiral later so planned the cruise and arranged for a three-day stay in Paris for the young midshipmen.

Once settled in the Hotel du Jardin des Tuileries, Jessie renewed acquaintance with her Paris friends and visited her sister, Madame Boileau, at her chateau. When the lively lot of midshipmen arrived, Jessie solved her chaperonage problems by keeping open house in her hotel suite. An all-day dining-room table was kept filled with cold meats, cakes, mountains of rolls and butter, and plenty of fruit. The butler François was amazed that the boys drank only syrups and seltzer and did not smoke. At the end of three exciting days wherein the midshipmen had dutifully visited historical monuments, they entrained for Cherbourg, and Jessie was free to plan for herself.

Upon receiving an invitation to visit the Danish Court where festivities were in preparation for the marriage of the Crown Prince, Jessie declared: "The Swiss mountains can wait, but royal commands don't arrive every day."

In Copenhagen the Frémont family were guests of General de Raesleff, attaché at the Danish Court. Through his wife, Mrs. Frémont was given a special morning audience with the Queen, and the Frémonts attended the ball given in honor of the Crown Prince and his Swedish bride.

The special delight of the whole European visit, however, lay in Jessie's meeting with Hans Christian Andersen. Her drives into the country, past farm houses with pompous storks perched on one leg beside the nest, prepared her to meet the fairy-tale man whom a *London Punch* cartoon had made familiar to her. This cartoon represented the tall, exceedingly thin, long-legged Hans as a stork with one foot resting on London and one on Copenhagen. Andersen sat with Jessie and her friends in the hotel window overlooking the street where the royal marriage procession passed.

"Good manners and an air of good will. That is Denmark," Jessie remarked as they took the train at the end of their visit.

Upon the family's return, Nellie Haskell received a letter from Hannah Lawrence, saying: "I have seen Mrs. Frémont; spent last Sunday with her in New York at the Darts'. We listened to her charming accounts of the delights of Denmark, Paris, and Pocaho. She never looked better or was more splendid in every way." Was it with prophetic sense that Jessie wrote to Nellie of her happiness, quoting:

> *If it were now to die,*
> *'Twere now to be most happy, for I fear*
> *My soul hath her content so absolute*
> *That not another comfort like to this*
> *Succeeds in unknown fate.*

Was it prophetic in that the last gay and colorful threads in the fabric of Jessie Frémont's life had now been woven? The busy shuttle was ready with the dark strands of pain and sorrow that were never fully to lighten again.

Frémont's business affairs had been in a more or less tangled state for several years, but he concealed all worrisome details from Jessie, and only when his income dropped from a fabulous sum to one threatening the family security, did he admit to her the seriousness of the situation. She had immediately cut down the household staff, lessened her contributions to charity, shortened her ceremonial visits to Washington, and steadied by an irrefragable common sense, she had carried on for the sake of her children and their friends. By now, however, no longer able to ward off evidences of approaching ruin, Frémont confessed the situation, one so involved that Jessie in despair told her only confidante, Nell:

Nellie Haskell, 1866.
Elizabeth (Lily) Benton Frémont, about 1880.
Commander John Charles Frémont, United States Navy.
Captain Frank Preston Frémont, United States Army.

It is an inextricable mass out of which I can glean only an impression of millions of dollars of railroad bonds floated abroad which brought profit only to the agent, advertisements published abroad that misrepresented the whole railroad picture, of which Mr. Frémont knew nothing. One thing, however, stands out perfectly clear: my husband was in Washington working for the rights of way for his road while his agents were selling bonds through misrepresentations. He has had no part in any dishonest transaction. Certain of that, I am strong for whatever is to come.

Though unpleasant publicity over the railroad company's affairs was imminent, the family stayed on at Pocaho, a sufficient income from other investments enabling Jessie to continue a cheerful and gracious hostess until after Charley's graduation as an ensign in July, 1873. Nellie Haskell that year became Mrs. George Browne, and Jessie's pleasure in this congenial marriage with a man of a fine old Salem family lightened many a heavy hour.

That Mrs. Frémont's courage still rode high is evidenced by the gay humor which played over her statements regarding the family. Nellie came up to Pocaho shortly after her marriage, and in quoting Charley's letter in which he declared, "Lil and I are especially glad of the safe haven our 'clipper Nell' has sailed into," the bride said regretfully, "I can't see why Lil has no serious suitor. She has many nice men friends."

Jessie laughed. "I can tell you. If a young man caller doesn't love horses, he is no friend of Lil's, and if he does love horses, by the time that subject is exhausted, it is time for him to go."

Jessie Frémont's capacity for inspiring affection now opened for her a new and welcome path of escape from stress in visits to Mrs. Browne in her home. George Browne realized from the first how much he owed Mrs. Frémont for her interest in his wife and for her approval of him as Nellie's husband. He gave the loyal affection of a son to Mrs. Frémont, whom he called in private "our mater." At his suggestion a room was set aside where she might feel free to come at any time, even when they were away. That room was destined to prove a retreat from which Jessie Frémont later sent forth her most remunerative bits of literary work and where she left many tender little notes of appreciation for the hospitality of "her Nell and dear G. B."

In the summer of '73, when the last of the Frémont fortune was being swept away, eighteen-year-old Frank, a cadet at West Point, was stricken with inflammation of the lungs. Frantic with anxiety, Jessie applied for leave for him and took him to Bar Harbor. Here he improved somewhat. Upon their return to Pocaho, when Frémont was called West again, a friend offered Jessie, Lily, and Frank transportation to Nassau, a change which proved a turning point in his cure. Here she wrote frequently to Mrs. Browne, who was expecting a child. A letter showing her usual tender concern for Nell concludes thus:

We all keep well, and Frank seems entirely so. He is on friendly terms with the garrison officers, and generally amuses himself in an unexciting way. I think sometimes I could step over the sea, so yearning for the General do I get. But it is not to be, and I am getting all the good I can out of this climate. Lil is doing charmingly. She is quiet and contented and has thinned remarkably. After the steamer gets in today, I can write much better. I feel like this is talking with you through a door when you are about to open it. I know I shall have a letter from you that will make rainy weather for Mrs. Frémont.

Upon Jessie's return, she was sufficiently restored in spirit to bear with courage the news of complete financial disaster that awaited her. She noted in love and pity the embarrassment with which her husband began the humiliating confession of his haste and poor judgment in placing his whole fortune in a project, allowing others to run it, and now sharing equally their disgrace in its spectacular failure.

Though "swooning" as did the poet Burns at the very thought of business, Mrs. Frémont asked for the whole story from the hour her husband poured his fortune into the maw of the Memphis and El Paso enterprise. She listened to his self-reproach over his foolish trust in his partners and his failure to learn of and check the fraudulent schemes at their source. She met him with assurances of her understanding as to his continuing trust in men who had once gained his confidence. She declared that with a clear conscience, fair health, and prospect for the settlement of the Black Point claim, they had reason for courage to face the litigation troubles looming ahead.

Afterward, during these lawsuits when blistering charges and counter-charges seared Frémont along with the worst of his offending railroad directors, Jessie declared: "Knowing him as I did, watching him make that humiliating admission of business ineptitude, I saw a mind filled with grief and sorrow and boundless anxiety, but with no shadow of guilty conscience."

At the worst, she felt his dreams to have been a little mad, his mind so filled with visions of those shining steel paths across the territories to the Pacific that he walked blindly along the dark alleys of tricky speculation with his associates. And so she defended him with savage courage and all the strength of her love. She worried over him, his health, his power to withstand what she felt to be yet another impact of cruel circumstances upon a sensitive mind. She suffered with and for him, but she never held herself to be suffering *because* of him.

Jessie Frémont's pride had already withstood many bitter blows, and the fact that she took this dizzying drop from wealth to poverty, from an ideal country home to a musty ill-lighted house in town, was due to the absence of petty vanity and of avarice in her nature. She liked money for the comforts it gave her family, for the opportunity to surround herself with her own kind, the men and women of culture who were her special delight, and for the power it gave her to help others. The loss of this power filled her with regret, but it brought no agonizing wrench to her heart.

The friends who rallied about her now and called her "gallant Jessie" failed to realize that her courage came from a substratum of character that had manifested itself in early childhood. The schoolgirl who saw no reason for social discrimination among girls of good character and good manners on the score of mere wealth or position anticipated no discrimination over her own loss of mere wealth. That same spirit now enabled her to accept the loan of a carriage and horses, a box at the opera, or gifts of gloves and books from those to whom she would formerly have made the same gifts. Nor was there any sense of special virtue in this attitude, for Jessie Frémont had no flair for martyrdom, even in its most delicate interpretation. So long as her family were together and in good health, no disaster seemed irremediable, even the loss of Pocaho. She said of herself at this time: "I am like a deeply built ship; I drive best under a strong wind."

Already she was formulating plans to increase the family income. She knew several publishers and editors to whom she might submit manuscripts. Out of the richness of her experience, she felt that some worthwhile material might be turned into travel articles or essays. She planned to consult these publishers as soon as Pocaho was disposed of.

While Frémont was testifying in a lawsuit in Washington, Jessie sent Lily to stay with Nell, while she herself went alone to Pocaho to tackle bailiffs and process servers and to interview prospective purchasers for the few items of intrinsic value that remained hers to dispose of. A letter to George Browne reveals the humiliating experiences she encountered:

> *Dear G. B.: The tax collector is here. He says he can levy on anything movable no matter whom it belongs to, even to one of the servants. Will you see Mr. Bryant about it as you come out? The collector is at the stable now, looking at horses and carriages with a view to moving them into the village, advertising them for six days, and if not redeemed, selling them. . . . Ask Mr. Bryant if he has a right to do this? He was so positive yesterday that nothing of the kind would happen. Mr. W. just tells me the collector consented to wait until Wednesday on condition a promise was given that nothing should be spirited away from the stable, the contents of which he listed. Meantime the promise was given, and there is a thirty-six-hour respite. . . .*

On Wednesday the horses and carriages went, and later the books, art objects, and her cherished Golden Gate painting. When the lovely things were sold, she parted with them dry eyed, as from friends who still held her secrets in their keeping.

One morning a stranger in passing asked to see the house with a view to purchase. When he exclaimed at the beauty and size of the rooms, Jessie agreed: "The rooms are large. They have held much happiness. The new owners will find few shadows on the walls."

CHAPTER XVIII

The Governor's Lady

Jessie Frémont was now settled in an ugly but comfortable house at Seventy-seventh Street and Madison Avenue in New York City. Here she enjoyed comparative leisure for the various literary labors that eked out the family income. Lily guarded her from casual callers and shared the household tasks with Marie, the French maid who had "adopted Madame Frémont' for her life."

Jessie's joy over the vindication of her husband in the matter of complicity in the railroad bond sale frauds was deepened by the implications of unblemished honor in his being given a receivership position in his defunct railroad corporation. This meant long absences from home and a meager compensation, but these facts only added strength to Jessie's determination to be of substantial help to him.

Robert Bonner of the *New York Ledger* and the editors of *Harper's* and *Wide Awake* offered to take her stories and sketches as fast as she could produce them. The rate at which her pen flew was a matter of amazement to publishers and the family as well. At the early stage of her writing, Robert Bonner had offered her a hundred dollars each for a series of articles. Thinking it would be months before she completed them, he was amazed to find her back with the lot complete after sixteen days of incessant labor. He could not know that a change of scene and climate for the ailing Frank had been the spur to her Pegasus. She wrote to Nell thus of her work:

Dear Kind Nelly: The patch of blue has enlarged to a resting place. I will tell you when I am with you all about it, and if it suits you, I will come down

*to stay a week. Coming perhaps Saturday. I am in the thick of two pieces of
work, the third and last part of the Harper writing and the new stuff for my
Philadelphians, and it will be very good for me to have a quiet corner to finish
them in. You bring me writing luck, you know. Frank will not believe you
said Thor might come. When he hears it officially, he will bring him down.
Be sure that you and G. B. are in the mind for our doggie, for we can board
him. Only if his affections can be spared the wound, we would like not to separate him from all the family even for a short time. Such good letters from
Captain J. C. Frémont, commander of the U.S.S. Pinta.*

Your loving, J. B. F.

(who writes for the Ledger! *Bonner is my good
fairy and I am regularly pleased with him)*

Mrs. Frémont's happiness over Charley's marriage to Miss Sally Anderson and his promotion to the position of commander of the *Pinta* had been
the highlight of the year 1877.

Another letter to Nell refers to her writings thus: "I am very pleased with
myself, for I have four columns all finished—four hundred dollars this week
already, and now it runs easily, for my mind is suited as to what it ought to be."

To Jessie Frémont, who had lived each experience from childhood with such
zest and whose pen had so often been in hand for long periods of intensive
work, those whimsical juveniles, the *Wide Awake* stories of Cherry Grove
and the *Will and Way* stories, were but in truth what she called them to Nell:
"A memory game where the cards get an occasional blob of tears as I play it
here—alone."

As for the sketches dealing with California and Panama and the review of
her experiences abroad, she said: "I have but to close my eyes to see the kind
face of Lady Bulwer taking the shakes out of my knees at Sion House and to
feel the welcoming smile of Madame Arcé."

When exhaustion sent her to bed for a few days, Dr. "Sandy" Morton came
to scold and doctor her. She had a profound respect for him as a "sensible doctor," the son of the Dr. William Morton who discovered the use of ether as an
anaesthetic.

But this author's life was not all slavish labor. She found that her poverty

[295]

did not lessen the demand for her presence at dinners and balls. We have her lively account of a charity ball in New York which netted twenty thousand dollars for the summer care of poor children. She as Martha Washington and Admiral Stephen Rowan as George Washington had opened the ball.

Many stories of Jessie Frémont's dignified and good-natured acceptance of complete bankruptcy had circulated among her friends. These friends old and new promptly rallied about her with offers of vacation trips and invitations to visit them in their summer homes. With engaging frankness and with no hint of self-pity, Jessie declined their tempting invitations on the score of being too busy with writing which was promised her publishers for a certain date.

She wore her made-over garments with as little self-consciousness as she had worn the tasteful and elegant costumes of earlier days, and to Nell she could even laugh over the success of her "petticoat contrivances." At one party in Washington given by Secretary and Mrs. Fish, the press reporter grew lyric over "the wavy sea of snowy shoulders, rounded arms, luscious eyes, and powdered hair, made more dazzling by the glimmer of satin and the glitter of jewels." In the list of names and costumes along with "Mrs. Judge Corwine, Mrs. Senator Ames" and others was "Mrs. General Frémont, pink satin." Jessie sent Nell this item underscored with the laconic line: "Two-year-old ball-gown made over and worn with hair well powdered by nature."

Among Jessie's most devoted and loyal friends in Washington was Olive Risley, niece and adopted daughter of William Seward. Jessie often stayed with her, and shortly after the inauguration of Rutherford B. Hayes in '77, she spent several weeks at the Seward home. She attended many dinners whose hosts were frankly annoyed at the President's "dry" theory and practices at the White House table. From Seward House she wrote to George Browne:

Dear G. B.: I came through most comfortably. Olive was at the station to meet me with a rose in her hand. It was quite cool. The wood fire was bright up here in the library, and the tea was good. The Stoughtons came in, and we had lots of political gossip with our tea.

On the late "wine question?" I heard what I made a mental note of for you. Wine in the soup was almost the rule, and half way through dinner always a

strong Roman punch. This was christened "the life-saving station." And fro-
zen puddings always. Your idea of economy being the real principle is be-
lieved by the habitués here, for elsewhere no objection was made by Mr.
Hayes to the wine cup.

I did not mean to write gossip, however, but to thank you for your care of
me up from the boat and across town. You don't like being thanked, but here
it is. I am so at home and so comfortably taken care of that I will do my work
with full energy....

One day early in '78, Jessie received an old friend, Zachariah Chandler,
who called in the interests of a political appointment for General Frémont.
He announced that President Hayes wished to send the General as Territorial Governor of Arizona. The salary would be small and the living conditions somewhat primitive, but the General's knowledge of the Indians and
of Western conditions generally would make his services of great value.

"What do you think of it?" Chandler asked.

"Very good," she answered. "If it appeals to the General as an opportunity
for honorable service, I am happy. As to primitive living conditions, they will
be no novelty to Lil or me, and I can supplement the salary with my own
work."

Her secret reactions may be easily surmised, for her *A Year of American
Travel*, just off the press, was going well, and other assignments were in hand.

This appointment was highly desirable to Frémont, and Jessie noted and
commented upon his eagerness to assume his new duties. Her pleasure in the
appointment of Frank to a station in Arizona because of his precarious health
took much of the sting from her separation from the other members of the
family. Frank insisted on taking Thor with him. Sheila and the female pup
Maida were entrusted to the Brownes, who had offered to keep them at their
home on Staten Island. Mrs. Frémont's faithful maid Marie was finally persuaded to stay at Nellie's until the Frémonts' return. Charley's wife was visiting the Brownes at this time. Jessie's farewell to Nell read:

Dear Nell: We go certainly tomorrow night. Thor is happy as possible. I
am sorry to leave my Charley. It falls well that he goes off tonight on duty,
not to be back till Thursday. Be good to him, dear Nell. He is an affectionate
beastie, and you have always gone deep into his best feelings, for your care of

*him and Lil and now of Sally. You have indeed been a daughter to me, and I
love and thank you. It is no good swelling over into tears, for now "I must turn
me richt and round about, turn me from the main," and we will make such
success out there that we can all be together again, I hope.*

*Mrs. Spence gave me a parasol I had once admired, a blue-satin cover with
white spots, the swellest thing I've seen since the Russian leather and quill
frieze days. Our humble trousseau is fortified by it....*

On September 9, 1878, Jessie writes from near Cheyenne:

*Dear Nell: I am up five thousand feet and feel perfectly well. That is good
for our six-thousand-feet perch at Prescott. Each one is well and happy. The
General has been getting fairly petted all along the way, in Chicago, and on
through. They telegraphed ahead and at every stopping place have farmers
and lawyers and ladies all saying kind things and giving us hearty cheering.
Me too (or I?). We had a good rest at Omaha at the house of Judge Savage.
His wife, a Boston lady, had one room built for her family belongings; it would
have kept you in Omaha a month. Wasn't that an oasis to strike? Picture your
brasses on the big open fireplace, a bedstead where she and her mother were
born. All hung round with red-silk damask. Chairs of odd shapes and a carpet eighty-four years old, real old English Brussels looking like a faded India
shawl. And such blue china and spindle-legged silver! And a Swedish cook
who has been with her for years and cooks like Frederika Bremer's novels.
My love to G.B. Thor is perfectly happy except the motion made him pit up
at first. He goes on harmoniously with all the baggagemen where he lives on
his rug and a pile of mailbags. Did you have Maida and Sheila in the country? Are you well? Don't forget your marraine who loves you!*

Upon reaching San Francisco, Jessie writes Mrs. Browne of having to press
her best clothes hastily "to try to look calm if not rested" at the reception given
by the Pioneer Association of California. She continues:

*Happy as all the adulation made me, my greatest thrill was in watching
the meeting between my Chief and his old scout Alexander Godey, who was
to accompany our party as far south as Los Angeles.*

*As the Southern Pacific made its slow way southward, General Moses
Sherman boarded the train and acted as official escort for the triumphal entry*

[298]

Jessie Benton Frémont, 1880.

into Los Angeles. A band met us, and as it played the stirring "Hail the Hero,"
Lily was the only one who spoke. The Chief and I were too busy with our
thoughts of another day long past.

Next morning we went up on Fort Hill and viewed the emplacement and
ruins of the demi-lune battery thrown up there to command the then little
pueblo of Los Angeles. Then we went into the little Church of Our Lady of
the Angels.

The Frémont party traveled by train as far as Yuma, Arizona. Here they
were met by Major Lord with Army ambulances and taken to spend several
restful days in the officers' quarters high on a bluff overlooking the Colorado
River. Jessie thus recounted this experience:

Surrounded by cottonwood and castor trees stood the Post Quarters, a
roomy comfortable adobe house. Here I saw my first corner fireplaces and
meat-safe beds. These were mattresses fitted into frames resembling cages,
the whole covered with fine wire netting to protect the occupants from too
friendly scorpions and tarantulas.

With my loathing of crawling things, I viewed these beds with horror.
Later when settled with Lil and the General in the ambulance drawn by six
stout mules, my thoughts turned fearsomely to the conditions that awaited
me in Prescott, two hundred miles away. I forgot my qualms, however, in the
desert drive enlivened by Indian settlements, our sunset camp, and our break-
fasts by starlight.

Upon arrival in Prescott, the Frémonts were welcomed by Governor Hoyt,
the territorial secretary, and other officials. Since houses were difficult to
secure, the family of Attorney Fitch, with true Western hospitality, turned
their house over entirely to the Frémonts and themselves went to camp in the
Fitch law office, coming to their own house for meals only. Jessie wrote later
to her daughter-in-law that "though speechless with fatigue upon arrival, this
generous act restored both strength and speech!"

With her fear of crawling things, she had secretly planned to rent or even
build a tiny plastered house set on a high place, but with cement at sixteen
dollars a barrel and wages for plasterers at seven dollars a day, she gave up and
was content with a four-room house of solid pine-planked walls.

When the family were settled, Frémont as Territorial Governor took up his absorbing duties relating to mines, the care of Indians, and projects of irrigation, while Jessie adapted herself with outward grace to the difficult conditions about her. She survived the shock of finding that on the Governor's salary of two thousand dollars, she faced such outgo as ninety dollars for house rent, forty dollars for cook's wages, almost prohibitive prices for canned goods, and the total absence of fresh fruit. The house rent she declared she would get lowered. The luxury of a maid could be foregone, and that of a horse and carriage as well, since hay was fifty dollars a ton.

These deprivations were cheerfully borne and gayly touched upon in her letters home, in one of which she declared: "Though we are beautifully located, we are four hundred miles from a lemon, and if I were offered the choice of one of my beloved La Marque roses and a fat ripe tomato just off the vine, I should take the tomato." The food problems of Thor she also noted: "He can't dig in this hard earth; so we bury his bones for him. He is greatly pleased. Tell Sheila and Maida that Thor is well. Being the husband of one and the father of the other, I don't know to which he would send the tenderer message."

The Frémonts were soon a part of the pleasant social group made up of the Army people at Fort Mojave and the villagers in this town of two thousand souls. And here as in every place where Jessie Frémont had ever sat within four walls came those who wanted good tea, stimulating conversation, and such fresh air as the mind of each guest might need. Here came General Moses Sherman and his gracious sister Lucy, afterward Mrs. Eli P. Clark of Los Angeles, widely known for her philanthropies. Here came also the young French curé, Father Desjardines, overjoyed at finding one with whom he could converse in his native tongue. He confessed himself "murderously lonesome" at times.

When Father Desjardines worried over the need for a good hospital with women nurses, Jessie wrote to the Sisters of St. Joseph, who had worked in the war hospitals with her in St. Louis. So eloquently did she plead her cause that Mother John and Mother Monica arrived shortly afterward, authorized to establish a hospital.

The day of their arrival was one of blistering heat, and as the two frail women sat sweltering in their heavy black dresses and veils, Jessie declared: "You can never wear such clothes in this climate."

"But what can be done?" they asked.

"I don't know," she replied, "but we shall see."

Next day a letter of protest was on its way, and within a short time the nuns were wearing habits more suited to a desert climate. In a letter to Nellie Browne, Jessie said of these women:

All those who indulge in fears and self-pity should see my little St. Monica. Before she came, a mule and a snake frightened her equally. Within a month she was riding alone through the sagebrush and rocks up into the mines, soliciting money for the proposed hospital and killing snakes with a manzanita cane. Of such stuff are Sisters made.

The stuff of which Jessie Frémont was made shows through the cheerful letters she wrote her relatives and Mrs. Browne:

This is not at all a frontier town with raw and petty ways. It is a splendid atmosphere for work. The General has renewed himself in it and is in perfect health and good spirits. As for Frank, his color is good and appetite steady. He is always jolly, and as for friends, you may as well call the roll from the public school to Whiskey Row where he has friends among the gentlemanly faro men. Gambling is licensed, under regulations. Doors must be open, etc. So there is no more sham to that than to anything else.

Jessie did not escape secretarial duties even here, and her writing of an occasional article was interrupted by the copying of Government reports and legal documents. After Frémont had secured with some difficulty certain needed legislation for the Indians, she writes:

Sunday morning we awoke to the happiest day we have known in years: the legislature gone and unable to undo its good work, the General sure of the good will and support of both the Democrats and our own people among the best men, and atop of all, this special mission for Indian reservations and the appropriation to do it on. Isn't it good to have the General in power again and supported?

In a letter thanking Nell for her affectionate interest in Charley's young wife, she says:

I am having a device on some Pacific paper made for you. I used up such a quantity of yours! When my turn comes to do something for you, it will be like these delayed rains here which can't wait to come in drops the regular way, but just burst the cloud and fall in a heap under it. Frank and Lil go to the window and take orchestra seats and listen to the thunder and oh! and ah! at the lightning which they say comes in two and four zigs at a time. Then the thunder makes a great go-bang. We are up here over a mile high in the air and see the factory turning out storms.

During Mrs. Frémont's stay in Prescott, her interest in child education prompted her to visit the local school taught by Miss Sherman. Chancing to arrive during a history lesson, she was asked to address the pupils. Her sprightly talk on Marie Antoinette led to her being urged to make history talks on Fridays throughout the school year. The care she gave to the preparation of these roused Lily to protest: "One would think that handful of village children were already critical students of history."

Jessie silenced her with: "Perhaps one of them may become so. I prepare my talks for him." Her work with these children was the basis of her later articles, *My Arizona Class.*

She also interested herself in the educational experiments being made with the Mojave Indians. Of these she wrote Nelly:

I have some modern Mojave pottery for you. The ladies of the Fort encourage the Indian women and give them models. One result I have seen is funny. A stray leaf from a spelling book served as model. On the little red pitcher were a cow and a bee on their beam ends, with the letters C O W and B E E interspersed agreeably just where the fancy struck Miss Mojave to put them.

Mrs. Frémont's letters referred to her health as good, but though her lungs had not "fought back," her heart became resentful of the high altitude. For months she suffered occasional attacks of vertigo and extreme lassitude. Refusing to yield to weakness, she kept doggedly on, making herself useful as copyist and writing an occasional article for *Wide Awake* or *Harper's*. She was often alone while Lily accompanied her father on inspection trips. One day after long hours in the saddle they returned to find her lying on the floor in a stupor from which she was restored with difficulty.

[303]

The Post physician upon being summoned talked to her cheerfully of "a little change," but to Frémont he declared: "Out of this altitude permanently." With another of those tender deceptions practiced for courage's sake, Frémont proposed a visit East for her, and she accepted eagerly, declaring: "Lil will take good care of the Governor, and I'm quite willing to go if I am to be of no more use to him than his stored luggage."

After an uneventful trip East she was met by the Brownes, and the warmth of her reception moved her to christen their new Staten Island home "Little Pocaho, for its warm welcome to returning Pocahese." After her visit, in referring to Mrs. Browne's little son George, she says: "I put in a note for Bebe, who was so good as to adopt me as his *marraine* too. There is something in the willing gentle little grasp of a baby that wants you to play with it that is the perfume of all tenderness." Established in a small house on Staten Island not far from the Brownes, Jessie continued writing travel sketches, essays, and juveniles that brought fair returns from the publishers.

During Frémont's official trips to Washington, Jessie joined him there, and they together with the Haskell heirs pressed their claims for a Black Point settlement. These claims were incorporated in the Black Point Compensation bill. That and similarly entitled measures were destined to become will-o'-the-wisp lures for the descendants of both the Haskell and Frémont families to this day.

Shortly after her husband's return to Arizona from one of these trips, Jessie received an inclosure of some verses Frémont had written while on the train journey just thirty-three years after his expedition of 1848, when youth, zeal, courage, and hope were a notable part of his equipment. Jessie at once sent a copy to Mrs. Browne with the message: "You can get the verses by heart and may show them if you like. I wish everyone could know the dear Chief for what he is." Jessie confessed afterward to Nell that the lines which broke her heart were:

> *Backward, amidst the twilight glow*
> *Some lingering spots yet brightly show*
> *On hard roads won,*
> *Where still some grand peaks mark the way,*
> *Touched by the light of parting day*
> *And memory's sun.*

But here thick clouds the mountains hide,
The dim horizon bleak and wide
*   No pathway shows,*
And rising gusts and darkening sky
Tell of "the night that cometh" nigh,
*   The brief day's close.*

Such were the lines whose implications Jessie Frémont more than any other could fully understand.

In 1883 Frémont resigned his Governorship and returned to New York, planning to reestablish himself in business. These plans were never to develop farther than the execution of various commissions for Judge Edward Silent and other Arizona operators in mining and irrigation projects, but they served to restore Jessie's "protectorate," Lily, to her arms, and shortly thereafter the General himself. On the day of his arrival in New York, Jessie sent flowers to Mrs. Browne with the message:

There is only one piece of news in the world today, the General is here. He tells me I am beautiful, but I tell him the truth. He looks young, rested, and as handsome as that day in '41 when I saw him swinging down the avenue in his new uniform.

This estimate was borne out by others than herself. As soon as the Frémonts were settled to routine living again, Jessie insisted upon his beginning work upon his long contemplated memoirs. Her prodigious memory and her meticulous care in having preserved letters, documents, and press clippings were of great service in blocking out the work. Her eager pen lay ready for use.

One evening while at work they were visited by young William Croffut, a journalist in search of a story. His impressions were later recorded in his volume, *An American Procession, 1855-1914*, published in 1931:

One of the most interesting figures in New York life at this time was General John C. Frémont, whose name and romantic career cemented two million men into the compact Republican party. He was one of the most attractive and best defined of our historic personages. I frequently met him on Broad-

[305]

way, swinging along uptown like a man of twenty. The illusion of youth was further encouraged by the close-cropped hair, the form still trim, the elastic step, the rosy face, and the cheery buoyant manner when he spoke. He generally wore a business suit of light-colored plaid. Time and trial had not soured him. It seemed impossible that this clear-eyed and agile man was that same stalwart pathfinder whose footsteps so many men followed with enthusiasm.

I called one evening on the General and his wife, Jessie Benton, at their Staten Island villa, where they were prolonging the romance of half a century before. Mrs. Frémont was a staid-looking, matronly woman with a remarkably strong face resembling the portraits of her distinguished father. They already had two stout boys grown up and married, with children of their own to bother about. "And one is in the Army and one in the Navy," said Mrs. Frémont. "So my feelings are completely triangulated," and she deftly drew on the table before her a triangle with its apex in New York and one leg in Montana and the other in the Southern seas....

"Your happening in this evening is timely," said Mrs Frémont. "The General is just putting the finishing touches to his memoirs in two bulky volumes. I need not say it is the splendid record of a very busy life. Well, do you know, it is so comprehensive and indeed ponderous that he finds it difficult to get a satisfactory publisher. One excellent firm will present it to the public under its imprint if the General will erase all of the unessential details; that is, all of the picturesque pages that give it animation and life. But he thinks that an autobiography without vitality would not be very valuable, even as a history, and I think so too. How about this firm that has just put forth your history of the Vanderbilts?" she asked.

I told her something about Belford, Clarke and Company, and briefly the conversation ended by the General and Mrs. Frémont going with me next day to the New York branch of my publishers, where a contract was entered into under which the first great quarto volume of the Pathfinder's memoirs was brought out in the fall.

When these interviews took place, Mrs. Frémont's hair was white as snow, but she showed few other indications of aging, and talked as brilliantly as ever. She greatly resembled her father, even in gestures and manner when animated by conversation, and with lineaments somewhat softened, inherited his studious and logical mind and his commanding spirit. Her sons were *both tall, black haired, black eyed, and "bearded like a pard." And both, like their sister, showed strains of Gallic blood, the influence of their grandfather, the poor scholarly French gentleman who came to Virginia at the beginning of the century and found their grandmother in her teens.*

CHAPTER XIX

Los Angeles Retreat

JESSIE Frémont's grueling labor on magazine articles and sketches had borne substantial fruit by 1887. That year saw the publication of those sketches relating to her girlhood and foreign travel under the title *Souvenirs of My Time*. This sprightly volume met with instant and wide sale. The first volume of Frémont's *Memoirs of My Life* was also published the same year.

Her special task on this volume had been to write the sketch of Benton's life which Frémont wished incorporated. Looking back with the perspective of her sixty-four years, she saw her father as a heroic figure for whose delineation she felt unfit. She made herself ill with anxiety to do him justice, often getting up in the middle of the night to rewrite, destroy, and write again. During these labors her only recreation was a short walk daily. In a letter to Nellie Browne, who was abroad, she said:

> *I have so many things I would like to gossip over with you, but I must use some of this Indian summer sunshine for a walk; and my hand gets tired. When I write much, I don't indulge in this handsome writing I give you, but I just save every old muscle and only scratch up and down. It gets over the ground in a kind of dogtrot, not much to look at, but it goes. Goodbye for this day, dear Nell. You have seemed very present through your letter.*

When the *Memoirs* appeared, the letters that came from friends who remembered her father warmed her heart, but the one she filed away with greatest pleasure was from George Bancroft. Jessie had last seen him in '77 on his return from the Embassy at Berlin where he had been Minister since '67.

JESSIE BENTON FRÉMONT: a Woman Who Made History

They had recalled the stirring days of '44 and '46, when as the young Secretary of the Navy he had been a frequent visitor at the Benton home and an enthusiastic member of the library round-table before Frémont's California expedition. Now at eighty-eight years of age, renowned as a historian and statesman, he was living out his life at Newport, Rhode Island.

Jessie Frémont, in writing about her father, had sought to obey a favorite dictum of Bancroft's: "Represent every man from his own standpoint; judge him from your own." She had sent to him an inscribed copy of the *Memoirs* and was gratified at the tone of his acknowledgment:

My dear Friends: I have just received the first of your joint tribute to Benton and the path to Oregon. I remember the days when the world turned to the bold adventurer who was to demonstrate that Oregon can be reached by a midwinter journey as well as by a trip through the wilderness in summer, and when Benton predicted to the Senate, in the lecture room, and in all companies the ease with which the East and the Pacific shore could meet together...and the consequent changes in the affairs of the world....It had been my desire to acquire California by all honorable means much before that (1846). I look upon the acquisition of California by ourselves as the decisive point in the perfect establishment of the Union on a foundation that cannot be moved. Up to that time the division was between the North and South. From that moment all division, if there were one, was between the North Center and West against the South. Now that we have got rid of slavery, it seems to me that all distinction between North and South has vanished, but the acquisition of California, making our country the highway between Europe and Asia and establishing domestic free trade through our almost boundless territory, promises for our institutions and for our Union perpetuity.

Best regards to Mrs. Frémont,

GEORGE BANCROFT

Gratification over this letter, together with a hopeful turn in the Black Point Compensation legislation, had lightened Jessie Frémont's weariness, and she was planning a little vacation trip with her husband when he became suddenly ill with a severe attack of bronchitis. Dr. Morton was sent for, and after examination of his seventy-five-year-old patient, he announced: "I'll stay a few days till we see him through." Because of Dr. Morton's skill and Jessie's careful nursing, the crisis was safely passed, but it left the patient extremely weak. The doctor's dictum, "A warm climate and at once," fell heavily on Jessie's spirit. While they were comfortable, there was no money for a long journey with an invalid. Knowing this, the patient declared he would recover quite as well at home and intended remaining there in any event.

With Jessie Frémont, in a battle between pride and love, pride always lost. From some underlying stratum of character she now called up her reserves. Anxious fears gave strength to her resolution and proved the last weapon against her pride. Learning that their old friend Collis P. Huntington was in New York, she made excuse for a trip to town and called upon Mr. Huntington at his hotel. Always a staunch admirer of Frémont, he heard her story with concern, declaring: "We must get him to a warm climate. California's the place for him. You should have my private car, but it's already lent. Go home and be anxious no more. I'll call upon you this evening."

It had taken courage to ask favors, even of so generous a friend as Mr. Huntington, but it took something more to tell her husband what she had done. A lifetime habit of frankness could not have been overcome for long in any case, but she afterward admitted this was the most embarrassing confession she had ever made to him. Frémont listened with attention but with no interest, announcing that such extreme measures as California were out of the question, and that while he appreciated his friend's generous offer, it would not be accepted. Jessie protested in tears, but he held firm. In recounting this scene afterward, she said:

Here we were, lovers for forty-seven years, having our first lovers' quarrel! The General, thin and pale, sat frowning, staring out the window, answering my questions and protests with the exaggerated politeness I had often seen him use so effectively when angry with the boys. I prepared his favorite chicken broth; he barely touched it. The papers came; he didn't feel like listening to the news. I was perfectly miserable, but whenever I looked at his sunken cheeks, I determined to see this thing through unless the General refused to stir, and I thought this quite likely as I waited for Mr. Huntington to come.

Mr. Huntington himself doubtless expected opposition, for he arrived at the cottage with railroad tickets, an ample check for expenses, and the announcement that he had already written letters to officials all along the line which would assure privacy as well as proper service. Of this visit Jessie said:

His heartiness, his solicitude for his old friend's health quite overcame Mr. Frémont's protests, and when he salved the General's pride with, "You forget our road goes over your buried campfires and climbs many a grade you jogged over on a mule; I think we rather owe you this," I saw that he had won his case, though mine was yet on the docket.

"Still silently uncooperative," Frémont watched hasty preparations for departure. In writing of this experience later, Jessie said:

Then the hurried start, the dropping of all other home ties, of all occupations and aims in life, to keep life itself; all the wrenching and uprooting, keenly felt but held under by necessity for action....The cold black Atlantic was washing against the snow-covered Jersey coast as we ran up to New York, and cold and snow were with us in that early, early drive across Washington, but not too early to find dear baby faces watching for us at the window to bring us in close to the bright fire, to pour out a happy confusion of joy and eager hospitality....

Night settled on us installed in warmth and comfort for the week's journey. We looked back through the gathering darkness and falling snow to the dome of the Capitol so often our last landmark of home, and though we spoke bravely of its welcoming us back on many happy returns, yet of what we felt most just then, we did not speak.... A stop for supper was called out at Manassas Junction, and at the name the years rolled back to that ordeal of the nation, the time of partings, of unreturning feet, of great aims and great deeds, and in its mighty shadow, personal pain felt rebuked.

The General's set unsmiling face had been a great trial to me, but toward night he beckoned me across to his section, and taking my hand, he said:"You were right to come. I feel better already." Whereupon I cried heartily. Instantly a young conductor was beside me with words of genuine compassion."Oh, it's not that," I said."I'm so happy the General says he feels better."...We came upon the Great River just above Memphis. A swell of far-past but never dimmed memories came with the view of the mighty waters shining in the glow of the setting sun....

[311]

Through it all, the trip was a neck-and-neck race with our enemy winter, a winter so exceptional and cruel that even in the low altitudes, sleet, ice, and driving winds kept pace with us. At Yuma, which disputes with Aden the palm for heat, there was ice on the grounds of the hotel where we breakfasted, but the blue sky and orange trees loaded with fruit promised return to usual conditions. Then followed the drop of three hundred feet below the sea level. . . . Coming up over the far side of the Basin, we met the fresh yet soft air of the Pacific Ocean and entered a region of rich valleys and gentle hills with pastures and orchards and pretty farm houses. . . . And into the town of Los Angeles we ran on Christmas Eve.

Before we were fairly in, Mr. and Mrs. Silent met us, and we realized from their look of sympathy what a haggard lot we were. . . . The cough was almost over, but later our friend told us he had feared there was to be no more "lift" for either of us. It had been a race for life against winter, and life had won. We had a wunderschön *drive and a Christmas dinner with our good friends the Silents before going to our hotel rooms. And that night my letter home was all out of shape with rose leaves and violets and such sweet vouchers that we were safe where winter could not follow.*

Soon the Frémonts were settled in a roomy cottage on Oak Street. Here General Frémont regained a degree of health, and he, Jessie, and Lily entered into the pleasant social life of the town. Early in '89 Frémont went to New York on a matter of legal business for Judge Silent and visited Washington again in renewed hope over the Black Point property settlement.

With the General definitely well again and interested in business, Jessie wrote her family and friends many letters, most of them "out of shape" with carefully pressed specimens of the flowers she loved. Early in 1890 her *Far West Sketches* were brought out in book form by D. Lothrop and Company. To her beloved Nell she wrote at this time:

If only there were a wishing carpet! How good it would be to have you in the big chair facing mine at this writing table. . . . Our flowers are arranged in a dull-pink jug full of white, yellow, and lilac. Some ripe pomegranates are by the flowers. Altogether you would feel fitly surrounded with beautiful things that tell of a most beautiful climate.

We have made new friends here. This is not a narrow atmosphere with taint

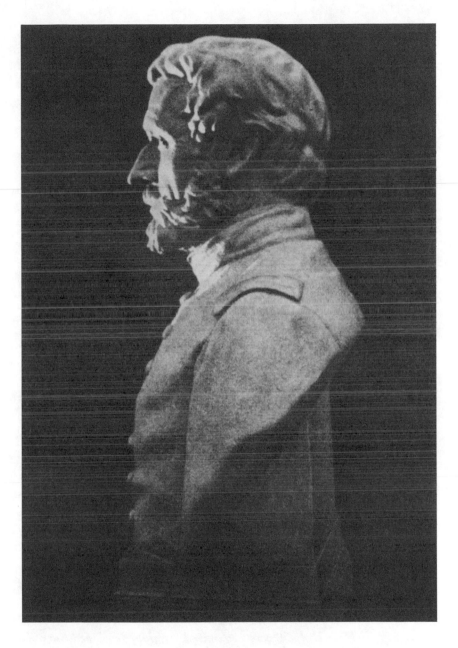

Bust of General John C. Frémont. From original by Austin James at the Museum, Monterey, California.

of village or a raw community.... Its component parts are too varied and too positive for that hideous binding down to small fetishes. The softer climate too keeps people in a healthy outdoor state.... Just by is a pretty park with a tennis court for its houses.... All about us live girls who go off horseback before breakfast. Later, donkey carts, village carts, little phaetons with pretty women and Kate Greenaway children; nice Army people, as General Miles has his headquarters here. She, you know, is a niece to Senator Sherman. A most musical coterie, lady violinists, pianists, men as good, forty active members. And a really fine public library, a real comfort that.... The librarian is allies with Lil and gets books we put on the list: French, Spanish, and English....

The General's being away makes us feel the width of this huge continent, but he writes every day as we do. Pretty soon now he can come back, and we shall have a good companionable time writing up the Second Volume.

When in 1889 George Browne's business interests took him and his family to live in Tacoma, Jessie Frémont was overjoyed to have her daughter-in-love so near. Later when officials from Washington were on the coast with the view of establishing a naval base at Tacoma, her letter to Mrs. Browne is that of the typical mother certain that her daughter will make the right impression, yet unable to refrain from uttering the tactful word that makes assurance doubly sure:

Los Angeles, May 15, 1889

Dear Nell: The Senate Visiting Committee you will see anyway, but they look forward to meeting you especially, as I went down with Mrs. Jones to Santa Monica on their special to stay the night and dine there with her. Allison especially you will like. Mr. Hale is my chief ally and old friend, but he was hurt in the accident near Monterey and may not be along. If he is, make much of him and Mrs. Hale. They are nice. You know they live near Bar Harbor. Next is Allison, and Miss Stoughton who will tell you lots of Sally and Charley, neighbors and always old friends with Sally.

Mrs. Hoar is very pleasant and interested in things. Mr. Hoar is very well but too much Hoar. Dolph is very well indeed, not fully developed, but right instincts; but he is at home and knows G. B., he tells me. I told him you were worth a million dollars' appropriation to Tacoma and local interests, and he soon caught on and saw it. It will please all those women to meet you. I will write you more fully by next mail. This is in haste.

I have been junketing, pointing out fig and blue-gum trees, big vineyards, etc.—dining, coming back this morning on a seven-thirty train, and being polite all the time, until I'm tired. But I wanted you to be under arms and make your mark, so this line of notice!

Your loving MARRAINE

During Frémont's absence in Washington, Alexander Godey, the guide who had accompanied Frémont in his Western travels, died January 20 in the Sisters' Hospital in Los Angeles. Jessie's letter to the General thus recounts her visit to the hospital and her talk with his widow:

Dear Heart: I would not send you this notice of Godey's death on your birthday. We went Sunday morning to the hospital and saw the Sister who was with him most. He got into town Wednesday and died Saturday morning, being barely conscious at the time. . . . Hamil and Denker, ranchers, cattlemen, and his millionaire friends, had insisted he come to this beautiful hospital, but it was too late. They took charge of all things and he had already been taken to the place from which he was to be sent to Bakersfield. I had a surprise in meeting his widow. Maybe you knew he had married again? This time to a really uncommonly pretty little thing, a genuine Californian of a delicate variety. She is very childlike, says: "He left me a good house and many silk dresses." She has the loveliest silky soft black hair, a clear good color in her dusky skin, great dark eyes, and exquisite small ivory teeth. Only twenty, but already six years casada. *She had on a swell little gown, "boughten" of black satin and velvet, for mourning; a large new black-silk mascara loose around her throat. Her little brown hands were firmly crossed over a new un-laundered handkerchief, man's size, with a black border. Her gold comb and earrings were natural to her. She was prim and intending to be quite correctly a mourner, but her eyes danced over* mia casa. *. . . There was no more I could do. The Sisters were happy to meet me and to show their house, as women can be. I promised to bring you there. But Godey's little wife was the astonishment to me! Lil and I are glad he had a kittenish young life around about his. I am getting all right. The weather is cold and bracing.*

Your loving, J. B. F.

At the time this letter was written, Frémont was in Washington making another effort to effect a settlement of the Black Point claim, which the committees of six Congresses had reported upon favorably but on which final decision had not been rendered. But if the authorities at the Capitol were criminally negligent, the Frémonts' friends on the coast and in Washington were not. They petitioned to have General Frémont, now seventy-seven years old, restored to the Army as a Major-General and placed on the retired list. In April, 1890, Congress made the appointment, which carried an annual salary of six thousand dollars.

Frémont's reaction to the now empty honor and the allowance of six thousand a year from a Government that owed him forty-two thousand dollars, bearing interest from 1863, we do not know, but we know that Jessie Frémont considered the honor itself "sadly belated" and the salary as "small payment on account."

Shortly after sending the wire to Jessie announcing this appointment, Frémont left Washington where he had stayed with the family of his son Charley, now on shore duty in the District of Columbia Navy Yard. In Frémont's daily notes to Jessie, he expressed his contentment of mind and his desire to start at once for Los Angeles.

A family friend in Washington had exacted a promise from him to visit the grave of her son in the Brooklyn cemetery on the following Sunday and "place birthday flowers above him." Always punctilious in carrying out a promise, Frémont took the long street-car ride to the cemetery in a broiling sun, and that night before retiring he wrote to the boy's mother and to Jessie. Next morning, though he felt ill and exhausted, he attended to several business matters before consulting Dr. Morton.

Jessie Frémont, receiving his daily messages and planning for his return, was wholly unprepared for ill news of him. On Monday morning she had just read a letter from him, speaking of "living out our years together in a content most absolute," when a telegram came from Charley: "Father is ill." And three hours later: "Father is dead."

In speaking later of that day, Lily Frémont said: "The awful impact of the shock numbed mother like a paralysis, and not until Charley's first letter came to me, did she fully awaken from this merciful state." Charley's letter of July 13 read:

[316]

Jessie Benton Frémont: a Woman Who Made History

My dear sister: It is impossible for me to write what I feel, and I can't write mother at all. So I will just tell you of things as they happened, and let the rest wait till we meet. I was called by telegram yesterday from Dr. Morton, saying father was seriously ill. I got there at five p.m., saw that he had a high fever, and he complained of pains which I recognized as peritonitis pains. I immediately got a trained nurse. Dr. Morton came in and stayed till near midnight. The fever had gone down a great deal, and he looked as if he were now on the mend. This improvement continued till near morning, when vomiting set in, and I sent for Sandy at once. He found conditions changed for the worse, and we sent for several leading physicians. . . . We finally got Loomis, but it made no difference. They all said everything Sandy did was correct. . . . Sandy was so kind and worked so hard. When I first telegraphed you, there was no hope, but I tried to prepare you a little. The end came painlessly. It was blessedly quick and easy, and as I looked at him lying there so still and peaceful, I questioned whether I was not heartless, for I could find no sorrow or pity for him at all, but a feeling of relief that his life was over. And how thankful I am that the last few months were made more peaceful and happier for him and that he had a peaceful home life with us there in Washington. He was so fond of the children and they of him. It is useless to regret.

Of what the effect is going to be on mother, I don't dare think, and when I do think, I doubt whether the cruelest result would not be the kindest. They lived in each other; so I don't think there is any life for the one left. . . . I am too stunned and confused to write clearly, but I felt this letter I must write before the day ended. . . . My heart and home were always open to you and mother, but never as they are now. I'll write again tomorrow.

When Jessie Frémont awakened to full awareness of final separation, she had but one absorbing thought: to have her husband carry with him into the chill of the tomb "herself in miniature," which he had always carried with him since Kit Carson had placed it in his hand in '45. She wired Charley to take her telegram sent after receipt of his first wire, together with the miniature, and place them in her husband's hand where she would have placed them, were she there beside him. Charley's letter of July 17 tells of carrying out her wishes:

Dear mother: Your message and your picture I put into his hand as it lies

[317]

with the arm partially crossed over his breast. I folded up the telegram and wrapped it and the miniature in the ribbons which were tied to it. And I want to tell you that he looks peaceful and so quiet. I can find no sorrow in me for him. Remember that the last few weeks for him were happy and cheerful, full of renewed hope and free from that worrying care. He never was let to know how ill he was; it would have just been useless cruelty. So his last impressions were peaceful and happy. Remember him as you last saw him, for, but that he is pale and looking thin, he is exactly as you have seen him asleep. In looking at him, all my sorrow for him vanished and went out. But for the regret that he could not have lived on to realize the many plans he had, and the comparative peace that was now his, I have no sorrow for him. I did everything in the last arrangements as I thought you would have wished. I am hoping the Los Angeles papers have told you of it all. Only the simple service in the church, and a few of us took him to where I had to leave him, the Trinity Receiving Vault at One Hundred Thirty-fifth Street. I gave him your message there, the last thing. I will write you soon.

Your CHARLEY

A note that day from Dr. Morton told of the General's last words before his final collapse:"If I continue as free from pain, I can go home next week." Seeing the eyes closing, the doctor leaned closer and asked:"Which home?" The patient's lips curved in a smile as he answered:"California, of course."

Deprived of the"kindness"which she agreed with her son would have been happy release to her, Jessie Frémont made the last and most difficult adjustment of her life. Never addicted to useless brooding, she turned instinctively to the task that would still be one more service to her Chief. She wrote to Dr. Morton and asked him to get the unfinished manuscript of Frémont's reply to an article by Josiah Royce concerning Frémont's services in California in '46. Her plan was to complete it. She received Dr. Morton's reply, written July 22, 1890:

My dear Mrs. Frémont: I received your letter about the Century *article yesterday and went at once to see Mr. Johnson and wrote to Jack [Charley] to send the manuscript. Mr. Johnson told me that the article had just been sent on to you to complete and that was just what he wanted.... I need not tell you that there is nothing in the world I would not do to aid you and doubly*

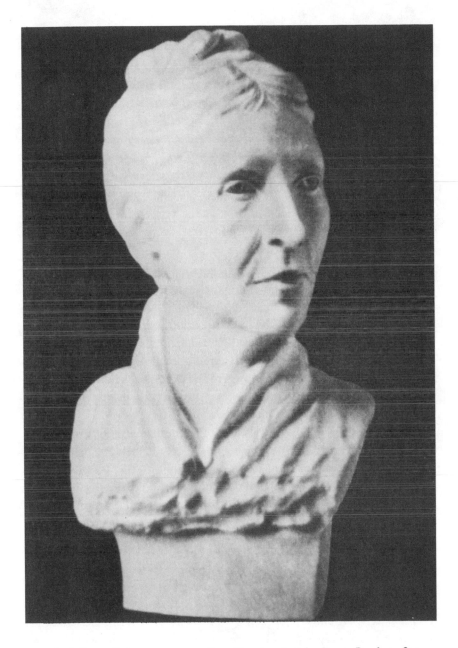

Jessie Benton Frémont at 70 years of age. From bust by John Gutzon Borglum, 1894.

so in memory of the General.... Again and again his lovely and noble char-
acter was impressed upon me....His death affected me deeply, for I loved the
General. He was an ideal to me. But it cannot be helped. The California pa-
pers speak of his going out to sail and getting a chill. That is all reporters' talk.
The progress of the attack was unattended by any very marked symptoms
prior to the collapse. He died without any suffering, and peacefully. Just sank
away. I feel for you deeply and for Miss Lily also as deeply. You have much to
do now, and I want to help when I can, as in the old times when you helped
me so much.

Yours ever,

WILLIAM J. MORTON

Jessie Frémont spent many weeks following her husband's death in the
difficult but well-loved task of replying to the letters that came from all quarters of the globe. The press of the country had given wide publicity to the
passing of Frémont, and the opposition press paid homage to the character of
the man whom on occasion they had reviled. Clipped articles from as far as
Australia and China came inclosed in letters of condolence. Jessie sat far into
the night in attempt to reply fittingly to the expressions that so comforted
her, and Lily refrained from comment, for she knew these letters were more
healing than sleep to her mother.

But the reply to the Royce article had to be completed, and Jessie set herself resolutely to this task. The article was a brief but adequate digest of Frémont's early explorations and a résumé of the political events leading up to
those Benton fireside conferences of the Committee on Military Affairs prior
to Frémont's third expedition. As to the controversial matter bearing on Frémont's authority for entering California as a military leader, he is quoted thus:

Some years ago, when publishing a volume of memoirs, I wished to be espe-
cially accurate on the subject of Lieutenant Gillespie's coming to me from the
Government. Gillespie had been directed to commit his dispatches to memo-
ry before reaching Vera Cruz, then destroy them. I asked Mr. George Bancroft,
who as an accurate and reliable historian kept the data of this California pe-
riod, which was solely in his charge, for his recollections; and he was so kind
as to take much trouble to verify the subject from his record. He sent me full
and distinct memoranda to use, marked "Not to be printed." With his con-

*sent I have used the following extracts from these official and personal papers; now such of them as are needed here are given to show how subsequent events were governed by these instructions brought me by Gillespie. They were to be known only to Gillespie and myself. Commodore Sloat had his separate, repeated, definite orders.**

From memorandum by the Honorable George Bancroft, Secretary of the Navy, made for General Frémont:

Newport, R. I., 2d September, 1886

Very soon after March 4, 1845, Mr. Polk one day when I was alone with him, in the clearest manner and with the utmost energy, declared to me what were to be the four great measures of his administration. He succeeded in all the four, and one of the four was the acquisition of California for the United States. This it was hoped to accomplish by peaceful negotiation; but if Mexico, in resenting our acceptance of the offer of Texas to join us, should begin a war with us, then by taking possession of the province. As we had a squadron in the North Pacific but no Army, measures for the carrying out of this design fell to the Navy Department. The Secretary of the Navy, who had good means of gaining news as to the intentions of Mexico and had reason to believe that its Government intended to make war upon us, directed timely preparation for it.

In less than four months after the inauguration, on the twenty-fourth day of June, 1845, he sent orders to the commanding officer of the United States naval force on the Pacific that if he should ascertain that Mexico had declared war against the United States, he should at once possess himself of the port of San Francisco and such other ports as his force might permit. At the same time he was instructed to encourage the inhabitants of California "to adopt a course of neutrality." The Secretary of the Navy repeated these orders in August and in October, 1845, and in February, 1846. On one of these occasions (October, 1845) he sent the orders by the hands of an accomplished and

---

*Undue value has been given by a few writers to the dispatch sent by the Secretary of State to the Consul at Monterey. It could in no way affect other and different instructions from the President and the Secretary of the Navy or the Secretary of War, who alone could govern the actions of officers. It would seem needless to state so simple a fact, but it appears the writers do not know that the different branches of the Government cannot interfere with each other; and though the President as Commander-in-Chief commands both Army and Navy, their respective officers are otherwise solely under the orders of their respective departments.—J. B. F.

thoroughly trustworthy officer of the Navy as a messenger (Gillespie), well instructed in the designs of the department and with the purposes of the administration, so far as they related to California. Captain Frémont having been sent originally on a peaceful mission to the West by way of the Rocky Mountains, it had become necessary to give him warning of the new state of affairs and the designs of the President. The officer who had had charge of the dispatches from the Secretary of the Navy to Commander Sloat and who had purposely been made acquainted with their import accordingly made his way to Captain Frémont, who thus became acquainted with the state of affairs and the purpose of the Government. Being absolved from any duty as an explorer, Captain Frémont was left to his duty as an officer in the service of the United States, with the further authoritative knowledge that the Government intended to take possession of California.

The Navy Department had no cause for apprehension that the movement upon California would lead to a conflict with any European power, and yet it was held that the presence of armed ships of any other power in the California harbors before annexation might be inconvenient. Therefore no orders were given to use force against any European powers; but the utmost celerity was used by the Navy Department in conveying to the commander of the American naval forces on the California coast orders in the event of war by Mexico to take instant possession of San Francisco and as many other places in California as the means at his disposal would permit. The information which the department possessed made it reasonably certain that if the United States commander in California should act with due celerity on receiving orders, California would be occupied before any European government or any armed ship in the Pacific could be in motion.

Newport, R. I., 3d September, 1886

My motive in sending so promptly the order to take possession was not from any fear that England would resist, but from the apprehension that the presence of an English man-of-war in San Francisco harbor would have a certain degree of inconvenience, and that it was much better for us to be masters there before the ship should arrive; and my orders reached there very long before any English vessel was off California. The delay of Sloat made a danger, but still he took possession of San Francisco before the British ship arrived. . . . *After your interview with Gillespie, you were absolved from any orders as an explorer and became an officer of the American Army, warned by your Government of your new danger, against which you were bound to defend yourself; and it was made known to you on the authority of the Secretary of the Navy that a great object of the President was to obtain possession of California.*

If I had been in your place, I should have considered myself bound to do what I saw I could to promote the purpose of the President. You were alone; no Secretary of War to appeal to; he was thousands of miles off; yet it was officially made known to you that your country was at war, and it was so made known expressly to guide your conduct. It was further made known to you that the acquisition of California was become a chief object of the President. If you had letters to that effect from the Secretary of War, you had your warrant. If you were left without orders from the War Department, certainly you learned from the Secretary of the Navy that the President's plan of war included the taking possession of California. The truth is, no officer of the Government had anything to do with California but the Secretary of the Navy so long as I was in the Cabinet. . . . *

With this necessary digression to make clear my subsequent acts, I return to our camp of May 9 (1846) on the Tlamath Lake. We had talked late, but now tired out, Gillespie was asleep. I sat far into the night alone, reading my home letters by the fire and thinking. I saw the way opening clear before me, and a grand opportunity was now presented to realize fully the far-sighted views which would make the Pacific Ocean the western boundary of the United States. I resolved to move forward on the opportunity, return forthwith to the Sacramento Valley, and bring all the influence I could command. This decision was the first step in the conquest of California.

Then followed rapid résumé of Frémont's march into California with supplies and money provided by Captain Montgomery at Gillespie's request, his organizing the battalion, and the receipt of news by express from Captain Montgomery that Commodore Sloat had raised the flag at Monterey and that he himself had hoisted one at Yerba Buena (San Francisco). Frémont's entry into Monterey, his interviews with Sloat and Stockton, his march

---

*End of quotation from Secretary Bancroft.

south, and the capitulation of Cahuenga were recounted together with his appointment by Stockton as Governor. The article ended thus:

In closing this paper, the following letter of George Bancroft, the historian, referring to errors in a History of the Pacific States *by Hubert Howe Bancroft (no relation of George Bancroft), will prove of interest. The points noted are from a review of the* History *contained in the* New York Sun *of August 29, 1886, and the errors mentioned have been repeated by other equally unreliable historians.*

Among pointed examples of the "blunders" referred to by George Bancroft in this letter are these statements:

There is conclusive evidence that Frémont did not act in pursuance of instructions secret or inferential from the United States Government, and the Pathfinder is accordingly set down as a mere filibuster. . . . The conquest of California was the outcome of accident and of fitful irreflective effort rather than any forecast of its superlative importance.

Newport, R. I., September 6, 1886

*Dear Mr. Frémont: My letter of Friday last crossed your inclosure to me and answers it in advance. I return the California newspaper (*New York Sun *of August 29) as enjoined by you.*

How can a man commit such blunders as are found in the New York Sun *of Sunday, August 29? I thought the paper Mrs. Frémont sent me was a San Francisco paper. Can it be our* New York Sun? *If so it is, I shall get a copy of it.*

Dear Mrs. Frémont: P.S.—As I close this letter, yours of Saturday arrives. If anyone contests anything stated by me to you, I am ready to be referred to as its voucher.

Your most truly, G.B.

The foregoing article has been edited by Mrs. Jessie Benton Frémont from the manuscript and notes of John Charles Frémont.

One morning in July, Mrs. Frémont was called upon by a young out-of-town press reporter. During the conversation he spoke of the talk of a fitting San Francisco memorial to the General in honor of his having named the Golden Gate. Then he spoke of the Royce article and other controversial matters. Jessie Frémont's reply was characteristic but without bitterness:

Jessie Benton Frémont: a Woman Who Made History

Our friend Mr. Greeley said near the end of his career:"Fame is a vapor; popularity, an accident. Character is the only thing that endures." I know better than most the questionable value of contemporary judgments. Time will vindicate General Frémont. I am past sixty-six years old. I may not live to see his enemies sitting in homage at the unveiling of his statue, as in the case of my father, but John C. Frémont's name can never be erased from the most colorful chapters of American history. From the ashes of his campfires, cities have sprung.

CHAPTER XX

Chapter's End

JESSIE Frémont was now to have practical proof of the love and veneration of the people among whom she was rounding out the Indian summer of her days.

Hopeful always of the success of her Black Point claim, her life filled with stimulating contacts, she experienced no sense of struggle with a narrowing fate. And scarcely had she begun to realize her straitened circumstances due to the fact that but two months of the General's pay had been turned over at the time of his death, when influential friends secured from Congress the two-thousand-dollar pension allowed the widows of Major-Generals. At the same time, the women of Los Angeles, aware of their good fortune in having Jessie Frémont among them, built and presented to her a comfortable cottage at the corner of Hoover and Twenty-eighth Streets.

This house she called her Retreat, and here she set up her household treasures. She superintended the placing of the furniture, the beloved books, and the portraits of Colonel Benton, General Frémont, and herself. When Lily declared that her father's portrait over the desk was being hung too high, Jessie left her own task and came to sit in the desk chair. "No," she said. "Leave it so. I've always looked up to him."

Jessie Frémont soon found that her plan of retiring into seclusion with a few close friends about her would have to be greatly modified. She was still too much a personage, one to whom came visitors of note from all over the world, to cut herself off from the world.

When her article appeared in the *Century* in March, 1891, she received letters from both detractors and defenders of her husband's name. These letters she answered with patient attempt to understand the personal animus revealed in the criticism of his detractors. In the case of one such she complained to Lily:

> *The personal element in these attacks bewilders me. It isn't as though the writers sought for the truth in a controversial matter. It is as though in using the authority given him verbally in Washington, the General had violated the Constitution and the moral law, with subsequent harm to the personal reputation of his accusers. If blame must rest with him, it is that he did not oftener come to verbal grips with his implacable enemies.*

But it was not all "bewilderment" for Jessie Frémont. One of the General's strongest protagonists was Charles F. Lummis, a Harvard graduate and an authority on the Southwest. He had been editor of the *Los Angeles Times* from '85 to '87 and was now editor of that authoritative magazine of the Southwest, *The Land of Sunshine*. As a close student of American history, Lummis had followed Frémont's career and the part both he and Jessie had played in matters vital to that history.

He came to congratulate Mrs. Frémont upon her article and remained to talk with her about his own literary ambitions. He had spent five years among the Pueblo Indians of New Mexico and was already an authority on the Indian dialects and Indian arts and crafts. He had traveled extensively through Mexico and South America, but despite his command of the Spanish language and his splendid facility in writing, he declared to her that his pen was no longer trenchant, merely "irritable." Responding to her lively interest in his material and deeply impressed with her general knowledge, he brought to her the manuscripts which were later to develop his stories of New Mexico and South America into *Spanish Pioneers, The King of the Broncos,* and *The Enchanted Burro.*

Lummis, whose pen was often dipped in gall and who took criticism from whatever source with ill grace, received at her hands not only criticism of his writings but also occasional rebuffs, which he declared well merited. One day he asked to present a young woman from Boston whose mental capacities had greatly impressed him. In making his request, he said that she had a man's mind.

Jessie fixed him with a look: "By that I suppose you mean to make her a supreme compliment. A *good mind!* If so, let us say it so. You can safely accord woman a fair share of brains, you who are so ready to allow her a monopoly of the duller virtues." In reporting this he said: "If Jessie Frémont had been born in '58 instead of '24, she would be an Agnes Repplier with the bark on."

The close friendship which grew up between Charles Lummis and Mrs. Frémont was such that when in special need of suggestions over an article he was at work upon, he would telephone: "I'm coming out. Send the others away." In the copy of Frémont's *Memoirs* which she gave to Mr. Lummis, she wrote beneath her own portrait: "With sincere regards to my pleasant peremptory friend."

Jessie Frémont's influence upon the writings of Lummis is happily reflected in the opening paragraph of his series, *The Awakening of a Nation*, published in *Harper's Magazine* in February, '97, and the next year in book form as *Mexico of Today*. Such inveighing against insularity as this often arose in their discussions at Mrs. Frémont's:

A course of travel shall be compulsory for all able-bodied adult citizens. No traveler shall print anything about a country whose language he cannot speak.

By this two-edged ukase, my friend who is much of a bigot in some matters would bring public enlightenment to bloom by cutting off the twin taproots of ignorance. When no one can longer sit still in that birthright prejudice, whereby we despise everything we know nothing about, nor anybody again disseminate the uninspired guesses of a traveled bat, then it will be impossible for the world to keep on so stupid and turbulent as now.

The "turbulent world" of the sixties was recalled to Jessie's mind by her special invitation to be present at the unveiling of the statue of Thomas Starr King in Golden Gate Park in San Francisco. Not being strong enough for this journey, she contented herself with rereading the cherished letters of her "hilarious friend" and glorying in this acknowledgment of the state's indebtedness to him as orator and patriot. The much later acknowledgment of placing him beside Father Junípero Serra in the American Hall of Fame would have gratified her equally.

Jessie Frémont was to have one of her most interesting experiences with artist visitors during her seventieth year. John Gutzon Borglum, twenty-seven-year-old painter and sculptor, had lately returned from a year in Spain, following his triumphs in the Paris salons of 1891 and 1892. As early as 1889 Mrs. Frémont had visited his studio on Fort Hill, Los Angeles, and upon seeing his equestrian casts and drawings, had exclaimed: "How spirited! Here is a young sculptor who will ride to fame on horseback."

And now in 1894 young Borglum was sitting in the cottage on Twenty-eighth Street at work upon a bust of Jessie Frémont. Her small granddaughter Juliet was visiting her at the time, and Jessie was much amused at the child's concern as to how grandmother's "head" would look after being wrapped up all night in a wet cloth. She was always surprised when it looked just the same.

While the young sculptor worked, Jessie listened with pleasure as he told of his life on the Idaho border where, the son of Dr. James Borglum, a Danish pioneer, he was born. He described his childhood years at a Catholic board-school in Kansas where he shocked the good monks by insisting upon drawing Indians and wild horses instead of saints. He had finally run away from the school, traveling by stage to San Francisco. There he studied with the painters, William Keith and Virgil Williams, and was greatly encouraged by their praise.

Later he went to Los Angeles, and from that tiny Fort Hill studio he had sold enough of his work by 1890 to enable him to depart for New York with a collection of forty canvases. After the sale of these, he and his young wife went to Paris. There he studied sculpture under the great Norwegian Sinding. Borglum's *Mort du Chef* and *Scouts* brought him fame. Then had followed a year of study in Spain where he made background sketches for the heroic painting *Noche Triste* upon which he was now at work in the intervals between commissions.

When Borglum finished the bust of Mrs. Frémont, she and her family declared themselves well pleased, for the young sculptor had caught the warmth of her as well as that classic line from cheek to chin, the beautiful nose, and noble brow. His enjoyment of his stay with Mrs. Frémont caused him to say long afterward: "I loved Mrs. Frémont, and I know she thought a great deal of me."

Though Jessie Frémont lent her name to all good causes, she sought to avoid public appearances "from pure vanity," as she remarked to Lily, but that astute"protectorate"knew that her mother's vitality was failing rapidly and must be conserved. Mrs. Frémont did, however, accept the honor of becoming the first regent of the Los Angeles chapter of the Daughters of the American Revolution, but when urged by the President General of that body to serve on an essay prize award committee, she made frank reply:

My dear Mrs. Main: I am much obliged by the compliment you make me, but it is only fair to notify you at once that I cannot serve on the committee to"award prizes for the best essay on the patriotic women of the Revolution."I do not think I am quite fully informed enough on the whole subject to do justice to the many well-thought-out papers they should bring in, and I am quite sure that I have neither time, health, nor leisure to go into the subject.

I am in unusually good health for my age but have to practice what Carlyle calls"enlightened selfishness"to protect and retain it. The letters to my family and some old and dear friends and reading for pleasure are enough occupation, with exercise and some, very few, visits. I keep as much as any thinking creature can out of the rush of life. And find it wise, for its mere echo as it reaches me in the day's news still deeply interests me. But nature has her inflexible law of retirement and I obey it and interfere no more.

Pray accept my sincere thanks for being included in your intended work, and understand it is from no want of interest that I must only read of it as an outsider. I send through you my regards to the President General. It quickens my pulse to address to the dear old city of my preference, and I am

Very truly yours,

JESSIE BENTON FRÉMONT

October 16, 1896
Los Angeles, California

Not only did Jessie Frémont"get the echo"of the rush of life, but she also kept pace with the changing thought of the time. She was not embittered by discovering the fallacy of many of the early tenets she had held sacred. She already sensed the growing homogeneity of our culture, already foresaw a time when music, painting, and literature would be of the world rather than of the country which produced them. What she had said of her father's portrait could well be said of her, for she too showed the same"energy, will, and

"Retreat," home of Jessie Benton Frémont, presented by the women of Los Angeles, 1892.

directness, but all softened by time and the influence of a mind constantly freeing itself from purely personal views."

Though the classics were most often in her hands, she avowed delight in the contemporary writers of the day. Her letters sparkled with humor over what she termed the "reform articles which pepper the pages of our periodicals and irritate the nostrils of the readers who want to enjoy the fiction writers and essayists."

To an elderly visitor who was shocked at her frank enjoyment of George Du Maurier's *Trilby*, then running as a serial, she replied:

Why not? I was always drawn to him as the son of a French emigré. *I laughed with the boy for years in his* Punch *drawings of those delicious French ladies speaking a French that never was. He couldn't write a poor novel after* Peter Ibbetson, *and he hasn't.*

Of George Moore's *Esther Waters* and its banning from certain public libraries, she said:

How can one dispute the moral value of this book? It has a Balzacian fidelity to life. I read it as I would view a masterpiece of painting. While Esther is his central figure, we see them all, Sarah and William and Ketley in beautiful perspective.

Mr. Lummis had just finished reading *Tess of the D'Urbervilles* and was anxious to get her reaction. "A good piece of work," she said, "but I resent as libeler the reviewer who says Thomas Hardy is French in his understanding of women. Perhaps I shouldn't say this. I seem to read reviews as father read Mr. Greeley's *Tribune*, just to quarrel with them."

"Then would you call Hardy typically English?" urged Lummis.

"No! Just a kind of Old Adam," she countered. "He is too willing to blame his women for his troubles, making them mere creatures of impulse. I only hope he doesn't expect to inherit George Meredith's mantle. Ah, there is a man who is poet enough to understand women. Diana, for instance."

"Have you read *The Ordeal of Richard Feverel?*"

"Yes. That will live. I recall reading it at Olive Seward's home in Washington. She had it in the two-volume Tauchnitz edition."

The immense variety of Jessie's literary interests was a constant source of amazement to Mr. Lummis. One day he would find her sitting with Lily in her sheltered corner of the garden, reading aloud in her beautiful French Alexandre Dumas' *L'Etrangère* and laughing heartily over some example of his trenchant wit. Once he came upon her poring over a rare volume of Montaigne's *Essays*. She passed it over to him, saying:

Did you ever see the bookplate of John Randolph of Roanoke? This book is one of a four-volume set printed in 1802 and bought by him at Firmin Didot's in Paris. He gave it to my father. But my favorite of all the books I have owned are the two little volumes of Homer's Odyssée *in French prose, printed in Paris in 1819. One or the other was my French dessert when my father took me rabbit hunting. He carried it in the pocket of his shooting jacket and brought it out while we ate our luncheon of apples and biscuits under a tree.*

Another time Jessie Frémont was sitting before the fire reading the Dickens-Collins letters when Charles Lummis dropped in. She recalled with delight having seen the plays *Pickwick* and *Our Mutual Friend*, the success of which was referred to in the correspondence. "Listen to this. How human!" she exclaimed to him.

Tavistock House, August 29, 1857

My dear Collins: Partly in the grim despair and restlessness of this subsidence from excitement, and partly for the sake of Household Words, *I want to cast about whether you and I can go anywhere—take any tour—see anything—whereon we could write something together. Have you any idea tending to any place in the world? Will you rattle your head and see if there is any pebble in it which we could wander away and play at marbles with? We want something for* Household Words, *and I want to escape from myself. For when I do start up and stare myself seedily in the face, as happens to be my case at present, my blankness is inconceivable, my misery amazing.*

I shall be in town Monday. Shall we talk then? Shall we talk at Gad's Hill? What shall we do?

Ever faithfully, C.D.

One day Lummis came when she was autographing a copy of her *Far West Sketches* for a friend. As the book lay open for the ink to dry, he looked at the inscription:

My dear Mrs. Scott: I hope you will like these skeleton photographs of my long-ago experiences here. They remind me of a time when I and I alone could be of fullest value in our home. Ordinary life is so parceled out and provided for, one has only a small part, but in our mountain life all that was in me found happy use.

JESSIE BENTON FRÉMONT

Thus did she refer to those grueling labors that for ten years had added materially to the family income.

When Lummis found her deep in the current press from Washington and New York, she declared she was enjoying the political drama from a safe and comfortable "orchestra seat." Lummis was much amazed by her pithy comments upon the coming election:

The national character is in as much of a state of fermentation as it was when Irving declared it to be so in his time. I have a great liking for William McKinley, and I predict that if elected, he will have much the same sort of courage as Zachary Taylor.

When the war clouds began to gather in '98 and war was declared in April, Jessie Frémont expressed herself thus: "The President will need great courage and great wisdom. I believe he has both. If we must have another war, I am glad to know that I have sons equipped for their country's service." When word came that her son Captain Frank Frémont had been made Assistant Adjutant-General of Volunteers and that her son Charles in command of the torpedo boat *Porter* was proceeding to the war front, she expressed no personal fears, even to her daughter.

About this time Jessie received an eagerly awaited visitor, Nellie Haskell Browne. In speaking of this visit long afterward, Mrs. Browne said:

As soon as I had recovered from the feeling of desolation over the extremely fragile appearance of my marraine, I had occasion more than once to appreciate the vitality of her mind and the unquenchable gayety of her spirit.

Echoes of old controversies reached her even here in this vine-clad, rose-embowered retreat, for Lily's wisely exercised authority over her mother did not extend to the reception of visitors. One morning the telephone rang, and we heard Lily saying: "I scarcely think so, but I will speak to Mrs. Frémont." Then turning to her mother, she said: "He is a student from the University; wants to talk about the taking of California, etc."

"*Let him come. I feel very well today with Nell here.*"

In half an hour there came a young man of very good appearance and a respectful though embarrassed manner. Mrs. Frémont put him at ease by saying:"Has anyone ever told you how much you resemble John Hay?"He admitted that one or two persons had so complimented him. With that, he settled in his chair and took from his wallet clippings from the controversial Royce article and her reply.

Mrs. Frémont's eyes twinkled as she said:"Though Mr. Royce and I quarrel, we travel about together quite unconventionally. You are the third visitor to produce us from his wallet. The last was from Australia.

"*To your questions, my young friend, I can make but one answer. I have no new material to offer. As my father's secretary, I was present at discussions involving not only the authority given Mr. Frémont for whatever eventuality might arise so far from Washington, but in Mr. Gillespie's last visit to our home, matters of expediency in case of conflict between him (Frémont) and the Mexican authorities were freely discussed. My memory of these matters is sharpened by the anxiety I suffered over what seemed to be a change in Mr. Frémont's status in such event. I did not want him an Army man. His talents lay along the line of his early explorations and scientific surveys. So anxious was I that I got my father to talk with Mr. Bancroft and President Polk, who gave their promise that this military duty should not interfere with his later work. I could not know Mr. Frémont's mind fully in this regard, but in the letter I sent by Mr. Magoffin I wished him to know my own relief over this assurance.*

"*A woman's fears and anxieties often sharpen her memory. My anxieties caused me to be very clear upon the authority Mr. Frémont was invested with at that time.*"

The young man sat making rapid pencil notes while Mrs. Frémont spoke. She watched him; then with a quizzical look she said:"Please add to your notes my parting admonition. You are young. Keep an open mind upon all matters of controversy and leave the truth for Time to declare." With these words the interview closed.

After Nellie's departure, Mrs. Fremont felt more than ever separated from her own family, but her love of youth now expressed itself toward the young people of the neighborhood who came to pay homage to her and remained to sit at her knee listening avidly to travel stories and reminiscences. Later they came for advice and went away comforted. One of these women thus described her first meeting with Jessie Frémont:

I had purchased a copy of Souvenirs of My Time *and very much wished to have Mrs. Frémont autograph it. Too timid to approach her alone, I got a young woman friend to accompany me. We found Mrs. Frémont sitting in the garden watching the sun set behind the acacia trees. Though as fragile as a china figurine, she sat up very straight in her chair. Her white hair was covered with a lace cap, and about her shoulders was a fleecy white shawl. Her keen appraising glance was offset by her welcoming smile, for my friend was one of her favorites among the young visitors.*

Mrs. Frémont called our attention to the new La France roses just set out and spoke petulantly of the border plants "grown weary in well-doing." While she spoke, the brilliant sky darkened suddenly to swift twilight; the air grew chill, and ominous growls of thunder came from the mountains. We all arose hastily, and as we walked up the steps with her, there came a sudden rush of slashing, sluicing California rain. We went into the house and found tea already set for four.

I found Miss Lily Frémont a dear, as my friend had described her. The animated conversation among the others gave me an opportunity to look about casually. My glance rose to the portraits on the wall. Directly above the desk was the life-size portrait of General Frémont. Just below it stood a bowl of heliotrope and white roses. Facing this portrait was that of a girl whose soft brown hair was drawn with a Madonna sweep over the oval cheeks; her lips were full and red; her eyes, deep and serious. Her gown was of soft luminous white stuff with a twist of light-blue ribbon at the neckline. Suddenly this vivid portrait of youth in contrast to that white-haired, exquisite figurante of age gave me a sense of unreality that remained until our visit ended.

I forgot my errand completely and returned home with the unautographed book under my arm. However, this was the first of many visits in which I was to sit beside her, enchanted with her travel stories and reminiscences.

Invariably did Jessie Frémont win her overawed young visitors by the flattery of her friendly interest. She listened whole-heartedly, and when she re-

Last photograph of Jessie Benton Frémont, 1902. From original by Alice Elliot, Los Angeles.

plied, it was not in the patient detached manner of the old. She would look up with alert attention, her voice holding a note of eager speculation as though youth might hold an answer, fresher if not truer, to her own questionings. She never checked their volatile or explosive moods; it was as though their innocent self-revealment had the approval of her heart whatever might be her mental reservations. Her humor had a delicacy derived from her sense of values. Since she always laughed in the right place, it became easy for them to fancy themselves interesting and amusing to this interested and amused old lady. With her superbly "selective" memory, she made her past live for them, and as she played again her part in it, she looked noble, beautiful, and by some magic process, *youthful*. She held to a freshness and casualness that accorded well with her hearers' sanguine spirit and viewpoint. This made them wholly forget her age and her many disillusioning experiences.

In recounting her travels, each person she presented became significantly alive, for in "remembering" she saw no alluring mirage of youth. She was looking upon living horizons. The fine cadences of her voice so vitalized details as to make the simplest of them expertly romanticized. The listener became at once oriented with her in the scene, a part of the setting, the people, the very air they breathed. She did not exaggerate; she merely whittled down the facts to make them servants of reality.

How much of the zest she gave to casual conversations came from her long habit of letter writing, one may only surmise. In this day when letter writing is a lost art, one wonders how much of Jessie Frémont's unquenchable liveliness over daily happenings throughout the world, her freshness of viewpoint when with her young visitors, her fine philosophy with the elders was the result of reliving her experiences in fancy for family and friendly letters. When a young visitor complained that she hated writing letters, Jessie sighed and said:

Ah, my child, you miss one of the greatest delights in life—the privilege of thinking aloud to another. I laugh with Sydney Smith's: "I quite agree with you as to the horrors of correspondence. Correspondences are like small clothes before the invention of suspenders; it is impossible to keep them up." But as for me, I wait for the postman as a child does for Santa Claus, even though an occasional letter makes rainy weather for me.

[338]

One day when Lily came upon her reading a complaining letter from a relative, she handed it over, saying:

This is the sort of letter my friend, N. P. Willis, referred to when he said: "A letter to be read understandingly should have marginal references as to the state of the thermometer, condition of the writer's digestion, and the quality of pen, ink, and paper at the time of writing."

On another occasion when she received a somewhat uninspired letter from a young relative abroad, Jessie showed her disappointment thus: "I've never been through Saxony, and after reading this little Baedeker I could find my way about easily enough, but I wouldn't meet a soul!" So much for letter writers with no sense of drama.

As time went on, the physical strength of Jessie Frémont might have continued indefinitely to sustain her gallant spirit, but in 1900 a fall with its resultant permanent injury to her hip reduced her to what she termed the "hated dependent state of a wheel chair," and it was then that those close to the household found that they had taken the "protectorate" Lily rather too much for granted. She had ruled the practical side of her mother's life with a skill and forthrightness very excellent for the personage she attended, but she who had been lady-in-waiting to a queen now became a benevolent despot, ruling over a none too compliant subject. Lily's nursing skill was of the kind that by its very efficiency emphasized the helplessness of the invalid. And her invalid often showed high-spirited resistance to service she deemed unnecessary. Lily, herself a person of character who chose her task and executed it with competence and pride, held herself no despot but still lady-in-waiting to a queen, a wilful queen too weak to see that her commands were executed but quite strong enough to issue them. Lily's eyes were ever watchful; her mouth drooped anxiously, her manner became uneasy when her patient grew restive; then she would look appealingly at her mother, a smile transfiguring her plain face. That smile was Lily's best weapon, and toward the last, her only one. Her mother's obstinate look would soften; she would reach over and catch Lily's fingers gently between her own, then take her tonic or submit to the ugly red-flannel wrappings about her injured limb.

From her wheel chair, however, Jessie Frémont still reigned, and here at the instigation of Mr. Lummis, she began the rough draft of an autobiographical manuscript. This was intended to complete a manuscript memoir begun in 1889 by Frémont and herself. She had at command a mass of valuable data covering the entire period from the capitulation of Cahuenga in 1847 to Frémont's death in 1890. Despite frequent interruptions from illness, she held grimly to her task, and by November, 1901, she had a rough draft of a hundred fifty thousand words. For this work Lummis offered to secure a publisher. In a letter to him she thus refers to the manuscript and F. J. Browne's suggestion as to a preface:

Dear Mr. Lummis: Thank you for thinking for me. Decidedly I approve the McClurg idea. Your friend Mr. F. J. Browne has the combination I wish: the making a stand for Western books and the "zeal." Talk to him by all means if it comes conveniently to you. And I shall thankfully accept your revision and oversight. I too want it to come out quickly and fitly. Where else than the West should my father appear? He was the West for a long time. Through him came the acquiring of our farther West. ... This will be a book for the coming Fair in St. Louis, and the swan song of the seventy-seven-year-old writer who has every confidence in you.

JESSIE BENTON FRÉMONT

In the intervals of work, Jessie Frémont still received her little group of young friends, and on occasion rallied her forces to talk with visitors from afar who came to pay homage to a personage. Among the distinguished visitors, perhaps the last ones, President McKinley and Secretary of State John Hay, gave her the most pleasure. She had heartily approved the President's acts during and after the Spanish War. Especially had she admired his courage against the attacks from Thomas B. Reed and George F. Hoar in his own party. Upon reading these she exclaimed: "The family lash always cuts deepest. I learned that in '56." She recalled John Hay as a good-looking modest young man, who was reported to wear his honors as Secretary of State with the same dignity that had characterized him as Ambassador to Great Britain in '97. She was familiar with his poetry, her favorite verses being *Two on a Terrace*, reminding her of those days when she and the General had stood where:

Warm waves of lavish moonlight
The Capitol enfold,

[340]

As if a richer moonlight
Bathed its white walls with gold.

When the two visitors called, the President bowed low over her hand and gave her the gardenia from his buttonhole. She thanked him and remarked to the Secretary of State: "My goodness, John, how you have grown!"

In the autumn of 1902, Jessie Frémont realized that the shadows were fast drawing about her. She appeared to welcome them, wrapping herself about in them, becoming at times remote and inaccessible. Then would come a "good day," and the fortunate visitor would see this woman, the last of that long procession of women, containing them all, still herself, at the mercy of no one, not even the loving mercifulness of her daughter. When she was confined to her bed, she became a gracious and patient invalid, asking only that her favorite photograph of the General be placed within reach "for my eyes to rest upon last."

A few days before Christmas, a privileged young neighbor asked whether she slept well. "I always sleep well," she replied, "for no matter where my thoughts sail by day, they sail safely home to the same harbor every night."

When she found on Christmas eve that many packages and letters had arrived, she quickened with a touch of her old-time gayety. "Let me have my Christmas tonight! Somehow this year I can't wait." There were gifts and messages from her sons' families, from Nell, and from friends in Washington. Lily and the nurse read the messages and took her dictation of acknowledgments. Then she said: "I am very happy over such attention from *mes enfants*, but I am very tired. Now I will sleep." These were her last words. She slept on and did not awaken again.

On the morning of the twenty-seventh the end came. So peaceful it was, just a shorter breath and then silence. Death had come as Jessie Frémont would have wished. That heart now cold had held to the last a warm and living fire. In death her sleep looked restful as though she dwelt upon some quiet moment in memory along that colorful time-line.

News of her death was sent to her sons, Commander John Charles Frémont on duty in Washington and Captain Frank Frémont stationed in Manila. The United States flagship *New York* was lying in the harbor at Santa Barbara, and on it was General Frémont's grandson and namesake, Midshipman John Charles Frémont. He was given leave to attend the funeral, which was set for December 30. He and a young family friend, Hugh Gibson, supported Lily Frémont through the ordeal of the services.

Despite the desire of the city officials for a public funeral, Jessie Frémont's last wishes for a simple service to be followed by cremation and the return of the ashes to lie beside her husband were carried out. Those who dressed her remembered her preferences in fabric and color. She lay within a gray casket with violets in her hands, and later great sheaves of violets lay above the closed lid. When the hour came to carry her to Christ Church, she was borne by the young men whose families had been nearest to her in these closing years.

When the cortège reached the church, every pew was filled, and along the walls stood many, both old and young, come to pay last tribute to a friend whose life had in some happy manner touched their own. The violet-covered gray casket stood before a chancel embowered in white roses and ferns. The organ softly played Chopin's *Funeral March* as the morning sunlight slanted across pulpit and chancel, touching this last scene to warmth and beauty. The reading of the burial service was followed by the singing of *Lead Kindly Light*. The last public tribute to Jessie Benton Frémont had been paid, and in hushed silence the throng slowly dispersed.

It was all as she would have wished, for at the very last, the ashes of her "friendly flowers" mingled with her own. The urn was received by the relatives in New York and taken for burial beside General Frémont at Piermont-on-the-Hudson. There overlooking Tappan Zee and Pocaho, these two lie beside an impressive monument of granite with bronze flag, sword, and bronze medallion head of the General, a monument that records at length Frémont's titles and achievements. This too is as Jessie Frémont would have had it, for of all the wishes that lay in her loyal heart the most often expressed was: "How I wish everyone could know the dear Chief for what he is!"

APPENDIX

PERSONAL RECOLLECTIONS OF JESSIE BENTON FRÉMONT

OF THE many authentic sources from which the material for this volume has been assembled, the most fruitful is that acquired from my own intimate acquaintance with Jessie Benton Frémont during the last six years of her life from 1896 to 1902.

During this period my parents, Tristram and Susan Coffin, were Mrs. Frémont's next-door neighbors on Twenty-eighth Street, Los Angeles. With her they shared mutual New England friends and New England memories. My father had sailed from Boston to California by way of Panama in 1851 and had been interested in California mining from '51 until '59. These facts and the added fact of his ardent admiration for the General formed a strong bond between him and Mrs. Frémont.

An anecdote of the first meeting between my father and Mrs. Frémont has become a Coffin family classic. In referring to the various types of "pioneering" courage, my father said that his father, Tristram Coffin, had been "read out" of the Quaker church in Boston for marrying an outsider. Whereupon Mrs. Frémont said: "That took more courage—in Boston—than your own departure as a boy for Panama!"

Mrs. Frémont and Lily shared with my mother a passion for flowers and a flair for experimenting with new varieties. The sheltered corner of the Frémont garden and a similar corner in the Coffin garden became a casual family meeting place for conversation and tea.

I was one of that fortunate group of young visitors who approached Madame Frémont with awe of the kind that brightened our eyes and made us smile pridefully at being thus honored, even while it parched our throats and stiffened our tongues. This feeling was soon lost in happy affection for Jessie Frémont as friend and mentor during those changeful days of the nineties.

When we talked of the transition from the old ideals to the new, she foresaw breaking down of traditional life patterns and disciplines for the young. "This is truly *fin de siècle*," she would say, "but I have a robust faith in youth. It pleases me to have it even now staging a play I shall not be here to see. I only hope that the youth of this country will learn to evaluate the past in the light of our heroes' dreams as well as their achievements, and this for their own sakes, since by the largeness of our dreams do we truly live."

Too young then to appreciate fully our privilege in her friendship, we took for granted the youthful zest and gayety of her; yet even then somewhere deep within us was being stored a wealth of memories against that far-off time when we too should be remembering.

I was away from Los Angeles during the visits of Nellie Haskell Browne, but while pursuing my research for this volume, I was privileged to meet her at her home on Garden Street, Santa Barbara, California. In her eighty-sixth year, herself a figurante of age, she still possessed a vigorous mind and vivid memories of her *marraine*.

At our first interview she said: "I am eager to assist you in every possible way, for it has long seemed strange to me that no one has attempted to put between book covers some adequate picture of that rich and glowing personality that was Jessie Benton Frémont."

Mrs. Browne had preserved all the letters (more than one hundred) written her by Mrs. Frémont and twenty-five from Elizabeth (Lily). Over the period of a year, as suited Mrs. Browne's strength and convenience, she read these letters to me a few at a time, explaining, elucidating, and often wandering afield in anecdote and characterization, as the names of people and places might suggest.

During this time I found myself on much the same intimate terms that had characterized my visits with Madame Frémont. She showed the keenest interest in the progress of the manuscript, and when on my last visit to her I found her very ill, she said: "I think I have been spared for just one more letter and one more anecdote. Though I shall not live to see the finished work, I am happy to have shared in this tribute to a national figure who is yet to me first and last my *marraine*."   C. C. P.

Letter of Jessie Benton Frémont to John Greenleaf Whittier, 1889. (Continued on next page.)

Letter of Jessie Benton Frémont to John Greenleaf Whittier, 1889.

BIBLIOGRAPHY

BENTON, THOMAS HART. *Thirty Years' View*. New York: D. Appleton and Company, 1854.

BIGELOW, JOHN. *Life of John Charles Frémont*. New York: Derby and Jackson, 1856.

CARVALHO, S. N. *Incidents of Travel and Adventure in the Far West with Frémont's Last Expedition*. New York: Derby and Jackson, 1856.

CLELAND, ROBERT GLASS. *The Early Sentiment for the Annexation of California, 1835-1846*. Austin, Texas: Texas State Historical Association, 1914-1915.

COWAN, ROBERT ERNEST. *A Bibliography of the History of California and the Pacific West*. San Francisco: The Book Club of California, 1914.

COWAN, ROBERT ERNEST, AND ROBERT GRANNISS COWAN. *A Bibliography of the History of California, 1510-1930*. San Francisco: John Henry Nash, 1933.

CREEL, GEORGE. *Sons of the Eagle: Soaring Figures from America's Past*. Indianapolis: Bobbs-Merrill Company, 1927.

DELLENBAUGH, FREDERICK S. *Frémont and '49*. New York: Putnam's Sons, 1914.

ELLET, ELIZABETH FRIES. *Queens of American Society, a Memoir of Mrs. Frémont*. New York: Charles Scribner's Sons, 1867.

FRÉMONT, ELIZABETH BENTON. *Recollections of Elizabeth Benton Frémont, Daughter of the Pathfinder, General John C. Frémont, and Jessie Benton Frémont, His Wife* (Compiled by I. T. Martin). New York: Frederick H. Hitchcock, 1912.

FRÉMONT, JOHN CHARLES. *The Exploring Expedition to the Rocky Mountains, Oregon, and California*. New York: George H. Derby and Company, 1849.

FRÉMONT, JOHN CHARLES. *Memoirs of My Life, a Retrospect of Fifty Years*. New York: Belford, Clarke and Company, 1887.

GOODWIN, CARDINAL LEONIDAS. *John Charles Frémont, an Explanation of His Career*. Stanford University: Stanford University Press, 1930.

GOODWIN, CARDINAL LEONIDAS. *The Trans-Mississippi West*. New York: D. Appleton and Company, 1922.

GREELEY, HORACE. *The American Conflict*. Hartford, Connecticut: O. D. Case and Company, 1864.

GREELEY, HORACE. *An Overland Journey from New York to San Francisco*. New York: Saxton, Barker and Company, 1860.

HOWARD, JOHN RAYMOND. *Remembrance of Things Past*. New York: Thomas Crowell and Company, 1925.

JONES, WILLIAM CAREY. *First Phase of the Winning of California*. San Francisco: Bosqui and Company, 1887.

McNEIL, EVERETT. *Fighting with Frémont, a Tale of the Conquest of California*. New York: E. P. Dutton and Company, 1910.

MEIGS, WILLIAM M. *Life of Thomas Hart Benton*. Philadelphia: J. B. Lippincott Company, 1904.

NEVINS, ALLAN. *Frémont, the West's Greatest Adventurer*. New York: Harper and Brothers, 1928.

NICOLAY, JOHN G., AND JOHN HAY. *Abraham Lincoln, a History*. New York: The Century Company, 1890.

PEACOCK, VIRGINIA TATNALL. *Famous American Belles of the Nineteenth Century*. Philadelphia: J. B. Lippincott Company, 1901.

ROOSEVELT, THEODORE. *Life of Thomas Hart Benton*. Boston: Houghton, Mifflin Company, 1886.

ROYCE, JOSIAH. *California from the Conquest in 1846 to the Second Vigilance Committee, 1856*. Boston: Houghton, Mifflin Company, 1886.

SMITH, WILLIAM ERNEST. *The Francis Preston Blair Family in Politics*. New York: The Macmillan Company, 1933.

SMUCKER, SAMUEL M. *The Life of John Charles Frémont, His Explorations and Adventures in Kansas, Nebraska, Oregon, and California*. New York: Miller, Orton, and Mulligan, 1856.

STEPHENSON, NATHANIEL WRIGHT. *Abraham Lincoln and the Union*. New Haven: Yale University Press, 1920.

STEUART, GEORGE RIPPEY. *Bret Harte Bibliography*. Berkeley: University of California Press, 1933.

UPHAM, CHARLES WENTWORTH. *Life, Explorations, and Public Services of John Charles Frémont*. Boston: 1856.

WILLEY, SAMUEL HOPKINS. *The Transition Period of California from a Province of Mexico in 1846 to a State in 1850*. San Francisco: Whitaker and Ray, 1901.

PERIODICALS AND PAMPHLETS

BARD, THOMAS ROBERT. *Jessie Benton Frémont*. Paper relating to the claim of Mrs. Frémont presented in Washington, 1901. Original in the Henry E. Huntington Library, San Marino, California.

BERING, WILLIAM. *Letters on the McDowell Family*. Virginia State Library, Richmond, Virginia.

The Bookman, Vol. XVI, February, 1903. *The Late Jessie Benton Frémont*.

COLFAX, SCHUYLER. *Frémont's Hundred Days in Missouri*. Speech delivered in Washington, 1862. From the files of the Henry E. Huntington Library, San Marino, California.

DAVIS, REBECCA HARDING. *In Remembrance*. Article in *The Independent*, January 29, 1903.

JESSIE BENTON FRÉMONT: a Woman Who Made History

DOBSON, ELEANOR R. *Jessie Benton Frémont*. Article in *Dictionary of American Biography*, 1931.

DUFFUS, ROBERT LUTHER. *Frémont and Jessie*. Article in *The American Mercury*, November, 1925.

FRÉMONT, JOHN C. *The Conquest of California*. Article in *The Century Magazine*, April, 1890.

FRÉMONT, JOHN CHARLES, JR., AND FRANK PRESTON FRÉMONT. *Chronological Data upon Their Navy and Army Careers*. United States Naval Academy, Annapolis, Maryland.

GILLESPIE, CHARLES V. *Statement on Conditions in 1848*. Manuscript in Bancroft Library Collection, University of California.

The Independent, Vol. LV. *Senator Thomas H. Benton*.

KENDALL, MARGARET C. *Jessie Benton Frémont, a Woman Who Has Lived History*. Article in *Overland Monthly*, Vol. XXXVII.

LUMMIS, CHARLES F. *Borglum and His Work*. Unsigned article in *Land of Sunshine*, Vol. IV.

LUMMIS, CHARLES F. *Jessie Benton Frémont*. Obit in *Land of Sunshine*, January, 1903.

Missouri Historical Review, Vol. I. Articles on *Thomas Hart Benton*.

MOODY, DR. J. D. *How a Woman's Wit Saved California*. Article in *Publications of the Historical Society of Southern California*, Part II, Vol. IV.

ROYCE, JOSIAH. *Montgomery and Frémont: Light on the Seizure of California*. Article in *The Century Magazine*, Vol. XIX.

NEWSPAPERS

Daily Union, Washington, D. C. June 16, 17, 18, 19, 26, 1845; May 26, June 15, December 9, 1846; February 12, 1847.

Jefferson Enquirer. September 9, 1847. Item on the return of Frémont. From the files of the State Historical Society of Missouri.

London Daily Telegraph. July 16, 1890. Obit of Frémont.

Los Angeles Times. December 28, 31, 1902. Obit of Jessie Benton Frémont.

New York Evening Post. January 20, 1890. Article by Josiah Royce in answer to Frémont.

New York Independent. January 29, 1903. Obit of Jessie Benton Frémont.

St. Louis Anzeiger des Westens. August, 1847. Account of Frémont's arrival at Westport Landing and meeting with his wife. From the files of the St. Louis Public Library.

St. Louis Daily Missouri Republican. May 25, 1868. Account of the unveiling of the Benton statue. From the files of the State Historical Society of Missouri.

Washington Post. September 24, 1934. *Half-forgotten Romances of History*.

FRÉMONT FAMILY PAPERS
In the Bancroft Library Collection at the University of California

Miscellaneous materials upon Frémont, copied by Allan Nevins from newspapers, Chase Mss., Bigelow Mss., etc.

Newspapers and magazine clippings upon Frémont in California, collected by Allan Nevins.

Manuscript papers by John C. Frémont.

Elizabeth Benton Frémont's notebook.

Autograph Mss. by Jessie Benton Frémont.

Typed Mss. Memoirs by Jessie Benton Frémont.

Letters from Dr. Morton and Charles Frémont relating to General Frémont's death.

Photographs.

PUBLICATIONS OF JESSIE BENTON FRÉMONT

The Story of the Guard, a Chronicle of the War. Boston: Ticknor and Fields, 1863.

An article signed *Lisa* in answer to one signed *Vixen,* in *The Atlantic Monthly,* 1868.

A Year of American Travel, in *Harper's Magazine,* Vols. 55-56, 1878.

My Arizona Class, in *Wide Awake,* Vol. 17, 1883.

My Arizona Class, in *How to Learn and Earn,* in joint authorship with Pratt and others. Boston: D. Lothrop and Company, 1884.

Souvenirs of My Time, in *Wide Awake,* Vol. 19, 1884.

The Bodisco Wedding, in *Wide Awake,* Vol. 19, 1884.

A Virginia Wedding, in *Wide Awake,* Vol. 19, 1884.

Grant, Words of Our Hero Ulysses Grant, 1884. Edited by Jeremiah Chaplin with personal reminiscences by Jessie Benton Frémont. From the original in the Henry E. Huntington Library, San Marino, California.

Washington in Past Days, in *Wide Awake,* Vol. 20, 1884-1885.

Family Life of the White House (illustrated), in *Wide Awake,* Vol. 20, 1884-1885.

Mrs. Madison and Mrs. Hamilton, in *Wide Awake,* Vol. 20, 1884-1885.

The Talent in the Napkin, in *Wide Awake,* Vol. 20, 1884-1885.

Crazy Sally, a Negro Story, in *Wide Awake,* Vol. 20, 1884-1885.

A Queen's Drawing Room, in *Wide Awake,* Vol. 21, 1885.

Queen Marie Amelie, in *Wide Awake,* Vol. 21, 1885.

Uncle Primus and Dog Turban, in *Wide Awake,* Vol. 21, 1885.

The Big English Bull (illustrated), in *Wide Awake,* Vol. 21, 1885.

St. Louis, in *Wide Awake,* Vol. 21, 1885.

New Orleans, Panama, San Francisco, in *Wide Awake,* Vol. 21, 1885.

William Rufus (illustrated), in *Wide Awake,* Vol. 21, 1885.

California, in *Wide Awake,* Vol. 21, 1885.

General Grant (illustrated), in *Wide Awake,* Vol. 21, 1885.

The Queen and the Peasant, in *Wide Awake,* Vol. 22, 1885.

A Military Fête Day in Paris, in *Wide Awake,* Vol. 22, 1885.

A Nobleman of the Old Régime, in *Wide Awake,* Vol. 22, 1885.

Paris, in *Wide Awake,* Vol. 22, 1885.

Men, Women, and Things, in *Wide Awake,* Vol. 22, 1885.

American Midshipmen at the Tomb of Napoleon, in *Wide Awake,* Vol. 22, 1885.

The Little Princess Thyra, in *Wide Awake,* Vol. 23, 1886.

A Morning Visit to the Queen of Denmark, in *Wide Awake,* Vol. 23, 1886.

A Midsummer Night with Shakespeare, in *Wide Awake,* Vol. 23, 1886.

Salzburg, in *Wide Awake,* Vol. 23, 1886.

Taffy and Buster, in *Wide Awake,* Vol. 25, 1886.

Ways to Do Things, in *Wide Awake,* Vol. 25, 1886.

Baby's Shoe (illustrated), in *Wide Awake,* Vol. 25, 1886.

Tied to a Christmas Tree, in *Wide Awake,* Vol. 25, 1886.

At Niblo's, in *Wide Awake,* Vol. 25, 1886.

Their Last Appearance, in *Wide Awake,* Vol. 25, 1886.

Hans Andersen at Home (illustrated), in *Wide Awake,* Vol. 25, 1886.

Souvenirs of My Time. Boston: D. Lothrop and Company, 1887.

The Cruise of the Coverlet, in *Wide Awake,* Vol. 26, 1887-1888.

Off Barnegat (illustrated), in *Wide Awake,* Vol. 26, 1887-1888.

Farragut's Flagship, the Hartford (illustrated), in *Wide Awake,* Vol. 26, 1887-1888.

Chist-a-Pah-ens, or Swordbreaker (illustrated), by Lieutenant F. P. Frémont, U.S.A., in *Wide Awake,* Vol. 26, 1887-1888.

How the Good News Came out of the West, in *Wide Awake*, Vol. 28, 1888-1889.

My Grizzly Bear, in *Wide Awake*, Vol. 28, 1888-1889.

Besieged, in *Wide Awake*, Vol. 28, 1888-1889.

The House that Jack Built, in *Wide Awake*, Vol. 29, 1889.

The Deck Hand, in *Wide Awake*, Vol. 29, 1889.

Snowshoe Thompson's Run, by Lieutenant F. P. Frémont, in *Wide Awake*, Vol. 29, 1889.

Camping near the Giant Trees, in *Wide Awake*, Vol. 29, 1889.

Kit Carson, in *Wide Awake*, Vol. 29, 1889.

Sierra Neighbors, in *Wide Awake*, Vol. 29, 1889.

A Picnic near the Equator, in *Wide Awake*, Vol. 29, 1889.

Play and Work, in *Wide Awake*, Vol. 29, 1889.

The Ball; and the Camp on Mt. Bullion, in *Wide Awake*, Vol. 29, 1889.

A Long Horror, in *Wide Awake*, Vol. 29, 1889.

Miss Miller, in *Wide Awake*, Vol. 31, 1890.

The Two Wills, in *Wide Awake*, Vol. 31, 1890.

The Hat of the Postmaster, in *Wide Awake*, Vol. 31, 1890.

The Good Samaritan, in *Wide Awake*, Vol. 31, 1890.

Far West Sketches. Boston: D. Lothrop and Company, 1890.

The Origin of the Frémont Explorations, in *The Century Magazine*, 1890.

The Will and the Way Stories. Boston: D. Lothrop and Company, 1891.

Sterilized Milk as Food. S. S. McClure Newspaper Syndicate, 1892.

A Home Lost and Found, in *The Home-maker Magazine*, 1892.

Dolores, in *Land of Sunshine*, June, 1897.

The Animal Story Book, as joint author with Maude Howe (Elliot) and others. Boston: D. Lothrop and Company, 1898.

BIRTH AND DEATH DATES OF THE FRÉMONT FAMILY

JOHN CHARLES FRÉMONT. Born, Savannah, Georgia, January 21, 1813. Died, New York City, July 13, 1890.

JESSIE BENTON FRÉMONT. Born, Cherry Grove, near Lexington, Virginia, May 31, 1824. Died, Los Angeles, California, December 27, 1902.

ELIZABETH BENTON FRÉMONT. Born, Washington, D. C., November 13, 1842. Died, Los Angeles, California, May 28, 1919.

BENTON FRÉMONT. Born, Washington, D. C., July 24, 1848. Died, near St. Louis, Missouri, October 6, 1848.

JOHN CHARLES FRÉMONT. Born, San Francisco, California, April 19, 1851. Died, Boston, Massachusetts, March 7, 1911.

ANNE BEVERLY FRÉMONT. Born, Paris, France, February 1, 1853. Died, Silver Springs, Maryland, July 12, 1853.

FRANK PRESTON FRÉMONT. Born, Washington, D. C., May 17, 1854. Died, Cuba, 1931.

INDEX